Wool Exchange

Furniture

Moorgate

Guild Hall

The Bank

Bishopsgate

Houndsditch

Baltic Mercantile Shipping Exchange

Cheapside

Banking & Stock Exchange

Royal Exchange

Lloyds

ALDGATE

Leadenhall St.

Minories

Lombard St.

Metal Exchange

King William Street

Fenchurch St.

Port of London Authority

QUEEN ST.

STREET

The Monument

Corn Exchange

London Rubber

London Commercial Sale Rooms

Cannon Street Station

EAST CHEAP

Coal Exchange

THE FINANCIAL NEWS

The Tower

POULTRY ST.

Billingsgate

Southwark Bridge

PROSPECT OF The City of London

Being a Map for the MERCHANTS, BANKERS, BROKERS & other VENTURERS trading into that City

19 34

DOUBLE HARNESS

Memoirs by
LORD DROGHEDA

WEIDENFELD AND NICOLSON
LONDON

To Joan

DOUBLE HARNESS

Contents

LIST OF ILLUSTRATIONS   vii

ACKNOWLEDGMENTS   x

PREFACE   xi

PART ONE *Prelude*   1

PART TWO *The Financial Times*   109

PART THREE *Covent Garden*   223

PART FOUR *Coda*   355

INDEX   369

Illustrations

Between pages 84 and 85

1 Moore Abbey by William Ashford
2 My father and mother soon after their marriage
3 Myself aged six months
4 In the nursery
5 My mother drawn by J. S. Sargent in 1911
6 My mother with my sister Patsy and myself, 1917
7 My stepmother Olive
8 My mother on the beach at Biarritz
9 On the Croisette at Cannes with my mother and Patsy, 1923
10 Polo at Cannes
11 Schoolboy
12 Londoner
13 Alvilde Bridges
14 Emerald Cunard
15 Freda Casa Maury
16 Penelope Dudley Ward
17 Patsy with her son Richard
18 Chatin Sarachi
19 Barbara Hutton
20 Francis Baring
21 Joan in 1937
22 Newly-weds, 1935
23 My portrait by Princess Marina, 1939
24 Derry's Christening, 1937

Between pages 180 and 181

25 Bracken House
26 View of St Paul's Cathedral from Bracken House

27 My father at his desk at the Ministry of Economic Warfare
28 Oliver Lyttelton
29 Brendan Bracken in front of 10 Downing Street, 1941
30 Sir Robert Sinclair
31 Brendan Bracken in the early 1950s
32 Geoffrey Crowther
33 Lionel Robbins
34 Abram Games' *FT* poster design
35 Sidney Henschel with a client
36 Group photograph at dinner given on Lord Beaverbrook's eighty-third birthday, 1962
37 Alan Hare and myself arriving for a meeting at the TUC, 1970
38 Gordon Newton with Fredy Fisher and myself
39 Making my speech at the *FT* 25,000 Issue Dinner, 11 November 1969
40 Jack Jones arriving at the dinner
41 Jeremy Thorpe between Lords Camrose and Thomson
42 Denys Sutton with Sir Thomas Monnington
43 Richard Powell being received by Lionel Robbins
44 Alan Hare with Lord Cowdray
45 Joan and myself with David Palmer at the launching of the trimaran *FT*
46 The *FT* garden at the Chelsea Flower Show, 1973
47 Joan with me at my *FT* farewell party, 1975
48 Arnold Goodman, Pat Gibson and myself

Between pages 276 and 277

49 The auditorium of the Royal Opera House
50 The front entrance to the building
51 David Webster
52 Ava and John Waverley
53 Ninette de Valois
54 Rafael Kubelik
55 Margot Fonteyn
56 Frederick Ashton
57 Franco Zeffirelli
58 Georg Solti
59 Margot, Fred Ashton and Rudolf Nureyev, October 1961
60 The same trio sixteen years later
61 Antoinette Sibley and Anthony Dowell in *The Dream*

62 Lynn Seymour in *Manon*
63 David Webster greeting the Queen Mother and Princess Margaret
64 Ninette de Valois with Sol Hurok
65 Otto Klemperer in the Crush Bar
66 On stage at the end of David Webster's farewell gala
67 Isaiah Berlin
68 Burnet Pavitt between myself and Bill Bundy
69 Jack Donaldson and John Sainsbury
70 John Tooley
71 The Queen and Queen Mother with John Tooley at my farewell gala, July 1974
72 My shadow on stage
73 The Queen Mother talking to Jennie Lee and Ken Davison
74 The Queen with Colin Davis and his wife, Shamsi
75 John Sainsbury presenting my bust on behalf of The Friends of Covent Garden
76 Sergeant Martin
77 Joan seated at the piano, 1977
78 The Garter Procession, 1972
79 Derry photographed by himself

The fanciful maps reproduced as endpapers were specially commissioned from Rex Whistler by the *Financial News* for publication in the newspaper's Annual Reviews in 1933 and 1934.

Acknowledgments

The author and publishers would like to thank the following for kind permission to reproduce the photographs: *The Tatler*, 6; Keystone Press, 14, 59, 78; The *Financial Times*, 25, 26, 33 (photo: Vijay), 34 and 37 (photos: Freddie Mansfield), 39, 40, 41, 42, 43, 44, 45, 46, 47, 48; Radio Times Hulton Picture Library, 29; Camera Press, 31 (photo: Karsh of Ottowa); Godfrey Argent, 32; The Royal Opera House, Covent Garden, 49 (photo: Reg Wilson), 50 (photo: A. F. Kersting), 51 (photo: Zoë Dominic), 54 (photo: Donald Southern), 56 (photo: Reg Wilson), 57 (photo: Zoë Dominic), 61 and 62 (photos: Anthony Crickmay), 64 (photo: Donald Southern), 66, 68 and 71–76 (photos: Donald Southern); The Press Association, 52; Mike Davis, 53; Angus McBean, 55; Peter Fisher, 58; *Daily Express*, 63; Bern Schwartz, 67; Clive Barda, 70. The author and publishers have made every effort to trace the sources of the photographs and to make due acknowledgment wherever possible. Any omissions will be repaired in the event of a future reprint.

Preface

When my old friend George Weidenfeld asked me to write a book of memoirs, I told him that I had no idea whether I would or indeed could do so, but I also undertook that since he alone had asked me I would not do it for anyone else.

In the following pages, after recounting something of my early life and my wartime experiences, I have confined myself to an account of my association with the *Financial Times* and Covent Garden, with both of which I was for so many years identified; and my title 'Double Harness' is intended to convey the feeling I had of being yoked simultaneously to these two contrasted and complementary enterprises, devoting to them all the time, thought and energy that lay within my power.

The book is essentially a chronicle of events, and does not pretend to be in any way an autobiography, still less a self-portrait, or essay in self-analysis. Here I have referred only incidentally to my private life; and therefore there are a number of friends of whom I have not written as I should have liked to do. There are also many business colleagues and acquaintances, and likewise performing artists and staff at Covent Garden, to whom because of limitations of space I have not been able to refer. I express to them a general apology, while realizing that there are those who will in no way object to the omission of their names.

I am most grateful to those friends and colleagues who have agreed to my reproducing various passages from their letters, and especially I thank Isaiah Berlin for leave to quote from two very long letters of his. To Andrew Wheatcroft I express appreciation for the help he has given me in making suggestions for the compilation of the material; and I particularly thank my former secretary Pam Law for the great assistance she gave me in checking facts and dates, as well as for typing the manuscript for me after she had retired.

PART ONE

Prelude

Chapter 1

My name is Irish but my blood is mainly Scottish. I was born in London on St George's Day, 23 April 1910, and ever since then my home has nearly always been in England.

For many generations my father's family had lived in Ireland. They were supposed to have come to England at the time of the Norman Conquest, and the family was then called de More. They settled at Benenden in Kent, where no doubt still to this day I have distant kinsmen. The first of my ancestors to go to Ireland was named Edward Moore. He was born in 1530, and he crossed the Irish Channel in 1550, to find fame and fortune serving the Monarch with the expectation of lands and revenues, and his hopes were not disappointed. He married the widow of Sir William Brabazon in 1563. Three years later Queen Elizabeth conferred a knighthood on him and he was granted the title deeds to Mellifont Abbey, adjacent to the town of Drogheda, which had been taken from the Church in the reign of King Edward VI. It remained the home of my family for nearly two hundred years with a somewhat painful interlude at the time of the Civil War, when it was sacked.

Edward Moore was succeeded by his son Garrett, whose Christian name appealed to my parents, and after whom therefore I was christened. He played a major role in the various negotiations with Hugh O'Neill, Earl of Tyrone, who had ambitions to free Ireland from the English yoke, and whose life is far more dramatic than that of any member of my family. Garrett was made Viscount Moore, and on the arms granted to him appeared the family motto 'Fortis cadere, cedere non potest.'* His son Charles was a passionate Royalist, and on the Restoration of the Monarchy in 1661 his eldest son Henry was given the Earldom of Drogheda. A grandson of Henry, another Charles, married an heiress named Jane Loftus, who was descended from a Lord High Chancellor of Ireland. Their son, who was born in 1700 and who with deplorable lack of originality was also named Henry, succeeded to the Loftus estates on the death of his maternal grandfather; and it must have been then that the family moved to Monasterevin in County Kildare. Henry had no offspring, and his brother

* The brave may fall, but cannot yield.

Edward became the fifth Earl, marrying Lady Sarah Ponsonby, by whom he had a number of children, headed, you will be surprised to learn, by another Charles, the sixth Earl and first Marquess, this being a reward for his services as a field marshal and as Master General of Ordnance. The Marquess lived to a very great age, and was very extravagant. So were his sons, who, I was always told, were given to gambling on a princely scale; likewise his grandson, yet another Henry, who, I should think, judging by Hay's caricature of him, was a real *bon viveur*, too busy having a good time to have any children, so the Marquessate became extinct; and my grandfather, who was a second cousin, being descended from Edward, the fifth Earl, succeeded to the title as ninth Earl. He was a mild and kindly man, quite unacquisitive, an attribute or defect, depending upon how you look at it, which he handed on to my father, and he in turn to me.

My grandfather died on 28 October 1908 before I was born, and indeed before my parents married; and my father's mother died while I was still very young. She was born Ann Moir and was entirely Scottish. Her father had held the position of Sheriff of Stirlingshire from 1858 until 1868. My grandfather and she were painted in peers' robes, and at any rate in the artist's eyes they bore a striking resemblance to King Edward VII and Queen Alexandra. I remember her nursing me when I had a bad attack of the flu towards the end of 1918. I think of her as small and kind and good, but otherwise my recollection of her is faint.

My mother was born Kathleen Pelham Burn, and she too was entirely Scottish. Her father's name was Charles Maitland Pelham Burn. His family was very extensive. It came from the region to the east of Edinburgh. They were tenants and subsequently owners of an estate near North Berwick although this was sold in the nineteenth century. The branch of the family to which my mother belonged had for three generations added to Burn the name Pelham, without hyphenating it, for the simple reason that John Burn had married a Miss Pelham Maitland whose father had had as his godfather the first Duke of Newcastle; and the Duke, being extremely attached to his family name Pelham, had asked that it should be handed down from generation to generation by one or other of the offspring of his god-children. I like the name because it has a kind of euphony about it, and my Scottish cousins should be grateful to the Duke.

By his children my maternal grandfather was always referred to as Pog. I know little about him except that he was in the Gordon Highlanders and that he married an heiress named Isabella Romanes Russell whose family had made money exploiting the ironstone and coal deposits in the region of Blackbraes, where they had lived for many generations.

The Industrial Revolution had turned Blackbraes into a hive of industry. It formed part of the 'Black Country' of Scotland, and as the Russells prospered they purchased Dundas Castle, an imposing house in Linlithgowshire near Hopetoun and Dalmeny with a fine view over the Firth of Forth. It was there that my grandmother was married, and she and my grandfather set up home in Edinburgh. He died in 1916. I never knew him, but I remember her as an extremely formidable character. 'Tremble and obey' could well have been her motto, despite her ridiculous nickname, Boo. She was intensely superstitious, and she had a great belief in fortune-telling. I loved staying with her, because of her kindness to me. I can still see her on the golf course as quite an old lady, doing her eighteen holes with a steady rolling gait. She lived until 1929. I sense that she was a stronger personality than her husband, rather matriarchal. She produced three sons and three daughters, all of them tall and handsome, the brothers greatly distinguishing themselves in military service in the first war.

Of the actual meeting of my parents I know nothing. I suppose that my mother came south for a London season, and to be presented. She had fallen in love, I was told, with Lord Malise Graham, but whether or not her love was reciprocated it was my father she married in St Giles's Cathedral in Edinburgh on 3 March 1909, assuredly with great pomp and ceremony, whatever the depth of their attachment to one another.

I was born at No. 40 Wilton Crescent in London, where my parents lived for the greater part of the year because my father had entered the Diplomatic Service, for which he passed the entrance examination with distinction. It is sad that under the rules as they then were my father was obliged to leave the service when my parents were divorced in 1921, for he would have had an outstanding career, probably ending as Permanent Under-Secretary of State.

The house in Wilton Crescent in which I spent my very early childhood was decorated by my mother in what must have taken the conventionally minded by surprise. The two rooms I remember in particular were the drawing room and the dining room. The walls of the drawing room were covered with a sort of silver foil paper, and dotted about the room were several blue glass balls resting on columns the colour of lapis lazuli which were reflected in the mirror-like surfaces of the walls. There were masses of cushions lying about everywhere and there was a generally exotic feeling about the room, and I imagine that my father must have felt very much more at home in his study.

The walls of the dining room were covered with black velvet, and all around the cornice there was an abstract frieze, painted in somewhat Miró-esque style by the Vorticist, Wyndham Lewis. The lighting came from translucent yellow alabaster lamps, which glowed warmly but somewhat dimly. At the time it seemed novel and daring, but it is now lost without a trace.

My memories of life at Wilton Crescent are very faint. We must have left the house soon after 1920, because of the separation and divorce of my parents. I remember walks in Hyde Park and sailing boats on the Round Pond in Kensington Gardens. I remember riding, as part of a group of children, in Rotten Row, and attending Miss Vacani's dance classes, where we were all beautifully turned out in muslins and velvets, and the horrors of war were simply never mentioned or thought of. My mother for a while had a very elegant electric car, black outside with grey upholstery, which glided silently along the streets of Belgravia; and why with their general excellence these cars were never properly developed passes understanding. I remember my mother's lady's maid, Lamport, a strict and severe woman who seldom smiled but who was loyal to my mother all through to her second marriage, and who, if she had any thoughts about the goings-on around her, kept them completely to herself. I remember my nurse, Miss Lavender, who was one of the real old school and extremely strict, although she always addressed me as Lord Moore and never by my first name. In Hyde Park she would say, 'Now then, Lord Moore, don't make your white gloves dirty on the railings.' When my sister appeared, two and a half years after I was born, the household was enlarged to include a nursery-maid, whom I did not like and once bit in the leg, causing my father to spank me with his bedroom slipper, saying in the approved style, 'This is going to hurt me more than it hurts you.' As I grew a bit older the nursery-maid was replaced by a French governess who taught me most of the French I know. Mlle Lemosse was her name, a plain but elegant lady whom I liked very much. There was also an elderly gentleman called Mr Nurse who came to give us drawing lessons, all this in the middle of the war. I used to play a lot of games. L'Attaque was a great favourite, and my unfortunate sister always had to take the German side, as she also did when the toy soldiers were brought into use. I had a passion for a model steam locomotive made by the renowned firm, Bassett Lowke and Company. I started collecting stamps, which fascinated me, and butterflies, and birds' eggs; and even for a while cigarette cards.

I do not suppose I saw much of my parents. For one thing, in the days of my childhood, children were mostly in the nursery, and only appeared rather briefly at tea-time, having been specially dressed for the occasion (in my case a sailor suit was a particular favourite). But beyond that, my father was working hard at the Foreign Office, where he was one of Lord Grey's private secretaries and my mother was extremely active in different kinds of war work. For some months she was away in Belgium, working on a barge bought by the legendary Maxine Elliott and used to distribute supplies of food and clothing to poor Belgian families who had been cut off when the Germans had made their initial advance through Flanders.

Maxine Elliott was an intimate friend of both my parents despite the fact that she was sixteen years older, being born in 1868. She was an astonishing beauty in an age of great beauties. She conquered the New York stage, and then she conquered London society, although she always gave me the impression that she treated her admirers with immense disdain. She is even supposed to have declined Lord Curzon's offer of marriage. Her story* has been very well told by her niece, Diana Forbes Robertson, the widow of the American writer Vincent Sheean. We used to go to Hartsbourne, a house she acquired in Hertfordshire, where she entertained the tennis-playing elite, her great love being an early star of Wimbledon, Tony Wilding. Years later I remember staying with her at her villa, the Château de l'Horizon near Cannes, where Winston Churchill was a frequent visitor. She must then have been eighty. One day playing backgammon with her I looked at her through the screen of smoke emitted from her long cigarette holder, which seldom left her mouth. I saw her astonishing velvety brown eyes and I had to say, 'Maxine, what marvellously beautiful eyes you have!' She replied, like a coquettish young girl, 'You're teasing! Tease me some more.' But the conversation was interrupted by her horrible little lemur, Kiki, which although far from house-trained had the free run of the house, clambering all over her guests: and she showed no sympathy for anyone who protested.

My mother was on Maxine's barge in Belgium during the early months of 1915. After her return she spent much time travelling up and down the British Isles with an air exhibition which she had largely organized herself and which was designed to recruit volunteers for the Royal Flying Corps. In planning the exhibition she was much helped by John Hodgson, who with his family owned the famous book auction business in Chancery Lane, and who in his spare time for relaxation wrote an authoritative history of aeronautics. He was a kindly and scholarly man, wholly unpretentious. The exhibition contained examples of every type of equipment, British or German, and an impressive collection of balloon prints which Hodgson helped my mother to acquire and which she presented, I believe, to the Royal Aeronautical Society. For her work she was awarded the CBE.

My sister and I spent a good deal of each year in Ireland at the family home, quite unaware of the country's troubled state, and our parents were surely very seldom there. I have some vivid memories of Moore Abbey, but they are completely disjointed, which is perhaps not wholly surprising since we cannot have lived there at all after 1919, when I was still only nine years old.

The house was excessively large, and the stables were almost as large as the house, for my family in the previous century had been addicted to horse-racing and riding generally, and they had founded Punchestown racecourse, which

* Diana Forbes Robertson, *Maxine*, Hamish Hamilton, 1964.

achieved great fame and is still in regular use. Moore Abbey was, I believe, built in about 1770 in eighteenth-century Gothic style. It was built on the site of the Monastery of St Evin, founded in the sixth century and like Mellifont Abbey taken from the Church in 1539. It was a well-proportioned stone building, with battlements and pointed windows, facing southwards over a romantic park containing deer, and a large beech wood carpeted in spring time with bluebells, and a stretch of the River Barrow, dark-watered and full of fish in the pursuit of which I one day nearly drowned, being heroically rescued by the More O'Ferrall brothers, our neighbours at Kildangan Castle nearby, with whom we constantly exchanged visits.

Our other neighbours were the Portarlingtons at Emo Park. Lord Portarlington was immature and spendthrift, but Winnie, his wife, an intimate friend of my mother, was a wealthy Australian, who lived in style, and was able to gratify his whims. They had a delightful son, Carlow, just my age, who was killed tragically in the last war when flying to join Fitzroy Maclean in Jugoslavia. We used to spend Christmas together in Ireland. Lionel Portarlington, being rather childish himself, was a great success with children. He had a fearful trick with an orange which I always pressed him to perform. It consisted of sticking in matches to represent the eyes and other features of an imaginary face, cutting a slit for the mouth, placing a cloth over the top of a glass and resting the orange upon it. He would start pulling the cloth from side to side, gently at first, then faster, until at last he would say, 'I'm afraid the poor fellow's feeling very sick'; upon which he would squeeze the orange, and the juice would pour out through the slit. I thought this enormously funny, goodness knows why; and he could do no wrong in my eyes.

The rooms of Moore Abbey were dull and lacking in ornamentation. There were few amenities. Bathrooms were conspicuously absent. The heating was primitive, log and delicious-smelling peat fires, and one large open vent in the hall emitting warm air, heated from a boiler in the basement of the house. There was a sizable garden, in which I remember my mother had planted two wide herbaceous borders, one essentially blue and mauve, and the other all the shades of red and pink, both leading up to a great copper beech tree. The garden was approached from one side by an ancient yew-tree walk, said to be haunted by a wretched knight who had been beheaded in the remote past and who emerged at night carrying his head under his right arm; so after dusk I kept well away.

There was one clear proof of ghostly presences when we engaged once in table-turning with my father's sister, my Aunt Betty, who was said to be psychic. I remember that we sat solemnly round a small table which after a short while began to agitate violently, spelling out by means of question and answer a message from a group of unquiet spirits, restless because they were lying in unconsecrated ground near to the house. We received spirit messages guiding us to the spot, the ground was dug, and sure enough we came upon a large quantity of human bones and a number of skulls, which were gingerly lifted from the soil in which they lay and were then reburied in the church graveyard.

I fancy that two of the characters most concerned with this rather grisly operation would have been Mr Pilgrim, the head gardener, a splendid Englishman with a striking resemblance to an Edwardian squire, as dependable as they come; and the house carpenter, McAsee (no Mr in his case – that was how it was), a lovable Irishman with a Kitchener-style moustache, who turned his hand readily to any task inside or outside, and who lived on to a great old age. McAsee used to take my sister and me for outings, and one I particularly enjoyed was to a small island in the River Barrow occupied by a most delightful brother and sister, Tim and Bridget Behan, who lived in a tiny damp cottage and earned a living cutting willow shoots or withies. Whenever we arrived, piping hot griddle cakes were produced, the excellence of which has never been surpassed. Bridget Behan was very devout. When she went to church she had to propel herself to the river bank in a small rowing boat, in which she frequently used to take her donkey with her for the subsequent ride. They were truly good people, who would have hated what has been happening in Ireland in the recent past.

During the 1920 and 1921 'troubles' which preceded the creation of the Irish Free State, Moore Abbey was empty, but it was left unmolested. The separation and divorce of my parents was imminent, and after their parting my father had neither the means to maintain a property of that size nor the desire to live in it. Instead he rented the house to the famous Irish tenor John McCormack and his family. I did not see the house again until Joan, my wife, and I went to stay with the McCormacks after our marriage in 1935. John had a pure effortless voice equally at home with Irish ballads or with Mozart. He played us one or two of his records, and a beautifully sung phrase always drew from him, 'That was nice, wasn't it?' – as indeed it was. He was a great charmer. Success, I think, rather went to his head. He lost a lot of money in the Wall Street crash, and he made some very unsuccessful investments in bloodstock. Yet no better tenant could have been wished for.

McCormack gave up his lease of the house in 1938, and shortly thereafter negotiations for its sale commenced. The purchasers were an order of nuns, the Sisters of Charity of Jesus and Mary, the intermediary being my Aunt Betty, who after her husband Robin Kerr Clark was killed in the First World War was converted to Roman Catholicism, becoming even more devout than Bridget Behan. The purchase price for this great house with its park and gardens, and its stables, and its stretch of river, was no more than £5,000, but to my father it meant the saving of £500 a year to keep the roof in order; and also he had no sentimental attachment to the place, while I saw the dark tunnel of war ahead, and little light at the end of it.

The sale of the house was completed early in 1940. The nuns, however, did not move in until well after the end of the war. My sister went there in the autumn of 1946 and wrote to my father describing the emptiness and coldness, the furniture all gone, the pictures and books all stacked in one room where occasionally a fire was lit to keep out the damp. Many of the books were sold by my father, with help and advice from John Hayward, a brilliant man of letters crippled by some rare form of paralysis when still very young, whom I first met at Cambridge with Victor Rothschild. In the main the pictures were of little value. My father allowed me to keep the few that I wanted. The rest were sold for modest sums, the exception being a lugubrious painting of a Franciscan monk contemplating a skull, said to be the work of Caravaggio, and if this were true it would mean that the £950 received through a well-known London dealer was grossly inadequate.

I have no regret over the sale of Moore Abbey. As the Irish political situation has developed, I should have found it positively painful to be obliged to live in Ireland. However shameful the story of English rule for over three centuries, nothing can condone the atrocities committed by the IRA and the Provisionals, which the Irish Government seem powerless to prevent. It would have been impossible for me to become in any way identified with the country. I loved my childhood days at Moore Abbey, but I have no sense of nostalgia and a great feeling of relief that England was to be my home.

Chapter 2

The war was nearly over by the time I was sent to Ludgrove, a private school which in those days was situated at New Barnet. The headmaster in my day was G. O. Smith, who had been a famous Amateur Association Football player. He ran the school together with his sister, whom I remember because every Sunday evening we all assembled in the drawing room and she used to read Victorian novels to us.

My general recollection of the school is hazy. There are two masters whose names have stuck in my mind: W. J. Oakley who had, I recall, an outstanding collection of stamps of the British Colonial Empire which he used to show us with great pride, whetting our appetites to become collectors in our own right, and W. P. Blore, whom I treated with terrible disrespect but who had something of a crush on me as can perhaps be gauged by a letter that he sent to my father, which made me sound fearfully priggish:

20th February 1921

In spite of all my sermons to Garrett on the theme of taking things quietly this term and getting the prize next term, he is top of my Mathematical Division this week, and from what I hear will probably occupy the same position in Classics in another week or two.

He is a most determined person.

I said to him yesterday, 'You haven't got much chance of getting the prize which your Father offered you for being bottom!' and he replied, 'No, I don't want it: I mean to be top.'

Though I have preached my best to him, I can't help rejoicing secretly in my heart at his determination, and at his refusal to be tempted away into easy paths. He seems to be like Alexander, and never happy unless he is conquering new worlds. However if you had seen how very much happier he has been during the last week or so, and how he has ceased to worry and fuss, as he has got on more successfully towards the object of his ambition, I think you would agree that there is nothing much to be anxious about, and that success does him good.

He evidently means to live up to the family motto: 'Cedere non potest.'

It is probably and also sadly true that I reached my intellectual peak while I was at Ludgrove. Mr Blore had high hopes that I would be capable of taking a scholarship into Eton. Fortunately those less prejudiced in my favour knew that, whatever might be my other attainments, I should surely come a cropper over Greek. So I played safe, and succeeded in taking what is called Remove in the Common Entrance examination, nothing to be ashamed of but with little glory attaching to it.

This must have been in 1923. By then my parents had separated, divorced, and indeed both remarried. I remember that while I was at Ludgrove my father came down to see me in order to tell me of their intended separation. I have no recollection of having been distressed, or shocked, or even surprised. They had never existed for me as a combined entity, but as two distinct individuals with very different lives and interests; and family life in the conventional sense had scarcely existed for us: this was partly of course an inescapable by-product of war, but I feel sure that it would in any event have been true, for they were fundamentally incompatible.

Their differences were striking. My mother had much the more colourful personality. She was slightly larger than life. Physically she was tall and well built, Juno-esque she could have been described, although in her later years she was pathetically bent and crippled with arthritis. She had strong artistic feelings except for music, yet she was not in the least intellectual, and she seldom opened a book. She had a natural eye for quality in furniture and the applied arts. Her dress sense too was excellent, particularly when it came to others. Nothing gave her greater pleasure than to choose clothes for her man of the moment. At all times until my marriage she liked to be consulted about any clothes I might order, and I readily complied because her taste was good and she frequently not only chose but also paid. One of her favourite establishments was Lesley and Roberts, a leading men's tailors whose head cutter, Mr Robinson, had a large and devoted international clientèle. He judged people almost exclusively by the cut of their clothes. He lived for his work, and after he retired, at the age I think of eighty-four, he very soon died.

My mother when young was physically brave, being one of the first women to fly as a passenger, but as she grew older her courage changed to extreme nervousness; she fussed endlessly over my sister and myself, and for this I cannot thank her. All her life she was attracted by men and women who lived for speed; she knew intimately Donald Campbell, Alan Cobham, Kaye Don, Jim Mollison and Amy Johnson, and plenty of others besides. She played golf and tennis avidly, and was an early playing member of Wimbledon. Like her mother she was tremendously superstitious, and believed in the occult. Also, she was spontaneously kind and generous. If she had a friend in need or distress, there were no limits to which she would not go to help. It was fortunate that she had a small amount of money in trust, because otherwise it would all have flowed away. Apart from my father, she had indifferent taste in men. She had numerous passions, a veritable procession in retrospect. Only one or two will appear in this story. Most will not. She must have strained their patience, for she was very demanding and very possessive.

Save for a love of golf and tennis, my father was in most respects the anti-thesis of my mother, although like her he had an immensely kind nature, tending to make allowances for people and give them the benefit of the doubt. Physically he was quite short, and very spare. He held himself erect, with his head slightly bent to one side. His eyes twinkled and he had a quizzical smile. He was modest, shy, unpretentious and retiring by nature. He was also very industrious. When he was obliged to express himself in speech or on paper he did it extremely well, for he had a clear logical mind which enabled him to view situations dispassionately, and to analyse their implications. He read a lot and was a skilful bridge player. He loved the stage, and knew many of the leading theatrical personalities of his day, but was otherwise no great lover of the arts. *The Times* crossword puzzle he polished off every morning in a matter of minutes, and on Sunday mornings *Webster's Dictionary* was usually open as he struggled with Torquemada in the *Observer*. He had great humour and a great sense of the ridiculous, enjoying teasing people for their idiosyncrasies, although he would never do so in a hurtful manner. After marrying my stepmother Olive, he led a very quiet sequestered life, rarely going out, except for his public duties, and yet he always took a passionate interest in people drawn from all walks of life, without regard to their class. Everyone who knew him loved and admired him. To the best of my knowledge he was without an enemy, often said to be a sign of a negative personality, which in his case was certainly not true.

I left Ludgrove at the end of March 1923, and went to Eton earlier than I should have done, presumably because of my parents' divorce. My first term, or half as a term is perversely called at Eton, was spent in the Waiting House, Mr Cattley's house where I was to board being full until the autumn when I was expected. The master in charge of the Waiting House was a friendly but tiresomely ingratiating clerical character by the name of Chaffey. To be under his supervision meant that one was gently broken in. There were only a small number of boys in the house, a dozen or so, compared with the normal forty to fifty, and they were all in the same age group. This in turn meant no fagging; but it also effectively meant two first halves.

Having taken Remove in the entrance examination, the next best thing (although much inferior) to a Scholarship, I only had to spend one year as a so-called Lower Boy and accordingly only three halves in which I could be called on to fag; and since one of the three had been spent under Mr Chaffey's wing, my length of time as a fag was mercifully short.

The duties of a fag were not very arduous, principally preparing teas and, in winter, fires for one's fag-master, and running errands on his behalf or for others in a senior position in the house. 'Boy' was the familiar cry to which those in the Lower School were expected to respond if they were within earshot, regardless of what they were doing, and woe betide them if they failed to do so.

John Morrison, now Lord Margadale, was my fag-master. He was a kind and easy-going person, not at all sadistic, so I escaped lightly at his hands. I had however been warned by my father in a very circumlocutory way to be careful of advances from older boys, so that although I had not the slightest idea what to expect I was always scared stiff if I was fagged to take a message to a boy in another house. I remember my absolute consternation on being sent once to the room of a senior boy who when I arrived was wearing his shirt and nothing else; I was quite certain that it had been carefully timed and that he was bound to leap on me, to do what I surely had no idea.

My house-master, Tom Cattley, was ill-equipped to put one at ease because he himself was both shy and formidable. He was bald, and his skin was white and tightly drawn, so that he had a rather skull-like appearance. He was very scholarly and he had small, neat, precise handwriting, which denoted to me a pretty narrow attitude towards things. He was a real misogynist. If ever I wanted permission to do something out of the ordinary, I would ask my mother to speak to him. I knew that he would comply with almost any request because he found the company of women distasteful, and wanted to be rid of them quickly. My mother's visits were always welcome to me because besides bearding Tom Cattley she was apt to be intensely spoiling. Also, she owned at that time a silver Rolls-Royce in which I took great pride, expecting to gain the admiration of my fellow Etonians for this splendid status symbol.

When Cattley came round the house in the evening to say goodnight to us, well anyway to some of us, he would sit on the bed, put his arm around our shoulder, and rub his by then rather bristly chin against our cheeks: and one felt that there was someone warm and loving aching to break free from his constraints. My most upsetting memory of Tom Cattley goes back to the time of my confirmation, when it was the custom for the house-master to give one a talk about the facts of life, and the snares and perils we should encounter. Mr Cattley's shyness produced first of all a lengthy silence, and then, 'I have been told that you have been seen playing with yourself as you walk along the High Street.' I cannot imagine what I replied, but it was the sort of remark that needed a quicker wit than I possessed at the time. It would not surprise me to learn that he used it as an opening gambit quite often. Anyway, I question the accuracy of the charge in so far as it related to myself.

This is not to say that sex played no part in my early days at Eton. Basically, though, it was more a question of romantic attachments. There were two or three older boys of whom I was immensely fond, above all Bob Laycock. I developed a faithful, dog-like devotion to him. He was about three years older than me. For a short while I used to try and follow him wherever he went. When he played football for the school I was there, cheering him on. I must have made myself a great nuisance, but the original initiative came from him, with a meeting in the gramophone shop carefully planned by our mutual friend, David Herbert, one always eager to assist the path of love; and we saw one another quite often, although our relationship was at no point physical. With David I had many escapades, which usually involved breaking one or other of the many restrictive rules which controlled the school bounds or hours, but in other respects were wholly innocent. Indeed the only occasion upon which I had active sexual relations with another boy was in my last half at Tidworth Camp, where the so-called Eton Officer Training Corps used to go in the summer for a week of manoeuvres. The episode was with a boy of my own age who like me was also about to leave the school, and we had a sudden spontaneous urge under the tent in the middle of the night which once relieved faded away for good.

Apart from this occasion my romantic attachments were usually with boys older than myself. I enjoyed being admired by my seniors, and therefore I suppose I egged them on a bit. This led to my being subjected to a fair amount of bullying by some of the boys in Cattley's house during the early part of my time at Eton. No doubt I brought it upon myself, but it marred the enjoyment of my first year or two, while leaving no indelible scars.

I worked quite hard at my lessons, particularly when up to (which meant in the class of) certain masters like A. B. Ramsay, the Lower Master, who taught classics, and C. H. K. Marten, the historian, who knew how to fire one's enthusiasm. I had a fairly competitive spirit, and I won my quota of prizes, including nothing of great distinction.

Among them was the Duke of Newcastle's Spanish prize, worth £25 in books, a lot in those days. It was easy money because I was the only entrant, although I had attained a modest standard, having taken Spanish as a so-called extra study, being nicknamed El Moro by Mr Evans, the master in charge. There were about six boys in the Spanish class, and one summer we were taken on the inaugural cruise of a ship sailing from Southampton to Santander. The Bay of Biscay was horribly rough. Only two people were not lying prostrate in their cabins, myself and an attractive girl named Conchita Villamediana. We had the ship to ourselves, flirting outrageously as the ship lurched: and after reaching Santander I borrowed enough money from my fellow Etonians to hire a taxi to drive quite a long way, hoping to see her. But instead her father blocked my path, and I left disappointed.

I used to try hard at games, but I was only given my football house colours because Cattley's got into the final of the inter-house competition, and in cricket I never came near to the first or second eleven. I greatly enjoyed squash rackets; and also Eton fives, a splendid game full of subtlety, involving gloved hand and ball, which was played in three-sided concrete courts modelled on one of the buttressed spaces on the north side of the School Chapel, where the game had once originated.

It must have been while I was at Eton that my first glimmerings of appreciation of music emerged, for they had no encouragement at home, or rather I should say during the holidays, because by the time I went to Eton I effectively had no home, my parents being divorced and both remarried, the house in Wilton Crescent sold and Moore Abbey on the point of being rented to John McCormack.

I was able in those days to sing in tune, well enough anyway to be a probationer in the Lower School chapel choir: and later, when my voice broke, I joined the Eton Music Society and used to engage in a good deal of choral singing. At one moment I hoped to study the violin, but it was far beyond my competence. My great Eton friend, Francis Baring, a member of the illustrious banking family of that name, beside whom I sat in class and in chapel daily for many halves, was himself intensely musical, playing the clarinet with considerable skill. He did much to stimulate my love of music. He was almost my exact contemporary, and while we were at Eton he was my intimate. There were no romantic or homosexual overtones to our friendship, but we had immense fun together, and I frequently stayed with him and his family in Paris where his father was head of the Westminster Foreign Bank in the Place Vendôme. Francis was a real life-enhancer, whose death in France shortly before Dunkirk was a tragedy.

The Eton master with whom I established the most friendly relations was my so-called modern tutor. This figure of speech denoted the master who had responsibility for overseeing one's educational progress in the later stages, regardless of subject, as opposed to the house-master, who had the overall responsibility for general behaviour, deportment, and so on: and inevitably there was an overlap and a playing off of one against the other. My modern tutor was named J. D. Hills, a history master, who left Eton in 1929 to become headmaster of Bradfield College. He had done very well in the war, was much decorated, and received rapid promotion to the rank of colonel at an early age. He had grown a military moustache, which he retained as he did his rank. He took himself a little bit seriously, and by many of the boys he was referred to, not without affection, as the man who won the war. He had bright, twinkling eyes and a warm manner, the antithesis of Tom Cattley. Once or twice a year he used to take a group of us up to London to visit the National Gallery, giving us lunch at the Criterion Restaurant, and he did much to arouse our interest in the visual arts, although he was not exactly adventurous in his taste, having a great preference for the Dutch School. It was usual at the end of each half for one's tutor to send a report about each pupil to his house-master. I have two letters written by John Hills to Cattley. In December 1927 he wrote:

Moore continues to work hard, read fast and improve very slowly. His essays are beginning to show, here and there, a little originality of thought and almost always there is visible something of a style. At present there is no sign of scholarship in him, unless it be as a linguist . . .

He is a light-hearted boy, full of good humour, whose company I enjoy in pupil room. He read his many parts in *The Dynasts* with much gusto, albeit complaining that I gave him all the shady characters—quite untrue of course.

In all things I think he goes on well—the addition of house colours will all help to establish him in his own and others' estimation as a good mixture of aesthetics and masculinity.

Then when I was leaving in July 1928 he wrote:

I shall be very sorry to lose Moore from my pupil room. He has two great merits: he is not afraid of hard work and he is willing to be interested. I wish I could add that he has learned to express himself in reasonable English, but . . . his essays are singularly disappointing—styleless and confused. He is not muddle-headed, for his conversation proves him perfectly capable of clear thought; but on paper, narrative and discussion, fact and fancy are all hopelessly jumbled . . . There is undoubtedly a danger that with his languid pose, liking for Maurice Baring and lack of enthusiasm for violent games, he will fall into the hands of the exotic gentry who flourish at a University—most of whose intelligence is far inferior to his, whose talk is vile and behaviour impossible. But they may prove to be the only men who can talk about some of his own particular loves. I hope he will soon see through them.

He has been a most amusing and friendly pupil and the picture he leaves behind is of a somewhat impertinent opponent – always ready with a challenge, frank comment or lie direct to keep his tutor up to the mark. Life will be more somnolent without him. I wish him the very best of luck.

John Hills was a pretty good friend to me. He certainly erred on the side of kindness in what he wrote. I was far from well educated, either academically or in practical everyday things which, at any rate when I was at school, were quite taken for granted. All that I and many of my contemporaries learnt was to be acceptably gregarious, undoubtedly of value in later life; although at the time I should think I was utterly maddening, and for this I partly blame my muddled home life. Truly I salute the name of Hills, for I owe him a lot.

I cannot leave Eton without mentioning the most memorable figure during my time there. This was without question the headmaster, Cyril Alington. I only knew him from a distance because I never attained the top or sixth form, and I was never elected to 'Pop', as the Eton school society was called, an exclusive club of the elite, self-electing save for certain boys, the captain of the school, the captain of games, and so on, who were automatically made members. However, Dr Alington made a deep impression upon us all. He had a fine, long, rather austere face, and a distinguished presence. He used quite often to deliver a sermon in the School chapel. When he did so, he wore a scarlet cassock. He had two candles burning on either side of the lectern in the pulpit, and very little lighting elsewhere. The effect was supremely theatrical, and inspired awe in even the most irreverent of us.

What surely above all stays in the mind when thinking of Eton is the romance and the beauty of the buildings. The chapel, dating from the reign of Henry VI, the founder of the school, has a simple splendour seldom bettered elsewhere. The proximity to Windsor with its castle and its forest, and to the River Thames, helped to give a sense of the continuity of English history, even to an undistinguished pupil like myself.

Chapter 3

In one of the more famous entries in *Who's Who* Osbert Sitwell wrote that he had been 'educated during the holidays away from Eton'. Education is not the right word in my case, but certainly the divorce and remarriage of both my parents shortly before I went to Eton meant that while I was there I had during the course of my holidays some strangely contrasting and even conflicting experiences. These may have contributed towards my indifferent state of health at the time. I used to suffer regularly from agonizing sinus pains. I was told that I should have an operation, but my mother had a great fear of what she always termed 'the knife', so fortunately I had none, and the pains gradually faded away. Also I suffered from a fearful complaint in hot weather, when tiny water blisters would form on the palms of my hands and between my fingers, and I had to apply calamine lotion in large quantities and wear cotton gloves to contain the irritation. This condition, which may have been what is termed psychosomatic, likewise ceased after I left school.

Under my parents' divorce settlement my mother had the custody of my sister, Patricia, who was two and a half years younger than me, whilst during the holidays we both spent half of the time with one parent and half with the other. When I was away at school Patricia, or Patsy as we all called her and as I shall call her from now on, was with my mother. She never went to any kind of boarding school, and since my mother was constantly on the move I do not suppose that Patsy had a very steady or regular schooling. She grew up to be a beautiful young woman with romantic illusions about life. She read a great deal in a haphazard way, and she used to write poetry of an execrably sentimental kind. My mother, whose judgement was always overruled by her affections, encouraged Patsy to believe that she was a budding Omar Khayyam. I myself did nothing to persuade her otherwise, but I could never feel really close to her because she inhabited a private world of make-believe which one could not seriously enter. We loved one another, though, and we had this particular bond of being shuttled to and fro between our parents.

My mother's second husband was a Mexican named Billy de Landa. I do not know where she met him. He belonged to a distinguished family, Mexican grandees they might be called, wholly Spanish, with all the haughty attitudes of that country's aristocracy. The father, Don Guillermo de Landa y Escandón, had, I believe, been close to President Díaz at the time that Mexican oil was first being discovered and exploited. The family therefore had a little money. Billy, my stepfather, was totally improvident, and never to my knowledge had any kind of a job. He was shorter than my mother, tubby and chubby, with sleek dark hair, mentally underdeveloped, pretty simple: but he had considerable personal charm, and my mother with her usual susceptibility was captivated. As I recall him, he had two chief passions, polo and baccarat or chemin de fer. My mother built a small villa at Biarritz, where Billy's tastes could be suitably provided for. I was constantly on the polo field watching his somewhat indifferent performance. That he could play at all was an achievement, because he had usually been up late the night before disporting himself at the casino. I used to observe him from my bedroom window entering the villa at five or six o'clock in the morning, carefully removing his shoes, and tip-toeing up the stairs, my mother having long since retired to bed. He was not a heavy drinker, but with his weird hours he must have imbibed his fair share of alcohol. He used to take me with him occasionally to the casino, although that would have been to the early evening session; and I suppose that he must have lied convincingly about my age to get me in. To me it was the acme of excitement. I became hypnotized by the weird characters whose eyes were endlessly fixed on the roulette wheel or the chouette from which the cards at chemin de fer were dealt, and I sensed the compulsiveness of gambling, although mercifully never succumbing.

There were other pleasures at Biarritz. The villa for instance was built very close to a newly created golf course, named Chiberta, which was carved out of a pine forest close to the sea, and my mother and I played there regularly. So did Billy, rather against his will for golf was not a game which came to him as naturally as it did to pretty well every member of my mother's family, and as it might have done to myself had I persevered.

Then there was the sea itself, the turbulent Bay of Biscay, in which we used to bathe despite waves that seemed immense and water that was seldom warm. My great hope when I went on the beach was to meet Barbara Hutton. In those days, by which I mean 1926 and 1927, she was my dream girl, and she was indeed a dream of beauty. She was four years younger than I was, but she was very precocious, and she developed the outward signs of femininity at an early age. Her figure was exquisitely proportioned, with feet so tiny and narrow that no ready-made shoe could ever fit them. Her mother had died when she was only five. This was the major cause of her life being so unhappy, for her father fundamentally neglected her yet showered material possessions upon her, paid for by what had been her mother's money, to the extent that she was grotesquely spoilt while she was still a child. She was a prototype of the poor little rich girl, but she was very, very attractive and there were plenty of adolescents besides myself who had succumbed. My chief rival was Bobby Lowenstein, whose father was an international financier, and likewise the possessor of a villa at Biarritz. Bobby used to dance well, which made me envious: I can still see him dancing the charleston in his bedroom for my benefit, wearing co-respondent shoes and nothing else. His father disappeared mysteriously from an aeroplane over the English Channel at the time of the 1929 crash, and I have heard no word of Bobby for many years. Barbara remained a good friend of my sister Patsy and myself long after the period of adolescence, and when I married in 1935 Joan, my wife, likewise came to know and love her.

When with my mother I was not only at Biarritz. We also visited most of the other French watering resorts. Once or twice we went to Deauville in the north, and several times to Cannes. The pattern was always rather similar, polo by day and casino by night for Billy, and various excursions and expeditions for Patsy and myself, tennis lessons, ballroom dancing lessons from a handsome Greek named Maurice who taught me the tango and slow waltz, and meals in expensive restaurants and in the villas of the wealthy. From Cannes we would go to Monte Carlo which aroused visions of deposed kings waiting to be restored; and international financiers and other sinister figures who controlled the destiny of nations from their Hôtel de Paris suites. Sir Basil Zaharoff, we fancied, was constantly there although seldom seen. It was a Baroness Orczy world in which reality scarcely existed, but to which I longed to gain admittance.

There was also a villa at St Jean Cap Ferrat (close to Monte Carlo) where we stayed although I think before my mother remarried. This was the Villa Fiorentina, belonging at the time to Sir Arthur du Cros, a wealthy businessman who in those days largely controlled the Dunlop Rubber Company of which for a short while he made my father a director. It was from the Villa Fiorentina that I first visited the opera. The work was *Parsifal*, at the opera house in Monte Carlo, an unsuitable work for a boy of eleven or twelve and an incongruous setting: and it would not be true to say that my love of opera stemmed from that evening. After the war, when I was married and the Fiorentina belonged to Enid Kenmare and her son Rory Cameron, Joan and I visited it often, as did my mother, for Lady Kenmare was a very close friend of hers: but by then the villa had been transformed into a decorator's dream.

Arthur du Cros also owned a large house named Craigweil on the south coast of England, at Aldwick near Bognor; and for a while (it must have been just after the war) my parents had a cottage close at hand, so that we saw him regularly, and also his very pretty ward and constant companion, Winnie Birkbeck. Craigweil House was lent to King George V for his recuperation after a very serious illness in 1929, and it was thus that Bognor became Bognor Regis. Today the house and grounds are gone, and in their place is a housing estate.

My holidays, or rather that part of my holidays spent with my mother, were not exclusively spent in France. We went quite often to Scotland, where her brothers and sisters mostly lived. My favourite was Vera de Falbe, nicknamed Vubby, whose husband, William, was of Danish extraction. He was a member of and worked at Lloyd's. They had no children of their own, and they lavished kindnesses upon their nephews and nieces. Uncle Willie knew of my love of stamps, stimulated first by W. J. Oakley at Ludgrove and then much assisted by my mother going round the world in 1921 with Lord Furness on his yacht *Sapphire*, when she sent me unused sets of the stamps of the various British colonies and dependencies through which they passed. Uncle Willie gave me his own collection which was strong in Danish and other foreign stamps, but the whole lot was sold by me a few years later to pay a trivial debt.

The de Falbes' home was in Inverness-shire, close to Kingussie, in the shadow of a mountain called Creag Dhubh. The name of the house was Biallaid. It was a simple two-storey building, unpretentious and welcoming, with character-istic white harl walls, the doors and window-frames painted black, and dark slate roof. There was a small grouse moor, and birch woods resembling olive groves, in which I tried to shoot game: but because being left-handed I fired from the left shoulder, with a gun intended for the more customary right shoulder, I was usually wide of the target, comforting for the birds but dis-couraging for me, although in later life I did not regret having abandoned shooting at an early age, for it is both addictive and costly. In any event, a visit to my de Falbe uncle and aunt, whether to Scotland or to a small house which they owned near St Albans, was always something to which I greatly looked forward. At each house she had a dairy, and I loved milking the cows, separating the milk and making butter and cheese. Likewise, she was an enthusiastic gardener, and this surely kindled one of my own later passions. She was a talented mimic, doing little sketches in the manner of the versatile American artist Ruth Draper, and we used to beg for a nightly treat, for she was both funny and moving. Her health was poor. She suffered from dreadful asthma before any of the modern palliatives had been developed. She used to inhale the fumes of some kind of red-hot charcoal-like substance, which gave her tempor-ary relief. She died before she was sixty, but not until she and her husband had been involved in one of the most terrible rail disasters of all time, the Blue Train Express to the South of France, in which Uncle Willie was killed but she survived, heroically succouring the injured, despite her tragic bereavement.

The house near Kingussie is now lived in by Katherine, the warm-hearted courageous widow of my mother's eldest brother, Harry Pelham Burn. He was a grand man, a distinguished soldier with strong features and a strong personality, intensely masculine, born to command, but with a great twinkle in his eye. In the First War he had commanded the 51st Highland Division, the youngest general in the British Army, and for years afterwards he had fearful nightmares, being haunted by memories of the Passchendaele bloodbath. I held him in real awe. He had very strict standards; I am sure that he took the poorest view of my mother's French watering resort life, although in character they had many similarities, and like her, indeed like all the family, he was extremely super-stitious.

There were two other brothers, Pelham and Jim. Pelham I knew the least well. He was said to have been fond of Scotland's native beverage. In any event his health was poor and he died while I was still young. He had a delightful son, Ronnie, to whom my aunt Vera had bequeathed Biallaid. In fact he did not stay there for long, perhaps because of marriage; and he sold the house to his uncle Harry and moved to London to work, achieving a measure of success as a business efficiency consultant. He had been an officer in the Seaforth Highlanders, and was taken prisoner in 1940. His life I fear was seldom happy and like his father he died before he was sixty.

Jim was the youngest of the three brothers. He was a softer and gentler version of Harry, a great golfer and shot, extravagant like my mother, with a real Achilles' heel, an irresistible urge to order suits of clothes, many of which I am sure were scarcely worn. At one moment when he was growing older, he decided to reduce the size of his wardrobe, and he disposed of a quantity of suits. Two of these I acquired, notably one made of brown vicuña, which fitted me perfectly without alteration and which I still wear regularly, although it is well over forty years old.

In addition to Vera, there was one other sister, Dorothy, the wife of Colonel Moncrieff Skene, who owned Pitlour, a beautiful house in Fife, and who also was an outstandingly fine golfer and sportsman. Dorothy shared the strong and distinguished looks of the rest of her family. I did not see her as often as I would have wished. Her daughter Helen was and still is very handsome. In my ado-lescent years I found her physically most desirable, although I do not suppose that my feelings were at all reciprocated; but in any event I was told that intimacy between first cousins was not to be encouraged, and so the matter was never put to the test.

My holidays with my father were a total contrast. He married my stepmother Olive in 1923. She had previously been married to Lord Victor Paget, the younger brother of Lord Anglesey and of Lady Pembroke. By him she had had two children, Peggy and Sandy. Before that she had been a star of the musical comedy stage, appearing at the Gaiety Theatre as Olive May, one of George

Edwards's band of beauties, several of whom had married into the peerage and all of whom, or so I was convincingly told, were extremely correct and *comme il faut* in their behaviour. Victor Paget's marriage with Olive did not last very long. He was, I fancy, not at all a good husband to her, and certainly when they parted his family wholly took her side, for he was in the words of one of them 'an old blackguard', profligate and promiscuous.

I do not know where my father first met Olive, but I know that he saw her quite frequently at Wilton, the home of the Pembrokes, and I think it was there that they became engaged. Once they were married their devotion to one another was extreme. Olive was always exceptionally kind to me, yet I could not help feeling the odd one out, for there were not only my stepbrother and stepsister, but also Olive's sister, Gertrude. Gar, as she was unattractively called, who had been her dresser in theatrical days and who then moved in as a kind of housekeeper, was a tiny little woman with a rather large, rather over made-up face, lacking any real life of her own. During the summer holidays, on two or three occasions my father rented a private school near Haywards Heath; and of those weeks, goodness knows why, my most vivid memory is of shelling and peeling walnuts for Olive, which she used to soak in a glass of port before eating them. The school was presumably rented to give us space and grounds in which to exercise. We were always joined by Olive's mother, who went by the unfortunate name of Mrs Meatyard and whom I see in my mind's eye dressed in black bombazine, resembling the photographs of Queen Victoria in old age; and by her brother Ralph, a large florid man who managed the Mayfair branch of the National Provincial Bank with notable success. Thus I, and my sister too when she was with me, felt rather outnumbered, and outclassed, particularly when it came to competitive sports.

I remember also that we stayed in lodgings at Littlehampton, where my father took me to play golf on the local sandy seaside course with a delightful professional named Riseborough, and I rode on the beach, falling off the horse and breaking my right fore-arm, which was then badly set; and my mother in her rather bossy manner took me off to a clinic near le Touquet, I think at a place named Berck, where the fracture was re-set. Fortunately I was left-handed, and afterwards for two or three weeks I was able to play one-armed golf, hitting the ball a surprising distance with my left arm while the right remained in plaster and a sling. Any love which I might have had for riding was thus discouraged at an early age.

The essential thing about my holidays with Olive and my father, Hengoo as she called him, was that they were utterly unsocial and domesticated, whether we were at the private school at Haywards Heath or in lodgings by the seaside or at No. 6 Victoria Road, Kensington, the large solidly-built and commodious house which they jointly bought and where they stayed until towards the end of the war, when my father bought a house at Cobham in Surrey. It was called Leigh Hill House, and it belonged to Sir Philip Warter, who asked me to sell it back to him after my father's death. It was quiet, secluded and nondescript but my father and Olive were very happy there, although for all too short a time, since she died very suddenly in 1947, after which my father continued to live there alone for another ten years. There was, I thought at the time, an element of dullness missing from my holidays with my mother, when we moved in a strange cosmopolitan world of intrinsically meretricious but, to an ignorant schoolboy, rather glamorous and intriguing people. One thing must be true, that these contrasted and conflicting worlds largely contributed towards making me the schizophrenic character I am.

I left Eton at the end of July 1928. My mother had by then fairly well parted from Billy de Landa. They had increasingly realized their basic incompatibility, and in the later stages of their marriage there were endless rows, with my mother's faithful lady's maid an involuntary witness. On more than one occasion I remember my mother's punch-line, 'Pack the suitcases, Lamport,' following which mock preparations for departure would be made. It is certain that when my mother took me to stay with Sir Basil and Lady Montgomery in Scotland that August Billy de Landa was not with us, and arrangements for their divorce the following year had I fancy already been set in train.

The Montgomerys were living in an imposing house named Kinross on the borders of Loch Leven. It was and surely still is a beautiful setting for romance. I knew that there were to be two fellow guests, Lady Bridges and her daughter, Alvilde, whom I had not met. Whether the meeting had been in any way planned by either of the mothers or by the hostess I do not know. I should think it unlikely because I was only just eighteen. In any event, long before getting to Kinross House, without having seen or heard anything of Alvilde I had made up my mind that a great moment was approaching, and I had in a sense almost fallen in love before we met. Therefore when a young girl appeared, not obviously pretty but very attractive, not unlike a film star named Dolores del Rio, capable then, as she has steadily remained, of making pretty sharp observations, taking nothing at its face value, I was fairly smitten: and my feelings and my courage were strengthened by the great kindness shown to me by her mother. We were not there very long, but we saw a lot of one another, going for long walks and rowing over to the island in the centre of the loch where Mary Queen of Scots had once been kept a prisoner; and when I left, I felt I was head over heels in love.

I went from Kinross to Hanover intending to study German for two or three weeks preparatory to going up to Cambridge. I stayed with a family whose

name I have quite forgotten but who had two very sympathetic young children
with whom I was to my astonishment a great hit. While I was in Hanover, I
tried to study. I spent much of my time at the post office, though, for I wrote
daily to Alvilde, and each letter became more expressively emotional than the
last. On returning to England I found my epistolary professions of love had far
surpassed the true extent of our intimacy with one another, and when we met
again I felt rather sheepish and our first conversation must have been very self-
conscious and stilted.

It was in the autumn of 1928 that I went up to Cambridge. It had been
decided that I should study foreign languages as a necessary preliminary to
sitting for the Foreign Office entrance examination. In so far as I had an aptitude
it was for languages, but it was never properly developed. The fault was largely
mine for allowing too many distractions to interfere with my work. However,
I should have been more strongly urged by my father to spend far more time
studying abroad. Apart from three brief sojourns with families in Germany at
Hanover, Munich and Heidelberg, the last of these being the only place where I
really worked, I went nowhere else. I was not for instance encouraged to go
either to France or to Spain so as to absorb their languages into my system. The
result was that although I was capable of taking a II (1) in German and a II (2)
in Spanish in Part I of the Modern Languages Tripos at Cambridge it was done
basically by the book and not through a true inner understanding: proper
mastery of idiom and accent was denied to me, and this is something which I
have always deeply regretted. Today, with the great advances there have been in
methods of language teaching, it perhaps matters less, but in 1928 it mattered
enormously, especially if one was destined, as at first it seemed I was, for the
Diplomatic Service. It is all the more strange that my father did not insist, for
before he passed into the Foreign Office in 1908 he himself had spent a great
deal of time abroad. But, however expert I might have become, it is unlikely
that I should in the event have sat for the examination. I knew how intensely
competitive it was. Also, and this became the dominating factor, I decided to
leave Cambridge after two years in order to get a job in London as a necessary
prerequisite of marriage, whereas for the Foreign Office the full three years at
Cambridge would have been necessary, followed by a further two years of
study, with an uncertain result at the end of that time.

My reason for going to Trinity quite simply was that my father had himself
been there. At no moment during my rather short stay at Cambridge did I
develop any real sense of identity with the place. This was in part because I was
so much in love with Alvilde that I worried above all about my next meeting
with her, and I absented myself from the University as often as I dared. Also,
however, I am sure that the Cambridge system (as it then was), whereby an

undergraduate's first one or two years were spent in lodgings rather than in college, greatly lessened the possibility of establishing a sense of identity. Indeed, for this as well as for other reasons, I regret that I did not go to Oxford, where it was the custom to live in college from the start, only moving out to lodgings during the last year: while for those destined for any kind of public life it has always seemed to me that the products of Cambridge have tended to be too introverted and specialized. There was a remarkable impersonality about it, and a sort of remoteness between dons and undergraduates. No member of the academic staff left any distinct impression on my mind, not even I fear my tutor F. J. Dykes.

There were only two exceptions, and with them my contacts were social and had nothing to do with work. They were George Rylands, known as Dadie to his friends, and Steven Runciman, both of them Fellows, one of King's and the other of Trinity. They acted as magnets for aspiring undergraduates. Both of them were kind and hospitable. Steven was a member of the famous shipping family, entertaining on a generous scale. He had a terrific sense of drollery, stretching his eyes wide as he told his outrageous stories. He was above all a great scholar, and he developed into a highly respected historian, making the Crusades his particular subject.

Dadie made English literature, above all English poetry, his subject. He played a major role in the theatrical life of Cambridge, being the moving spirit of the Marlowe Dramatic Society, which was originally founded in 1907 to perform neglected Elizabethan plays, with Rupert Brooke as its first secretary. Dadie both acted and produced, tackling all the leading Shakespearean roles. Later, together with Peggy Ashcroft and Cecil Day Lewis, he started the Apollo Society; and over the years he was responsible for a large number of distinguished poken word gramophone records, covering all the plays and poems of Shakespeare and much else besides. He had an eager, shining, new-pin look about him, generating a sense of enjoyment in those about him; and so he has remained for half a century.

My room-mate at Cambridge was Cuthbert Fleetwood-Hesketh, who had been with me at both Ludgrove and Eton. We shared lodgings together in Park Parade. He was a very charming sweet-tempered person, something of an eccentric, addicted in those days to absinthe, which I could perceive at close quarters to be most pernicious in its effects. Fortunately his addiction did not persist. He tried for the Foreign Office examination, failed the oral test, and after the war became a stockbroker. He died in 1969.

I made a number of new friends of whom by far the most important was Victor Rothschild. He had come up from Harrow where he had been a brilliant performer at games, and he was to develop into a distinguished scientist, as well as holding a number of important public appointments. He and I used to play golf often on the famous nine-hole course at Mildenhall, as well as bridge in the Pitt Club. I saw him frequently, visiting his home during the vacation, and I grew to know well several members of his remarkable family. Until the outbreak of war we continued to meet regularly, both before and after our respective marriages, and my wife and I were frequently his guests. No one I have known could be more charming or more impossible. He was immensely attractive to women, not because of his name or his wealth, but because of his striking good looks, his penetrating insight, his outspokenness, his ready wit, and his originality of mind. He had a sadistic streak too, enjoying treating people as though they were on the dissecting board in his laboratory. As a very minor instance, a favourite trick of his was to put three-star brandy in a Napoleon brandy bottle, so that the more gullible could savour their glass of cognac convinced that they were drinking some kind of nectar. But if he did treat someone harshly he would usually, although not always, compensate for this subsequently by an exceptional display of kindness.

Among those destined to play a continuously important part in my life was Jack Donaldson. His name will recur quite often. While at Cambridge I did not know him well, because he was a couple of years older and his academic and intellectual life was on a very different plane from mine. He took a double first in law and philosophy, and when he was not studying he played serious music on the violin and jazz on the saxophone, the latter in Fred Elizalde's band. Through him I made a rare collection of jazz records, which, like a dolt, at some point in my amorous strivings I presented as an act of homage to a girl of great beauty, named Betty Snagge, without the desired result being achieved.

I suppose that my most consistently close friend at Cambridge was Francis Baring, my Eton contemporary. He had an aunt, Lady Mar and Kelly, his mother's sister, who lived at Alloa in Scotland. By careful contriving it was arranged that my loved one, Alvilde, should be invited to stay at Alloa and that I should drive up with Francis from London for what promised to be a delectable holiday, planned to follow a visit I was to make to the United States in August 1929, together with my mother and sister.

I waited eagerly for my return, being impatient to get to Alloa, but it turned out otherwise. Soon after crossing the border into Scotland, in Dumfriesshire, Francis and I were involved in a really grim accident. It was a true accident in that no one could be held blameworthy. The chief victim was myself. I was catapulted out of Francis's car, which then proceeded to turn a somersault over me.

This is an extract from a vivid and touching letter he wrote to my mother who was still in America:

Alloa House, Alloa   *Sunday, 3rd September 1929*

. . . It happened as follows. We were going north on our way here and there was a motor
cycle coming towards us, followed by a Morris Saloon. The first thing I saw was the motor
cycle swerving all over the road as if out of control. It appears his back tyre was half off,
so he can't be blamed. He then stopped dead in front of the Morris and left the Morris
driver in such a position that he *had* to hit either the motor cycle or us. He pulled slightly
to his right, and just caught my right front wheel. That sent us literally spinning. My car
turned over twice completely. I stayed in it all the time, but poor Garrett was thrown out,
I haven't the least idea when or how, nor has he. I was trapped in the car as all the doors
had jammed; I expected it to catch fire any moment, but it didn't God knows why. I
could see Garrett lying in awful pain in the edge of the road, and got to him as soon as I
could . . .

My father, who never liked writing to my mother, wrote somewhat drily:

Buccleugh Arms Hotel,   *1st September 1929*
Moffat, Dumfriesshire
Dear Kathleen,

I am very sorry to tell you that Garrett had rather a bad motoring smash while coming
up to Scotland with Francis Baring.

They were run into about ten miles from here, and Garrett was thrown out on to
some flints at the side of the road. His right arm was broken, and he had a lot of cuts
though mostly superficial ones. Also slight spinal concussion.

They brought him to the very nice cottage hospital here, and I have come up to look
after him. He is going on very well, is in no sort of danger whatever, and we hope to
move him to a nursing home (14 Drumsheugh Gardens) in Edinburgh on Friday. I
expect he will only have to stay there about a week. Then he will probably go to the
Mars at Alloa, and then back to us in London.

It is very bad luck, but it might have been so much worse that one must be grateful.
And all the people at the Cottage hospital here are delightful, and the doctors most
efficient.

Garrett sends his love to you both. He is getting on *really* well, and I hope will be quite
all right by the time you get back.

Love to Patsy.
                          Yours,
                          D.

Apart from extensive cuts and bruises and a broken arm, I was also paralysed
from the waist downwards for two or three weeks. I vividly recall the Moffat
Cottage Hospital where I shared a room with Francis. He sobbed all through the
night while I floated on pink clouds evoked by heroin, unaware at first of my
precarious condition.

There was no question of my getting to Alloa. Instead, I was moved after two weeks to a nursing home in Edinburgh, where I stayed the best part of a month recovering. My family came to see me, and also poor Alvilde, but my general appearance was so dreadful that I had no desire to see anyone but my nurse, whom I regarded as my adored saviour and a dream of beauty.

I must surely have returned late that autumn to Cambridge to resume my studies, and above all to resume my regular visits to London to see Alvilde, returning by the last train in an ecstasy of frustrated desire.

All through this time Alvilde's mother treated me with the utmost sympathy. She had a grand sense of humour, and we developed a real rapport. However, Alvilde's father, Sir Thomas Bridges, terrified me. He was 6 feet 6 inches tall. He had been a distinguished general in the First War, and even before that he had a considerable military career; and I always found it hard to think of him in any other terms. I felt that he did not welcome me as his daughter's suitor and regarded me as a trespasser, although I went constantly to their house, so perhaps he was less intolerant than at the time I supposed. In any event both of Alvilde's parents must have consented to her coming with me for a ski-ing holiday one winter in Mürren, rather audacious for those far-off days, for she was accompanied only by an older woman friend of hers, who came as an unobtrusive chaperone. We had a wonderful fortnight, the only flaw being that we were a couple of rabbits on the nursery slopes at the resort which we realized too late was the spiritual home of the cream of the British ski-ing community.

During my second and as it turned out final year at Cambridge my father suffered a considerable blow. At some point during the late twenties he had succeeded Lord Churston as the London representative of an American private bank, Hallgarten and Co. of New York. After Wall Street crashed in late 1929 they decided they must economize. The first thing to go was the London office and my poor father, who had made immense efforts to master the theory of chart reading and so on, surrounding the walls of his office with beautiful charts drawn by himself plotting the movements of the various indices, suddenly found himself out of a job. And it was at this point that he decided that he had had enough of being the servant of others, and resolved to be his own master, and to read for the Bar, with a view to practising as a barrister. He in fact passed the examination in 1934 at the age of fifty, taking a first in Roman Law, after which he entered the chambers of Victor Russell, a KC with a massive divorce practice, until at the outbreak of war he was recalled to public service.

A further blow to my father around this period, or at least a considerable irritant, was the fact that my mother, following her divorce from Billy de Landa, decided to resume not her maiden but her former married name. She accordingly became Kathleen, Countess of Drogheda, to the intense and not unjustified annoyance of my father. My mother always said that she did it for the sake of my sister and myself, but I fully sympathized with my father's irritation.

Before I left Cambridge in 1930 there was a brief discussion as to whether my future prospects would be enhanced were I to stay on at the university for a further year, in order to study economics. I remember going to see D. H. Robertson to seek his guidance. He was most emphatic that for me to do a two-year course in only a year, in a subject so alien to me was totally unrealistic. Accordingly I left, contenting myself with spare-time reading of Marshall's *Principles of Economics* and later Keynes' *General Theory*. The other books I read in those days tended to be earnest and radical, notably G. D. H. Cole, R. H. Tawney and Bertrand Russell, who as a rule was way above my head. I became obsessed as well with the writings of Freud, feeling for a while that I really had found the key to human behaviour; and to complement Freud I wallowed in Havelock Ellis's *Studies in the Psychology of Sex*, with Casanova for lighter relief, whose exploits I always envied.

Chapter 4

When I first came to London I had no clear idea what I was going to do. I recall visiting Vichy with my mother, why Vichy goodness knows, where we met Solomon Guggenheim, a member of the family which then controlled the American Smelting and Refining Company. Among the interests of Asarco was a large investment in a British company, the Mining Trust, which controlled the Mount Isa mine in Queensland, later to become one of the world's great copper mines, but in those days only thought to contain payable lead and zinc with silver as a by-product.

As a result of this chance encounter, Sol Guggenheim spoke to Leslie Urquhart, chairman of the Mining Trust, who before the war had had a major stake in mining in Russia which naturally disappeared with the Revolution, although he still appeared to have more than a competence, with a large mansion in Kent and a generally prosperous air. It was accordingly agreed that I should be taken into the company's offices in Adelaide House, in King William Street, opposite the Fishmongers' Hall, becoming part of the crowd flowing over London Bridge. Before I started my somewhat dispiriting time there, where my humble task consisted largely in laboriously entering mining assays in long columns as they were received each week from Mount Isa, it was thought desirable that I should learn the elementary principles of book-keeping and accountancy. Accordingly I enrolled at the office of Messrs Foulks Lynch, who ran regular courses of instruction for young hopefuls, and for all I know still do so to this day.

Just before I started going to work in Adelaide House my father wrote to me on 15 November 1930:

Dear old man,

Just a line to wish you the best of luck for the beginning of what will, I hope, be a very successful career, on Monday. I have been thinking a lot about Guggenheim's telegram, and though it is absolutely non-committal, I feel that he does probably mean to look after you and that much, if not everything, will depend on the report he gets about your work from Urquhart after a few months time.

So do your utmost even if the work itself is dull as I suspect at first it will be. And don't think me interfering if I make the following suggestions:—

Make up your mind to get to your office always five minutes too early rather than five minutes too late.

Don't keep too keen an eye on the clock when 5 o'clock is coming along, and be ready to stay on past the time without a murmur if there is any work unfinished.

Do everything cheerfully however beastly it seems, and if there is any particularly unpleasant job to be done volunteer for it.

Make up your mind to get on well with the office staff even if they are somewhat unpleasing as some of them probably are.

If you have any slack hours in the office, as one has in most offices, don't waste them but read up about something that it will be useful to you to know in your future in the Guggenheim concerns.

If possible keep up your Spanish.

I do feel that for your future its probably tremendously important to put in all you know while you are in Urquhart's London office. Hence the foregoing homily which is now off my chest!

I think that I did my best to comply with his admirable precepts, but my destiny lay elsewhere.

Meanwhile, my passionate but frustratingly unfulfilled love affair with Alvilde was all the time raging, and by moving to London I was able to see her a good deal more often. She became very friendly with both my parents. Her mother was fond of me, but her father was convinced, rightly, that I was quite unready for marriage. Financially my prospects were poor. I was insecure and unsure of myself, and this expressed itself in really dreadful, unforgivable bouts of jealousy, the sort of agonizing insensate feelings which by those not a prey to them simply cannot be comprehended. Poor Alvilde was the sufferer. If she smiled at anyone I thought it an open invitation to flirt, a raised skirt seemed to be a deliberate provocation. I wanted to know her every move and every encounter. At one moment, seeking respite, she escaped to Rome with her mother. I persuaded my mother to accompany me to Rome in pursuit. It was too late, though, to prevent the inevitable and indeed necessary separation. Nothing but a fundamental change in me could have prevented that. How we came finally to part I forget, but it happened without leaving any permanent scar. She married in 1933, and we have remained close and intimate friends to this day.

Initially, after leaving Cambridge and coming to live and work in London, I stayed in my mother's house in Park Row, a group of tiny Queen Anne houses in a cul-de-sac off Knightsbridge, looking out towards Hyde Park, now regrettably demolished with much else besides to make way for Bowater House. It was however not long before I wanted a place of my own and I rented a service flat in Ryder Street, St James's, in a building which likewise later was pulled down (without architectural loss) as part of a redevelopment scheme resulting in *The Economist*'s building. From there I went daily by bus or tube to my workplace in the City, but in the evenings I was out and about quite a lot. Several of my Cambridge friends were in London, and these I continued to see.

One of our stranger diversions was the Worst Play Club. This had been formed before I left Cambridge, and its membership was not confined to the products of one university. The purpose of the club was very simple. It was to dine early, and then head for theatreland, choosing a play to which one could gain admittance in the cheapest seats without previous booking, and laugh noisily at what seemed to us the more ridiculous lines in the play, which was painful to the artists, maddening for the audience, and not creditable to us. All the more is this true when one reflects that the members included Jack Donaldson, later to become Minister for the Arts; Heywood Hill, who became London's most exclusive bookseller; Peter Fleming, gallant soldier, author and explorer; Gilbert Debenham, a successful psychoanalyst; Ralph Jarvis, a charming, attractive eccentric, and a very able banker; Victor Hinchingbroke, a delightful but disappointed Tory MP; Tom Mitford, handsome breaker of hearts and brother of six remarkable sisters; and then Nigel Birch, enamoured in those days of Tom's sister Nancy, a highly skilled stockbroker who retired before he was thirty because he foresaw what disasters lay ahead, joined the Army where he distinguished himself, and after the war entered Parliament, becoming the scourge of the Government when in opposition and a minister of great integrity when in power.

Although it was a time of economic depression and poverty, the social life of London went on in its carefree fashion. As a potentially eligible young bachelor, I received my full share of invitations to the debutante dances which took place almost nightly during the so-called Season, white tie and tails being the compulsory garb.

Two of these occasions have stuck in my mind. White tie mishaps they might be called. The first was at Derby House, where I was invited to dine before a dance. Getting ready for dinner I cut myself shaving. I did what I could to stop the bleeding, but while I was straining my neck to fasten the butterfly collar the cut reopened. Within seconds the collar and tie and stiff shirt front were all stained red. Frantically I applied whatever I could to the wound, and struggled to transfer studs and links to another shirt, forcing them through the starched front and cuffs. All seemed to be well when just as I was fastening the last button the bleeding recommenced, and again everything was spotted. A third change of clothes was inescapable. At last I arrived, frantic, and half an hour late. The dinner had started, and I was guided shamefacedly to the one empty chair, which to my horror was next to the hostess, who did everything she could to put me at my ease: but ever since that day I have regarded the evening tail-coat as an invention of the devil.

The second occasion was at Belvoir Castle, the home of the Duke of Rutland whose elder daughter Ursula was a friend. The occasion was a shooting party, but I did not shoot. Very early after dinner all the men retired to bed so that their eyes should be clear in the morning. Ursula and I, together with two of her friends, Virginia Gilliat and Ruth Primrose (the grand-daughter, as it happened, of old Lady Derby), decided to go to the still-room to make some cocoa. We were there for half an hour or so, joking and laughing in a most innocent manner. As we were going up to bed, when we reached the first-floor landing a figure emerged from the shadows in a white dressing gown. I saw it was the Duke. 'Go to your room,' he said to Ursula, and then followed me to mine. 'I want you to leave my house at once,' he angrily said, without any request for an explanation, evidently assuming that I must have been doing some dreadful thing to his daughter and her friends. I pointed out that at that time of night I might find it hard to get my car from the garage. Reluctantly he agreed that I should stay until the morning. At dawn, after a sleepless night, I packed my case and crept away to the garage, smarting under a monstrous sense of injustice, for, whatever sins I might have committed elsewhere, on this occasion I was wholly innocent, except of having caused His Grace to make an egregious ass of himself. Sure enough within a few days I received a handsome letter of apology, but memories of the episode never left my mind.

During this period I went for the first time to Salzburg, staying in a hotel with my Cambridge friend Martin Debenham, and succeeding in making myself quite seriously ill through an idiotic attempt to become beautifully bronzed by the sun within twenty-four hours of arriving. I have been to Salzburg when it has rained day and night for a week, but upon this occasion the weather was superb. I went to one of the lakes, lay all day in the sun, became lobster-red, and halfway through the *Magic Flute* that evening passed completely out, overcome by sunstroke: and then I spent the rest of my holiday in bed with a high fever, all the skin on my face and body cracked and peeled, a punishment for my vanity and a lesson never to be forgotten.

Among the country houses I used most frequently to visit was Plas Newydd, the house of Lord and Lady Anglesey, he being the brother of my stepmother Olive's first husband, Victor Paget, and she the sister of the choleric Duke of Rutland. I loved the whole of the Anglesey family, but my particular friend at the time was the eldest daughter Caroline, later to become Lady Caroline Duff, who was roughly my contemporary. She did not have the spectacular beauty of her younger sister, Liz. She was however a great breaker of hearts, not through any conscious effort on her part, nor because of her tall slim figure, her thick brown hair, her deep-throated infectious laugh, nor the mischievous twinkle in her eyes; but because of her strange, enigmatic quality and an irresistible fascination.

My friend Jack Donaldson was a regular visitor to Plas Newydd and he was captivated by Caroline. The three of us used to meet together frequently in London, going to concerts and then returning for supper to Jack's mother's house where he was then living. After his mother's death he invited the members of a string quartet being formed by the violinist Harry Blech to stay in the vacant rooms in the house, which they also used as a studio, while Jack went to work in the City. In those days the lot of a musician was far from easy. Apart from his immense help in the early development of the Blech string quartet, Jack also conceived the idea of a small music society which would give both employment and pleasure. He spoke to me, and jointly we launched the Quartet Society, later named the Chamber Music Society, the members of which were drawn from among our friends and the friends of our friends. Each member paid a modest annual subscription, and in return was able to enjoy half a dozen or more chamber music concerts during the autumn and winter months, each concert being given in a different private house, usually the house of a London hostess known to enjoy or at least to respect serious music, and willing to lend her drawing room for the occasion. The names of the hostesses and of many but not all of the members would read a little like a page from Jennifer's Diary, but there is no doubt that the various artists engaged found the concerts helpful and beneficial.

One of the hostesses we had approached was Lady Wimborne, whose daughter Cynthia I knew. Wimborne House, which has now been pulled down, was run in style. The drawing room, where the concerts took place, was lined with mirrors and was entirely illuminated by candle-light from four or five large chandeliers as well as from wall brackets. The effect was striking. Furthermore, not only did Wimborne House offer the most splendid setting, but Lady Wimborne provided us all with a delicious cold supper after the concert. It was clear that the idea of our society appealed strongly to her, despite a somewhat slender knowledge of serious music, and it therefore seemed to me that it would be right and proper to invite her to become our president; with the result that after the first season all the concerts took place at Wimborne House, Alice Wimborne becoming a close and intimate friend of mine.

She was not a beauty but she had great elegance, and she had something of the *femme fatale* about her, perhaps more in her own imagination than in reality. She liked wearing rather languid tea-gowns, and she took particular pride in the long silky hair under her arms, reputed to be irresistible to men although not so in my personal experience. Alice was an eager smoker of cigars, and she had curtains installed in her car so that between appointments she could smoke unobserved. She was fairly uninhibited in her approach to life. She once told me that she regarded my mother as a child of nature, but the description could have fitted herself every bit as well.

There was a small committee to advise upon the planning of our concerts. It consisted of Malcolm Sargent, who was a fine pianist as well as conductor and a man who did much to promote the appreciation of music; Ivor Newton, a distinguished accompanist, and considerable wit; Patrick Hadley and Humphrey Procter-Gregg, both later to become professors of music, the latter with a particularly thankless task as head of the London Opera Centre. A subsequent addition was a young and brilliant composer, William Walton, the possessor of a sharp tongue, and a very quick wit. He was already a close friend of the Sitwell family, having collaborated with them in the composition of *Façade*: and they in turn were friendly with Alice, so that a ready-made bridge existed, over which Willie very soon passed, and an intimacy developed between himself and Alice which quite eclipsed my gentle *amitié amoureuse*.

Among the artists who performed was a friend of mine, the pianist Harriet Cohen. She was the great love of the composer Arnold Bax, and she did much to promote an interest in his and other British music. I found her attractive, with a beautiful body, very white skin and long black hair. She had a number of friends in the world of letters. On one occasion I was at a literary party she gave and Lytton Strachey was present. I had not been introduced to him, but when he left I was talking to Harriet. He glanced at me, said goodbye to her, and then went downstairs, paused, returned, took a gardenia from his button-hole and, to my embarrassment, without saying a word presented it to me, turned and departed, never to be seen by me again.

I said that in the first season of the Quartet Society we held our concerts in a number of different private houses. One of these was 7 Grosvenor Square, the home of Lady Cunard, who must then have been about fifty-five years old. I do not recall how I first came to meet her, but she was to play an important part in my formative years in London. By the time that I knew her and indeed for a number of years before then she was a widow. She had come to England from the United States before the turn of the century and in 1895 had married Sir Bache Cunard, a wealthy man with a home in Leicestershire, and Emerald (as we all called her) had conquered her fears and rode actively to hounds. At some point she had met Sir Thomas Beecham who gradually, and then swiftly after the death of Sir Bache in 1925, became the dominant force in her life. Thereafter London was her only home. She played a leading role as a hostess, although a number of the great ladies of the day regarded her with some disapproval as an upstart from across the Atlantic, somewhat outrageous in her behaviour, and not to be encouraged. The loss was theirs, for she was a major stimulant. She must also when young have been very attractive. She was small and fair, with tiny neat ankles and wrists, holding herself very erect and moving briskly. Lord Berners once described her as a canary of prey, which was pretty apt, for she had sharp bird-like features, and a gay chuckling laugh.

All her life she worked on the principle of keeping her acquaintance in constant repair, and it must have been because of this that I and several of my contemporaries less than half her age were admitted to her circle. I was invited quite often to lunch at her house. She had a disconcerting habit of entering the room twenty minutes after her guests were assembled. The reason was simply that she was an insomniac, and she used to read through half the night. Occasionally I slept in her house, and I would hear her drawing a bath at 5 o'clock in the morning. Her parties were gay and amusing. She provoked lively discussion, and she could animate the dullest gathering, turning the most boring of her guests into the star of the occasion. For a while I was one of her favourites, being nicknamed 'Lord Paramoore', and when I married in 1935 she was at first very displeased, although later she became even more closely my wife's friend than mine.

Thanks to her I was able to hear far more music than I could otherwise have done. She played an important part in finding financial support for Sir Thomas Beecham's activities in the field of opera, at Covent Garden in particular, where she had a regular box. She also took me to many concerts at the Queen's Hall, and through this I came to know much of the basic classical repertoire. Beecham himself always rather frightened me. He was eccentric in manner and speech, given to saying outrageous things, rotating his protruding eyes as he spoke. One example of his eccentricity always delighted me. Walking along Bond Street one day he was wearing a heavy overcoat. It was warmer than he had expected, so he hailed a taxi, threw the coat on to the seat, shut the door, and proceeded on his stately stroll, saying to the driver, 'Follow me.' He was not handsome, but his appearance was assisted by his monocle and his white spats, his large pearl tie-stud and his neatly groomed imperial. He was arrogant and could be cruel; but there is no doubt that he made a very great contribution to the musical life of Britain at a time when there was no official support or encouragement for the performing arts.

Among the group of young people to whom Emerald showed special kindness was a ravishingly beautiful girl, Penelope Dudley Ward, who was to become my second great love. She was more than four years younger than me, and she was barely eighteen when I first met her. Her mother Freda in those days was the particular friend of the Prince of Wales, who used to frequent Emerald's house, and this may have been the reason that Penelope came into the circle so young. Whatever the cause, the good fortune was mine – I fell deeply in love with her.

She had the beauty of a fairy princess. She was tall and slender as a reed, with lovely fair hair and blue eyes, delicate features with perfectly formed lips, slightly parted in gratified amazement at the joys and wonders of life, showing faultless teeth whenever she smiled. Each time that one saw her was a new revelation. To me in my enamoured state she seemed to convey a picture of pure innocence, seeing, hearing, and thinking no evil, radiating light and gaiety wherever she went, making allowances for the shortcomings of others, always anxious to help those whose lot was less happy than her own.

I was enthralled. I seized every opportunity of being with her. She had been spending a good deal of time in Munich, studying German. Since I already knew Munich slightly, upon one occasion I followed her there. The Intendant of the State Opera House, Clemens von Franckenstein, whose brother George was Austrian Ambassador in London, had met Pempie, and had been completely vanquished by her ethereal beauty; and she and her friends had free access to his box, from which I benefited during my short stay.

Pempie had a slightly younger sister, Angela, who was likewise a beauty. They complemented one another marvellously. Angie, as we called her, had immense sweetness in her nature, but lacked Pempie's quality of romantic other-worldliness. She was more of a tom-boy and far more of a realist. She attracted I think more admirers than Pempie and was much sought after. She married very young, her husband being by complete coincidence Bob Laycock, the boy I had most hero-worshipped and doted upon when I was at Eton.

I came to frequent Pempie's house; and Freda, her mother, always showed the greatest consideration towards me. At that time she was barely forty years old. I am not sure that she had ever had the beauty of either of her daughters, but she possessed a uniquely attractive quality, and was surrounded by adorers. She had a lovely slim figure, walking and holding herself very straight, with narrow highly-bred features, and constantly laughing eyes. When she was together with her daughters, they were like three sisters. They were closely knit, with no secrets from one another.

Freda was an important influence in my life. She could not be called an intellectual, but she had a very strong intellect, with penetrating insight and clarity of vision. She was extremely direct, and would not tolerate humbug or nonsense, hating cant and insincerity, and excelling at deflating the pompous without causing them pain in the process. She had a tremendous sense of fun, and of the ridiculous. Above all she had a charm which nobody could resist, and a true heart.

Although born in the last century, no one was more contemporary in her outlook. She perceived the social trends more sharply than anyone, and this I fancy was an important part of the bond between herself and the Prince of Wales, who in those days of slump suffered deeply from the evidence of widespread distress and poverty. Her maiden name was Birkin, a leading family of Nottingham where in Victorian times they had prospered in the manufacture of lace; and Freda's awareness of the impact of change was I feel sure heightened by her experience of the decline of that industry. Her mother was American, nicknamed Pearly because of the beauty of her teeth. She had become a grandmother when barely forty, an example followed by Freda, who now, at the age of eighty, is a great-great-grandmother.

When I first knew Freda she was living in St John's Wood, exercising a remarkable talent for acquiring rather conventional houses and then modernizing and decorating them along clean and simple lines, spending a few months in residence and then reselling them, together with the furnishings, for a very acceptable profit. She helped the Prince of Wales considerably with the redecoration of Fort Belvedere. Later she was to engage in new building, and carried out one most attractive development in Wells Rise, not far from the Regent's Park Zoo. Had it not been for the war this talent of hers might have been expanded on a considerable scale. She led a very lively social life, with a host of friends rather suggestive of café society, whom I tiresomely labelled frivolous, although I was always delighted to see them, wishing to stand well in their eyes because of my love for Pempie, not to mention her mother.

Freda though was anything but a social butterfly. She was profoundly aware of the poverty and distress which abounded in the early thirties, but unlike many others she was not willing merely to wring her hands. She decided to take positive action. Selecting a particularly depressed district of London, with the help of the Kensington Housing Association she opened the first of a series of clubs designed to provide subsidized meals and social amenities for some of the poor families of the neighbourhood, and the Prince of Wales became Patron. Encouraged by the success of the first club, she opened a second and a third, and then more, until eventually seven clubs were running simultaneously, all in the same general area. They were named the Feathers Clubs after the Prince of Wales's emblem. The name gave them a cachet, and I am sure that it helped with the raising of the funds required to launch and run them. Billy Rootes of motor car industry fame and one of Freda's devotees became the first Hon. Treasurer. He was at an early stage of his career, and he made immense efforts to justify her confidence in him. Freda in her teasing way blamed my nagging for her initial involvement in the clubs (which still exist to this day, over forty years on), but more than that was required to stir her, and I neither claim nor am entitled to any of the credit.

My close and intimate friendship with Pempie lasted for perhaps two years. During that time I saw her as often as I could, for her beauty and her youthful eagerness had transfixed me. I remember one wonderful holiday, I think in 1933, when a friend of Freda's had taken a house in Austria for the month of August. Freda and her two daughters were invited to stay, and so was I as Pempie's beau. The house was in Carinthia, in dramatic mountainous country. After only a few days Freda was called home because of the serious illness of one of her very close acquaintances, and our unfortunate host was left alone with three youngsters and his son, who was aged twelve. Pempie and I tried to go for walks, but the son developed a kind of fixation on me, and used to stalk us. We could only escape by using my car, and we used to drive through the wild countryside with the car open and the wind and rain beating down on us while Pempie would sing Bavarian folksongs against the noise of the storm.

My passion for her was intense. For a while she returned it, but gradually her affections began to drift away. She fell in love with the stage, and she decided with great courage and determination to take up acting as a career. Brendan Bracken, a man of whom in future chapters I write at length, had met her through me. He was struck dumb by her beauty, and he persuaded himself that he was in love with her. Until his death twenty-five years later her photograph was always by his bedside. He urged Alexander Korda to give her an opening in films and in order to develop her acting ability she joined the Liverpool Repertory Theatre company where she played a wide range of parts. Before this, though, she had met my old Cambridge friend, Victor Rothschild, who like many others was dazzled by her beauty as well as by her mother's charm: and of course when he chose to exercise *his* charm lesser beings were eclipsed. They saw one another quite often; and on these occasions I frequently saw Barbara Hutchinson, the girl whom Victor subsequently married and to whom he was indeed most deeply attached. She became an intimate friend of mine and of Joan, my wife, and was always to remain so.

Barbara's home was in Albert Road near Regent's Park and the zoo, which we visited often. She always directed our footsteps towards the giraffe house because she insisted that I bore a striking resemblance to a female giraffe named Maudie, a sobriquet she has never allowed me to shed.

Her teasing habit she derived from her father St John Hutchinson, a highly successful barrister at the criminal bar, although it was seldom that a client of his was acquitted; and he used to say that their reason for turning to him was that he helped them to get lighter sentences than they otherwise would. He was a great philosopher and wit; his presence enlivened any gathering, and his death when only fifty-six was a tragedy.

Barbara's mother lived to be ninety-three. She was born Mary Barnes, a cousin of the Stracheys. She carried with her a strong aura of Bloomsbury. Most of the leading figures in the world of art and letters were her friends, Henry Tonks, the head of the Slade School, and Clive Bell being prominent among them; and she had an intimate literary salon to which through my friendship with Barbara I was occasionally admitted, although I felt unworthy of the privilege. They were physically dissimilar, yet unmistakably mother and daughter. Mary had very sharp pointed features, a narrow face with fair hair drawn tightly back, and the svelte look of a ballerina. Barbara's face was softer. It could light up in a way that made more obvious beauties look insipid. She had an infectious laugh and large misleadingly innocent eyes which sparkled with mischief. She had extraordinary charm, and could be dangerously seductive, seeming at once innocent and sophisticated, arousing expectations of a store-house of delights waiting to be discovered. Since she also had a highly perceptive and responsive mind, it is not hard to see why when she wished she could sweep all before her.

Chapter 5

It was some time during 1932 that I met Brendan Bracken. I think that I first met him through one of Pempie's friends, Pamela Smith, the strikingly beautiful and formidable daughter of F. E. Smith, the first Lord Birkenhead. I met him again in Brooks's Club, of which I had been made a member by a strange and rather snobbish character named Courtauld Thomson, a gnome-like figure with a shrewd business sense, who was the chairman of Brooks's Club and who had befriended me. (He was the owner of a house called Dorneywood, which before his death he bequeathed to the nation, being in consequence ennobled.)

My chance encounter with Brendan was a turning point for me, and he was to become the major influence in my life. Towards the end of 1932 I was still working with the Mining Trust. The job was as dull as ever; metal prices were uneconomically low, and prospects of advancement seemed remote. Therefore, when Brendan offered me a job with the *Financial News*, I leapt at the chance of escape.

The *Financial News* was part of a group he had formed in the late twenties on behalf of the family trust which owned Eyre & Spottiswoode, of which he had been made a director by Colonel Jack Crosthwaite-Eyre, who became head of the business following the death of his father-in-law, James Bristow Eyre. Brendan had been recommended by Lord Beaverbrook. He was only twenty-four years old when he joined the board, and most of the other directors were past retirement age, and his rampageous nature seems to have been allowed free scope.

He was without question one of the most extraordinary men of his generation. His background was wrapped in mystery, and he preferred it that way. He had been born in Ireland, was sent to Australia as a child, and then appeared at Sedbergh (a public school in Cumberland) at the age of eighteen, cheque book in hand, persuading the headmaster that he was only fifteen and thus gaining admittance. When he left the school after two terms he had a spell as a school-master, and then contrived to attach himself to Winston Churchill during a by-election in Dundee, from which moment he became Churchill's self-appointed and dedicated servant for life.

His appearance was unforgettable. Some of his friends nicknamed him affectionately Tarzan. Wherever he went he created a vivid impression. He was tall and well-built, with an immense shock of unruly, crinkly red hair. He had powerful features, with prominent lips and a rather large soft nose, and being very short-sighted, he always wore spectacles. His voice was deep and penetrating, and it seldom tired although it was in constant use.

His first duties at Eyre & Spottiswoode were as manager of a short-lived magazine named *English Life*, which was edited by Hilaire Belloc and which was intended as a sophisticated *Country Life*, although it failed to make inroads into that solidly based publication. Brendan's initial venture into financial journalism came with the founding of a monthly magazine called *The Banker*. He had seen a copy of the *Banker's Magazine*, which belonged to Waterlows, the printers of bank notes, and which he observed was full of advertising. Unfortunately he had not troubled to learn that the charge for advertising was only £5 a page, so that *The Banker* which charged double was at some disadvantage. However, Brendan with his brash personality persuaded Montagu Norman and other leading figures of the world of international banking to contribute to his magazine; and although his knowledge must have been minimal (the year was 1926, when he was only 25) he bluffed his way through, *The Banker* became established and respected, and today it makes a very handsome profit.

His appetite being whetted, he persuaded his Eyre & Spottiswoode colleagues to bid for the Argus Press, which owned and printed a daily newspaper, the *Financial News*, although the Argus Press itself was disposed of together with a contract to print the paper. At that time the stock market was lively, a large number of dubious companies were being floated, and financial papers were profitable.

Brendan extended the empire further. A weekly paper, the *Investors Chronicle*, was purchased. This was owned and edited by one G. J. Holmes, a very shrewd judge of markets, but no literary genius. The paper was profitable but undistinguished; Brendan thought that its quality must be enhanced. He brought in several good writers, and eventually in 1938 he invited Nicholas Davenport, a radical-minded stockbroker with a brilliant talent for writing, to contribute a weekly article under the pseudonym Candidus, the magazine being thereby transformed.

Two further additions were made. A 50 per cent share in *The Economist*, Brendan's pride and joy, was acquired for £50,000 from the descendants of the founder James Wilson, the other 50 per cent being acquired by the then editor Walter Layton, together with a number of his (Walter's) business and other friends. An unusual trust deed was entered into, designed to protect the independence of the editor, who could only be dismissed with the trustees' consent, and stipulating that all share transfers required their approval. There were four trustees, each of them eminent and respected for his impartiality, and they were self-electing, being themselves responsible for filling such vacancies in their number as occurred through death or otherwise. The company's articles also provided that the *Financial News*'s holding could never exceed 50 per cent, and therefore that the *FN* could not have control. Brendan would naturally have preferred to obtain full ownership but over the years the 50:50 arrangement worked well and I have no doubt that it was in the best interests of *The Economist* that it was not dominated by any single interest. A condition of the new partnership was that the *Financial News* should appoint the managing director, and accordingly Brendan assumed this position from early in 1929; and apart from the war years he kept the title until 1956 when he was succeeded by Geoffrey Crowther.

The final acquisition was a monthly medical paper, *The Practitioner*. If the interest in *The Economist* was acquired to give respectability to the group, *The Practitioner* was acquired to give stability. It was a learned monthly of the highest quality, strongly supported by the medical profession and full of the most ethical pharmaceutical advertisements. Apart from the excellent appointments he made to the staff of the magazine, Brendan's chief contribution to *The Practitioner* was to ordain that each issue should in the main be devoted to a review in depth of one or other major aspect of medicine: and so the magazine continued, selling at a reasonable price to large numbers of doctors who are deluged with endless quantities of free periodicals, until in 1977 it changed hands, as I shall later relate.

With the passage of time, I was to become closely involved with the personalities and problems of the various publications in the group formed by Brendan (in which it should be said that, contrary to popular opinion, he had no personal stake at all). When I first joined, after Brendan had asked me in a casual off-hand manner whether I would like to work with him, I was offered the job of collecting financial advertising. It was a time of deep depression, and the *FN* had a minute sale, under five thousand copies a day. The company was losing money, and had to be reconstructed. My knowledge of finance and of advertising was nil, and I do not know what Brendan saw in me. He never interviewed me at all, which is just as well, for I was very undeveloped and inexperienced. As with nearly all his actions and nearly all his appointments, he went by hunch and not by reasoned judgement, but looking back on it, he must have been reasonably pleased with his decision, because we remained firm friends and colleagues until his death in 1958.

In any event, within a short space of time after joining the *FN* at the beginning of 1933 I found myself going the rounds of the offices of stockbrokers, merchant banks, and financial and industrial companies in general, urging upon them the merits of our humble newspaper. My immediate superior was a delightful man named E. C. Fisher who was quite indefatigable in the pursuit of revenue for the paper. He had a bright pink look about him, as though he had just been scrubbed. He was an ardent Freemason, and his letters were written in the most extraordinary English which I felt must have embodied some masonic code. He took me to the offices of the various City advertising agents. Before long I had picked up their special jargon, although I cannot in the beginning have spoken with great conviction because I was so ignorant. However, I had the good fortune to join the paper when times were hard, at a point from which our fortunes could only move upwards. My father, who had himself had a spell in the City working for an American brokerage house, was able to give me a handful of letters of introduction to people in some of the leading firms; and the patience and courtesy they showed towards a callow youth of twenty-two was comforting and gratifying.

I cannot for the life of me imagine what arguments I could have used to persuade people to advertise in the FN with its minuscule circulation. Promises of editorial puffs were certainly not among them. The standards set by Brendan in this regard were as high as they could be. There was one notable example, before I had joined the paper, of a very dubious flotation which was not going to be advertised in the FN. Brendan thought it would be wrong to criticize without at the same time publishing the advertisement. It was therefore printed in full free of charge, Brendan's accompanying comment being simply that the issue was reminiscent of a company floated at the time of the South Sea Bubble which in asking the public to subscribe for shares had merely stated that the money was being raised 'for purposes to be disclosed later'; in other words that a subscription was no more than a vote of confidence in the promoter, to which in Brendan's view he was emphatically not entitled.

It was in fact only rarely that Brendan contributed to the newspaper or attempted to influence the editorial line to be taken. His relations with Oscar Hobson, who was the editor when I first joined, were extremely strained. Hobson was a *laissez-faire* liberal, whereas Brendan was a rather right-wing Tory, having been elected to Parliament in 1929 as member for North Paddington. They were both appallingly obstinate, and the atmosphere was often unbearable. Hobson eventually left, but while he was there Brendan accepted that the responsibility for editing was his.

Hobson's doctrinaire attitude sometimes made my job as advertisement canvasser very difficult. An important part of our revenue came from mining companies and at a time of depressed prices there was a sensible movement to control production and to build up buffer stocks so as to even out fluctuations and to keep prices at an economic level. Hobson held that natural forces alone should operate. A leading figure in the mining world was Oliver Lyttelton (later to become the godfather of our son, and my wartime boss from 1942 till 1945). He was closely identified with a scheme to restrict the production of tin, anathema to Hobson. When I saw Oliver to ask for his advertising he would ask why he should subsidize us to attack him, to which I never had any convincing reply; although to his credit he always gave us the advertisements. Brendan's sympathies were entirely with him, but he would not interfere with Hobson's prerogative.

I knew Brendan for a quarter of a century, and during that time I established a great intimacy with him without ever knowing any single detail of his origins or early life. He was at all times for me a figure of mystery. I loved him dearly, although at times, I hated him for his unreason. I respected him immensely for his loyalty and his courage, and for his integrity. A favourite quotation of his was Lowell's, 'Once to every man and nation, in the strife of truth with false-hood, for the good or evil side, comes the moment to decide.' He was totally in-corruptible. He made his own way without any help from others. He had great heart and great warmth but he despised weakness and loathed pomposity. The civic side of the City he dismissed with the phrase 'Turtle-fed Aldermen'. 'A too highly developed bump of reverence' was a favourite expression of his; 'Never trust a pipe-smoker' another, looking backwards I suppose to Baldwin and forwards to Wilson. Men of the Left were 'the class warriors'. Keynes 'made inflation respectable'. The House of Lords he called the Morgue: although Churchill made him accept a peerage in 1952, he never once took his seat. The support and encouragement which, with one or two painful exceptions, he gave to those working under him were remarkable, and he earned the undying loyalty of his staffs both at the *FN*, and at the Ministry of Information, where he achieved outstanding success.

There were of course those who could not abide him; and it was undoubtedly the case that to those he disliked he could be insufferably rude, and at times intolerable. His attitude towards new acquaintances was quite unpredictable. I remember once introducing someone I particularly wished him to meet with a specific job in mind. This man came for luncheon at the office. Brendan spoke without ceasing. Occasionally my friend interjected a question, each time drawing forth a lengthy flow of words. Finally, after almost three hours, having hardly spoken at all, he left. I asked Brendan whether by chance he had been able to form an impression. He replied: 'I thought he was quite a nice fellow, but he talked far too much.' And I suppose that he really believed this to be the case. Then there were other times when he himself hardly spoke, and they were the worst. It was as though a thick black fog of depression had descended, and it affected anyone else who happened to be present: for Brendan was an extremely positive character, rather larger than life, with enormous facility of phrase, a rapier wit, and a disconcertingly good memory; and it was usual for him to be the focal point of any gathering at which he was present.

There were few people in public life who filled him with any kind of awe. He had a profound respect for scholars and for men of the church, but most politicians and businessmen he despised. Among those he loved came first and foremost Winston Churchill, in a class quite apart, to whom Brendan had attached himself at a very early age and to whom he remained constantly true. Christopher Sykes, in his life of Evelyn Waugh, says that Brendan encouraged the belief that he was the illegitimate son of Winston. Churchill, when asked if the story was true, is supposed to have reflected carefully and then replied 'The dates don't fit.' Anyway Brendan never made any such suggestion and it is unmitigated nonsense.

Then there were a handful of others who at different times and in different ways were father figures to Brendan. There was the great Australian, W. S. Robinson, a man I knew well not only through Brendan but also through Oliver Lyttelton, and likewise through Freda Dudley Ward, opposite whom, for a while, he owned a house in St John's Wood. He had played a major role in the development of the massive deposits of lead and zinc at Broken Hill in New South Wales. He was at all times, and especially during the war, a trusted adviser to successive Australian Governments. He was intensely realistic, seeing vividly before the war what was happening in Germany, and giving repeated warnings which were ignored. He was spry and dapper, and he had a great sense of fun, which bubbled out both in talk and in writing. He was rather deaf, and he used a hearing aid which he quietly switched off if he was bored by the conversation. Money meant little to him: he was not in the least acquisitive, and he died quite poor.

There was Lewis Douglas, more nearly Brendan's age, not dissimilar from W. S. Robinson in his philosophy and attitude to problems. He was American Ambassador in London between 1947 and 1950, and it was then that Brendan's friendship with him ripened. He was one of the most considerate of men, very modest and never pushing himself forward, but always willing to accept responsibility when asked. His father had been a successful mining engineer, and Lew had a clear understanding of politico-economic and business problems, being able to set current events in their historical context. Jack McCloy, another great public servant, was his brother-in-law, because they had married sisters. When Lew was in London, Jack was head of the American-occupied zone in Germany. He was a lawyer by profession, and he enjoyed tackling difficulties, having a most forceful personality. With their respective wives, they made a remarkable quartet. Peg Douglas had a special quality of humanity and understanding and a very affecting appearance which made all men and women fall in love with her. Happily for us she liked Joan and myself, and we met regularly, continuing to do so long after she and Lew had left London.

Another of Brendan's father figures, who also became a very good friend of mine and of Joan's was Alexander Korda, the Hungarian-born film producer, who perhaps more than anyone else helped to put the British film industry on the international map. By a curious coincidence, when he first came to London he occupied the house next door to Freda Dudley Ward and therefore opposite to W. S. Robinson. He was born in 1893, and when Brendan first met him he must have been some forty years old. I do not know whether the meeting came about through Freda, who knew him as a neighbour; but Brendan by that time believed himself to be in love with Pempie; and she had adopted acting as a career, so that Brendan may well have thought that by cultivating Korda he could assist her on the path to stardom. It is indeed the case that he was helpful to him in his early days in Britain, but Korda needed little help, for he had great talent and a compelling charm. He had real panache, aiming high, and more often than not achieving his aim. His style of living was not extravagant: he simply wanted the best of everything. We dined with him sometimes in his penthouse in Claridges and I remember one lovely meal, when we had twelve oysters each, not six, a whole grouse each, not a half, and then a large chocolate soufflé to round it all off. By buying the post-war rights of his pre-war films, he made a good deal of money after the war, more it must be said than did his pre-war backers, and this enabled him to form a valuable collection of paintings. At all times Brendan was close to him, but never with any financial involvement. His death in January 1956 left a sad gap.

Then there was Max Beaverbrook, who in fact was quite a bit older than Brendan. He was a spell-binder, a dominating personality, with real creative brilliance, a penetrating mind quick to spot the chink in people's armour and to exploit any weakness. He made money by the courageous development of his own journalistic ideas, but money meant little to him except for the power it gave. Brendan's relationship with him was complex, a kind of love-hate, with love and admiration predominating. I only knew him slightly, and I found him frightening: but he accepted me as Brendan's colleague and therefore treated me with a degree of consideration although never seeking to draw me into his circle.

One half of Brendan envied Beaverbrook's Edward G. Robinson toughness of manner and studied ruthlessness. With his other half he wished rather to emulate his second great hero and father figure in the world of newspapers, Lord

Camrose, who was born in the same year as Beaverbrook, and together with his brother Gomer (Lord Kemsley) had built up a substantial press empire. He himself had developed the *Daily Telegraph* to its commanding position among large sections of the middle classes, realizing the immense importance as a circulation builder of classified job advertisements. Camrose was of course himself extremely tough, but in his business dealings, not in the pages of his newspapers, which steered clear of banner headlines or anything with a hint of sensationalism. Beaverbrook's *Daily Express* was compulsive reading for its lively stimulating presentation, its masterly typography and its splendid cartoonists. Camrose's *Telegraph* was staid, but it gave (and still gives) all the news, home, foreign, political, sport, so that if it was not compulsive reading it was certainly compulsory. It was from Camrose that the group presided over by Brendan bought control of the *Financial Times*, and of that I later relate.

With these various people, each of them pretty distinguished, Brendan had a kind of father–son relationship. Collectively they took the place of his own father, who had died when Brendan was still a child. There were others to whom Brendan acted as though he was their father, and it was to this group that I belonged, although I was less than ten years younger than him. What it was in me that drew him in my direction I cannot tell. We were very different in character, but on the big issues we usually saw as one, and it is undoubtedly the case that I too lacked a highly developed bump of reverence, even though, mercifully for the *FN* and later the *FT*, mine was rather more developed than his.

Chapter 6

During my first months of working with the *FN*, my mother told me in great secrecy and in a state of great excitement that my sister was on the point of becoming engaged. Her fiancé was Paul Latham, Conservative MP, London County Councillor, and a wealthy baronet. I had never met him, indeed his name meant nothing to me. Instinctively I felt that the choice was unwise. From his description he sounded the very opposite of everything that appealed to my sister. She was completely uninterested in politics, and she had always dreamt of impoverished romance. When and how they met I have no idea, but I am certain that my mother for quite the wrong reasons did everything in her power to promote the marriage. My father acquiesced.

Paul's father, Thomas, had died when Paul was still quite young. He left a substantial fortune. He had been managing director of Courtaulds in the very early days, and I always understood that it was through his initiative that Courtaulds had made their initial investment in artificial silk, having previously been above all concerned with the production of mourning crêpe which in Victorian days had been in constant heavy demand.

Paul himself was notably handsome. He was unnaturally blonde, and his eyes were strangely wide apart, almost equine in appearance. He had lost a leg in an accident at a railway station, but this was scarcely noticeable when he walked. He had a strongly developed sense of public duty. He was kind and generous, but he also had a rather cruel streak and the misfortunes of others amused him. He enjoyed bringing ill-assorted people together, and he laughed mercilessly at their discomforture.

He was pleased to be marrying my sister because he had a passionate desire for a son and heir (which she gave him), but his natural affections were very much more for his own sex, and thus from the beginning the seeds of disaster were there. Disaster in fact struck during the war, when Patsy was away in America, and Paul found himself cashiered, prosecuted and imprisoned for a homosexual relationship. But that was still several years away.

The marriage took place on 29 June 1933, and after their honeymoon they went to Hurstmonceaux Castle in Sussex, a beautiful ruined rose-red brick façade which Paul had bought from Claud Lowther and which he was in the process of rebuilding and restoring to its original design, courtyards and all. The work was splendidly completed but the outbreak of war in 1939, and Paul's subsequent tragedy, meant that the reconstructed castle only provided them with a home for a very short time. I used to stay there regularly, both before and after my marriage, and I was constantly amazed by the simple beauty of the original façade.

After Patsy's wedding my mother suggested that I should move back into her house in Park Row, giving up my service flat. I was delighted to do this, but only on a temporary basis, for I had my eye on a small house which was being built in Jubilee Place, Chelsea, as part of a private development scheme involving a number of houses on both sides of this attractive little street off the King's Road. The houses were small and compact, but well planned and well built; and remarkably cheap, costing under £3,500 for a longish lease with a very low ground rent. When I first moved to Jubilee Place, my mother most considerately allowed her tall willowy Irish maid, Kitty Foyle, to accompany me, a noble sacrifice on her part: and Kitty remained with me until after my marriage, when she returned to her native land and married the house carpenter, McAsee, at Moore Abbey, which was still at that time occupied by John McCormack.

However, that was some way on. I stayed for over a year with my mother, and while I was there I met an American girl who for a few months was to dominate my life. It happened thus. My mother had been over in New York, and returning by sea she had met and fallen in love with an Albanian diplomat named Chatin Sarachi. He was close to King Zog, and he was either Minister or First Secretary at the Albanian Legation in London. He went fairly regularly to the United States, Paul Getty being among his intimates. Women found him attractive, and he was a considerable womanizer. He was versatile and talented, for having been educated in Rome and Vienna he spoke several languages fluently. He was also an excellent cook, understanding equally both Mediterranean and Central European cooking; a very good handyman, he had an enviable knowledge of the techniques of plumbing, electrical wiring and so on, indeed pretty well anything about the house. His looks were striking, for he resembled a sophisticated buccaneer; I christened him Münchhausen because of the colourful tales he told. My mother was utterly dazzled, and of the numerous loves of her life he became the most important.

When she first met him he was extremely close to an American showgirl who was coming over to London to appear in a midnight revue at the Dorchester Hotel. My mother thought, or so I have always supposed, that she could both ease my virginal state and detach the American beauty from Chatin by introducing her to me. Therefore, they and a few others (I forget who) came for drinks. When I first set eyes on her, it was as though I had had an electric shock. She was very tall and slender, with extremely blonde hair, hands that surpassed in shapeliness any others I have ever seen, and a face suggesting a sensual Marlene Dietrich. I was well and truly smitten. I could scarcely wait to be alone with her, and she made me believe that her feelings for me were the same. Within a short space of time, we started to meet regularly.

After her show had opened I was only able to meet her very late at night, after 1 a.m. I used to wait for her at the hotel, and then as often as not we would go out to a night club. Three or four times a week I would not get home to bed before 4 a.m., and I must have had some stamina because I had to be at my office by 9.30, ready to set out on my advertisement getting rounds. Frequently on our night club outings she and I were accompanied by a girl-friend of hers, who was also appearing in the show and who brought with her a budding film producer, no less a man than the young Sam Spiegel. His subsequent career was spectacular, but in those days he only had his feet on the lower rungs of the ladder. I envied him his easy charm for women and his talent for making whichever girl he was with feel that she alone mattered: but it was a technique which could not be learnt or taught.

To me in my state of inexperience my American belle revealed a whole new world. I spent many hours of pleasure with her, and I think of her with affectionate gratitude. Soon after she returned to New York she married a dancer. I was sent a cutting from an American variety magazine containing a short news story about her, with the headline 'Jilts peer to wed hoofer', pithily expressed but inaccurate in two respects, since I was not a peer, and marriage was never in question. She came to London once or twice after the war, performing at a night club and always looking glamorous, singing mildly suggestive songs into a microphone in the style of Dietrich, a talent which she had very successfully exploited in America.

Work on the house in Jubilee Place progressed, and I was able to move in soon after the departure of my Dorchester Follies girl. In the actual decoration I was much helped by two talented women whom I had met through Freda Dudley Ward. They were Doris Howard Robertson, the wife of a well-known architect, and a gifted interior decorator with creative ideas in advance of her time, and Marion Dorn, a large and very handsome American who designed carpets and textile materials of high quality. Both became close friends. Marion lived with one of the most sympathetic people I have known, the American artist and graphic designer, E. McKnight Kauffer, a man with real creative flair. Marion and Ted (as he was called) returned to America at the outbreak of war. Both died young, and both are sadly missed.

As time passed my work at the *FN* became increasingly interesting, while my friendship with Brendan Bracken was steadily developing. He began to talk of putting me on the board of the company and indeed did so quite early in 1934. There was no one else on the staff who had the same special relationship with him. I looked forward to the future with reasonable confidence. Business was beginning to show some revival, and modest profits were beginning to emerge. My calls on stockbrokers and others continued, and wherever there was a hope of advertisement revenue, I was there knocking on the door.

One of the most active firms of brokers was Myers & Co. The founder and senior partner was Mossie Myers. He was a tiny little man, lively and imaginative, who had been extremely successful during the stock market boom of the late twenties. Among his clients were the Berry family. He had acted as broker to their various flotations in the field of newspapers and publishing, one of the companies being the *Financial Times*, the powerful competitor of our little *FN*, with its far lower sale. It followed that there was a double reason for the issues with which Myers was associated to be advertised in the *Financial Times* in preference to ourselves, and therefore I made particular efforts to establish friendly relations with his firm. The partner who undertook the responsibility for dealing with newspaper canvassers was named Edward Beddington-Behrens. I had fairly frequent occasion for calling on him, and we established a superficial friendship, although I could never warm to him. He lived in Regent's Park around which he used to run every morning before going to work. He had a charming wife, the daughter of Montagu Burton the tailor, from whom he subsequently parted. Later he was to leave Myers, and establish his own issuing house, the Ocean Trust, with offices in Park Lane. He made a considerable fortune, and assembled a good although cold collection of modern painting. In the later stages of his life he played an important role in the foundation of the European Movement, working closely with Harold Macmillan and being knighted in recognition of his work.

Brendan did not like him at all. This was known to a leading publisher who had best stay nameless. One Christmas as a joke he sent Brendan not a box but a cabinet of cigars, with a card inside inscribed 'From your old friend E.B.B.'. Brendan failed to spot the joke, and learning that Edward collected modern painting deputed me to choose something to send to him. When the picture arrived, Edward in his turn of course was highly embarrassed, so back came a further batch of cigars. Their friendship however never ripened.

During the course of 1934 I was invited to spend a weekend with him at his country house. I did not wish to accept, but I felt that I should assist the interests of the *FN* by so doing. Perhaps, too, some inner and deeper voice guided me, for had I not accepted I should in all probability never have met Miss Joan Carr, who less than a year afterwards was destined to become my wife, and so remain to this very day, more than forty years on.

The reason that Joan was visiting at Edward's house was simple. He was a nephew of Violet Schiff, who, together with her husband Sydney, had befriended Joan from an early age. They had first met her at the Royal Academy of Dramatic Art where she had been attending a dancing class. They were there to see a young friend of theirs act, and they fell into conversation with Joan during the interval. She was only nine years old, but they were taken by her gay manner and her long brown hair. She told them of her musical aspirations. They invited her for lunch and to play to them; and from then on, partly because they had no children of their own, she became their protégée. Joan effectively had no parents. Her mother had been beautiful but unfaithful, and her father had disappeared from view when she was born. She was left to be brought up in very simple surroundings by an exceptional woman who formerly had been her mother's nurse, a person of fine character and very strict standards.

The chance meeting with the Schiffs greatly influenced Joan's future life. As well as helping with her musical and dramatic training, they also stimulated her intellectual awareness. Violet Schiff, whose maiden name was Beddington, was a remarkable woman with a strong personality. She had spent much of her life in musical and literary circles. She was very good looking, with a powerful head, rather too large for her body, and penetrating eyes and a delightful smile, although she could be severe and even forbidding if she disliked someone. Her eldest sister was Ada Leverson, known as the Sphinx, a clever and witty novelist who befriended Oscar Wilde during and after his trial. Sydney Schiff was a man of independent means, civilized, courteous, and most talented. He wrote semi-autobiographical novels under the name of Stephen Hudson, and after the death of Scott-Moncrieff he translated the last volume of Proust into English.

Already before knowing the Schiffs, Joan's musical gifts had revealed themselves. When she was only six she had played to Harold Craxton, who was a well-known teacher. He had been impressed by her potentialities, and for a while taught her for nothing. She next went to RADA, and her histrionic ability looked like emerging on top; and then when she was still very young she was encouraged by Violet Schiff to go to the United States, partly because Violet thought Joan might find greater opportunities there, but also I fancy because she wanted to stop short of assuming full responsibility for her future. In any event, Joan had an adventurous and fearless temperament, and she sailed to America with some letters of introduction and enough money to live on for a few months. She succeeded in finding work with the New York Theatre Guild and also in Hollywood in one or two films: but it was a time of depression, and the going was hard. Also, of course, her potential as a pianist had to be neglected. Thus, although she had valuable, interesting and character-forming experiences, it would be difficult to argue that Violet Schiff's advice was wholly beneficial.

When I first met Joan at the house of Edward Beddington-Behrens she told me that she had only come over to England to visit the Schiffs, and that she would quite shortly be returning to America. Before long I determined it would be otherwise. Her opening remark to me was scarcely endearing, 'I hear that you like Dorchester show girls!' Who would have said this to her, I asked myself, and why should she be so challenging and provocative? I liked it, though, because she was so extremely attractive. She had a lovely heart-shaped face, framed by dark brown hair, with soft grey-blue eyes and full sensitive lips, a beautifully proportioned body, and above all an enchanting laugh. Beyond this, her attitudes, her varied and unusual experiences, her fundamental lone-liness, all appealed to me very strongly. I had no other emotional involvements at the time, and I did whatever I could to stand well in her eyes. During the weekend I pressed her to play the piano as often as I could, and I was enormously impressed that someone so attractive should be so talented. I was eager to see her again as soon as possible. I had discovered that she was living in a small studio flat in Upper Cheyne Row, Chelsea. I did not know her telephone number, so I simply took a chance and went to call. As bad luck would have it, rain was pouring down. I stood outside waiting for an answer. Finally she came to the door, wrapped in a bath towel, furious that I had disturbed her while she was having a bath. 'Go away,' she said. I went, only to return twenty minutes later, when I was admitted.

From that moment onwards our friendship blossomed. She introduced me to Violet and Sydney Schiff, and to her most intimate, stimulating friend Fabia Drake, a great figure of the Shakespearean stage, through whom she had come to know John Gielgud, Laurence Olivier and others in the world of theatre. I introduced her to both my parents and to Brendan. I took her to Hurst-monceaux. She met Freda Dudley Ward, Jack Donaldson, Barbara Hutchinson (by then married to Victor Rothschild), and many other friends besides. She was a success all round. Finally she met my old school friend, David Herbert, who said to me in his simple direct way, 'You would be mad if you don't ask her to marry you.' And so it was ordained.

The question then arose where we should be married. The *FN* were planning to publish a large special number devoted to the United States. It had been decided by Brendan that I should go there together with our trade advertise-ment manager, Grahame Martin Turner, to try and obtain the necessary advertising support. I thought that it would be an extremely sensible idea for

Joan and myself to be married quietly in New York. My parents were divorced, and the idea of a conventional wedding in a church in London seemed to me both sham and costly: too many marriages launched with orange blossom and bridesmaids had ended disastrously. I did not want one, nor did Joan, and besides her friends were largely in America. So to New York we went, but on separate liners, a week apart.

When Joan arrived, we stayed at the Ritz Tower Hotel. We were married in the City Hall on 16 May 1935, and in the evening after our wedding we invited some of Joan's New York friends for drinks, mainly drawn from the theatrical and literary worlds: for instance there was Sam Behrman, a lovable witty man, a master of the wisecrack, and a brilliant writer and playwright; Alfred de Liagre, at the time an aspiring impresario, with his sister Eleanor Labrot (who was later to marry the actor Brian Aherne), both of them warm-hearted, gay and delightful; Nelson Rockefeller (no hint of the politician about him then) who took us to the top of the Empire State building, and was kind and hospitable; Conde Nast, the moving spirit of *Vogue*; Carl van Vechten, the author; Alfred Knopf, the publisher, and others who to me were unknown; and I very much had the feeling that my intrusion and my removal of Joan from their lives was thoroughly unwelcome.

Brendan had asked me particularly to see a close friend of his, the famous Bernard M. Baruch, who was to him almost another father figure. I had telephoned to the great man, and he had bidden me to breakfast on the morning after our wedding night; and so, far too frightened to request another appointment, I arose sleepless and bleary-eyed, and presented myself on his doorstep at 9 a.m. His hawklike, formidable appearance fully matched his legendary reputation as the man who had made millions as the stock market collapsed; and any pronouncement of his was listened to and treated with the deepest respect. After breakfast he made me walk with him in Central Park, and we sat on his favourite seat, a bench which later I believe was presented to him by the City of New York, although I suppose he left it in the Park and did not take it home. Brendan had latched himself on to Baruch in a way which he always successfully did with anyone to whom he was particularly drawn, and I was therefore treated with great consideration as Brendan's emissary; but I would rather it had not been the morning after my wedding night. Two or three days afterwards he and his wife very kindly gave a dinner party for us. I forget who was there, but I vividly recall the most delicious southern fried chicken, with sweet corn and bananas and all the necessary appurtenances.

On a later visit of mine to New York Barnie Baruch told me that he had a sister living in London. He asked me to call on her. I found a charming old lady, in a very humble flat in Kensington, and I could not help wondering whether he had done as much as he might have done to assist her or even enquire about her condition.

From the point of view of the *FN* the New York visit of Martin Turner and myself was a success. He and I complemented one another admirably. He was a formidable salesman, a master of convincing overstatement whereas my gift was more for what is known in advertising jargon as the soft sell, an expression I understand but could never define. Together we gained a lot of advertising support, and we returned satisfied. I was delighted to have met Joan's New York friends, many of whom later adopted me as a friend as well, doubly gratifying since in those days my American acquaintance scarcely existed.

Initially we moved in to the little house in Jubilee Place. We knew that should there be a question of a family this would be too small, but equally we felt that it would be tempting providence to find anywhere else before there was unmistakable proof of the need. Such proof in fact came within less than a year. At first though our concern was to become accepted as a couple rather than as two individuals; and if in New York the acquaintance was nearly all Joan's in London it was the reverse. She had to adapt herself to my family, to my *FN* colleagues, and to the particular friends who in my three or four bachelor years in London had become an integral part of my life. Several of my closest friends were at the same time in the process of marrying, so that we were quite a group of newly-weds. I took great pride in Joan's beauty and her talent as a pianist, above all in her gift for friendship; and effectively bringing with her no family of her own, so that I had no in-laws to contend with, she fitted in naturally and easily to the contrasted lives of my two parents.

We could not immediately go away on a honeymoon because I had to complete the work arising from my American visit, and June and July were always busy months for the advertising department. It was not therefore until August that we could get away. We did however pay a number of weekend visits to friends and relatives. We often went to Hurstmonceaux Castle, the home of my sister and my brother-in-law Paul Latham. We went to stay with Alice Wimborne at Ashby St Ledgers near Rugby, where luxury and ease reigned. We paid frequent visits to Alice's nearby neighbours, Georgia and Sacheverell Sitwell, who lived in a historic house named Weston Hall, and who did much to stimulate our intellectual curiosity. Then I thought Joan would wish to see Moore Abbey, our family home in Ireland, which was still tenanted by John McCormack. He invited us, and we spent two enjoyable days there, although neither of us had any sense of deprivation at not being able to live there permanently.

On the way to Ireland we stayed at Plas Newydd, the home of the Anglesey family overlooking the Menai Straits, which for many years I had visited regularly. While we were there Joan had a minor accident which could have ended more disastrously than it did. Before dinner she turned on the water in her bathroom and went to undress, having failed to realize the pressure of the water and the speed with which the bath would fill. Returning, she found the floor more than an inch deep in water. Every kind of mopping-up device was mobilized, and the situation was brought under control: but as ill luck would have it the bathroom was directly above the dining room, and the water had percolated the plaster of the ceiling, so that throughout the meal there was a pattering accompaniment of the sound of water dripping into half a dozen buckets strategically placed around the room, none fortunately being needed on the dining table itself.

Marjorie Anglesey behaved with immense understanding of poor Joan's embarrassment, and what could have been a most painful occasion ended as a cement of friendship. She was a woman of exceptional gifts and exceptional charm, lovely to look at, whose death before she was sixty caused widespread grief.

Our honeymoon was spent in a romantic German castle near to Passau on the river Inn. It belonged to a Count and Countess Arco, but when we were there he was away in Africa, where he spent much time. They occasionally took in paying guests since, like so many of the older landed families in Germany in those days, they were poor. We drove out in our car because we wanted to see something of Bavaria. We went through Bamberg, Würzburg, and Nuremberg, where Joan became quite seriously ill with what was thought might be diphtheria but happily was not. Before we went there we had not realized that there would be such strong evidence of Nazi activities. We were astounded at the extent of parading by para-military detachments; and in one town, I think Würzburg, I remember rashly emptying the contents of a jugful of water from our hotel bedroom over a contingent of Brownshirts who early in the morning were marching past the hotel. I remember also pretending to be Jewish in order to be turned out of a restaurant which displayed prominently the sign '*Jüden hier unerwünscht*'. It was extraordinary, looking back on it, that so long before the war the evidence of everything Hitler was engaged in was there for anyone with eyes to see, and our statesmen of those days let it all happen, just as their successors would today. We went to the Arcos' castle on the recommendation of a friend, 'Chips' Channon, an American who had adopted England as his home, entering Parliament in 1935 as member for Southend, one of the safest of all Conservative seats, which he represented until 1950. He was married to Honor Guinness, a daughter of Lord Iveagh, head of the famous brewing family; and he was well placed to endorse the truthfulness of that most famous of all slogans, 'Guinness is good for you'. He was an immensely kind man, with many acts of generosity to his credit, although those who did not like him regarded him as something of a snob, which would be hard to deny. He had himself stayed several times at the Arcos' castle, during the time that he wrote his very readable life of the 'mad' King Ludwig II of Bavaria, a monarch to whom anyone who appreciates the music of Wagner should feel constantly indebted.

Chapter 7

Among other newly-weds of 1935 were two old friends of mine, Daphne Finch-Hatton and also Jack Donaldson, with whom three years before I had started the Quartet Society. Jack married Frances, or Frankie as everyone called her, the daughter of the very gifted and successful playwright Frederick Lonsdale, a marriage which turned out to be one of the happiest and most fulfilled of all my contemporaries. We saw them constantly then, and save for the war years we have continued as intimates ever since. They complemented one another perfectly. Jack was a great idealist; Frankie shared his idealistic aims, but she was far more of a realist. He always had a powerful radical streak. When he came down from Cambridge he had been taken into Lloyds Bank, where he was earmarked for rapid promotion. However it was not long before his social conscience got the upper hand, and he left the bank in order to work for a nominal salary as secretary of a new institution about to be built at Peckham. Its name was the Pioneer Health Centre. Whatever Jack undertook he set about with enthusiasm. He largely raised the finance, and did most of the administrative work. The underlying concept was prevention of illness rather than cure. Families from the surrounding neighbourhood were asked to enrol as family units. Attractive club facilities were provided, including a heated swimming pool, and members were asked to agree to automatic regular check-ups as a condition of enjoying the amenities. It was an idealistic concept, designed for the scientific study of health. A number of people benefited, and the Centre aroused much interest, but the idea was never adopted by the Ministry of Health and the intervention of the war helped to bring the experiment to an untimely end, although the actual closure only took place in 1951.

Jack and Frankie had built an attractive modern timber house, designed by Walter Gropius, on some land in Kent giving Jack easy access to the Pioneer Health Centre. During the war Jack was sent overseas, the house in Kent was sold, and Frankie very bravely decided with practical good sense to study farming. A farm in Warwickshire was bought, and then when Jack returned after the end of the war he adapted himself to her new way of life, entering into the spirit of it with tremendous zest. She discovered too that she had inherited her father's talent for writing, producing first a slim volume giving an account of her life as a farmer, and then together with Jack a most useful handbook dealing with the basic principles of farming in a way intelligible to the uninitiated. Later they gave up farming and moved back to London and I invited him to join me on the board of Covent Garden, where he was to prove an invaluable colleague. Frankie's career blossomed; she wrote a book about her father; another about the Marconi scandal; and her life of King Edward VIII had the stamp of real authority. At the age of sixty-five Jack was invited by Harold Wilson to enter the Government: and together their lives have become fuller and richer as time has marched on.

Daphne Finch-Hatton I had known for several years since she was Penelope Dudley Ward's best friend. She too had exceptional beauty. She resembled a piece of fine porcelain, and her sensibility matched the delicacy of her features. Ballet was one of her passions: had her circumstances been different she might successfully have adopted it as a career. Whitney Straight, whom she married in July 1935, was strongly contrasted. He was powerful and masculine, and he loved speed. At an early age he took up motor racing, and from this switched to aircraft, playing a prominent role in the RAF, first of all as a fighter pilot in the famous 601 squadron, and later in other branches of the service. Both his parents were American, but his father died young and when his mother remarried she settled in England and together with her husband founded Dartington School, which defied convention by being co-educational and allowing the pupils far more freedom than was usual elsewhere. Whitney adopted England as his home and British as his nationality. His marriage with Daphne withstood the stresses to which our generation was subjected, and endured very happily, as also did Jack's and mine.

When it was clear that Joan was expecting a child, it became necessary for us to sell the little house in Jubilee Place and find something larger. We chose a solidly built Victorian mansion in Lansdowne Crescent, off Ladbroke Grove in North Kensington. In those days the area was not greatly sought after and property there was cheap: but the house had a garden and a good open view, and we turned a basement room into a garage. Our friends Doris Howard-Robertson and Marion Dorn helped with the work of redecoration. Built-in cupboards and fittings were a principal feature, and a powerful gramophone loudspeaker in the upper part of the wall dividing the living room from the dining room which in the later months of the war helpfully drowned the sound of buzz bombs and anti-aircraft fire. We had very few pictures to put on the walls, and those we had were mainly given to Joan as a wedding present by Edward Beddington-Behrens, an Augustus John sketch for his famous portrait of Suggia, a John Nash watercolour landscape, a William Roberts drawing of a scene in the Café Royal, and a Richard Eurich seascape; very generous of him, looking back on it.

On 14 January 1937 our son Derry was born. He was christened Dermot, a name chosen for no better reason than that we wanted something Irish which would blend easily with the surname Moore. Daphne Straight agreed to be one of his godparents (I was to become godfather to her daughter Camilla), and the others were Brendan Bracken and Oliver Lyttelton.

At this point of time my income was £1,500 a year, Joan effectively having no separate income of her own: and yet we were able to employ a nurse and a cook and a maid, all three living in the house with us; we had a car, we travelled quite a lot, and had it not been for the ever-present shadow of Hitler, life would have been pretty good. But it really was an ever-present shadow, something which anyone born less than fifty years ago – and that means most of the popu-lation – has never experienced. It cast a blight over any attempt to look into the future, or to make any forward plan. There was a certainty of impending nemesis; the question was not whether but when, coupled with a sense of great helplessness as one watched the international statesmen allowing Hitler to get away with one knavish trick after another. Men of the Right tended to regard him as a bulwark against Communism, turning a blind eye to his more mon-strous deeds, while liberals and men of the Left organized peace votes and opposed suggestions of rearmament. It was thus a grey backcloth for the happiness of early married life. There was of course much enjoyment, but nearly always the feeling, which grew as 1939 approached, that it was all very temporary.

As to my job, the interest and enjoyment broadened after I had been made a member of the board of directors during the course of 1934. The board was small, and very much dominated by Brendan. The chairman was Colonel Jack Hills, a political colleague of Brendan's, whose contribution to the affairs of the group never seemed to be particularly significant. The word group is mis-leading, for we were very small, and not at all profitable, losing an average of £25,000 a year in 1931, 1932 and 1933, and making profits of that order in subsequent years. To know everyone by sight and by name was not difficult, and I made a number of good friends. Besides Martin Turner, the advertisement manager, I also developed a close friendship with Maurice Green, who had been appointed editor of the paper in 1934 at the age of twenty-eight in succession to Oscar Hobson. He had an effortless brilliance which always astonished me. When I first knew him he was the principal leader writer, and I remember well how often we would have a drink together in the local pub before I left to go home while Maurice had to return to the office to turn out a lengthy leader upon some complex subject with only an hour or so in hand: but he was never rushed or fussed, and in the morning sure enough there was his leader, full of good sense, and written in impeccable prose. When at Oxford he had taken a First in Greats. He must have worked harder than he conveyed to me, for when I asked him how he had achieved such academic distinction he replied that he had done it on gin and strychnine, a statement which I suppose must have contained some element of truth. Music and fishing were his two passionate hobbies, and quite often musical scores provided his bedtime reading. He left to become financial and industrial editor of *The Times*, where he stayed, save for the war years, until 1961, when he joined the *Daily Telegraph*, of which he became editor in 1964. As editor of the *FN* he did much to earn respect for the paper, and a good deal of the credit for the postwar success of the *Financial Times*, with which the *FN* merged, must be due to him. He established a standard which earned widespread respect. Many of the qualities he imparted were handed on to the *FT*. More important, Maurice Green recruited several exceptional men to the *FN*, notably Gordon Newton and Harold Wincott, who belong essentially to the postwar period. Gordon was to become the oustandingly successful editor of the *FT* from 1950 until 1972, while Harold, who started humbly at the subs' table, was to develop into one of the most brilliant financial writers of our time and a successful editor of the *Investors Chronicle*.

In addition Maurice did much to develop the talents of Richard Clarke, known to all of us as Otto. He followed Maurice as chief leader writer when only twenty-four years old. I have seldom met anyone with a clearer or more ruthlessly logical mind. Because of the war he was taken into Government service, initially in the Ministry of Supply; and in due course he became an established civil servant, rising to high rank. He was the most unlikely person to produce as his son a communist president of the National Union of Students.

Maurice's recruits included two other men who were to become illustrious in different fields. One was Hammond Innes, a strikingly handsome member of the staff with much routine work assigned to him; and none of us in those days foresaw that he was to develop into a star among thriller writers. The other was Harry Fischer. He had come to England as a refugee from Hitler, and he was content to take a job for £8 a week in charge of the library, which meant above all supervising the filing of company reports and related material, and ensuring that the reference books were kept up to date. This was indeed a humdrum job for someone who was to emerge from the Pioneer Corps at the end of the war as a joint founder of an art books business from which evolved the highly successful Marlborough Fine Art Gallery with its wide-ranging tentacles. (Later Fischer was to leave Marlborough in order to set up his own Fischer Fine Art.)

The deputy editor was Paul Bareau, and the assistant editor Wilfred King. Paul was half Belgian, and he never lost his attractive slightly foreign intonation.

Both he and Wilfred had a deep understanding of economic and monetary matters. Paul was the more suave and less specialized, and his contributions have always been greatly in demand because of his gift of lucid exposition. Wilfred was the more scholarly: he was to become a pundit among writers on banking and the money markets. After the war he was appointed editor of *The Banker*, which he made almost too learned for the banking community, as I tried vainly to impress on him. Another colleague of pre-war days was Paul Einzig, who stemmed from Central Europe. He had been appointed editor of *The Banker* by Brendan. I found it hard to believe that he was the ideal choice because although he was very clever he was incapable of considering any problem objectively, and he loved intrigue. He also contributed the so-called Lombard column in the *FN*, a daily unsigned but personal commentary upon the monetary scene. The column was the cause of numerous complaints from people in high places. Brendan usually brushed these aside, except once or twice during the war when he was Minister of Information and colleagues of his in the Government complained of harm being done to the British cause, and he felt obliged to take notice. After the war, Einzig discontinued his column in the merged *FN/FT* paper because in a moment of aberration (and blame must attach to Brendan rather than to the editor, Hargreaves Parkinson) he was appointed lobby correspondent, in which capacity he was freely able to indulge his lack of objectivity. He had an astonishing facility with his pen. As well as his work for the newspaper, and for *The Banker*, he managed also to produce an average of at least one book a year, and I remember his great pride when Opus No. 50 appeared, a history I think of primitive money.

Brendan had given me responsibility for the business oversight of the *Investors Chronicle*, and thereby I came into close contact with G. J. Holmes, the editor, who really was a wily old bird, far too wily for me. He was old enough to be my father, and what he thought of my being set to keep an eye on him I cannot imagine. His editorial staff was incredibly small, and disgracefully underpaid. The magazine's opening feature was entitled 'A Stockbroker's Notebook'. It was mainly written by Frank Leighton, no stylist, but a man with uncanny flair and knowledge, and completely honest, although the temptation to profit from the undoubted pulling power of the feature must have been strong. Indeed in those days we had to be very strict about not allowing the magazine to be placed on sale before the close of the stock market on Friday afternoons, and people used to hang about by the printers in the hope of getting hold of a waste copy before the market had closed so that they could see what shares were recommended and buy some that afternoon with a view to selling them on Monday when later buyers would be appearing. Distribution arrangements were such that in those days it was possible to send out copies of the magazine on

Friday afternoons, and have it on sale throughout the country by Saturday morning. It is not so today. Printing has to be earlier, and efforts are made to ensure that the magazine is available everywhere by Friday morning; but the importance of simultaneous sale is not what it was, for people are more sophisticated, and far greater influences upon the course of markets are at work now than they were then.

One of the pleasures I derived from being made responsible for the management of the *Investors Chronicle* was my friendship with Nicholas Davenport. He was a breath of radical fresh air in the City. He had been a stockbroker for a number of years, starting, I think, with Rowe & Pitman, a famous rather conventional firm lacking the foresight to make him a partner, and he therefore left to join Chase, Henderson & Tennant. (Subsequently he joined Messels, but that was after the war, and it was by his own choice that he did not again become a partner.) His first journalistic efforts were for *The Nation*, continuing to write for it after the merger with the *New Statesman*, but in due course Brendan persuaded him to agree to write the Candidus column in the *Investors Chronicle*. Politically Brendan and he were poles apart, but each delighted in the other's company. Nicholas wrote in a peerless style, and no one was better at clarifying the issues. In 1953 he resumed writing a weekly column, not in the *Investors Chronicle* but in the *Spectator*, to which he has been faithful to this day, the one constant feature throughout its confusing changes of ownership and policy. Harold Wincott could never have achieved the success he did, writing as Candidus and later editing the *Investors Chronicle*, had he not had the example of Nicholas to guide him.

Brendan had another bond with Nicholas in that both were infatuated by the film business, Brendan through Alex Korda, and Nicholas through Gabriel Pascal, although Brendan had no financial involvements owing to what he used to call the 'safety catch' in his mind, whereas Nicholas did. Joan and I used to visit him at his home near Oxford, first of all when he was single and later with his gifted wife Olga, who had been an actress and was to become a successful painter.

We left London as often as we could at weekends. We went frequently to the house of Oliver and Moira Lyttelton in Kent. They lived at Wittersham, close to Rye, where there is a famous seaside golf course. I used always to play golf with him when we were there. He was a natural games player, having inherited some of the skill of his father, Alfred Lyttelton, who had commissioned Lutyens to build a most attractive house named Greywalls near to the clubhouse and first tee of the famous Muirfield course, so that Oliver came to understand the game from a very early age. He played far better than I did, but it did not matter, for golf is one of the few games in which unequal skills can be evenly matched through judicious handicapping. He also immensely enjoyed card games, especially those outmoded games, piquet and bezique. He pretended to enjoy music, but he was something of a philistine in the musical field, with conventional tastes. The written and spoken word were what he appreciated, and he was an extremely amusing raconteur. He had a fund of good stories, and I was an ideal audience, for I did not at all mind hearing the same story being retold several times, although I fancy that Moira, his wife, heard parts of what he called his anecdotage a bit too often. She was a real *grande dame* in all but stature; physically they were strongly contrasted, he being large and powerfully built while she was delicate and fragile.

There were others that we stayed with. Notably there was my old school friend David Herbert, who had played such a key role in my marriage to Joan. He lived at that time in a delightful little single-storey house in the grounds of Wilton, his family home. Ever since I had first known him at Eton he had always seemed to me one of the great life-enhancers, one who generated a sense of happiness and well-being in all around him.

Through David we met Edith Olivier, a writer who lived in a house on the Wilton estate and was a friend of all his family and all his friends. We used to stay with her from time to time, always looking forward immensely to the visit for she was the embodiment of warmhearted kindness, a talented eccentric, full of character. She had a passionate attachment to Wiltshire, which she seldom left, and one of the great moments of her life was when she was elected Mayor of Wilton. She was a cousin of Laurence Olivier, and daughter of one of the canons of Salisbury who was also private chaplain to the Pembroke family. Her most intimate acquaintance was Rex Whistler, a sensitive and gifted artist, seeming to have been reincarnated from the eighteenth century. To this day the walls of her home, now lived in by her niece Rosemary, are adorned by many of his paintings. He was killed tragically on active service in 1944, a senseless death if ever there was one. I recall that from Edith's house we went to a unique party given by Cecil Beaton at Ashcombe, a romantic pink brick house which he then owned, a house with a quality of mystery enhanced by its situation all alone in a hollow surrounded by chalky slopes. The party puts me in mind of the dreamlike otherworldly atmosphere of Alain Fournier's *le Grand Meaulnes*. The guests were all in eighteenth-century costume, and this increased our sense of remoteness from the hideous realities of Hitler and Mussolini. No one wanted to go to bed and thus shatter the illusion, so we stayed up all night, laughing and dancing, with Cecil, most versatile of men, the glorious animator.

Another house that we visited often was Merton Hall, the home of Victor and Barbara Rothschild close to Trinity College, Cambridge, where he was then a science research fellow. The house had a splendidly informal atmosphere, and credit for this is due to both of them. Laughter was continuous; occasional arguments, storms, disagreements, reconciliations, leading back to calm and gaiety. Sometimes we were allowed to see Victor's most recent additions to his valuable eighteenth-century library, for which special protection had wisely been constructed in the house; and we also admired the sophisticated air raid shelter which with a vision of the shape of things to come he had constructed in a corner of the garden for the protection of his family. Once too we stayed with them as their guests in the Beach Hotel at Monte Carlo, where my general sense of inferiority was heightened by my inability to learn to water-ski; while Victor took to it instantly and effortlessly. Also tennis was a great humiliation, for he had a cannon-ball service which quite defeated me, and he usually ended up playing with the professional.

For our holidays we did in fact generally try to go abroad. Twice we went to Venice, where my mother had rented the top floor of the Palazzo Morosini on the Grand Canal, undoubtedly at the instigation of Chatin Sarachi, who had become her constant companion. The rooms were small, but there was access to the roof, which she converted to a kind of garden with splendid views of the domes and campaniles, and of the lagoon itself. We did our modest share of sightseeing, but in August it was always intensely hot, and we usually found ourselves upon that overcrowded overrated beach, the Lido, where my mother had a cabana: and Chatin played backgammon by the hour, ready to take on all comers, usually winning, for like most Albanians he had learnt the game from childhood and he played it very well. In his spare moments he used to teach me the basic principles, and for a while I became an addict, although I never felt good enough to challenge a real expert.

Among those we saw in Venice was Doris Castlerosse who was at the time sharing a Palazzo on the Grand Canal (now the Peggy Guggenheim Gallery) with an American lady friend whose name I have forgotten. Doris was a legendary character in her day. She had a number of wealthy lovers. Her maiden name was Delavigne, but Valentine Castlerosse, a prototype of the *bon viveur*, physically vast and temperamentally gay and expansive, wanted her for his own and in 1928 had taken her to the registry office. She had an exquisite figure, and was desirable and welcoming, kind and generous. St John Hutchinson, the father of Barbara Rothschild, called her the fox terrier with a diamond collar. Fidelity was not her chief virtue, and predictably her marriage did not last. In the early stages of the war she went to America, but she returned to England in 1942, not long afterwards dying through an overdose of sleeping pills, to which at the time I was told she had been driven by poison pen letters, although she was certainly also pretty penniless.

We had two very enjoyable holidays with Freda Dudley Ward, who for two years running rented a small villa in the South of France belonging to a Madame

Python at what was then a quiet little town called Lacroix, near Hyères, far removed from the social life of Monte Carlo and Cannes. It was approached through a pretty vineyard, and surrounded by pine trees. The sea was within a few yards, and we were in and out of it constantly. Freda was either just married or about to be married to Bobby Casa Maury, who came from Cuba, styled himself a marquis, and who had made England his home. He had charm, usually knowing just what to say to evoke a positive response, and also how to touch an exposed nerve. Many ladies loved him, although his looks were marred by what I had always thought to be a broken nose, said to have been caused through a motor-racing accident, a sport to which he had been addicted. He was one of the pioneers in London of the small intimate comfortable theatre, specializing in showing the best continental films, particularly from France. He achieved this by building the Curzon Cinema, and stimulated by its success, Bobby conceived the idea of a second cinema, to be called the Paris and following the same policy. A suitable basement in the Haymarket was found and a number of friends combined with Bobby to provide the necessary finance. Among these was my father who had been urged by me to make a small investment. Unfortunately the war intervened, thus cutting off the supply of films, and the investment was lost; sad, for the idea was a good one. The Curzon Cinema managed to survive, and is still an accepted landmark.

Freda we saw regularly in London. Indirectly through her I had my portrait painted for the only time in my life until I was approaching retirement, when Derek Hill was commissioned to paint what seems to me a very skilful likeness which as I write still hangs on the *FT* office walls. The earlier picture was by Princess Marina, wife of the Duke of Kent. Freda had invited us for dinner one evening when the Duke and Duchess were going to be with her. I could not accept because I had to be in South Wales for the *FN*, but she insisted that Joan should go without me. Despite her instinctive shyness she obeyed. After dinner the party went to the 400, the fashionable night club of those days. The evening was hugely successful, and the next morning there came an invitation for us to join the Duke and Duchess that very night at the theatre. From then on we became firm friends, meeting frequently and staying with them at their home. And so it was that in 1939 Princess Marina asked me to sit for her, and while she scrutinized my features I was able to fasten my eyes upon her unique loveliness, which seemed to have been shaped by the past tragedies of her own family and perhaps presaged the tragedy of her husband's death in 1942.

In the pre-war years I had a considerable passion for serious movies. I joined the Film Society, and we went regularly to see the films of Serge Eisenstein, Fritz Lang, René Clair, Jean Renoir and others. I also took up still photography.

A small part of the basement of our house was turned into a dark room, where I used to develop my own films and make my own enlargements, some of which were not at all bad. But the war brought the hobby to an abrupt halt. Music was our main relaxation and pleasure. Joan used to play a great deal, but only at home or for friends, not professionally. A close friend in those days was Joe Cooper, whose most outstanding popular success came later with his television programme *Face the Music*. When we first knew him he was very young. He was studying to become an organist, and he earned the necessary wherewithal to pay his fees by giving piano lessons to a number of elegant young society ladies with musical aspirations. Joe was always a great charmer with a tremendous sense of fun, easy and extroverted, with a particular gift for musical mimicry. (Once he played a popular tune 'Today I Feel so Happy' as a Bach fugue on the organ of King's College, Cambridge, persuading everyone that it was a piece of early Bach.) We saw him there often at our house, and at the homes of other good friends of ours who were also enthusiastic music lovers, such as Alfred Beit, a much sought-after MP, and Hamish Hamilton, the enterprising publisher, to whom I had introduced Nancy Mitford, thereby rendering service both to her and to him. He was especially kind to us when our son Derry was only a year or two old, and he frequently invited us to stay at his cottage in Sussex.

In general we heard a lot of music. I doubt whether standards were as high then as they are today. They certainly should have improved, with all the money expended, and the conscious endeavours made. But if the average level of performance is vastly better, there were some very great artists in the years before the war; and thanks mainly to Emerald Cunard, never, I regret to say, to my parents, we went to the Queen's Hall often. Frequently, it was to hear Sir Thomas Beecham conduct, but also Toscanini and Furtwängler whenever they appeared, and also of course soloists like Cortot and Schnabel, who seemed then respectively to be, as they still would today, the authentic interpreters of Chopin and Beethoven.

There were splendid sets of gramophone records which we collected. Schnabel recorded all the Beethoven piano sonatas, and Cortot most of Chopin. The Pro Arte Quartet produced a fine series of Haydn quartets. Beecham recorded most of Delius, Koussevitzky and Kajanus the main orchestral works of Sibelius, for whose music we developed a major passion, hearing Beecham conduct the complete cycle of his symphonies and other works at the Queen's Hall. The operas of Mozart were recorded by Fritz Busch, with the forces of Glyndebourne, to which we went regularly. John Christie, its creator, had been a master at Eton from 1906 until 1922, leaving just before I went there. He was vividly remembered by everyone at the school for his jocular eccentricities. I used to see him in Brooks's Club and he told me of his plans to build an opera house in the grounds of his family home. He owned an organ-building business: at first he formed the idea of placing a number of keyboards in the orchestra pit, each of them linked to different organ pipes representing the various wind instruments, the object being to keep down running costs; but the practical disadvantages soon became clear. His wife Audrey Mildmay was a gifted soprano. Had it not been for her he would not have had his dream, and the dream would not have become a reality.

Chapter 8

During the years before the war Joan had been given quite a lot of broad-casting work. She had auditioned for Eric Maschwitz, who was in charge of light entertainment at the BBC. Together with Jack Strachey, a composer of popular music and a cousin of Lytton, he produced a series of monthly radio revues, aimed at a sophisticated late night audience. Joan's speaking voice appealed to him, and he engaged her to perform various monologues and other sketches which he wrote specially for her. She asked him to write a song for her. In his book *No Chip on My Shoulder* Maschwitz said:

> To her desire to add singing to her other achievements I owe part of the small regular income which gives me the opportunity of writing this probably unprofitable book. She had a small voice of considerable charm; the problem was, where to find a song for her? Jack and I decided to write one ourselves.
>
> One Sunday morning in my flat in Adam Street, only half-recovered from six eighteen-hour days in the studios, I sat in pyjamas, unshaven, considering the problem of a song for pretty Miss Carr. . . . By some accident I hit upon the title 'These Foolish Things' and, then and there, between sips of coffee and vodka, I drafted out the verse and three choruses of a song.

Jack Strachey composed the music, and Joan gave the first performance of 'These Foolish Things'. This turned out to be one of the really great popular hits, but not until the black night club singer Leslie Hutchinson – 'Hutch' – had adopted it into his repertoire.

From a national point of view, 1938 was a deeply depressing year, culminating in the shame of Munich. As the inevitability of war became increasingly clear, I decided that I must join the Territorial Army. Meanwhile, Joan and I accepted an invitation from Billy Rootes to accompany him to Berlin, where his company had a stand at the Motor Show. The other guest was Freda Casa Maury. The actual date I forget, but it was some weeks after Neville Chamberlain's 'peace in our time' surrender. We bowled along the fine new autobahn, all ready one suspected for military traffic. Our car was a Rootes product, a

Humber I suppose: and I remember Billy's consternation and chagrin when it broke down on an empty stretch of road, although fortunately his chauffeur managed after some delay to put things right; and we duly arrived at the Adlon Hotel. The next day the show opened, and Hitler was expected to be present. Billy I think was the only British exhibitor. A master salesman, he was in personal attendance on his stand, and he asked me to be with him. Not long after the opening we saw a group moving towards us, and we could scarcely believe our eyes when not only Hitler loomed into view, but also Goering, Goebbels, Himmler, the lot, all smiles and post-Munich contentment, and sickening handshakes all round. What a chance I missed!

Because of Freda's interest in youth clubs and other welfare centres we were shown several examples, designed to impress on us the good things the Nazis were doing. What essentially impressed itself upon us was their astonishing ruthlessness towards anyone that stood in their way, and above all, more and more, towards the large Jewish community. There was one Jewish family that we had promised to visit. They were the relatives of a dress designer named Joe Strassner, who had made good in London, and from whom Joan had obtained a number of clothes. He was a man of taste and intelligence. We liked him, and we were only too happy to do anything we could to make ourselves useful. His family in Berlin were touchingly welcoming. They laid on a magnificent tea, with cakes and delicacies, which we knew must have meant sacrifices on their part. Joan asked whether there was anything she could do to help them in their precarious state. They gratefully handed over to her several rings and a watch, and a letter for her to take to Joe in London. We wanted to return their hospitality, but they declined, for they said that as Jews they could not walk along the Unter den Linden, let alone enter the Adlon Hotel. Joan and Freda returned from Berlin by train, while I stayed on for a day or two with Billy Rootes. Joan had a nerve-wracking journey, wearing the rings on her fingers, one of them on her thumb because of its size. But nothing was observed at the frontier, and the modest treasure was duly handed over to Joe. What happened to his family I never heard, though I think that some of them managed to join him in America.

Our son Derry was meanwhile learning to walk and to talk. He was lively and engaging, and he laughed and chuckled a lot. St John Hutchinson, who always had the *mot juste*, nicknamed him Little Beamers. It was an apt description, which still holds true forty years on. As we moved into 1939 and the outlook grew even darker, Joan, knowing that I would be mobilized instantly at the outbreak of war, if not sooner, joined the temporary staff of the BBC. I had enlisted in a heavy Anti-Aircraft Territorial Regiment, the 53rd HAA, which was largely manned from the City of London, with bank and insurance company officials predominating: and by dint of evening study and regular attendance at a gloomy drill-hall I mastered the elements of ballistics and of King's Regulations, and became a 2nd Lt RA, without feeling in the least born to the military manner. Derry it was arranged should go to Bodnant, the home of Lady Aberconway in North Wales, in company with a number of other children; and Joan headed for Evesham where for some months she acted as a BBC announcer, while continuing to do her sketches. During August our unit was mobilized; and as Neville Chamberlain was making his declaration of war and the first air raid siren sounded, I found myself standing behind a gun on a gun site in Hyde Park only a short distance from Grosvenor House, with a low wall of sandbags in front of me, as it might be a turf butt on a grouse moor, waiting for the waves of enemy bombers which happily never arrived (not, that is, for many months) for we knew that they would have been very unlikely to be hit, let alone shot down. But the siren had sounded a false alarm, and the period of phony war had started. From Hyde Park my battery was moved to Primrose Hill, where visibility was not blocked by any Grosvenor House: and from Primrose Hill to Enfield, and thence within a short space of time to Arborfield near Reading, which one knew meant that we were headed overseas, almost certainly of course to France.

The day before the departure of our unit for embarkation, Joan came to Arborfield, accompanied by Brendan; we went to a small hotel for tea, and for our final tearful parting Brendan discreetly left Joan and myself alone, went to a desk and on the back of an envelope of the hotel wrote me the following note which I was told to read after they were on their way back to London:

This is the hardest day we have ever known.

I could not say goodbye to you because I am certain that our old happy days will, in some degree, be given back to us.

I wish I could find words to tell you the strength of my gratitude and friendship.

As words are of no avail I must restrict myself to saying that I shall not fail Joan and Derry.

Love B.

Let no one reading this say that Brendan was a man without heart.

The 53rd HAA embarked from Southampton for Cherbourg on 15 October 1939 and it was some time before we learnt that our destination was Reims, and that we were to have the responsibility for defending from air attack the airfields of what was designated rather too portentously the Advanced Air Striking Force. This consisted of some seventy-two night bombers of moderate quality, although manned by as fine a body of men as one could wish to find anywhere, drawn from the Commonwealth as well as from the UK. Our feeling that we might not quite be up to our task was heightened by seeing very clearly the date 1917 stamped on the 3-inch guns (not 3.7 inch as in Hyde Park) allotted to us when we set forth from Arborfield: but we all had a sense of relief that we were on our own and not part of the main British Expeditionary Force. We realized soon our good fortune in being based upon Reims, a city of great character, with a superb cathedral, in the heart of the land of champagne, the qualities of which as an aperitif swiftly impressed themselves, for at that time we were able to buy very drinkable wine for the equivalent of 10p a bottle.

Within a few weeks of arriving at Reims I was seconded back home to England for special duties. I had to report to Sir Campbell Stuart, a vulpine character who was concerned, in a way never quite clear to me, with psychological welfare. There is little doubt that the suggestion had emanated from Brendan, but it was evident that there was no niche into which I could be sensibly fitted, so back to Reims I went.

It was not long after my return that I was appointed assistant adjutant, under a most delightful adjutant, Archie Savory, and a CO of great humanity, Colonel Vere Krohn, who showed consistent kindness towards me. Throughout the winter and early spring of 1939/40 the phony war raged, and we in the army were the spoilt ones with little to do and ample food and drink to do it on. Reims was far from provincial, and there was plenty of social and other life to divert us. Among the diversions was the local *maison close*, which was supposed, probably rightly, to belong to the head of one of the prominent champagne families, and which was ornately decorated with plenty of plush and ormolu, and of course mirrors. I visited the establishment on more than one occasion, developing a friendship with a girl named Lili who was extremely attractive save for a rather prominent gold tooth. My arrival was always greeted with 'Le voici, Monsieur le Vicomte.' My colleagues were highly impressed; and no doubt some of them thought what a wise choice it had been to appoint me assistant adjutant.

However, Lili was not my only French friend. During the period of phony war I met several of the leading figures in the world of champagne, but my closest acquaintances by far were Prince and Princess Jean and Jacqueline de Caraman Chimay. He was the head of Veuve Clicquot, a man of immense charm, intelligence and wit, bubbling – appropriately – with fun, never taken aback, for he understood the foibles and weaknesses of his fellow men. Jacqueline gave me French lessons while I was at Reims. She was talented and cultivated, with a number of books to her credit, notably on gardening themes, as well as an excellent short book about the founder of the house of Clicquot, the original Veuve Clicquot Ponsardin, with an introduction contributed by Evelyn Waugh, and an interesting work jointly with her nephew Jean Poniatowski,

who later became President Giscard d'Estaing's right hand man, about Talley-
rand's years in America during the period of the French Revolution. She was
very well read, but also a good shot and keen fisherwoman. She touched the
social and charitable life of France at many points. She was a woman of remarkable style and taste; never, I suppose, a beauty, but always a most attractive
woman, with a lovely laugh. She was born Hennessy, and the marriage of
champagne and brandy resulted in an outstandingly happy couple, a happiness
that lasted until his death, which quite simply broke her heart and for a while
looked like destroying her utterly.

When I was in Reims their kindness to me was an immense solace. At one
point this kindness went to the point of harbouring Joan for a few nights. She
had contrived to obtain a Red Cross job in Paris, and from there, against all the
rules and regulations, she had found her way to Reims: and the Caraman
Chimays most sweetly allowed her to stay in their house. I realized that I would
have to tell my commanding officer, Colonel Krohn, what had happened, for
to see one's *own* wife in wartime was strongly discouraged. He was very understanding, and we all had a celebratory dinner together before her departure.

Early in 1940 two elegant creatures descended upon Reims from London to
create and open a club for the flying crews and officers of the Advanced Air
Striking Force. They were Dorothy Beatty and Leslie Benson. No more
glamorous ladies in uniform can be imagined. Their club had a short and sad
history. The opening day was fixed for 10 May 1940, the date chosen by Hitler
to strike through Belgium (proving the worthlessness of the Maginot Line which
only extended from Belfort to Sedan, and unbelievably did not continue
through to the coast), so the club was deserted, and I was one of the few at the
inaugural party.

Within five days of the German attack sixty-seven of the seventy-two aircraft
of the AASF had been shot down, being used for day work, trying to stem the
advance, when they had been intended for night bombing; and with nothing
left to defend, our regiment was ordered at very short notice to quit Reims in
the middle of the night. The thought of departing without a word of farewell
to my dear friends Jean and Jacqueline, the idea that they should wake up and
find us all gone, was to me unthinkable; so at about 4 a.m. I drove to their house
and beat upon the door until I had roused their elderly manservant and asked
him to explain our overnight disappearance. Then followed a drive to Dijon,
whither initially the unit was ordered. I was alone in a tiny car with my batman,
a touching character named Jackie Allan, whose letters home I had to censor,
mainly love letters to his sweetheart, more moving than any I have ever read,
and one of which I copied out and have kept to this day.

The drive away from Reims can only be described as nightmarish. The roads were packed with French peasants and other refugees fleeing from the invading army, taking such belongings as they could hurriedly assemble piled up on any available form of conveyance; while in the opposite direction would pass from time to time coachloads of troops who were, I suppose, being transferred from the white elephant Maginot Line in order to slow the German advance in the north. There was the occasional low-flying aircraft, strafing anything in sight; and so swiftly did alarm and despondency spread that any rumour, however improbable, was quickly believed; for instance that the railway signal boxes were manned by fifth columnists, and that German paratroops were being dropped disguised as nuns. All the time the sun was shining warmly down from a clear and cloudless blue sky, Hitler weather it was called, and so it continued throughout the critical weeks.

Of Dijon I remember nothing. The regiment's stay there was brief. Within two or three days we were on our way again, an unreal but beautiful drive along the River Loire almost to the sea, to Nantes, where the countryside had all its early summer glory, and the fact of war seemed hard indeed to believe. And yet at this very same time the mass of British and other troops who had been cut off to the north of the German advance were in the process of being evacuated from Dunkirk, and all we could do was to follow tensely this marvellous rescue operation, feeling blessed by good fortune that we had been stationed south of the German breakthrough, but profoundly unhappy and unsure what the future held in store.

When the regiment arrived in Nantes we were all billeted in different lodgings. I was with a most delightful French family called I think Marquisan. At this distance of time the picture is very hazy in my mind, but our regiment was certainly not the only body of British troops converging upon Nantes. Thick and fast they came, a mixed and motley group totalling some 75,000, including many Poles, the organizing of which presented many problems; and I was detached from the regiment to work on what was called the Nantes Base Sub-Area Staff. I was made an Acting Staff Captain (Q), and I found myself doing what I could to help with the establishment of some semblance of order.

At first the expectation was that a new Expeditionary Force would come out from England, the French forces would be regrouped and a great counter-offensive would be mounted; but few of us I think believed in our heart of hearts in the likelihood or feasibility of this. After only a few days, on 8 June, my own regiment, the 53rd HAA, was moved away from Nantes to the South of France in anticipation of Italy's declaration of war, Mussolini's contemptible yet predictable stabbing of France in the back, which in fact came on 10 June. I was left behind on the Base Sub-Area Staff; and as we witnessed the rapid disintegration of French resistance, when Churchill's offer of joint citizenship was declined, we longed for only one thing, to leave for home as quickly as we could, realizing that at best the alternative was a prisoner-of-war camp.

In the meantime, Joan was still in Paris, and whenever she telephoned to the British Embassy she was given calming answers. I tried desperately to reach her by telephone, finally succeeded, and persuaded her to leave for Nantes on what must I fancy have been one of the last trains to depart. She arrived with no luggage, save for a hat-box containing one very feminine, chic and totally useless hat, her suitcase having been mislaid on the Paris platform (somehow by a miracle it appeared at Nantes after she had left for England, and I rescued it from mountains of baggage at the station depot, my final last search before embarking). With difficulty she was persuaded to join a body of Auxiliary Territorial Service ladies who were being returned to England via St Malo, although before she left she embarrassed me greatly by running away and hiding; for she had visions of me staying behind in France, with some ghastly fate in store, and this she wished to share rather than to be separated for an infinity of time by the English Channel.

After she had left, I was profoundly relieved. The emotional strain of her presence was great. I feared for her safety, while the pressure of work grew from hour to hour. The French requested an armistice with Hitler on the night of 16 June, although it was not to be signed for a week. The final departure of the Nantes Base Sub-Area Staff took place after the fall of France, and during those last days the French hated us for what they regarded as our callous and selfish abandonment of them to their fate, although what else we could by then have done, beyond Churchill's offer of joint citizenship, it is very hard to see. Only the immediate entry of the United States into the war might have saved the situation. It was a most painful time, made especially so by the successful bombing of the troopship *Lancastria* on 20 June, as she was setting sail from the bay of St Nazaire with five thousand troops on board, many of whom were drowned or seriously burned, a terrible happening which cast a cloud of blackest gloom over our final day.

The *Lancastria* was a large ship. I was most fortunate to be on a boat too small to be an easy target. We sailed on 21 June. We took a wide sweep out into the ocean, and twenty-four hours later we landed at Plymouth, blessing English soil, and thanking the Almighty for his goodness towards us. Joan and I were soon reunited. A few days' leave followed, after which I was ordered to report to Aldershot, and we had to discuss and decide what she and our son Derry, then aged three, should do.

When I wrote in an earlier chapter of my schoolboy holidays with my mother, I told of my friendship with Barbara Hutton in Biarritz. That friendship persisted, and was strengthened after my marriage, when Barbara decided to make her home in London, obtaining permission to rebuild Winfield House on the site of the old St Dunstan's in Regent's Park, a mansion which she later presented to the American Government to provide the Ambassadorial residence. At the time she was just embarking upon the second of her catastrophic series of marriages, marrying Count Kurt Haugwitz-Reventlow, whose title was Danish but whose character seemed essentially Prussian, a bully if ever there was one. She was sincerely attached to Joan, as well as to my sister Patsy. By June 1940 she was in the United States, in California. Always intensely generous as well as concerned, she sent a succession of telegrams and other messages pressing Joan and Patsy, and their sons, to come by the fastest means to America, to be her guests there, staying for as long as they wished.

A similar spontaneous urge to do anything they could to help was shared by many people in North America, and plans were made at Governmental level for the evacuation of considerable numbers of children across the Atlantic. Looking back on it after many years, I fear that I was quite wrong to encourage Joan to accept Barbara's invitation. In the hysterical atmosphere of the summer of 1940, having witnessed and to some extent experienced the impact of German aggression, believing that for so long as the war lasted Joan and I were destined not to be together, and knowing that in the United States, under Barbara's protective wing, she and Derry would at least be safe, I encouraged her to go. My father and mother both concurred, and my brother-in-law Paul Latham added his voice in support, so far as concerned Patsy and my nephew Richard. Thus it was that after several weeks of agonizing debate, passages were arranged in a ship sailing from Liverpool, and we all journeyed up there by train from London for another desperate farewell. I returned to Aldershot, a lonely lieutenant without a regiment, to await the pleasure of the War Office.

Encouraged I suppose by Chatin Sarachi, who foresaw what was in store for London, my mother and he became camp followers. They rented a mock-Tudor cottage at Chobham, some five miles from Aldershot, and I was allowed to stay with them there, thus freeing other accommodation: and since both he and she were excellent cooks I knew I was jolly lucky.

I was not to remain long at Aldershot. On 20 July 1940 I received instructions to report to the 8th Anti-Aircraft Reserve Regiment at Cleethorpes in Lincolnshire, a posting which scarcely made my spirits rise. However, I duly reported to this somewhat drab seaside resort adjoining the fishing port of Grimsby. The colonel, named I think Hayley, turned out to be a perfectly delightful man, anxious to make something of a job which had little to offer since, as the name of the regiment implied, the personnel was in a state of constant flux; and, although a certain amount of refresher course training was undertaken, in the main the purpose of the unit was to provide a temporary staging post for anti-aircraft officers and other ranks, available to fill gaps as and when the need arose. Within a relatively short time, I was appointed adjutant, and this gave a semblance of permanency to my job in comparison with the others, who apart from the colonel were very much birds of passage, and therefore to me names and numbers rather than individuals.

It must have been around this time, August or September 1940, that I began to frequent a palmist. She called herself Madame Dubois. She never knew my name, and she elected to call me Captain Luck, because she sensed, or so she said, that good fortune would smile on me. For perhaps eighteen months I visited her regularly at her flat in Marylebone. Each time I had to listen first to a ten-minute eulogy of Sir Roger Keyes, whom she revered; and then Captain Luck would have his turn, and I always came away comforted and reassured. It was above all the pressure of work which caused me to stop my visits, but she was a great help during a very dark period.

After I had left Aldershot the *raison d'être* for my mother's staying at Chobham ceased, and continuing her camp follower existence she and Chatin decided very nobly to join me in this remote town in a distant corner of Lincolnshire. We searched for a cottage to rent, and decided upon an isolated characterless dwelling on the side of the main road from Grimsby to Lincoln. The living room was all shiny brown leather and brass, but by judicious rearranging my mother succeeded in conveying an atmosphere of home. There was a small garden which before long we had turned into an allotment, growing as many vegetables as we could, while on one side we built a run for a few chickens and ducks, and eggs provided our staple fare. I recall too that we grew a remarkable crop of sweet peas, having filled their trench with basketfuls of rotting fish which could be had for the asking at the fish docks at Grimsby.

The owner of the cottage was a cheerful Jewish shopkeeper named Louis Furman. He was short and square, and he had a great desire to please. He owned a well-stocked shoe shop over which he lived when he rented his cottage to us. I visited his shop quite often, buying a number of pairs of shoes from him to present to a pretty young married woman named Linda whom I had met in the course of my daily round. Her husband was serving overseas in the Navy, and we provided one another with a temporary solace. She was short and neatly proportioned, with large brown eyes and tiny size 1 feet: and since I had a weakness for well-turned legs in high-heeled shoes I asked our landlord what help he could give. It turned out that he had a fair stock of very feminine shoes of the right size for which in those austere times he was surprised and delighted to find a buyer. So I took four or five boxes and proudly presented them to Linda, who was even more surprised and delighted, and I am sure rewarded me suitably. After my stay at Cleethorpes I only saw Linda occasionally, but I bless her for her transient goodness to me.

Despite this agreeable diversion, I was all the time desperately missing Joan and Derry who were on the far side of America. After a brief stay in Los Angeles she realized that she had to escape from the atmosphere there. The people were resentful of the war and terrified of the possibility that they might be dragged in. Therefore, although most of the people were kindly, some of them were very anti-British and did not disguise their feelings. Joan went to New York in search of a job. Through mutual friends she met a pianist with the not very inspiring name of Harold Triggs to whom she played, following which he arranged that they should give a series of two piano concerts together, being billed as duo pianists. He was a pupil of the great Josef Lhevinne who in turn was very kind and helpful in giving Joan lessons and above all encouragement. She worked up a new repertoire with Triggs, and they had a quite considerable success. She rented a tiny furnished flat, where through the kindness of Barbara Hutton and with the aid of small concert earnings she was able to have Derry with her in New York.

Whenever I could, which was only seldom because of the distance, I would escape to London in order to see Brendan and to have some contact with the world of great events. In the early months of my time at Cleethorpes the blitz was raging over London and the south-east and we only experienced the occasional raid at Grimsby and at nearby Hull. London was suffering most terribly and Churchill's leadership was all that the country had to lean upon. Brendan was his Parliamentary Private Secretary, installed at No. 10 Downing Street, and rendering immense service to his master. He was also supervising the *FN* and its various associated interests, and this he continued to do until in July 1941 he was appointed Minister of Information. It was an appointment he did not seek, for he wished to be constantly at Churchill's elbow, but it was surely an inspired choice, for he made a major contribution to the strengthening of public morale, filling a number of the key posts in his Ministry with persons of exceptional talent.

For me the appointment of Brendan as a Minister of the Crown was an important turning point. He was required instantly to give up his directorships, and he could not continue to run the newspaper. A request was made for my temporary release from the Army. Three months' leave of absence was granted to me, and my poor mother was left to wind up matters at Cleethorpes, and hand back the key of his cottage to Mr Furman. I wrote him a letter of thanks at the time of my departure and he was good enough to send me this very touching reply:

71 Freeman Street, Grimsby   *28th July 1941*
Lord Moore,

Please accept my sincere wishes for your good health, happiness and success in your sudden change. I may say, that no one has ever made so deep an impression on me, as your wonderful personality, and I feel rather embarrassed to accept the thanks you so kindly rendered me in your note. The Boundary House has at last been made worthy of its building by housing your lovely mother and yourself.

Believe me, that if at any time, myself, property, can be of any service to you, I would consider it a very great honour to be so.

With best wishes and regards,

I remain,
Yours sincerely,
L. Furman

Chapter 9

On my arrival in London I had nowhere to stay. With Joan and Derry in America our house was closed down. I rented a small furnished flat in Hallam Street near Portland Place. It was a pretty cheerless place, but that was no matter for I was never there except at night, and it was a joy to be away from the dead end of Cleethorpes. My mother returned to her ground floor flat in Chesterfield House, into which she had moved from Park Row shortly before the war. I used to see her frequently, and also of course Chatin, in regular attendance. Through him she met Oscar Kokoschka, who had chosen to settle in London and who became a British subject. He was an egocentric genius with a highly developed moral sense, a somewhat tortured spirit whose split personality is revealed by his brutally realistic portraits, and his poetical watercolours of animals and flowers. Oka, as his wife called him, took a great liking to my mother. He was intrigued by her striking appearance and unconventional personality, and he asked to paint her portrait. She gladly agreed, although she might have decided differently had she known that nearly one hundred sittings would be required for an immensely unflattering end-product which became Chatin's property and is now I know not where.

She had two other friends, both of them doctors, whom she saw regularly with Chatin. One was Janos Plesch, the brother of the financier Arpad. He was a Hungarian Jew who practised in Berlin and who wisely decided to move to Britain in 1933 while the going was still good. He had a brilliant brain, but was a fearful name dropper and he had for me a pretty displeasing personality. The other was Jack Spira, a great authority on the abdomen. He and his wife lived in the same block of flats as my mother, and they were endlessly kind to her until the moment of her sudden final illness in 1966, when Jack escorted her to the hospital and eased her last hours. By good chance I was able to repay something of their kindness when I proposed the name of their son Peter, who had been a scholar at Eton, as a possible recruit for Siegmund Warburg, thus helping a very bright young man to be launched on a considerable career.

My father was also in London, working in a senior position at the Ministry of Economic Warfare of which within a short space of time he became Director General. We met often, and my affection and respect for his abilities steadily strengthened. He had evidently won the strong regard of the Ministers and officials of his department. He had a simple natural manner which put people completely at their ease. He was never pompous, and he had great humour. Above all, he had a highly developed sense of right and wrong, and a powerful sense of duty, to which he rigidly adhered.

I made my way regularly to the offices of the *FN* in Bishopsgate, as well as to the offices of *The Practitioner*, the *Investors Chronicle* and *The Economist*. The staff in Bishopsgate had been reduced to skeleton proportions, the account books were housed in the home of the company secretary at Alton in Hampshire, the paper was reduced in size to a daily four- or six-page sheet, and total outgoings had been cut by Brendan through rigorous economies, reductions in salary and so on, to under £100,000 a year. It really was a shoe-string operation.

The editor was a good Lancastrian named Hargreaves Parkinson. He had been appointed in 1938 when Maurice Green left to become financial and industrial editor of *The Times*. For quite a while he had worked simultaneously for both the *FN*, for which he used to write a daily investment column known as the Lex column, and for *The Economist*, of which he was Stock Exchange editor, becoming in 1935 associate editor under Walter Layton, who himself was dividing his time between *The Economist* and the *News Chronicle*. Hargreaves Parkinson was a man of exceptional goodness, willing to undertake any task allotted to him, and he was I fear somewhat exploited by Brendan, who could be a bully to those who did not stand up to him. During the war H. P. worked immensely hard in miserable conditions, and to him more than to anyone else, save only perhaps for Albert Knock, the company secretary, who also tended to be bullied by Brendan, is due the credit for keeping the *FN* alive during the darkest years of the war. Another stalwart was Leonard Shapland, the circulation manager, to whom Brendan had given the added task of supervising the running of *The Practitioner*. He was slightly self-important but a real pro at his job, coming into his own when the *FN* merged with the *FT*, and he became circulation manager of the combined paper. He was highly respected by all those who worked with him for his meticulous attention to detail and his remarkable industry. I remember his telling me that his grandfather had been born in 1760, which since he himself was born in the first years of the present century suggests that he came of vigorous stock. He used to own an MG sports car, and almost his only relaxation, in later years, was to drive very fast for thirty or forty miles along the M1 motorway on Sunday mornings. In London he and his wife lived in Dorset House, and after he retired they moved to

1 Moore Abbey by William Ashford (1746–1824)

2 My father and mother soon after their marriage

3 Myself aged six months

4 In the nursery

5 My mother drawn by J. S. Sargent in 1911

6 My mother with my sister Patsy and myself, *The Tatler*, 18 July 1917

7 My stepmother Olive

8 My mother on the beach at Biarritz

9 On the Croisette at Cannes with my mother and Patsy, 1923

10 Polo at Cannes: Billy de Landa on the right, my mother in the centre

11 Schoolboy

12 Londoner

13 Alvilde Bridges when we first met   14 Emerald Cunard
15 Freda Casa Maury   16 Penelope Dudley Ward

17 Patsy with her son Richard

18 Chatin Sarachi

20 Francis Baring

19 Barbara Hutton

21 Joan in 1937

22 Newly-weds, 1935

23 My portrait by Princess Marina, 1939

24 Derry's Christening, 1937

Dorset where he became the complete country squire, although sadly he did not live long after his retirement.

Each week I went to see Brendan at the Ministry of Information. He had taken instantly to his new job. His knowledge of Fleet Street, and his feeling for the English-speaking Empire and for the United States, coupled with the uplift given to Britain's morale by Hitler's baffling attack on Russia, resulted in his being successful from the start. Question Time in the House of Commons was hugely enlivened whenever he was at the Box. His quick wit and his gift for sharp repartee gave general pleasure to the House, which always filled up to hear him. My regular visits to see him at his Ministry kept him in touch with the modest happenings at the office, while I was able to learn more about the progress of the war than the official communiqués told.

His two private secretaries, Bernard Sendall and Alan Hodge, became good friends of mine. Sendall was nicknamed Sunshine by Brendan, simply I suppose because of his round smiling face. Later he was to become deputy director general of the Independent Television (Broadcasting) Authority, where he achieved success, although he was not thought to be sufficiently a public figure for the number one job. Hodge was highly literate. He was editor of Hamish Hamilton's attractively produced Novel Library, and together with Robert Graves he wrote two books, one of them, *The Reader over Your Shoulder*, mercilessly dissecting the prose styles of some of the greatest authors, and calculated to make anyone reading the book think very hard before putting pen to paper. At the end of the war Brendan brought him on to the editorial staff of the *Financial Times*.

After two months of my three months' temporary leave of absence I received a communication from the War Office instructing me to report back to Cleethorpes in four weeks. At about the same time Brendan told me that Oliver Lyttelton, who at the end of June had been appointed Minister of State in Cairo with War Cabinet rank, was in need of someone charged with the specific duty of keeping him informed of important developments at home, since there had been several instances where he had not been told of decisions for which he had collective responsibility until they were publicly known. I was asked to see Sir Edward Bridges, the Secretary of the War Cabinet, an arduous position which, incredibly, he held from 1939 until 1946. Within days of the due date for my return to military duties I received a War Office telegram dated 16 October 1941 countermanding the instructions; and shortly afterwards I was installed in an office in Great George Street (a street running from St James's Park to Parliament Square), with regular access to the great Bridges, from whom I was to learn what could or should not be transmitted to Oliver in Cairo. It all seemed unreal. It was hard to believe my good fortune in no longer being obliged to return to

Cleethorpes but finding myself attached instead to the War Cabinet secretariat, and thus at the very heart of things.

The specific duty assigned to me was to prepare a weekly letter to send to Oliver in Cairo giving him as far as possible a background picture of opinion, trends and events at home, enclosing such Cabinet papers as Edward Bridges authorized me to send, plus newspaper cuttings and so on, anything that I thought might be of value. This had nothing to do, of course, with operational matters, which were dealt with at a very much higher and more secret level; but from my point of view it was extremely helpful, for it meant that I was obliged to be properly informed myself about a wide range of subjects.

The letters I sent were submitted to Bridges for approval. Thus I saw this outstanding man pretty frequently and I developed immense respect for him. He devoured work. His working hours were endless. He worked a seven-day week, seldom finishing before midnight, yet by 9 o'clock the following morning he would be back at his desk, having as often as not been summoned in the middle of the night by Churchill, whose Map Room and Cabinet War Room were in the lower basement, directly under Bridges's office. (These rooms are still very properly preserved for posterity.) His example was followed by those around him and a fifteen-hour day seemed normal. Distractions were few: everyone shared a common aim; and the habit of work became ingrained. Many of the staff, as well as Churchill himself, had their own small cubicles in the catacomb-like basement, where they slept during the blitz or whenever their immediate presence was likely to be required. Quite often I slept there myself, for however insignificant we were all treated by Bridges as equals. The facilities were really primitive, but it was highly convenient and there was an illusion of security, which provided a kind of comfort.

Bridges's secretary, Ronald Harris, gave me much encouragement. Whenever I was in doubt I would go to him and he helped me to find my way around the office. His industry, and his hours, were those of his master, but he would always manage to find time to give guidance. He had a sharp tongue and a clear incisive mind, which matched his looks. It happened by chance that some years after the war I was for a while once more to come into regular contact with him. This was when I was chairman of Covent Garden and he was Third Secretary at the Treasury, responsible for Government aid to the Arts, in the days before the appointment of a separate Minister for the Arts, and before he had become chairman of the Church Estate Commissioners. (By another chance, to my regret, the transfer of responsibility for the Arts away from the Treasury was made on the advice of my old *FN* colleague, Otto Clarke, who after the war became an established civil servant and whose tidy mind disliked the idea of the Treasury being in any sense a spending department.)

There were two more people upon whom I (and many others besides) leaned heavily, Norman Brook and Ian Jacob. Brook became assistant secretary to the War Cabinet in 1942, having before that been personal assistant to Sir John Anderson, who was the Lord President of the Council, and the man upon whom Churchill placed the greatest reliance, making him the clearing house for discussion and decision upon all non-military matters. Later, Brook* rose to the highest rank in the Treasury, where in my Covent Garden capacity I frequently asked him for assistance, never withheld if my request was reasonable. Ian Jacob at the time held the rank of brigadier. He was assistant secretary to the War Cabinet. He was, however, far more than that. In the eyes of those who saw him, he provided an indispensable link between the civilian and service departments. He had a mind like a computer in its rapidity and its ability to unravel complex issues. The magnitude of his contribution to the successful prosecution of the war cannot be exaggerated.

There was one small episode of light relief during Oliver's time in Cairo. A certain general was despatched from London to fill a freshly created appointment on the staff of the Minister of State. Oliver sent a private and personal message to Churchill in the course of which he epitomized the new arrival by saying, 'I suspect that he wears a full row of medals on his pyjamas.' Owing to carelessness this telegram was given what was called Full Cabinet Distribution. This meant that pretty well everyone in Whitehall saw it, as they appear still to do today; and of course a copy went straight out to Cairo into the general's hands. He took it well though, and it may even have done him good.

In fact I only worked a few months for Oliver in the War Cabinet offices, from the end of October 1941 until the end of February 1942. The period seemed longer because of the length of the working day. We all took our pattern from Edward Bridges, and work anyway seemed the only thing that mattered. I had hoped to have the possibility of joining Oliver's staff in Cairo, but this was not to be for he was brought back to London at very short notice to become Minister of Production.

The prelude to his appointment was a drama involving Churchill, Beaverbrook, Bevin and others. For many months, indeed since the end of 1940, Churchill had wanted to give Beaverbrook responsibilities for production over a wider field than aircraft. Beaverbrook accepted appointment as Minister of Supply at the beginning of July 1941 in succession to Sir Andrew Duncan, who was to return to the same post a few months later. However, the need was increasingly felt for a Minister who could exercise a general authority over the various departments having powers of war supply procurement; and this

* Brook was created Lord Normanbrook in 1964. He died in 1967.

meant not simply the Ministry of Supply, which catered only for the War Office, but also the Ministry of Aircraft Production, where Beaverbrook had by his unorthodox methods and by cutting through all the red tape achieved truly remarkable success, perhaps saving Britain. (The Admiralty as the Senior Service managed to be excluded from the purview of the new department.) Beaverbrook had declared to Churchill that he would undertake the job of co-ordination, providing that he was given the full powers he needed over the allocation of materials and capacity, and – here was the real rub – over the allocation of labour. Ernest Bevin, toughest of trade unionists, a man of force and judgement, was Minister of Labour, and he would have no interference.

Working in Oliver's private office I was able to see most of the senior Ministers in the Government. Ernest Bevin made the strongest impression. I felt that he had by far the most penetrating vision; he had no great subtlety of manner, but he always seemed to me to see the fundamental facts of any given situation more clearly than his colleagues. If there was a tangled skein of arguments for and against any given course of action he was better than any of the others at brushing aside the inessential and appreciating where the country's true interest lay. And as Minister of Labour and former General Secretary of the Transport and General Workers Union he carried immense weight. When he had decided what he wanted no one except Churchill and perhaps Anderson could withstand him. He had a large head, a strong heavy body, and a rolling gait. His mannerisms at meetings were atrocious. He would yawn, grunt, burp, snore; but he was always conscious of the key points under discussion; and no one could resist him in a contest of wills. Beaverbrook knew he had met his match. He would not accept appointment. But both the need, and the outside pressures (in which the small voice of the FN was also heard) grew ever stronger: Churchill's persuasive powers were used to their uttermost; and Beaverbrook's resistance was finally overcome. Against his judgement and instinct, he accepted the terms of reference for the Minister of Production as laid down by Churchill, giving him no more than a co-ordinating job, with no authority in relation to labour; and his appointment was announced.

Within less than two weeks he had resigned on grounds of health, and never again did he hold ministerial office. In A. J. P. Taylor's life of Beaverbrook, which tells the story with a wealth of fascinating detail, it is also suggested that an added cause of his departure arose from a strong difference with Attlee regarding policy towards Russia and the so-called Second Front, Attlee urging that a fundamental condition should be a guarantee by Russia of the frontiers of the Baltic States, whereas Beaverbrook thought this a matter of trivial importance in comparison with the greater issues at stake. How far this was a significant contributory factor I cannot say. The simple fact is that Beaverbrook decided to go, and on 19 February 1942 Oliver Lyttelton was appointed Minister of Production in his stead.

I thought that this would inescapably mean my return to the 8th Reserve AA Regiment in Cleethorpes. I went to the airfield to meet Oliver on his return from Cairo. I greeted him, and his opening words to me were, 'Is there a job for *us* to do?', from which I instantly knew that my fears were groundless, and that he intended that I should continue to work for him.

As the new Ministry was only a few days old, there was virtually no staff. Everything had to be done from scratch, although happily we were given accommodation alongside the War Cabinet secretariat, and therefore for me there was no physical dislodgement. A leading, indeed almost the only figure was Walter Layton, for many years editor of *The Economist*. He had been recruited to Government service by Beaverbrook, first of all holding the position of director general of programmes in the Ministry of Supply, and coming to the Ministry of Production at Beaverbrook's special request, a real attraction of opposites, for no two men could have been more dissimilar in personality or character.

Oliver decided to retain me in his private office as one of his two private secretaries, my superior being an able, rather donnish fellow named Hilton Poynton, who seemed to read and write classical Greek in his spare time. He was only with Oliver some three months, after which he was succeeded by another experienced civil servant, Denis Rickett, with whom I was later to be associated when I was first introduced to the Covent Garden scene in the autumn of 1951. Denis was handsome and urbane, a Fellow of All Souls, and a great lover of music. Regrettably, he too did not stay long at the Ministry of Production since he was taken to work for Sir John Anderson, the Lord President, in connection with highly secret Anglo-American negotiations relating to the development of the atom bomb.

When Oliver arrived back from Cairo he was homeless; and he decided to move into the residential accommodation in the Great George Street building, overlooking St James's Park, which had been prepared for and lived in briefly by Beaverbrook. As there was a small spare room he suggested that I should occupy it, and this I very gladly did, since I had no proper home in London, and Joan was still in America. I thus saw him constantly. His company gave me immense enjoyment. In addition to his sense of fun, he had a robust quality which communicated itself to all those around him. The war brought out the best in him, as it had done in 1914–18, when he had served gallantly in the trenches.

Chapter 10

The first few months at the Ministry of Production were not easy, least of all for Oliver himself. There was inevitably a built-in resistance in the various departments to the setting-up of a co-ordinating Ministry, although no one denied that the co-ordination of effort was essential; and the rather vague nature of the powers conferred on the Minister gave some justification to Beaverbrook's decision to resign, even though under great pressure from Churchill he had reluctantly accepted office. Oliver, despite being powerfully built and physically very brave, was not a tough character nad he needed to be constantly reassured. Soon after taking over he realized the inadequacy of his powers, and Churchill who loved him dearly nevertheless failed to uphold him in one or two ministerial confrontations, notably with the Minister of Supply over the vexed question of steel allocations.

There was, however, one massive subject of fundamental importance, where the work of a co-ordinating department was in no way in dispute and where the Ministry of Production played a major role. This was the whole field of Anglo-American supply relationships. Within days of Pearl Harbor and the American entry into the war Churchill was in Washington for the Arcadia Conference, accompanied by Service and Supply chiefs, with Beaverbrook playing a prominent role. The broad strategy and the whole pattern for future co-operation between the two countries was largely set at this conference. Beaverbrook's particular contribution was to force up dramatically the level of American production targets, especially for aircraft.

One outcome was the creation early in 1942 of the Combined Raw Materials Board, the British chairman of which was Clive Baillieu, a member of a distinguished Australian family and by coincidence an intimate friend and business colleague of Oliver Lyttelton. The Combined Production and Resources Board was not brought into being until some months later, at the time of Oliver's first visit to the United States in his capacity as Minister of Production. This visit was made at the beginning of June 1942. Its purpose was described at the time as being 'to review the whole of the combined machinery for the production of munitions, and in particular to discuss with Mr. Harry Hopkins and Mr. Donald

Nelson the integration of the British and American production programme for 1942 and 1943'.

The party accompanying Oliver included officials from the Ministries of Supply and Aircraft Production, and the Admiralty. Ian Jacob from the War Cabinet offices came so that there could be liaison with the Chiefs of Staff at a high level. From our own department there came Walter Layton, Charles Morris and Otto Clarke, all three of whom had been transferred from the Ministry of Supply when the Ministry of Production was brought into being. Otto Clarke I had known as a colleague at the *FN*. He had been recruited by Layton to work on his planning staff at the Ministry of Supply. Charles was a distinguished academic figure, who like Layton was later ennobled. He was particularly concerned with raw material allocations, one of the functions of the Ministry of Supply which had been transferred, not without resistance, to the Ministry of Production. I was included in the party as private secretary to the Minister, with a general responsibility for co-ordination and liaison. My senior colleague in the private office, Hilton Poynton, stayed behind in London. The decision that I should be included rather than him was only partly because of the importance of the problems likely to require attention at home: chiefly it was kindness towards myself, since it was known that Joan, my wife, was still over in America, where she had gone in the summer of 1940.

By the standards of today the journey to Washington took a long time. We left from Hendon airport during the morning of 31 May 1942, changed into a Boeing aircraft at Foynes in Ireland, and arrived at Washington at 8 p.m. the next evening, that is to say some thirty-six hours later. We were in America for the best part of two weeks. Oliver had good reason to be satisfied with the outcome of his talks. Harmony prevailed. There were wide-ranging discussions. Oliver gave a moving radio talk (TV scarcely existed) about the united efforts of the whole British people in the face of the enemy. Most important, the Combined Production and Resources Board was formed, Oliver Lyttelton and Donald Nelson, the head of the American War Production Board, being named as joint chairmen. The official communiqué stated that the new Board would combine the production programmes of America, Britain and Canada into a single integrated programme, which would be continuously adjusted to the strategic requirements of the war. This clearly went far beyond what could in practice be achieved, but it unmistakably evinced the spirit of the talks and the spirit of Anglo-American co-operation which was to persist for the next three years.

It was agreed that the headquarters of the CPRB should be in Washington; and Oliver nominated as his deputy and full-time representative Sir Robert Sinclair, who after spending a year or so in America returned to London to become chief executive of the Ministry of Production, and in due course I was appointed his personal assistant. Rab, as he was known to all of us, was an object-lesson to me for his thoroughness and his meticulous attention to detail. He was a wise, thoughtful Scot, gentle and soft-spoken, with kindly eyes but a strong chin, rather short in stature and with a head slightly too large for his body. Before joining Oliver's staff, he had been director general of Army Requirements at the War Office. He had been educated at the Glasgow Academy and at Oriel College, Oxford; and his pre-war career had been with the Imperial Tobacco Company, to which he returned after the war as chief executive. Anyone working for him developed a true affection and respect for his qualities. He had one possible fault, a great inability to delegate; he was always reluctant to allow others to draft letters and memoranda for him, a reluctance which fortunately was not directed particularly at his personal assistant, but seems to have been the common experience of all his associates. My friendship with him persisted long after the war, and when I took my seat in the House of Lords on my father's death I asked him, and Clive Baillieu, to act as my sponsors.*

During the two years that she had been in America, Joan had become a very active pianist, giving a considerable number of two-piano concerts with her partner Harold Triggs. She managed, however, to get down to Washington while I was there, although she could not bring our son, Derry, with her because he was ill. We had a touching, moving reunion after a two-year separation, too long a separation which nearly ended tragically. While in New York Joan had met a young Frenchman who had escaped from a prison camp in France. He fell madly in love with her and she was for a time infatuated with him. He followed her to the hotel in Washington where we were staying, appearing in the lobby at breakfast time. It was obvious that he was in a distraught state, for he muttered to me that I must allow Joan to join him as he was being called up for the US Army and would have to leave in two days. I told him as gently as I could that his idea was out of the question for I needed my wife to be with me. Whereupon, to my astonishment, he drew a knife from his pocket – and stabbed himself in the chest. I had never previously, nor have subsequently, had to contend with such melodramatic behaviour, but I suppose I more or less kept my head and made Joan go up to her room. The young man was taken to

---

* It perhaps should be explained that my father had sat in the House of Lords as an Irish representative peer. Not long before his death he was given a UK barony. Had he not been, I should not have had a seat. It is the custom for all newly elected peers to be formally introduced, and to take the Oath of Allegiance; but since my father was already seated in the House, and was in fact Chairman of Committees, it was thought neither necessary nor appropriate that he should be introduced. The powers that be, however, ordained that I must act as though the title had been conferred upon me personally, and therefore go through the strange ceremony. Hence my need for sponsors.

hospital, and eventually recovered, while the incident mercifully was not reported in the press.

After this nerve-wracking experience I was able to go to New York to see Derry. My desire to get Joan and him back to England was intense. There was an elderly Frenchwoman looking after Derry who adored him and believed it was wicked that he should be allowed to return before the war was over. However, Joan longed to return, and I persuaded her that both she and Derry must do so. But to obtain passages back was immensely difficult, and it was in fact to be another five months before they arrived in England. Many of those who had left in 1940 wished to return: there was great jostling for position; air travel was simply unavailable for those not on official business; and it was largely a question of luck finding a cabin in a cargo vessel. A good friend of ours, Tommy Brand, who had been sent over to Washington to work under Rab Sinclair as the British Chief Officer of the CPRB, took infinite trouble on behalf of Joan and Derry. She should in fact have returned sooner than she did, but Derry developed a fever the day before the first convoy on which they were booked was due to sail, and she thought it unsafe to leave. I did not appreciate this at the time, and was convinced that Tommy in some way had slipped up. I wrote him an insufferably offensive letter, rebuking him quite wrongly for neglect, my only excuse being my eagerness that they should return quickly. He had the goodness to post it back to me, saying that it was the sort of letter to write and then not send, but also saying that in my circumstances he quite understood the state of mind I was in. As it happened, a kind of fate may have intervened, for the convoy suffered several losses, whereas when Joan and Derry left a month or so later their convoy was not molested, and they arrived safely.

My sister Patsy was still in California. She was in the process of obtaining a divorce from Paul Latham; and she stayed on in Los Angeles where she had fallen in love with an Irish film actor whom she married.

While Tommy Brand was concerning himself with Joan's passage back to England, I was arranging passages to America for his wife Leila and their children since he was clearly going to be stationed in Washington for quite a long time. I saw her regularly before she departed, and I developed a very strong affection for her. She was a cousin of Freda Dudley Ward, and they both had immense vitality, although as time passed Leila came to suffer from serious bouts of depression persisting sometimes for weeks, induced originally perhaps by the tragic death by fire of her eldest daughter in 1937.

In 1942 she and Tommy were tenants of a small farmhouse adjoining St Paul's Walden, the home of David and Rachel Bowes-Lyon, near Hitchin in Hertfordshire. I suggested that we might take over the lease, because it would provide an excellent base for Joan and Derry, easy of access from London, with the added attraction that Leila, helped by a young lady named Merrifield Jones, had been running a kindergarten school in the house which was attended by a number of children from the neighbourhood; and if this were continued it would clearly help with Derry's early education as well as easing the supply of fuel and other rationed commodities. From everyone's point of view a transfer of the lease was desirable, and it was duly effected. We spent over two years there, until David and Rachel Bowes-Lyon returned from America and moved into the farmhouse, their own large house not being available to them since it had been converted to wartime hospital use.

Within the constraints imposed by the war, which governed all our thoughts, it was a happy two years. We grew to love the Hertfordshire countryside, so close to London and yet so surprisingly rural. We loved David and Rachel's faithful old retainers. And my suppressed desire for a garden became greater than ever as I admired David's achievements.

There too we made friends in Christopher and Camilla Sykes, who were tenants of a flat in the farmyard buildings at St Paul's Walden, although for most of the time Christopher was on military service overseas and the decorative Camilla, whose beauty I nearly ruined in a car accident in Park Lane in the blackout, was alone with her irrepressible little son Mark: while Christopher whenever he was there kept us all in gales of laughter and when he was away sent Joan a series of marvellously illustrated letters.

Among the friends I made during our stay there was old Lord Hampden, the father of Tommy Brand, who lived nearby. Together he and I started a pig club, one of the permitted methods used in the war to increase the slender meat ration. The population of the club was never more than two, all we could manage to feed: but the help to our menu was tremendous. Lord Hampden was an outstandingly charming man but he never seemed to me to have the ability of his shrewd, witty and subtle-minded son, nor of his brother Bob, a very able banker, who during much of the war was head of the British Food Mission and then of the Treasury delegation in Washington. After the war both Bob and Tommy returned to Lazards; Bob made speeches in the House of Lords fairly regularly on economic subjects. Although he was on the board of *The Times* he always sent an advance copy of his text to other newspapers, not for personal aggrandisement but because he was convinced of the rightness of his views which he wanted as widely disseminated as possible. Take this as a quotation from almost his last speech (he died in 1963), delivered in July 1961, but even more relevant to the plight of Britain in the seventies:

It cannot be right for a democracy that our destiny and our fate, financial and economic, should be determined, not by the Government and Parliament, but by shop stewards;

that it should be they who determine whether we can or cannot control inflation, and whether, therefore, we are to go bankrupt or not. There must, however, be many leaders of trade unions, and also many leaders of industry, who wish to co-operate, who recognise the evils of the present situation, and who would be glad to set our country on an even keel again. This must be also what every Government and every Chancellor want. That this aim should be achieved is vital to our future.

He was sound and sensible; our currency and a good deal else would have fared better had his advice been heeded. In any event between them Bob and Tommy Brand rendered great service in Washington, playing an important part in Britain's victory.

The return of the Lyttelton mission from the United States was followed by intense activity. Oliver reported with justifiable pride to his Cabinet colleagues upon what had clearly been a successful visit, not only because of the new machinery established but also because of the reinforcement of good personal relations and the broad understanding reached on the principles to be used in determining the fair allocation of materials and equipment. However, the sense of achievement was short-lived. Two Conservative MPs, Sir John Wardlaw-Milne and Admiral Sir Roger Keyes, had decided to move a vote of censure on the Government for its conduct of the war. They were supported by only a handful of left-wingers and Tory mavericks. Churchill elected that Oliver, freshly returned from his Washington exertions, should be the first Government speaker in the two-day debate, which he himself would wind up. Neither Wardlaw-Milne nor Keyes had anything significant to propose, Wardlaw-Milne's chief contribution being that the Duke of Gloucester should be placed in command of the armed forces. Oliver's reply was a dismal failure. He lost the support of the House early on by not expressing sympathy for Keyes, whose son had just been killed in action. He dealt very feebly with interruptions, refusing to give way at all to Jimmy Maxton, the much loved left-winger from Glasgow; he failed to comment on Wardlaw-Milne's quite unrealistic proposal; and he was rebuked and criticized for appearing to read his speech (which of course he had a right to do on such an important occasion). The fact was that he was put off balance at the beginning and never recovered, although the matter of his speech was good.

I was sitting in the so-called box reserved for officials, conveniently situated to enable Government spokesmen to obtain quick replies to points raised; and I suffered acutely to see Oliver in his distress. He was a brilliantly able man, but he was not a parliamentarian, and his gift of repartee quite deserted him on the floor of the House. However, he was amazingly resilient, and that night he slept as soundly as he always did, whatever rebuffs he might have suffered. I slept less well. I sat up for hours writing a note, entirely for myself, which I kept, analysing Oliver's parliamentary position ('He has really got to work on the H. of C. if he intends to go ahead politically. Today he had a nasty set-back,' and so on), his position in the Government ('. . . there is general recognition at *present* that he is the right man for his job'), the additional powers he needed as Minister of Production ('(a) Power to direct in cases of disagreement. (b) Power over senior appointments in supply departments' (what a hope!) and so on), some thoughts about the American organization and Oliver's Washington appointments, and finally some observations about the office itself. Regarding this I wrote that there was 'much uncertainty among the civil servants as to what is to happen in the office, and especially what its future organization is to be, and who is to be the head official. My own view is that Self is the man because he is able, forceful and respected, backed by Wilson and Bridges, and knows America.' There was another official that I prefer not to name, because he was a good friend to me, who thought the job should be his; but he simply did not have the requisite qualities – although he never lost his facility of phrase, as can be judged from his writing to me after the war from the country to which he had been posted 'This is a grand place. The standard of living is 12/6 a bottle.' Prompt action though was taken about the Washington set-up, and Sir Henry Self did become Permanent Secretary of the Ministry of Production. But Oliver never gained mastery in the House of Commons: he was a man of wit and humanity, but he could not help showing his disdain for those he disliked, and he needed the intimacy of a drawing room or dining room to achieve his true effect.

There was someone else who sat up late writing Oliver a letter which was delivered to him the following morning. It was Wyndham Portal, Lord Portal of Laverstoke, head of the famous banknote business, a company with a built-in protection against inflation, since the higher the rate of inflation the greater the demand for notes. He was a member of the Government as Minister of Works, but he was also chairman of the Raw Materials Allocation committee, a function he had carefully preserved from his time as Parliamentary Secretary at the Ministry of Supply under Beaverbrook. In this capacity he had frequent contact with Oliver. He even arranged to share a flat with him in a building in Curzon Street which came under the control of his Ministry, and which he told me was intended for use by the Royal Family in the event of Buckingham Palace being bombed. The flat's windows had been bricked up, and it was lit by the most fearful blue neon lights which were supposed to simulate daylight, making everyone eerily hideous.

Wydham was rotund, with a head like a pumpkin, so that his appearance was that of a gouty squire, which since he lived off the fat of the land was not to be wondered at. He loved intrigue, and he made a point of cultivating the private secretaries in the different ministerial offices, presenting them with gifts of

game during the shooting season, and generally showing kindnesses, so that
when the need arose he could with a clearer conscience seek information, or
help in arranging appointments. Brendan Bracken he had installed in a small
house named Bere Mill on an islet in the river Test for use at weekends: and
since Brendan was at all times very close to Churchill, Wyndham's sense of
nearness to the centre of supreme power was enhanced. The letter to Oliver
discussed the question of his need for extra powers, and advised him to write to
Churchill staking out his claim, ending with the words, 'The debate strengthens
your hand enormously for making changes,' a point of view which was to say
the least open to argument. I am pretty sure that in fact no formal extra powers
were given, but Sir Henry Self helped greatly to ensure that such powers as
existed were recognized. He was a formidable character. He was very tall and
well-built, with a high-pitched voice and a head which in relation to his frame
was extremely small, yet crammed with brains. It is the absolute truth that he
studied to become a Doctor of Divinity exclusively while on his daily commuter
train, passing the stiff examination with distinction; and I believe he earned
other degrees in the same way. He did a lot to break down the Whitehall
resistance to a new department which, being superimposed, had much initial
opposition to overcome. He also did much to build up a cohesive structure in the
department itself. An economic and statistical section was started under the
benign Austin Robinson of Cambridge. A so-called Industrial Division was
formed which concerned itself with the allocation of capacity, and a panel of
industrial advisers, who played a sort of role as progress chasers, being headed by
Robert Barlow, who after the war became the chief executive of the Metal Box
Company and succeeded in marrying Margaret Rawlings, an actress full of
allure. There was a new regional organization division under Norman Kipping
(later of Confederation of British Industry fame); and an Industrial Information
division under John Rodgers (later the MP for Sevenoaks). Percy Mills, the
Controller General of Machine Tools at the Ministry of Supply, moved his
office to the Ministry of Production, and for the allocation of machine tool
capacity was made answerable to the Minister of Production, so that he had a
dual allegiance. And then Walter Layton, Beaverbrook's first recruit, was given
the position of Head of the Joint War Production Staff, a title implying a good
deal more than the reality, and which did not persist after Rab Sinclair's return
from Washington in 1943. Layton recruited as his number two Geoffrey
Crowther, his successor as editor of *The Economist*, that paper then being largely
edited by Donald Tyerman and Barbara Ward, although Crowther surely kept
his finger on the pulse, and he never really took to Government service, producing memoranda which resembled miniature leading articles. He resumed
the editorship well before the centenary luncheon in 1944, an occasion graced by

all the dignitaries one would expect to be present; and he delighted the audience by saying in a tribute to Walter Layton during the course of his speech that he had made a steady living for a number of years finishing Walter's sentences for him, a service badly needed, as I knew from frequent personal experience.

On the Anglo-American supply front things moved fast. Rab Sinclair went to Washington as the Minister of Production's deputy and his representative on the Combined Production and Resources Board, shortly followed by Tommy Brand who went as British Chief Executive Officer. Oliver Lyttelton's task in London was much helped by his close personal relations with W. Averell Harriman, who had been in London since March 1941 with the rank of Minister as Roosevelt's personal representative for all supply and other matters not strictly the ambassador's responsibility. He belonged to that special breed of wealthy Americans possessing an endless desire to give unselfish public service, always making himself available even after he was close to the centre of power and past retiring age, clearly loving to be in on the act, wishing to be able however slightly to influence the course of history.

As Oliver's secretary I saw Harriman fairly regularly, although always in a subordinate capacity. I also saw him away from the office, because his daughter Kathleen who was in London as the correspondent of *Newsweek* was a friend of mine: and then too he was mightily smitten by the charms of Randolph Churchill's glamorous wife, Pam, an affection which after much turning of the wheels of fate reached fulfilment when they married some thirty years later in Washington.

At the end of July 1942 Harriman sent Oliver a note saying that he was issuing instructions for all missions from the War Production Board in Washington to report to the Ministry of Production in the first instance, even though their principal activity might be with one of the Supply Ministries. He asked to whom they should report, and Oliver replied that the right people to ensure efficient attention were the joint secretaries of the interdepartmental North American Supply Committee, 'that is to say Mr. W. J. Hasler and Lord Strathallan who, although members of the War Cabinet Secretariat, are available to assist in the work of my own office in all matters concerning the United States'. Then a few days later Oliver circulated a note to the War Cabinet setting out revised terms of reference for the North American Supply Committee, of which he himself was chairman, and of the British Supply Council in North America, which tied together the work of all the civilian missions there and of which Rab Sinclair became chairman after his arrival. The terms of reference had been largely drafted by Bill Hasler, who like Sinclair believed in leaving as little as possible to chance in the matter of drafting and therefore did all that he could himself.

Bill was indeed a brilliant civil servant. He had a very clear idea of what he wanted to achieve, and he showed amazing skill in manipulating people far senior to himself in order to obtain his ends, which were never concerned with personal advancement, but to further causes which he believed to be right. He and his wife were drowned tragically soon after the war when swimming off the Cornish coast. His death was a serious loss to Whitehall. David Strathallan, who became Lord Perth on the death of his father, was similar to Bill in his desire to further causes in which he believed. He was not a civil servant by career. Before the war he had worked with Jean Monnet, the father of the concept of European union, spending much time in the Far East with him, and after the war he became a merchant banker and also head of the Crown Estates Office. His wife Nancy was a very attractive American, with a great capacity for laughter. He was an ideal servant of the cause of Anglo-American co-operation.

In October 1942 there was a small but important change in the position of the North American Supply secretariat. They were reconstituted as the Joint American secretariat, and David Strathallan, while continuing to sit and work with Bill Hasler, was transferred on to the strength of the Ministry of Production. Their duties, which had developed in a somewhat capricious manner, were spelt out in detail in an office notice. Less than a year later, I was to succeed David who for a few months was given a special co-ordinating task in connection with supplies for the growing US forces in Britain, before going to Washington to become British Chief Executive Officer of the CPRB (in succession to Tommy Brand). My actual promotion was conveyed to me in a note from A. S. Pankhurst, the Principal Establishment Officer of the Ministry, telling me that my salary as a Temporary Assistant Secretary was to be £1,000 a year; and he very thoughtfully added, 'I do most heartily and sincerely say how pleased I am, and that you've jolly well earned your new appointment,' which I humbly trust I was right to regard as an unsolicited testimonial.

But that was still some way off. In the summer of 1942 I was still in the private office, and it did not seem to be long before we were preparing for Oliver's second visit to Washington. On that occasion I remained behind, but I had the task of assembling the necessary departmental and divisional briefs for him. It was agreed that he and Averell Harriman should go together. They were away for the best part of a month. In his book *Special Envoy* Harriman claimed that the decisions reached 'laid the foundation for the enormous build up that made possible the Normandy landings in 1944'. He then went on to say,

... my one regret was that Lyttelton did not take up with Roosevelt and Hopkins the postwar situation that would result from the sacrifices the British were making for the common cause. I had been deeply involved in the effort to persuade the British that their traditional export programme be abandoned during the war.... I strongly urged Lyttelton to seek an understanding ... that Lend Lease would continue after the war, in order to give the British time to rebuild their exports. He agreed that such an understanding was essential, but for one reason or another, he failed to raise the question in Washington. I have no doubt that if he had taken my advice, he could have received a commitment that would have made our financial relations with the British a lot easier after the war.

Personally I question whether it was as simple as Harriman made out. It was less than a year since America had entered the war, and the war still had two and a half years to run. I am sure Oliver felt that it would have been premature to raise such a tremendous issue of principle when all efforts had to be concentrated on the immediate aim. I could be wrong, but I do not think so. Leaving that aside, the Lyttelton/Harriman visit was very successful. At all levels Anglo-American co-operation was immensely heartening. It was not long however before Harriman himself was to leave London to go to Moscow as US Ambassador. He was very much missed; but fortunately he had a splendid deputy, Philip D. Reed, who was able, willing and ready to step into the top position. The name of the mission was changed from the simple, personal Harriman Mission to the more formal Mission for Economic Affairs. Phil Reed was an outstandingly agreeable person, a lawyer by training and a handsome peacetime tycoon, who before the war when still very young was chairman of US General Electric, a post to which he returned after the war was over. He grew to be greatly loved in London, for he was a true friend to Britain while faithfully serving his own country.

There was one change in Ministry of Production appointments which caused some initial distress in Washington. This was the decision of Oliver to bring back Rab Sinclair in order to make him chief executive of the department, supposedly because a businessman was needed to keep the other businessmen on the staff in order; and to send to Washington in Sinclair's place Sir Henry Self, whom Oliver did not find a kindred spirit, although respecting his great ability. The change left the top civil service job vacant. Before it became effective, Tommy Brand wrote to me from Washington:

I don't like this change. Rab has created a position for himself which is much better than anyone else here since Purvis. He is in a position to begin to harvest a few apples and plums. If he goes we will have to create a new personal position, since everything here is personal not administrative, we can do our best to do this quickly but it is bound to take time and the new man's qualities are very different. Rab is an excellent sheep dog the sheep don't hardly know they are being driven or led at all. Whether Self has these gifts of co-ordination and getting people to work with goodwill is the only question.

His ability to do the job otherwise is clear. However I gather O.L. has made up his mind so that's that. Rab should be very good at the M. of P. but he is not a good delegator. You should warn people that they will just have to take the less important stuff off his hands and go along with it without bothering him. Otherwise you might get a bottle neck.

From my purely selfish point of view the change was advantageous. First of all, it brought back to London the man with whom, as I have already said, I was to be closely associated during the last year or so of the war. Secondly, it introduced into my life the most sympathetic and lovable of all civil servants, John Henry Woods, who at Rab Sinclair's special urging had been given a double promotion in order to be made top official at the Ministry. Quite early after he had taken over I had to have a somewhat unhappy encounter with him. Going to Kings Cross station to return to St Paul's Walden for the weekend, I left my briefcase in a taxi. I did not realize this until I was in the train, by which time of course the taxi had disappeared. I reported the loss instantly. Messages went out in all directions and I had an agonizing twenty-four hours. Mercifully the briefcase contained no very secret documents, and still more mercifully the taxi-driver himself spotted the case and handed it to the police. John Henry was obliged to send for me, and put me, metaphorically, across his knee. He did so in formidable fashion, and then said, 'This could easily happen to any of us. Don't worry. You are doing all right here. Just try to avoid a repeat perform-ance,' which I successfully did.

By his human, considerate approach to people and to problems he won the respect and affection of the whole department, and he made it a happy place to work. He was an extremely intelligent man, having taken a First in Greats at Oxford, but he was completely without side. He also had a keen sense of humour which greatly helped his and Oliver's mutual understanding. In the 1914-18 war he had been wounded very badly in his right leg. He was in pretty constant pain, and he died before he was sixty, a sad loss to public life.

The return of Rab Sinclair from Washington resulted in a considerable change in my personal position. I had already been taken out of Oliver's private office, and was performing general duties in the department. Rab started to hold a weekly chief executive's meeting, attended by all the various heads of divisions. I was chosen to take the minutes of these meetings, and thus I was enabled to have a pretty good overall picture. This, combined with the experi-ence I had gained in the private office, and before that in the War Cabinet offices, gave me a considerable insight into the workings of Whitehall. I was promoted to the rank of Temporary Assistant Secretary at the end of September 1943, when I joined Bill Hasler in the office of the Joint American Secretariat. I continued though to do the minutes of Rab Sinclair's weekly meetings, and my association with him was further strengthened when he asked me to become his personal assistant, a position which I shared for a while with David Strathallan, continuing also to hold my Joint American Secretariat title. (David and I were at that time nicknamed the Lords of Creation.) Rab said that he saw his need to build up good personal contacts with departments with which he had not previously had direct dealings, and he wanted, as he later told me,

. . . a couple of chaps whom I trusted and who had some standing, were preferably not permanent Civil Servants, but had enough 'natural' authority to go straight to anyone in these other Departments to discuss on my behalf problems in which M.O.P. had to take action which inevitably at first sight might seem to savour of an attempt to exercise 'control' in some measure whereas what we were, essentially at least, attempting to secure was co-operation in a general plan which made sense! And somehow or other you and David became with Oliver's approval the obvious possibilities – and how lucky I was! I honestly can't recall who first mentioned your name but it was, of course, a natural suggestion by reason of your previous work with the Joint American Secretariat. Although David, after a bit, had to go out to Washington, you, thank goodness, were able to stay with me and I will never cease to be grateful for that.

Looking back now, years afterwards, it seems as though I must have been immensely industrious. In a way I was. All the time I was anxious to justify my *raison d'être*, for I never forgot my good fortune in not being obliged to spend the war years in either a much more dangerous or much duller sphere. I was grateful too for being brought into close and regular contact with many of the leading Americans stationed in London, and sensing the strength of their ultimate confidence in victory. And my postwar career, such as it was, would certainly not have been possible without the experience I gained and the friendships I made in Great George Street.

Chapter 11

At the beginning of 1944 I thought that it would be interesting to keep a daily diary. For a few months I did so, the one and only time in my life. The diary was a curious mixture of private and office happenings, but since I referred to many of the individuals and the plethora of committees merely by their initials a lot of it has become meaningless to me. (For instance: 'Met Gilbert L. who has come into W.C.O. as P.A.S. to co-ordinate A.S.E., A.E.A., J.A.S., S.M.E., etc. It looks as though A.E.A. will not be transferred to M.O.P.' And so on.) My social life in the evenings was, it appears, largely an extension of my office life. I used to see many of the American officials with whom the Joint American Secretariat had regular dealings. Quite often Joan and I would entertain them in London or at the Bury Farm cottage, where Joan spent a fair amount of time because the small school started by Leila Brand was still in existence and our son Derry was there constantly. A new schoolmistress was in charge, a large and charmless lady with whom our relations were rather strained, for she never stopped complaining about Derry's lack of interest in things, which Joan said was merely a reflection of her own apathy and indolence. And certainly when our American visitors appeared, Derry who was then seven years old went out of his way to exercise his charm on them. We used to see Phil Reed, the head of the Mission for Economic Affairs. He often had with him the actress Frances Day, who brought with her her dog Done 'em, well named for he was far from house-trained. There was Walter Thayer, a lawyer by profession, dark and handsome, resembling the film star Conrad Veidt, very conscious of the public relations aspects stemming from the great build-up of American troops in Britain for whom it had been estimated that over half a million Britons were directly working. Walter was a tremendously urbane character, making himself well liked wherever he went. I turned to him for help and guidance more than to any of his colleagues. After the war he became lawyer to the Citizens for Ike movement, of which Jock Whitney was chairman. Through this Walter was invited to become Whitney's man of affairs, having among other things the melancholy task of closing down the New York *Herald Tribune*, the demise of which was largely assisted by the unwillingness of the *New York Times* to put up its selling price to a realistic level, thus leaving the *Tribune* either to increase its price in isolation and so lose sale to its rival, or else to expire as it did through shortage of revenue. Another American we saw regularly was Winthrop Brown. I remember him for his steel-rimmed spectacles, behind which he constantly blinked, and because he was a health crank, being convinced that to drink milk in England was to drink poison. He was very conscientious, and highly moral in every sense of the word: he could have made an excellent Methodist preacher, but in fact he was a career diplomat, concerning himself largely with commercial policy, but also after the war going to India as minister, as well as to Laos and Korea as ambassador.

There were many others with whom we worked. Names which linger are Charlie Noyes, who looked like the golfer Bobby Jones, and Pinkie Thompson, who wore exotic ties, and always had a friendly smile; and then Dave Ueber-lacher, who arrived with the unenviable job of 'screening' British lend lease requirements on the United States, to make sure that the UK was not in some way gaining advantage by requesting goods from America which it could supply for itself, thereby freeing capacity for the manufacture of 'relief' goods for liberated territories, which after the war could become export markets, a tricky and difficult subject without a simple clear-cut answer.

Although D-Day was still three or four months away, and the end of the war in Europe more than a year off, the problems of the postwar era were already looming large. Indeed Phil Reed had taken a major initiative in pro-posing the creation of a Combined Exports Board, a subject which for many weeks absorbed much of our time in the Joint American Secretariat office. Predictably, the British Board of Trade, who disliked the idea of combined programming, were critical of the idea, and the Treasury supported them. Being imbued with the spirit of Anglo-American co-operation Bill Hasler and I strongly urged a positive response, but we were up against the two great established departments. There were hours of talks but the practical outcome was negligible, and this, seeing the vast strength of the United States, can only be deplored.

It is strange to see from my diary how much of the work of the Joint American Secretariat was concerned with the postwar. Apart from Phil Reed's proposal, a tremendous amount of time was devoted to the interpretation of Article vII of the Lend Lease Agreement, which dealt with the 'final deter-mination of the benefits to be provided to the United States by the United Kingdom in return for aid furnished under the Act of March 1941' (the Act that Churchill described as the most unsordid and unselfish financial Act in history). Article vII said, in starry-eyed fashion, 'the terms and conditions shall be such as not to burden commerce . . . but to promote . . . the betterment of world-wide economic relations'. These were splendid words. Cynics, however, were convinced that the Americans intended to use them to force the UK to abandon Imperial Preference. Maynard Keynes was the principal architect of the various monetary plans for the postwar economic world although the framework that emerged differed in important respects from what he wanted, or might have achieved had he lived. He was riled by some of what he regarded as the nonsensical things being written. His wrath was directed particularly at Paul Einzig who was writing articles regularly in the *FN* calculated to provoke the Americans to great fury. He complained to Brendan, and persuaded him that Anglo-American relations were being jeopardized during the vital run-up period before D-Day; and Brendan, who was reluctant to intervene personally, requested me to speak to Hargreaves Parkinson, the editor, which I duly did, for I was sure that Keynes was right, knowing from past experience what a relentless propagandist for his own point of view Einzig could be. I noted in my diary that H.P. told me that after his talk with him Einzig was 'chastened', but I found it regrettable that the situation had been allowed by H.P. to develop to such a point.

My own contacts with Keynes were very limited, so far above me was he in status and in intellectual capacity. I had the good luck however to see him once or twice in connection with the preparation of the documentation he required for his negotiations over the American loan to Britain at the end of the war (a loan which incidentally was bitterly opposed by Brendan and by Beaverbrook); and I was able to see the extraordinary spell-binding quality he possessed. I remember a delightful story he told of a call he had paid in Washington on Harry White, the head of the Overseas Finance division of the US Treasury. While Keynes was with him, White continued to receive numerous telephone calls, until eventually in despair Keynes decided to return to his hotel and himself ring up White, because, as he told him, that was the only way he could be sure of getting his undivided attention.

There was one very agreeable aspect of Anglo-American relations at the time. This was the Churchill Club, founded at Brendan Bracken's suggestion by Pam Churchill, and Barbie, a daughter of Edwin Lutyens and wife of Herbert Agar. They obtained the use of Ashburnham House, one of the buildings forming part of Westminster School. The club was available to all Americans serving in Britain, a necessary qualification for membership being that in peace-time they had a professional career. As well as providing club facilities, discussion panels and recitals were organized for the benefit of the members. In the opening months of 1944 there were several such occasions. For instance, Kenneth Clark, Osbert Lancaster and Nicholas Bentley had a splendid evening on the subject of cartoonists; John Foster, Walter Monckton and Arthur

Goodhart engaged in witty and erudite exchanges about legal problems; I chaired a panel in which Geoffrey Crowther and others answered economic queries; Phil Reed gave a lucid balanced talk about Lend Lease; Malcolm Sargent presided over a musical brains trust, consisting of William Walton ('the *enfant terrible* of evening'), Vaughan Williams, Boyd Neel and David Webster ('a businessman who supports the Liverpool Philharmonic'); Peggy Ashcroft and Cecil Day Lewis recited verse and Natasha Spender played; so did Joan, on more than one occasion; and the three Sitwells read their own writings, the most dramatic moment being when a buzz-bomb, a frightening invention when it first appeared, was heard approaching as Edith was reading 'Still falls the rain', continuing to do so quite calmly as the engine cut out close at hand, and we all waited anxiously for the explosion, heaving a collective sigh of relief when the bomb exploded a short distance away.

Both Kenneth Clark and his wife Jane had a lot to do with the planning of events at the Churchill Club. We ourselves had first met them with Marion Dorn, and then we used to see them regularly with Emerald Cunard. We became very friendly with both of them. He had been appointed a director of the National Gallery in 1934, at the age of thirty. His love of painting had commenced while he was still at school, and he was to develop into a great pundit who influenced the aesthetic thinking of literally millions of people. Already before the days of television his lectures were to develop a legendary fame. He never talked down to his audiences, but lifted them up momentarily to his level of appreciation. Despite his scholarship and imagination he also had an intensely practical side to his nature. He administered very effectively, as well as having unerring artistic perception and judgement. His family were wealthy through the manufacture of cotton thread, and this enabled him to become a collector. He did not however confine himself to the past, but also did a great deal to promote the talents and assist the careers of living artists. To several leading British artists he was an extremely important influence and help, among them Henry Moore, Victor Pasmore, John Piper and Graham Sutherland, to all of whom he introduced us.

He and his wife Jane had married when they were both undergraduates. She played a major part in the development of his career, helping to promote his talents and aiding his self-confidence. Her appearance was striking, with large blue eyes and very dark hair. She had a generous and considerate nature, and she was highly imaginative in the dispensing of hospitality. With his brilliance, he was always destined for a distinguished career, but without her influence its path would have been different, and less I think in the public eye. Together they were a formidable combination.

We used to see them often, and during the worst of the buzz-bomb period we frequently stayed with them at their house in Hampstead. We had in fact reopened our house in Kensington which had been closed when Joan went to America and we had living with us an old Polish maid named Katie, whose age and background were unknown to us and who was without home or family. Her wrinkled face was set in an expression of unalterable gloom, unless some mishap occurred, when she would break into a ghoulish cackle. One night in March 1944 after seeing a new Terence Rattigan play we took K, Jane and William Walton home for dinner, eating turkey which though hard to come by was one of the few things not rationed. Soon the blitz started up and we decided to drown the noise by playing Elgar's First Symphony, with its stately march tune very loud indeed on the gramophone, because it seemed the most sensible thing to do.

There was another occasion when we had friends for dinner; and in the hope that it may still draw a smile or two I reprint what I recorded in my diary at the time.

Oliver Lyttelton, Bob and Angie Laycock, & Camilla Sykes dined. O.L. in terrific spirits, telling one story after another. He was started off by our telling him of Angie's alleged encounter with a young lady who had deposited a specimen of her water in an empty whisky bottle and this had been stolen while she was in the post office. Bob L. then told us about the blues trooper who when asked by his M.O. to pass water into a chamber at the other side of the room said 'Wot, from 'ere?' Then O.L. told of the Red Indian Chief who had tea at Windsor Castle in the days of Queen Victoria: when asked by the Lady Bertha Dawkins of the day if he was married, he replied that he had 13 wives: she asked what he did with so many wives, to which he blandly answered 'I fok them'. O.L. also had a very good story of an English Admiral who after dining with a Sultan at some Mediterranean port was asked if to round off the evening he would like a beautiful girl; at which he hotly replied that he was a married man. The Sultan said 'Ah, I understand. You would like a boy,' causing the Admiral to turn puce. The next evening the Sultan dined with the Admiral and the midshipmen in their little short jackets were lined up as he was piped on board: the Sultan eyed them carefully, turned to the Admiral, and then chuckled 'Farceur!'

Oliver was very fond of another story which I do not think is recorded in F. E. Smith (Lord Birkenhead)'s biography. During his early days at the Bar F.E. was briefed to act for a charlady named Winterbottom. In his opening statement he inadvertently began, 'My client, M'lord, Mrs Winterwoman, a Washerbottom, . . .' whereupon the judge stopped him to observe, 'A melancholy name, Mr Smith, and a still more melancholy profession!' How the case proceeded, I never discovered.

The evenings were pretty regularly disturbed by anti-aircraft fire. An attitude of lofty indifference towards the blitz was more strictly observed by Emerald Cunard than by most people. She was living on the seventh floor of the Dorchester Hotel, but nothing would ever induce her to descend into the basement when the sirens sounded. It is clear from my diary that we saw a great deal of her, for she had become an intimate friend of Joan's when they were both in New York in 1941 and 1942, and Joan was in fact one of the few people that she really loved. To dine with her was always enjoyable. The mixture of guests was quite unpredictable. The important thing was that they should amuse her. Then a kind of spontaneous combustion took place, and everyone came alive, even the dullest. She had a host of little quips and jokes, often showing her own sex in a poor light. Two that she loved were 'Il n'y a pas d'hommes impuissants, il n'y a que des femmes maladroites,' and 'Women should always marry, men never.' Occasionally she developed romantic attachments for men who were half her age. There was one she nicknamed 'the idealist' for no self-evident reason. With another, who was no woman lover but who wrote her ardent letters professing his deep attachment, calling her the Queen of the Night and that sort of thing, she fell madly in love.

She did not long outlive the war. Although she always maintained her spirits, the last years of her life were unhappy. Her great love, Sir Thomas Beecham, had remarried. She was basically lonely; and after her death it also became clear that apart from two or three quite valuable pictures she was almost penniless. I suppose that someone helped her with her hotel bill, perhaps Nika Hulton or Vera Lilley, who were both very good to her. But it was a sad end to a gallant spirit.

PART TWO

The Financial Times

Chapter 12

The real beginning of the end of the war came with the Allied landings on French soil. The date, 6 June, D-Day, must have been known in advance to thousands of people, and yet the element of surprise was astonishing. It was not long before one could feel confident that the end really was in sight. The incredible thing was that with the great mass of men and materials pitted against them, from the east as well as from the west, and despite incessant air attacks, the Germans could resist so stoutly for so long. They succeeded indeed in making life surprisingly trying and hazardous for people living in London. I remember going home one evening with Joan, a few days after D-Day, when we heard an unfamiliar droning sound which we could not identify. Then we saw a strange low-flying object with fire belching out of its tail. What it was we had no idea. It must either be an aircraft in distress or a thing from outer space. It turned out to be the first of the buzz-bombs, or V1's as they were called: and for some weeks until their launching pads were overrun by the advancing Allied troops they gave us a sense of active involvement in the war.

Such a sense was by then lacking at the Ministry of Production, where my work seemed to be almost entirely concerned with postwar matters, and I felt depressingly detached from the real world of action. I was overjoyed, therefore, when in the autumn of 1944 Brendan one day said to me, 'Camrose wants to sell the *Financial Times*. You'd better go and buy it.' I knew that if his information was accurate it presented the *Financial News* with a unique opportunity. It was clear to me that I must make every effort to ensure that the merger of the two papers took place. The *FN* was by far the weaker of the two, with a sale not more than one-third that of the *FT*. We were also much smaller in resources, with very modest profits. During the war the group kept its head above water, but a profit of £30,000 after tax in the year to 30 June 1945 was the best by far.

I decided that before taking any other step my first duty must be to see Lord Camrose and have confirmation from him personally of what Brendan had told me. I therefore went to call on him in his office at the *Daily Telegraph*. I had met him before with Brendan, and I had been at school with two of his sons, Seymour and Michael, both of whom I liked very much and saw regularly over the years. Seymour was to succeed to his father's title in 1954, showing particular kindness to Joan and myself after he became the owner of a yacht, taking us with him on a variety of cruises in the Mediterranean, Adriatic and Aegean, and thus giving us an infinity of pleasure. Old Lord Camrose was pretty awe-inspiring. (A former employee of his said to me that of his various employers Camrose was 'the best of the lot for fairness, *firmness*, and inspiration'.) There was laughter in his eyes, but his manner was tough and uncompromising. He confirmed what Brendan had told me about his willingness to sell. Together with his family he controlled 375,000 shares, which was 75 per cent of the ordinary capital of the *FT*. Before the war his son Michael had been placed in charge of the paper, but Camrose told me that after demobilization he wished Michael to concentrate his energies upon the *Daily Telegraph*. He told me that the price he wanted for his family's shares in the *FT* was 41s. 3d., the highest price ever reached by the shares since they were introduced to the public in 1928, although in 1941 they had fallen to 1s. On top of that he also stipulated that a similar offer must be made to the outside shareholders in the company, his point of view quite simply being that he did not want anyone to be able to say that he had caused them to lose money. We therefore had to find a sum in excess of £1 million, which of course was beyond us. Recourse was had to the company's brokers, Cazenove, Akroyds & Greenwood, who undertook to find purchasers for all shares beyond those needed to give the *FN* a bare 51 per cent controlling interest in the *FT*, as well as for the shares to be acquired from the outside shareholders of *FT*, most of whom rather foolishly sold out.

In order to assist matters Camrose himself took one half of all the shares sold by the outside shareholders, so that although he had disposed of his control he retained a significant stake in the company, an investment which he had no cause to regret. I myself was eager to invest in the company. Had I done so I could have enjoyed a very sizable capital appreciation; but I felt that it would have been both tempting providence and morally wrong; and I never bought a share.

It was evident that once control had passed the two papers would have to be merged: for one owner to be running two financial dailies was obviously unthinkable. It was also evident that although the *FT* was stronger than the *FN* it would be fully justifiable for the *FT* to pay a significant sum for the acquisition of the goodwill of the *FN*, since by absorbing the competition it would thereby be assisting both its own circulation and its advertisement revenues. Two leading firms of chartered accountants were asked to make an independent assessment of what the sum might properly be. The figure they arrived at was £280,000. By a happy chance, the *FT* owned a strange assortment of perfectly respectable industrial and other investments, none of them particularly appropriate for ownership by the *FT*. Camrose proposed that he himself should purchase these investments from the company at a fair valuation; and the effect of this was to place the *FT* in funds to the tune of over £300,000. Thus the transaction was completed to everyone's satisfaction.

Brendan at the time was still in the Government, moving from the Ministry of Information to the Admiralty during the brief life of the caretaker Tory administration. He could not therefore take part in our discussions. It was clear though that I must keep him informed; and sure enough he ran true to his occasional form, and when he heard the price which Camrose was asking for his shares he berated me, saying that I must be mad to contemplate paying a price for the shares not attained since 1929. It would in fact have been theoretically possible to conclude the deal without any reference to Brendan. Time would have been saved, and the transaction would not have been placed in jeopardy: but it would have been out of the question.

My efforts to convince Brendan took some weeks, and meanwhile Camrose did not exactly help matters by making a last minute tongue in cheek request that he should be paid compensation for loss of office as chairman of the *FT*, on the argument that under clause 90 of the company's articles of association he had been entitled to a commission on the company's profits which he had regularly waived. The sum involved was small, but I reacted strongly against it, and the suggestion was not pressed. I never understood why it was made, especially since he was determined, although he did not put it that way, that the deal should be concluded before the results of the 1945 General Election were announced. Camrose, with his well-developed political antennae, surely anticipated the big swing to Labour. I did not do so, feeling that gratitude to Churchill must give him the victory. If I had done, I might have shared Brendan's qualms, although these were not based on the probable result of the election. As it was, the deal was finally concluded and announced on 25 July. Labour's landslide victory with a majority of over two hundred became known on the 26th, polling having taken place three weeks previously, the delay being the result of the time allowed for assembling the votes of those still serving overseas.

When the acquisition was announced, with its indication of a coming merger of the two financial dailies, I recall no questioning or complaint, nor do I think that people had any subsequent cause to regret what we did. I was convinced that there was no need for two specialized financial newspapers; and being the weaker of the two would have meant a permanently uncomfortable position. It is a truism that with newspapers the important thing is not the absolute level of sale, but to be the leader in one's own particular field. I was convinced that for the *FN* to supplant the *FT* would have been a well-nigh impossible task, even though I knew – *of course* – that it was a much better paper. The habit of preferring the *FT* was ingrained in conservative City readers. To overtake its sale would have meant the expenditure of much money, which we did not have, with no guarantee of success; whereas the *FT* had considerable resources, as well as its own printing works, while the *FN* was printed outside under contract. There was no doubt that despite the excellence of some of the *FN*'s writers, the *FT* was regarded as the leading City paper for its stock market comment and greater volume of straightforward financial information; and, because of its greater sale, it attracted more financial advertising, which was itself news, at any rate for readers of financial papers, and this in turn attracted more readers, so that success bred success.

As the completion of the deal advanced but before it was concluded I saw and wrote a letter to John Henry Woods, the Permanent Secretary of the Ministry of Production. I explained what was likely to happen, and urged that on the assumption of the deal going through I should be allowed a partial release from the department, which was in the process of being absorbed into the Board of Trade and which was increasingly concerned with reconstruction problems, the war in Europe having ended two months previously and the end in the Far East being imminent. John Henry took me to see Sir Henry Wilson Smith, Under-Secretary at the Treasury, who seemed to have the ultimate say in the matter. John's consideration towards me, as towards all his staff, was extreme; he was always absolutely fair, and whenever he could he went out of his way to be helpful. As well as Wilson Smith, Rab Sinclair, the Chief Executive of our Ministry, also had to be consulted; and the upshot was that I was allowed to devote up to two days a week to the affairs of the *FN* and *FT*, providing that I did not for the time being join the board of the *FT*. The question, Woods said, would have to be reviewed in the light of developments concerning the future relationship between the Board of Trade and the Ministry of Production and also if after a short period I found it possible to devote less time to the two companies' activities.

The war was clearly drawing to its close, but all too slowly, and for those still working in the Ministry, and elsewhere, there was great uncertainty as to what the world 'post war' would be like.

Thus I was very fortunate, for the *Financial Times* deal was concluded and I secured a sufficient degree of release to enable me to plan the various steps preparatory to the merger of the two papers and other related problems. Brendan himself, after the fall of the Government, was not destined to return either to the old office of the *FN* or to have a room in the even older offices of the *FT*. He rejoined our various boards and in due course became chairman, but he was to conduct his business life from the offices of the Union Corporation, a leading South African Mining Finance House, of which on the death of Sir Henry Strakosch, at the latter's express urging, he had been elected chairman in August 1945. Strakosch had been born on the Continent, and had come to Britain before 1914. He was both businessman and trained economist, and he had been invited by Brendan and Walter Layton to become chairman of *The Economist* after the paper changed hands in 1928. He was exceedingly wise, giving great attention to the smallest detail without allowing it to obscure the broader picture. Brendan and he had become very close to one another over the years, and he chose him as his successor. I think that Brendan was immensely flattered. He threw himself into his new job with great eagerness. For me it was something of a mercy, since Brendan breathing down my neck at every stage would have been insupportable. I was in fact able to see him without difficulty, for the Union Corporation offices and those of the *FT*, into which I gradually moved, were only four hundred yards apart. Because the *FT* received much advertising from mining companies Brendan in fact took me out with him once to South Africa, which he visited regularly, for he loved his Union Corporation job, and he was particularly pleased to have a mine named after him. I was quite appalled by the whole business of apartheid. The callousness of the white population really shocked me; and it seemed to me that the English-speaking element were in a way worse than the Boers because they were happy to enjoy the benefits of the system while at the same time condemning it. I remember accompanying Father Trevor Huddleston through the township of Sophiatown, and walking with the Son of God could have been a similar experience. Alone I should probably have been assaulted. It struck me at the time what tiny concessions to the black people would have sufficed to give them some contentment. But these were not to be forthcoming for years to come, when it was far too late. During part of the time, I stayed with two very good friends, Alfred and Clementine Beit, who were living near Capetown. He had lost his parliamentary seat in the 1945 election and had decided to set up home in South Africa where he had extensive interests since his uncle had been the partner of Cecil Rhodes. However, they could neither of them accept the policies of racial discrimination, realized that they had not the power to bring about change, and moved instead to Ireland where they bought a house of outstanding beauty near Dublin, and did much to promote the cause of the Wexford Festival.

The second half of 1945 must have been intensely active for me, since for most of the time I was working three days a week in Whitehall, while also trying to plan the merging and integration of the two papers. The first issue of the combined paper in fact appeared on 1 October 1945. Soon thereafter I went to see John Henry Woods armed with a letter from Guy Dawnay, the chairman of both the *FN* and the *FT* pending Brendan's return, emphasizing the import-ance of my full-time release from Government service following the merger of the two papers. It was Dawnay's issuing house, Dawnay Day & Co., which had helped Brendan with the original *FN* issue in 1928, and ever since then they had remained close to one another. I urged upon John Henry that since the Ministry of Production had been absorbed into the Board of Trade and the matters dealt with were exclusively concerned with postwar reconstruction it was wrong that I should be at large in Whitehall. John Henry concurred, and within a few weeks I was free to concentrate solely upon the affairs of the *FN/FT*.

Joan and I were beginning to hunt for a house with a proper garden because the St Paul's Walden garden had given us a great enthusiasm for horticulture. In the summer of 1944 we had both spent many nights sleeping at Upper Terrace House, the Hampstead home of Kenneth and Jane Clark, and for a while it seemed to me that Hampstead offered a perfect compromise between town and country, possessing the best features of both. We saw a number of old houses there. I thought that the ideal among them was Cannon Hall, which belonged as I recall it to Mr Carroll Marx, a successful stockbroker. In earlier days it had been the home of the famous actor, Gerald du Maurier. The house dated from the early eighteenth century, and was built of dark-coloured London briek, with attractive linen-fold panelling in the corridors and bedrooms upstairs. The garden was very large, at least an acre I suppose, constructed on two different levels. There was a splendid view right across London to the hills to the south. Hampstead Underground station was only a short distance away. Everything seemed right, including the price, except that both my father and Brendan thought that I was suffering from a kind of *folie de grandeur* in wanting to buy such an imposing mansion; while Joan objected that despite the size of the house there was no decent-sized room suitable for music, and the circulation of the house was inconvenient. On top of this, it turned out that the house had dry rot: also the wall at the southern end of the garden was a good twenty feet high, and bulged ominously into the street below it; and I had visions of its giving way and of having to rebuild it at heavy cost. So I withdrew my pro-visional offer. Thus ended our house-searching in London, for after Cannon Hall there was nothing else available that we really wanted.

We then decided to search in the country, which from the point of view of Joan's health and her ability to concentrate upon her musical work had much to recommend it. We spent a number of weekends on visits of inspection, but everything that we saw was either too large or too small, too ugly or too costly or too dilapidated, or else too far from London. There was one exception: a most beautiful stone-built house near Wallingford in the Thames Valley, rather large but with splendid rooms and all that one could desire. Alas, though, the surveyor discovered that the house had slightly subsided on the front facing towards the river, and he could give no guarantee that the process would not continue until eventual collapse.

Again then no offer could be made. In some despair the house agents asked if we might possibly be interested in a leasehold. Against our better judgement, although not to our regret, the upshot was that we acquired the lease of Parkside House, Englefield Green, a house of no special beauty, but with character and charm; and there we have lived happily for the past thirty years, the lease still having a few more years to run, after which the crystal ball is clouded. But meanwhile we have made an attractive garden, giving us both interest and pleasure. We have our own gate into Windsor Park, and within a few hundred yards is the famous garden created by Sir Eric Savill, an able but irascible man, charming to one's face if not on paper, who while he was Deputy Ranger of the Park acted as our landlord.

The advantages of abutting Windsor Park were considerable. There was the attraction of having a gate directly into the park, which in those days was quiet and placid. It was still a number of years before the commercialization of the Savill Gardens and the introduction of polo on nearby Smith's Lawn, where the noisy loudspeaker running commentary, provided for the benefit of ignorant spectators, destroyed much of the calm. The house was only twenty-five miles from London, with a relatively easy drive up or down, and it was handy for the airport, Heathrow being only ten miles away (although I might have thought differently about this had I known that twenty years later I should be instigating and leading a deputation to the appropriate Minister, protesting against the noise of aircraft flying overhead, a deputation which mercifully achieved results because of the presence of a large teacher training college close at hand). Another advantage was that our son was about to go to a boy's preparatory school a few miles away, and was afterwards likely to go on to Eton, just across the river from Windsor. Later, although we did not then know it, he was to do his military service in the Life Guards, and for most of the time that he was serving he was stationed at Windsor. Finally, both my parents were living nearby, my father at Cobham and my mother in London; and we were thus able to see them regularly.

The problem of furnishing and decorating the house in the period of postwar austerity and shortages was considerable. We had sold our old house in Kensington for an absurdly small sum. The house had very little in the way of furniture because so much had simply been built into the walls: and what was movable was unsuitably modern. Therefore when we bought the lease of Parkside House we also bought quite a few of the contents, but the previous owner had a love of cupids which showed up as lamps or in some other guise in several of the rooms; and these we did not want. Joan had a very good eye for quality in furniture, and managed to obtain quite a few bargains. She had a natural sense of colour and she was extremely skilful in adapting materials for purposes for which they were not intended. Mattress ticking served in a variety of ways.

But it all took time. Before we were thoroughly installed at Parkside House we used to stay very often in Cornwall with Bertie and Diane Abdy. We met him first during the war with Emerald Cunard. He and Diana Cooper were her two closest confidants, and their friendship dated back to the days when she was regarded disapprovingly by much of fashionable society, not that either of them were ever likely to be deterred by that. From an early age Bertie had been interested in works of art in an amateur way, but a fire at a wharf which he owned and which he had failed to cover for insurance forced him to take up dealing professionally, and during the 1930s he was active and successful in London, Paris and New York. I was deeply impressed not only by his knowledge of the French seventeenth and eighteenth centuries, but also by his quick perception of merit in works of art of all periods. He was one of England's true eccentrics, capable of doing and saying most extraordinary things. Beauty in all its aspects used to delight him, but ugliness made him wince with pain. He was tall and handsome, with a short-sighted look and a gentle persuasive manner. He had taken a great fancy to Joan, and because of this and because his son Valentine was an exact contemporary of our son, we often visited Newton Ferrers, his beautiful, sadly romantic Cornish home where he was endlessly constructing a large water garden, having diverted a stream for the purpose.

If Bertie fancied Joan, I was captivated by his wife Diane. She was a complete contrast to him in every way. She was tiny, gay and pretty, bubbling with laughter, loving country life and gardening, milking the cows, feeding the chickens, even attending, suitably veiled, to the bees. She could draw and paint with professional skill, and her letters were a delight to read. She had numerous admirers but if they ever received encouragement, the fact was most skilfully concealed. Our visits came to an abrupt halt when she was involved in a most terrible motor accident in about 1953 driving her son Valentine across the Devon moors. She should have died instantly. Instead her life was prolonged for a number of years after the accident, and she had to reside in a home, where to visit her was pointless for she could neither recognize nor remember.

We often saw K and Jane Clark. One summer at the very end of the war we went with them and their three children to Portmeirion, the hotel created by the architect Clough Williams-Ellis, beautifully situated by the sea at the north-western point of Wales. It was among the first hotels built on the principle of giving guests their own separate cottages; each was a different pastel shade, only the main dining and living rooms being located centrally. The atmosphere was rather arty-crafty, and judging by the issue of *Country Life* dated 16 September 1976, it has become more so, but the situation with the mountains to the east and the sea to the west was splendid. K used to go there because the National Gallery paintings were kept throughout the war in the Manod caves, and he went regularly to inspect their condition. He took us over with him. It was strange to see some of the world's greatest masterpieces in such un-conventional surroundings, but the atmospheric conditions must have been satisfactory for they suffered no harm.

Among those who appeared while we were at Portmeirion were Arthur Koestler and his wife to be, Mamaine Paget. I think that they had a farmhouse somewhere close at hand. He had a strong but to me not very sympathetic personality. He seemed a restless spirit and it was hard to feel at ease with him. Mamaine we had known for a number of years. She and her sister Celia were very pretty, and they could not be told apart for they were identical twins; arriving anywhere they had to announce their name, rather like two Eton friends of mine, Geordie and Eddie Ward, who used to keep one another's dates, once changing over in the middle of an erotic evening, to the mortification of the young lady when she learnt the trick they had played.

Also visiting Portmeirion when we were there was my old school companion, David Herbert, who was shortly to be demobilized from the merchant navy, in which he had served gallantly during the war. At the time he was still living in his delightful little house in the grounds of Wilton, his family home in Wiltshire. He filled me with envy because he effortlessly radiated a sense of enjoyment to whomever he was with, and he was a great antidote to the nine to six mentality with which I was afflicted. As a second son he was not well off although his family had wealth, and therefore not long after the war he decided to go and live in Tangier where there were then no taxes (before it was absorbed into Morocco), and he could find domestic staff for a fraction of their cost in England while the need for fuel and other forms of heating was far less, clothing presented no problem, and private life could be quite uninhibited. Joan and I used to visit him in his new abode, always with pleasure; and if he admired my doggedness I admired his initiative in making a new life for himself, and I was most impressed by the way in which he swiftly became the moving spirit of Tangier, coming to know every part of Morocco intimately.

In England there were two or three grand and beautiful houses which we visited regularly in the days when the weekend house-party was less of a rarity and before I became irretrievably addicted to gardening, absorbed by its fascination, coming to realize the price of a few days' neglect. One of our most frequent visits was to Hatfield House, Robert Cecil's great Elizabethan monument, the home of Bobbety and Betty Salisbury. He was a prototype of the aristocrat, ever conscious of a sense of public duty, his inheritance fitting him like a glove, yet never pompous and always unpretentious and accessible. She could be very fiery, and even vindictive; but she was extremely amusing, magnetic and full of charm. And she was warm and welcoming, always greeting one with 'How *are* you?' as though she really meant it. Her chief passion was gardening. Both at Hatfield and at Cranborne in Dorset she created beautiful gardens, and from her I learnt a lot.

Through our visits, Bobbety's brother David Cecil became a very good friend, especially of Joan, to whom he dedicated his life of Max Beerbohm. Unlike the rest of his family, who devoted themselves to public service, he was a true artist. He used to be a professor of English literature at Oxford, where he was a very popular lecturer, being a great romantic, aiming above all to convey a sense of enjoyment to his listeners, as he did in his fine sensitive writing. Now over seventy years old he still conveys a feeling of youthfulness, as though his voice had not yet quite broken.

We went several times to Boughton in Northamptonshire, one of the homes of Walter and Mollie Buccleuch, and also to Drumlanrig, their fairy tale pink castle in Dumfriesshire. Both of their houses were storehouses of treasures. They were not in those days open to the public, so it was a rare treat to be shown around. Mollie in particular was a remarkable guide. Despite the richness of the contents, there was nothing she did not know, and she always made everyone feel that she was doing it for the first time, so fresh and eager did her youthful voice sound.

Close to Boughton was another house that we had already visited often before the war, Weston Hall, the home of Georgia and Sacheverell Sitwell. He was the youngest of the three Sitwells, resembling an elongated Modigliani; and he was a most refreshing companion, with extraordinary all-round knowledge which he imparted with an air of amusement and shocked surprise. He was addicted to foreign travel, writing many books into which he managed to compress art and architecture, ethnography, history and geography. I found his style rather literary, and his books harder to absorb than his conversation. Besides travel, music, the ballet and gardening were his other passions; and I envied him the ease with which he communicated his enthusiasm. Georgia, his wife, had a striking and pleasing appearance. She was warm-hearted, and she gave their house a very harmonious atmosphere. She was a very good foil to him, with her feet much more firmly on the ground; and she was far more capable of tackling difficult situations.

Another friend with whom we regularly stayed was Maud Russell. She was partly Jewish, extremely civilized, wise and witty, with a delightful sense of the ridiculous. Her home was called Mottisfont, a romantic and very comfortable house in Hampshire built on the site of a medieval abbey, with the River Test, famous for its trout fishing, flowing through the grounds. She had inherited money, and she always gave generously to causes in which she believed. When I came to be chairman of Covent Garden and started the Benevolent Fund, she was one of our first and most constant supporters. Mottisfont now belongs to the National Trust, and she lives in a small neighbouring property, but in its heyday it was a joy to visit, radiating *luxe, calme* and *volupté*.

Oliver and Moira Lyttelton were close friends of hers, and we often stayed with them after they moved into Trafalgar House, the home of Horatio Nelson, only a few miles from Mottisfont. Trafalgar was bought as an investment for Moira's brother, the Duke of Leeds, who did not himself wish to stay at the house; and it suited Oliver very well to be the tenant, for it gave him a stately home, which he could not himself have afforded; and then he loved the shooting. There was one particular friend of Oliver's whom we met both with him and with Maud Russell. This was 'Crinks' Harcourt Johnstone, a Liberal MP who was Secretary of the Department of Overseas Trade from 1940 to 1943, being appointed by Churchill in order, as he said, to make sure that we didn't have any exports. He was a great wag and wit, and a true bon viveur. According to Brendan he once consumed thirty plovers' eggs as an appetiser for lunch while flying from London to Paris. He loved champagne, dismissing the magnum as a very inconveniently sized bottle, too large for one but not enough for two. Not surprisingly he died when he was only fifty years old.

Our most frequent visits were to Ditchley Park in Oxfordshire. This was architecturally one of the most splendid houses, with exceptional interior decoration. It had originally been the home of the Dillon family, but before the war Ronald Tree and his wife Nancy had bought it and transformed it. They both had great taste, which he had the means to indulge. He was born American, but he was educated in England, became British, entered Parliament and for many years made his home here until high taxation forced him to leave. I knew him first through Brendan, whose Parliamentary Private Secretary he was during the war, when Brendan was Minister of Information, and Ronnie was able to make a valuable contribution to Anglo-American relations in this field. It was on Brendan's initiative that he made Ditchley available for use by Winston Churchill at weekends when it was feared that the Germans might attempt a moonlight raid on Churchill's own country home. Ronnie combined a love of good living with a strong desire to do good. He was fundamentally serious, and his handsome features usually wore a look of grave concern. He was kind and hospitable, and he brought together under his roof a wide variety of people; and the more they played an active part in public affairs the happier he was, for he himself was a frustrated statesman.

He was married twice, on each occasion to exceptional women, both of them distinguished in appearance, and both having very powerful and positive personalities, although there the similarities ceased. Nancy had a highly developed artistic strain, and she was able to put her creative talent as a decorator to practical effect some years after her divorce from Ronnie when she bought control of the decorating firm Sybil Colefax & John Fowler. His second wife Marietta was a statuesque beauty. While being a lover of works of art, her real bent was for politics, in which she took a lively interest, while later in life she also showed a strong aptitude for business, becoming a director of Pan American and CBS, and entering into a successful partnership with the firm of a British architect, Richard Llewelyn-Davies, the purpose being to offer the advantages of modern urban planning to underdeveloped countries, and to bring aspects of British experience to some of the 'ghetto' areas of American cities. Politically Marietta had always supported the Democrats in the United States, and she had a strong social conscience, which her partnership helped to assuage.

She had little opportunity to be chatelaine of Ditchley. Ronnie lost his seat in Parliament at the General Election of 1945, and soon after that was obliged to leave England by the penal taxation introduced by Hugh Dalton, the Socialist Chancellor of the Exchequer; and since Ronnie's income derived from the Marshall Field estate in the United States he betook himself there.

Joan and I were to see Ronnie and Marietta often in the years to come. At first it was on their regular visits to London, but later we stayed with them many times in Barbados, an island which he first visited in 1946, falling in love with it, buying land, building Heron Bay, a Palladian villa constructed from the local coral right by the sea, creating a splendid garden, and becoming the moving spirit and chief participant in the construction of a hotel and golf course a mile or two away, all done with the taste and practical good sense that he revealed in everything he undertook. As time went by he became an important presence on the island, spending half of each year there, much respected and indeed loved by the local population, and particularly by his own staff. 'The Heron has departed from the Bay,' his manservant Tull wrote to me touchingly after Ronnie's death. And he is certainly widely mourned.

There were two other houses we went to quite often in the early postwar years: Somerhill and Sledmere. Somerhill near Tonbridge in Kent belonged to Harry and Rosie d'Avigdor Goldsmid. It was an imposing seventeenth-century

pile, but comfortable and welcoming because of the warmth they both generated. In those days he worked in the City, where his family business was bullion
broking, but he had a desire to go into politics and so abandoned his business
career, which I always felt was a mistake because he was not meant for the
hustings, and ministerial office always eluded him. He had a characteristically
clear, dissecting Jewish brain, and he was capable of making people feel uncomfortable; but Rosie put it all to rights with her skill at humouring him.
They were outstandingly kind and generous, an object lesson to many others
equally well placed.

Sledmere was the Yorkshire home of Richard and Virginia Sykes. He was the
head of a leading Roman Catholic family, but she remained staunchly Church
of England. Her father, Jack Gilliat, was one of my father's closest friends, and
therefore I had known Virginia for many years. Indeed she had been one of
those present in the still-room at Belvoir Castle when, as I have described, I was
so unjustly treated by the old Duke of Rutland. She was among the most
rewarding and sympathetic people of all my acquaintance, a marvellously good
wife and mother, with an eager love of life, dying far too young after a minor
operation. Sledmere being a famous racehorse stud, it was possible to maintain
the house in style and to entertain lavishly. Virginia had natural talents as a
hostess, and Richard was wont to leave the responsibility to her, withdrawing
quite often to the dome of the house where he played, pretty loud, a powerful
organ that he had installed there. He took great pride in showing his guests
round the stud farm, which was handsome and beautifully maintained, and a
most enviable asset. In the evenings we were expected to play The Game, a
form of competitive dumb crambo, in which one had to take it in turns to
enact a word by mime and gesture. It was particularly enjoyed by Princess
Marina, who was a frequent guest. Its charm always eluded me, but it did help
to unbutton people and eliminated the need for conversation.

Richard and Virginia allowed me to use Sledmere as a staging post when
driving to Scotland. For several years after the war I went regularly with my
father to play golf at Muirfield. He asked me to accompany him there after the
death of Jack Gilliat, with whom he had been in the habit of taking an annual
golfing holiday. My stepmother Olive had died suddenly and unexpectedly
at about the same time. For a while my father was plunged into a state of deep
unhappiness. It was a mercy that in 1946 after closing down the Ministry of
Economic Warfare he had been elected Chairman of Committees in the House
of Lords, for this helped to distract him from his grief; and I should like to
think that our golf outings together contributed slightly towards the same
end.

I was never much good at golf, and I was always delighted if I went round the course in under ninety strokes. The course was marvellously situated, over-looking the Firth of Forth, with the hills of Fife across the water, undulating open countryside, conveying a real sense of freedom. The holes looked deceptively easy, but there was usually a strong wind and mistakes were always punished. I used to have a caddy named McGregor whose highest compliment to anyone was to say, 'That's a golf shot!'; and if I heard the words once during a round I was overjoyed. My father and I played two rounds each day, and then during the evening went into Edinburgh for the Festival. We stayed at Grey-walls which had been bought by Colonel James Horlick who presented it to his animated mercurial daughter Ursula Weaver as a wedding present; and she and her husband John converted it to a small, very personal hotel, making it feel like staying in a private house. Our annual visits continued until my father's death in 1957, after which I pretty well gave up playing golf, spending more and more of my leisure time scratching away in the garden.

For our holidays Joan and I usually went abroad. Not long after the war we had one most enjoyable motoring tour in France, visiting the Abbey of Vézelay, 100 miles south of Paris, a thirteenth-century masterpiece splendidly restored in the nineteenth century by Viollet-le-Duc, perfect for its form, colour and siting. On our way home we stayed at the British Embassy with Diana and Duff Cooper, making a new and intimate friend, Susan Mary Patten, whose husband Bill was on the staff of the American Embassy in Paris. He suffered from appalling asthma, and this weakened him so seriously that he died very young. Susan Mary now lives in Washington. She has more than her fair share of personal charm, and she is a model of elegance. Wherever she is, she contrives to be *au courant* with the latest events in political and social life. Joan and I often stayed with her in Paris if we had a business or other excuse to go there, and we owe her much for her kindness. When Bill Patten died she set up house in Washington and married Joe Alsop, the noted columnist, who steadily earned a large income, particularly at the time of Vietnam, as a modern Jeremiah.

We had two very happy holidays in Italy, once with Barbara Rothschild, Pam Berry and Julian Amery when we jointly rented a flat in Florence, and engaged in intensive sightseeing. It was Pam, as I related, who first introduced me to Brendan. I continued to see her regularly over the years, and I never ceased marvelling at her skill as a hostess or in adapting herself to the changing political scene. She and Barbara were old friends, and they were hilariously funny together, bickering like mad, while I was dubbed Mr Facing Both Ways by Pam for my feeble attempts at peace-making. Our return journey by train I remember because we had bought a large Gorgonzola cheese which smelt so powerfully that at the railway station we bought several bunches of tuberoses to counteract the smell. At the frontier, the customs officers nearly fainted, and had we been smugglers we could have brought anything through safely.

On the second occasion we rented a villa on the coast south of Naples jointly with another group of friends, headed by Tony Rosslyn, a beloved neighbour with whom in those days I regularly played golf and bridge, and Bertie Abdy, who could only have come because of his devotion to Joan, for swimming from rocks in a broiling sun was not at all his idea of fun. There were two women with us. One was Edwina d'Erlanger, an American beauty with a Southern drawl, given to complaining but immensely funny, always smartly dressed, with exquisite legs, and feet so tiny and slim that her shoes had to be specially made for her. Her husband Leo, who was also a good friend of ours, preferred not to come because he hated to feel caged up and unable to escape even if he was with people he loved. He was a man of original and creative mind, who before the war was a pioneer in the development of commercial air transport. He was to have more than his fair share of disappointments. Although he was wealthy, fortune did not smile on him. He was chairman of the Channel Tunnel Company, and fought very hard to bring this imaginative project to fruition, thinking he had succeeded until, at the eleventh hour, the British Government developed cold feet and drew back. On top of that, his large agricultural property in Tunisia was expropriated, just when his efforts were coming to fruition. And yet at all times his courtesy and consideration towards others were unfailing.

The other woman with us was Odette Massigli, the wife of the French Ambassador to London. She and her husband René first appeared in November 1944, and by the time they left eleven years later they were widely loved. They both made a great impact. He was shrewd and witty, with much personal charm, and like most Frenchmen in the upper echelons he was highly literate and informed. Odette had no intellectual pretensions, nor did she claim to have, but she was wonderful company, speaking excellent English, with a deep and attractive voice, and making rather challenging remarks which demanded a riposte. She had a natural talent for wearing clothes, and although it must have been very difficult in France so soon after the ending of German occupation, she appeared to all of us in clothes coupon Britain as the embodiment of French chic. At the villa in Italy because she spoke Italian she took natural charge of the domestic arrangements, ordering the food and generally supervising things until one day she rebelled, deciding she was being taken advantage of. Joan and Edwina then tried to take turns to relieve Odette, but within a day or two she resumed the responsibility, because she could not bear to see them struggling.

Odette Massigli was the first of three French Ambassadresses to whom I remain devoted. In 1962 Geoffroi and Martine de Courcel arrived in London. They stayed for ten years until he was appointed head of the Quai d'Orsay and they returned to Paris, leaving many friends behind them. I loved them both dearly. He was able and charming, and she was exceptionally pretty, with a sharp wit, gauging people very effectively and capable of devastating comment. To follow them at the Embassy must have been a forbidding prospect, but the five years that Jacques and Marie Alice de Beaumarchais spent in London were memorable. For most people they personified French elegance and sensibility. They were immensely gay, and she put me in mind more than anything else of a graceful fountain constantly playing.

In the early postwar years, Joan and I used regularly to visit the Villa Fiorentina at St Jean Cap Ferrat on the French Riviera. This was in fact the villa which I had visited many years before, when I was a child; but it had changed hands and was in the process of being transformed. It was the property of Enid Kenmare, the widow of Valentine, better known as Castlerosse until he succeeded to his father's title in 1941. Enid was rich because she had previously been married to Lord Furness (once an intimate of my mother), who died in 1940. Her eldest son, Rory Cameron, the offspring of an earlier marriage, was living with her. He was American and his father too had died. Four husbands in fact died while married to her, so that one could say that to marry her was to tempt providence. When we knew her she was very tall and striking looking, with silvery grey hair. My mother and she had been friends for years, being closely akin; and generally when Joan and I visited Fiorentina my mother and Chatin Sarachi were with us. The property was exceptionally situated on the point of Cap Ferrat, surrounded by sea on three sides, with a privacy missing everywhere else on the French Riviera. The main villa was in course of redecoration, this work being supervised by Rory. He had rare taste, and by the time he had completed the work, at goodness knows what cost, the Fiorentina was in a class apart for elegance and comfort, better than anything to be found in the pages of *House and Garden* or *Vogue*.

Close by there lived Willie Somerset Maugham, whom we saw regularly, often playing bridge with him. He became very fond of Joan, and we stayed in his house, the Villa Mauresque, more than once. He was a charming and attentive host, but he could make most cutting remarks when displeased. He always appeared very much in control of himself, but beneath the surface one observed a lonely and unhappy man; and this was all the sadder and harder to explain because he was so universally known and appreciated.

So much for our weekend and holiday life before we were installed in the house on the edge of Windsor Great Park. Let me turn now to an account of the *Financial Times* and a variety of related matters.

Chapter 13

The merger of the *FN* and *FT* took effect from 1 October 1945. In most ways the options open to us were limited by the general constraint imposed by postwar controls. Above all, newsprint was strictly rationed. Both papers had their own allocations, and these were added together, thus establishing the allocation of the merged paper. The size to which each paper was restricted was a mere six pages, with an occasional eight page issue. We thought that as there must be some overlap in the circulation of the two papers this would give us a little elbow room for a modest increase in size. It turned out differently. The daily sale of the *FT* was 30,000, and that of the *FN* 10,000. For the first combined issue, for which we naturally retained the distinctive salmon-pink paper on which the *FT* was produced rather than the *FN*'s plain white, we printed just over 40,000 copies and every copy was sold. Any overlap of sale was absorbed at first by the interest people showed in the new venture; and then the revival of business activity and the strength of stock markets, aided by the Chancellor of the Exchequer's outrageous cheap money policy, continued the process, so that within a short period the sale came to over 50,000, at which level we had to peg it until the beginning of 1947 when there was a slight easing of rationing and we were able to let the sale grow to over 60,000. Then once more it became pretty static. For several years any extra newsprint we were allocated went into enlarging the size of the paper so as to allow for more news and, let it not be despised, for more advertising. It was not until the later months of 1954 that we achieved any significant increase in sale; and by the middle of 1955 we were selling some 80,000 copies a day, which to us then seemed splendid.

We did not in those days engage in any kind of large-scale publicity. We did however produce one of the most brilliant newspaper posters ever devised. Rather, I should say that we asked a masterly graphic artist, Abram Games, to design a poster for us. He had first caught my attention as the inventor of the 1951 Festival of Britain symbol, and when he accepted our commission I was both surprised and delighted. I have included his original design as one of my illustrations. The design was used by us in various adaptations, and others imitated it, but none had the impact of the original.

Throughout much of the early postwar period the editorial content was largely predetermined. There was little room for anything beyond the essential stock market, company and commodity news. We preserved the daily investment comment columns from the *FT* and *FN*, which went respectively under the pseudonyms of Diarist and Lex, the latter being a daily column contributed to the pre-war *FN* by Hargreaves Parkinson. The problem of editorship of the merged paper was straightforward because Archie Chisholm,* the editor of the *FT* who had been away on National Service in the Middle East during the war years, had accepted a job with the Anglo-Persian Oil Company, for which after a stint with the *Wall Street Journal* he had worked before joining the *FT*: while his deputy, A. G. Cole, who had acted as editor throughout the war, an able, delightful and worthy man, did not seem to either Brendan or myself to have qualities which outweighed the claims of Parkinson.

H.P. had given yeoman service to the group over the difficult war and prewar years, and he was an acknowledged authority on investment, having developed his own particular theory, known as Hatch, which, he held, enabled investors to take advantage of broad market swings, although it was far from infallible. He was probably not the best choice as editor. His inability to delegate, and his excessive willingness to undertake tedious tasks, told against him. He was not a strong enough personality to weld the editorial staffs of the two papers into a harmonious whole, and he allowed himself to be overridden by Brendan too often.

One basically new feature was added to the paper. Before the war the *FT* had run a regular column entitled 'City Men and Matters', started I think by Archie Chisholm in 1937. The purpose of this column was to provide a home for notes of a mainly laudatory character about company chairmen and other dignitaries. Brendan decided to revive it, but on a once-a-week basis and with a very different aim, modifying the title to the more simple 'Men and Matters', so that his scope was in no way inhibited. Although he signed the column 'Observer', most people knew that he was the author. He used the column to praise his heroes and to hold up to ridicule his ministerial, aldermanic, and other *bêtes noires*. It is sad that an anthology of the column has never been compiled and published. Brendan wielded a lively pen, much influenced by Swift and Burke. The following extracts give a fair example of his style. Thus he castigated tax inspectors who left the Inland Revenue to·join private

---

* It was Chisholm incidentally who had made indirect soundings of Maurice Green on behalf of Geoffrey Dawson before Maurice left the *Financial News* in 1938 to go to *The Times* as Financial Editor. There was also a suggestion after the war that Chisholm might go to *The Times* himself as Manager.

industry:

> Members of the Spanish Inquisition had a reputation for coldbloodedness, though they were hardly less coldblooded than our tax gatherers in Somerset House. But, at least, the Inquisitors were not in the habit as our tax gatherers increasingly are, of seeking opulent employment in the ranks of the unbelievers. . . .

and when a committee set up to enquire into the preservation of houses of outstanding interest, stated in their report 'The Board of Inland Revenue did not think it proper to give evidence before us,' Brendan wrote:

> Did not think it proper! The Minister responsible for the goings-on of Somerset House is the Chancellor of the Exchequer. That Minister appointed a committee to enquire into an important matter of national interest, yet the Board of Inland Revenue refused to give evidence – was there ever a more successful example of a bunch of bureaucrats snapping their fingers in the face of the nation?

The column developed a following. If Brendan was away Alan Hodge, his secretary from the Ministry of Information, whom he had recruited to the *FT* to help him with the column, kept it going. Alan made gallant attempts at imitating the style, but inevitably it was shadow-boxing and not the real thing. Brendan's column appeared almost every Monday for nine years, and was only discontinued when he was struck by illness. It was not revived until after Brendan's death, and then, rather at my urging, on a five days a week basis, to fulfil its original purpose.

Looking through the early postwar issues of the paper, it is depressing if not surprising how little change there was from month to month. The reason stemmed largely from the hampering effects of newsprint controls, but also because Brendan exercised a strangely dominating influence over Hargreaves Parkinson. Until his last year, when he was gravely ill, Brendan's personality was very strong, while H.P.'s hard life had tired him. One day in early 1949 H.P. was sitting talking to me in my office when suddenly his jaw dropped slightly, and with difficulty he managed to say: 'I'm afraid I don't feel very well.' It was evident that he had had a slight stroke. We got him home, and he was away for several weeks. He insisted upon returning to work, but his liveliness was gone, and special arrangements were made for his early retirement. To small avail, though, for within a year he was dead, barely fifty-four years old.

Before he retired he made it very clear whom he thought the right person to succeed him. This was Gordon Newton, a pre-war colleague on the *FN*, a very able product of Cambridge where he had read Economics with conspicuous success, who might have found himself, had things turned out differently, running the family glass-manufacturing business. In indicating his preference so clearly H.P. did great service. Had he not strongly urged his view the decision to appoint Newton as editor would probably have been taken, but there were other possibilities. In particular there were those believing that Harold Wincott, who was both editor of the *Investors Chronicle* and author of a notable series of weekly articles in the *FT* (started entirely at Brendan's instigation), should have been offered the post. Wincott would surely have done a very good job, but the paper would have been far more market-orientated: and it would certainly have been more unequivocally right-wing (by which I do not mean Tory) in its policy. There would have been some deprivation, too, for Harold Wincott had a genius shared by few for presenting the basic economic and monetary issues in vivid and striking images, and exposing the prejudices and follies of the ministerial and administrative overlords of his day; and editing a daily paper leaves little time for writing. Gordon himself wrote admirably simple clear prose. Before the war he had written the Lex investment column in the *FN* and when he returned after demobilization his first assignment was to be the *FT*'s man in Berlin. But he did not have Harold's special gift of humour, so carefully concealed by a lugubrious expression.

Harold was in fact distressed that the *FT* editorship had not been offered to him. He left me in no doubt of this at the time. He felt that he had a prior claim since he had in 1938 been appointed editor of the *Investors Chronicle*, a post he was to hold for over twenty years, not that the jobs were in any way similar, as I constantly emphasized to him: and within a year or so of Gordon's appointment Harold told me that he recognized that our decision had been the right one.

In intellectual ability, in shrewdness about the likely course of events, and of markets, it would be hard to place one before the other. Both had remarkable antennae. But in toughness and in power to withstand the slings and arrows, Gordon won hands down. It would be wrong to say that Gordon was not someone who worried, for he did, immensely so. Solemn-faced Harold, though, was in a class apart in this regard: the strains and stresses of the *FT* would have been far too much for him.

After his death in 1969, on the initiative of Ralph Harris, the tireless head of the Institute of Economic Affairs, a charitable trust was formed, named the Wincott Foundation, the purposes of which were to perpetuate the educational work of Harold Wincott and to encourage and promote high standards in economic and financial journalism. The sponsors included Lords Cromer, Robbins and Tangley, and Knights Edward Lewis and Halford Reddish, two of the most successful free enterprisers, heads of Decca and Rugby Cement respectively. Hundreds of contributions were received, and a fund of over £100,000 was raised. The annual Wincott awards were to become an important feature in the world of financial journalism, and the winning of an award was regarded by the recipient as a real mark of esteem. Even those who disagreed with Harold Wincott's views respected him for his skill and his integrity; and the perpetuation of his memory was a gratifying idea.

Gordon Newton took over in 1950 and for twenty-three years he was an inspired editor. Our relationship with one another had its ups and downs, hardly surprising considering its long duration. In the early stages, we had the interesting task of dealing with Brendan, who at times treated us both like children, and thus bound us together. Brendan in fact interfered very little, and for this thanks is largely due to 'Men and Matters', the outlet he had established for his journalistic talents. He strongly encouraged the development of the paper's industrial coverage, and it was on his initiative that we introduced the words Industry, Commerce, Public Affairs on page one, under the title block, the purpose being to establish in people's minds that the *FT* was not simply concerned with finance. No one can say how much good this did, but the appearance of the page was not helped, and we dropped the addition in 1966 when we thought people had the message.

As to Gordon and myself, there is no doubt that at first we were quite good at getting on one another's nerves. In this respect I was the active and Gordon the passive agent. I made myself a great nuisance because if I felt a certain line of development was desirable I kept on pressing for action. (I do not mean the taking of a particular editorial line – I was always at pains not to interfere in editorial policy, although it was not unusual for me to criticize the line taken *after* an article had appeared.) Gordon once referred to me as his goad,* a charge to which I admit. His skill at resisting my goading was brilliant. However, I was very persistent, and fortunately we managed far more often than not to see eye to eye. We had the same basic values, and we both knew instinctively where we wanted the *FT* to go. For the initial period, the scope, as I have said, was limited by the constricting effects of newsprint rationing. In the early postwar years we had to remember the needs of the advertiser for space. With the gradual resumption of normal business life, businessmen had to use our columns for their announcements: but if we failed to accommodate them they would look elsewhere. What we had not expected was the extraordinary growth in the amount of trade display as opposed to financial advertising which we should be asked to publish. And for this credit is due, more than to any other person, to Sidney Henschel, the advertisement director, who in his way had as great a flair as Gordon Newton. Together, Sidney, Gordon and I came to form a sort of triumvirate, standing firmly together on pretty well every issue. But it was Sidney who really foresaw the revenue possibilities. Although I knew him well for many years I scarcely knew his background except that he was highly

* *Goad.* Spiked thing for urging cattle: thing that torments, incites or stimulates. *OED.*

literate and that he had been in advertising for some years. Had it not been for the First War he would have become an analytical chemist, for he had studied chemistry at a technical college which was part of London University. He was invalided out of the Army in 1918, and took a job on the advertising staff of the *Manchester Guardian*, later becoming advertisement manager of the *Yorkshire Post*. He joined the *FN* in the mid-thirties, having been recruited as his successor by Grahame Martin-Turner, who was to my regret leaving to join a mining company run by a somewhat controversial character named Claude de Bernales. In addition to his advertising work, Sidney wrote regularly on motoring matters for the *FN* and the *Investors Chronicle*. He was on friendly terms with most of the leading personalities in the motoring industry, and there was no motoring function of any importance at which he was not present. With the exception of classified advertising, where he had rather a blind spot, his judge-ment of revenue possibilities was uncannily good. It was seldom that he made a forecast that was not achieved or bettered. In the early postwar days he was put in charge of all forms of advertising, other than foreign, and so he remained until he retired in 1969, well past the age of seventy-five, after which he retained a small room at the office to which he came regularly, until he was over eighty.

All through his career he had unerring judgement about those most likely to help him in his efforts to increase the advertisement revenue of the *FT*, and an enviable skill in latching them to himself as friends. Shortly after the war there was one advertiser in particular who made a deep impression. His name was Bernard Sunley. His origins were humble. His father was employed by a market gardening firm but obliged him to take a job as a railway porter, which he did not fancy. At the age of sixteen, together with a friend, he had bought a field, from which he cut and sold turf: and this evolved into the making of sports grounds. He thus acquired a knowledge of the problems of earth-moving, and when the war came he turned his attention to open-cast mining. He obtained a concession from the United States for importing Euclid and Marion trucks and bulldozers, machines in a class apart for efficiency. In 1945 he foresaw the numerous postwar reconstruction possibilities: and it was at this time that Sidney Henschel met him and persuaded him to advertise exclusively in the *FT*. As a result, large spaces on behalf of Blackwood Hodge, his company, appeared regularly in our columns, representing at first a significant proportion of our total advertisement revenue. Sunley thought they were achieving results, and other companies followed his example until eventually display advertising, which in pre-war days almost never appeared in financial newspapers, became a major factor in our affairs.

Brendan was intrigued to meet the man who was so notably benefiting the finances of the *FT*. Sunley came for lunch, arriving with a vast box of chocolates which he presented to me saying, 'Give these to your wife' – whom he did not know. He himself was vast. He had a broad expansive style, well suited to his build. Brendan was delighted by him. He loved his brash, buccaneering manner, which went with a genuine warmheartedness. They clicked, to coin a phrase; and the lunch was hugely successful.

From then on they met regularly. Brendan opened a new assembly plant for him on the Hillingdon Estate near Glasgow, a transatlantic Boeing being chartered to transport the invited guests from London. Whatever Bernard did he did in princely style. He had a farm near Northampton which I visited. All the farm buildings could be floodlit by pressing a single switch by the front door of the farmhouse. He regularly took a party of thirty or more people to the Wembley Cup Final, giving them a large luncheon beforehand at his house in Hampstead. At Christmas time he used to invite friends to an office party on a choice of dates, his letter of invitation saying, 'There'll be some oysters and champagne knocking around here. Do come if you can.' Before Brendan became fatally ill, he fully intended to move into a flat which formed part of a small and exclusive block being built by Bernard in Amen Court, close to St Paul's Cathedral. And after Brendan's death it was Bernard who proposed and undertook to pay for a posthumous sculpture by Epstein to whom I took a number of photographs of Brendan and also one of his hats to help get his very large head-size right; but Epstein died before he could commence work, and the sculpture which stands in the entrance hall of the *FT* office building was completed by Uli Nimptsch, a distinguished Austrian, naturalized British, sculptor who undertook a number of Epstein's unfulfilled commissions, although he was better at nudes than at portrait busts.

Bernard Sunley's early support of the *FT* and the results he achieved from his advertising were important for the subsequent large build-up of industrial display advertising in the paper.

Another of Sidney's friends but one to whom Brendan did not warm in the same way was Arthur Whitehead, who indirectly was responsible for one massive item of *FT* revenue. Whitehead had been trained as a business efficiency expert. During the war he was recruited to the Ministry of Aircraft Production by Beaverbrook, whom he served as one of his progress chasers. After the war, he formed the Whitehead Industrial Trust, specializing in obtaining Stock Exchange quotations for the shares of some of the businesses which he had come to know during the war. In the main these were too small for the leading merchant banks to assist. One difficulty which Whitehead had to contend with was how to have the various share prices quoted in the press, and particularly in the *FT*. A suggestion was made and accepted by us that these should be listed in a small separate section headed 'Whitehall Industrial Trust issues' for which he would pay. The quotations were not supplied by Whitehead but were obtained from the Stock Exchange by our staff regularly each day in the ordinary way. It was not long before other merchant banks and issuing houses objected, to the point that we were obliged to discontinue the special Whitehead heading although we continued to quote the shares in the appropriate place. Soon other companies approached us, asking us to quote their shares, and there was no logical reason for refusing. Our yardstick was simple. Had the company's shares an official quotation on the London Stock Exchange? There had of course always been many companies whose shares we quoted without payment, mainly those with a lot of shareholders and a regularly active market; and there was no question of asking them to pay. But for the others I argued that for every line that we added something else had to be displaced, and therefore payment was not unreasonable. As the years went by the total number of companies whose shares we were paid to quote grew and grew until the total was over two thousand, and the revenue we received from this source went well above three-quarters of a million pounds. The service became far more than the mere quotation of share prices. It developed (thanks to Gordon Newton) into an elaborate computer-based setting of dividend yields and covers, price/earnings ratios, and highs and lows; and if profitable it was also costly to produce, requiring great skill and care. It is an interesting question whether without Whitehead's original initiative this development would have taken place. I suppose so, for the pressure became so great, but it might not have done, in which case the *FT*'s profit and loss account would have looked very different.

As to Whitehead himself, he was quite without Sunley's panache and charm. He was a hard-headed businessman, that and no more. In the conditions of the immediate postwar period he probably played a useful role, for the small companies which he financed did not have sources of finance available to them as readily then as they probably would today. Whitehead was not generally loved, but I fancy that the *FT* has reason to be grateful to him.

It was fairly soon after the merger that I decided we must appoint a foreign manager to build up foreign advertising for the paper. The man first appointed was Robin Bruce-Lockhart, the son of Sir Robert, the well-known intelligence agent and man of letters. The appointment was made too early, and it was not a great success. Robin was a slightly prickly person, finding it all too easy to rub people up the wrong way. After a while he left to take up another job.

The position fell vacant. I still believed it to be most important. Whom to appoint, though? When searching I received a note from the *FT* librarian asking whether he could be considered for the job. His name was Peter Galliner. He was of German Jewish origin, and he had come to England before the war as a refugee from Hitler. His parents had stayed behind. Both paid the price, simply being exterminated, along with countless others. Peter's letter of application was very compelling. I had a preference for promotion from within whenever it was possible. Since there was no other obvious applicant, and since I believed that someone with a strong conviction that he could do a particular job would exert every endeavour to prove himself right, Peter was appointed. He was outstandingly successful in obtaining foreign advertising for the *FT*, above all from his original homeland, and I have no doubt that Germany's deep sense of guilt was a major factor. They saw it as one very small way of making some partial amends. Peter established friendly relations with the Deutsch-Englische Gesellschaft, and attended a number of their conferences. He knew that Joan, my wife, was a pianist and he arranged for her to give concerts on the Society's behalf in Berlin, Munich and Düsseldorf. On these occasions, which were a success, he kept himself very quietly in the background. This was his natural way. He liked to plan and arrange things, but he hated any show of personal limelight. People often thought because of this that he was an intriguer, that he burrowed out of sight like a mole to achieve his aims. It was above all his shyness and a sense of insecurity which was the cause; but nevertheless he was outstandingly successful on behalf of the *FT*. During the course of his travels in Germany he met most of the leading businessmen. Among these was Axel Springer, publisher of the best as well as of the crudest of German newspapers. He offered Galliner a job, putting him in charge of the house of Ullstein in Berlin, as well as providing him with a splendid residence on the Wannsee. It was not a happy choice on either side. Things did not work out as hoped, and he was there for only two years, after which he returned to the UK disappointed but not uncompensated. He held one or two other jobs, but none of them for long; and as I write he is in charge of the International Press Institute, where he may well make a mark.

In the early days of Gordon Newton's editorship, that is to say in 1949, staff recruitment was one of his chief preoccupations. He established close links with the Oxford and Cambridge Appointments Boards, in fact later becoming a member of the Cambridge Board, and regularly, each year, he recruited two or three young graduates. In those days when our staff was very small I too used to see everyone other than clerical staff before they were engaged. It was almost unheard of for me to question any of Gordon's choices. My talk with them was something of a formality, although I often discovered facts about their private interests, hobbies and so on, which turned out to be subsequently helpful in establishing personal relationships.

Many of those engaged left the *FT* to go on to greater things. There was certainly no better training ground, or source of good material. The list of jobs filled from the postwar *FT* editorial staff is pretty impressive. There are one or two City editors, among them the very pungent Patrick Hutber; the editors of both *The Director* and *Management Today*; the arts editor and the political editor of *The Times*; the music critic of the *New Yorker*; two directors general of Chatham House; three MPs, including a member of the Cabinet; one of the nine EEC Commissioners in Brussels; the managing director of *The Economist*; one of the early moving spirits of Coronation Street; several successful merchant bankers, and others who have prospered in commerce and industry; and, to cap the list, William Rees-Mogg, the editor of *The Times*. In 1975 George Bull, the editor of *The Director*, conceived the happy idea of forming the Gordon Newton Society, the qualification for membership being to have been recruited to the *FT* by Gordon and to have left the staff for another job. I was the only member elected to whom the criteria did not apply. The purpose of the Society is simply to dine once a year, in order to do honour to Gordon; and the dinner is far more agreeable than any old school dinner could ever be.

The engagement of William Rees-Mogg was in fact almost the only example of recruitment to the editorial staff where the first initiative came from myself. It happened by pure chance, in 1952. In those far-off days we used to subscribe to a press cuttings service in order that we could be sure not to miss any references in other publications to the *FT*, so eager were we to learn where and how our existence had been recognized. One day I was going through a batch of cuttings when I came upon something unusual, a cutting from the Oxford University magazine, *Isis*. It was a whole-page profile of William Rees-Mogg, and the reference to the *FT* was simply that he read the paper every morning in bed. The reason for the profile was that he was president of the Oxford Union. I thought that this was a signal to me that I should find out more. I therefore telephoned to Roy Harrod, the well-known economist and biographer of Keynes, who used to write for us at regular intervals. He undertook to discover whether William might care to come for a talk, or whether his future after leaving Oxford was already determined. The answer came back, yes he would, and no it was not. Within a week or two he was in our office seeing first of all Gordon and then myself. Immediate success all round. He would like to join us, but before he could do so he was committed to going on a debating tour in the United States, to be pitted against successive adversaries as one of a team of two, his team-mate being Dick Taverne.

He returned flushed with success to say that only once were they defeated in debate, and that was in one of the better-known prisons. His recruitment proved from the point of view of the *FT* to be most successful. Within a year or two he was writing many of the first leaders. He was rather solemn and owlish in appearance but very able and much liked. He had political aspirations, and one day he asked permission to stand as a parliamentary candidate. The answer was made easy when he revealed that the constituency was Chester-le-Street, a solid Labour stronghold, and William, or Smog as we affectionately called him, was standing as a Conservative. Twice he stood, and twice he was defeated. He could, I told him, go on standing for Chester-le-Street for as long as he liked. But twice was enough for him. He stayed with the *FT* for ten years, and then he received a tempting offer to go to the *Sunday Times* as business editor, an offer which we could not match: and so he left bearing with him the greatest possible goodwill for his gentlemanly qualities and for the services he had rendered.

One of the other exceptions where I myself took the initiative in a matter of editorial recruitment was Derek Granger. He joined us in April 1953 to contribute theatre criticisms. I had suggested to Gordon Newton that it would help to leaven the contents of the paper if we could advise businessmen about London's theatrical offerings. I had been given the name of a possible contributor (whose name I have forgotten). It seemed to me that it would be a good idea to seek the advice of Laurence Olivier, who had been a friend of Joan's for many years and whom we used to visit regularly while he was still married to the exquisitely beautiful, unstable, highly strung Vivien Leigh. He instantly told me that by far the best person we could engage was one Derek Granger, the theatre and film critic of the *Sussex Daily News*. West End theatre managers, he said, often gave their plays an advance run in Brighton in order to get the benefit of Granger's critical notices, which he said were highly perceptive and never unfair. As our advertisement director, Sidney Henschel, used frequently to visit Brighton at weekends I asked him whether he could help. With his usual resourcefulness he had arranged within a few days for Derek to come and see Gordon Newton and myself; and it was not long before he started to do overnight dramatic notices for the *FT* as well as continuing his work for the Brighton paper. In addition, for a spell he also contributed film reviews to the *FT*. The strain to which he was subjecting himself soon became too great. He knew that he had to choose between London and Brighton; and he opted for us. He stayed with us for over five years, after which he was tempted away to the world of television, proposing as his successor as *FT* theatre critic Cuthbert Worsley, who was already well known through his contributions to the *New Statesman* and elsewhere. We were very fortunate that he agreed to join us: and he continued to write for us as television critic after poor health obliged him to leave London.

One day I urged upon Gordon that in order to give a complete theatrical coverage we should also review performances of opera and ballet where, being at the time secretary to the board of directors of Covent Garden, I had a kind of vested interest. Concerts at that stage we did not contemplate writing about; the idea was only to cover entertainments which, if a notice aroused their interest, people could sample for themselves. Granger's advice was sought, and thanks to him we recruited as a contributor and later as a member of the staff Andrew Porter, a precociously brilliant young music critic who had just graduated from Oxford. When he first came to London Andrew lived in the house of John Pope-Hennessy, sharing with him the same scholarly approach to his work, paying almost excessively meticulous attention to detail but helping enormously over the years to earn respect for the arts coverage of the *FT*, although of course it was to be some time still before we started to devote a whole page daily to the arts.

The free and easy methods of recruitment that we enjoyed in the early 1950s are much harder today. True, the *FT* house agreement with the National Union of Journalists provides for the occasional recruitment of an exceptional person from without the ranks of the union, but the insistence of the union that virtually all recruits to the editorial staff of a national newspaper must first have served on a provincial paper for over a year has undoubtedly had a discouraging effect on would-be entrants to the profession. It is a sad fact that what is best for the industry and for the public as a whole is not the union's chief motivating force. People ask, 'Why then give way to a demand which you don't accept as reasonable?' Why indeed? Unfortunately, though, in an industry where there are such closely overlapping and competing interests, if one publisher concedes a demand it is not long before the rest are obliged to do so. In any event, when Gordon Newton was first recruiting for the editorial staff no such inhibitions existed. Mercifully, on the business staff side, that is to say those engaged in promotion and in the getting of advertising, complete freedom to recruit still continues; and Sidney Henschel, the advertisement director, was as perceptive as Gordon in his recruitment of staff.

When we merged the two papers there were two others who were leading figures on the *FT* staff and who continued to play a major role. On the editorial side there was T. S. G. Hunter, known to everyone as Jim. His father, a genial Scots journalist of the old school, had been editor before Archie Chisholm, (whose father incidentally had been city editor of *The Times* from 1914 to 1919). Jim himself was totally imbued with the spirit of the paper. He became deputy editor, making a major contribution towards the integration of the two staffs. Later, when the general manager, Leslie Dearlove, retired, I thought that it would be a wise move to appoint Jim to succeed him. It was evident that he had little prospect of becoming editor himself since he was several years older than Gordon, and Gordon was firmly in the saddle. I felt that his translation to the business side would be popular with everyone. For one thing the editorial staff always tended to be rather suspicious of the business staff and seemed at times to look down their noses at them. I was firmly convinced that to move a key editorial man to the other side would help to promote understanding. I would not expect every similar move to have such good results, but Jim Hunter had a particular gift of understanding, and it was not long before the entire staff, business as well as editorial, were coming to him with their troubles. There were one or two people whom he could not abide, usually for good reason, but in the main he had helpful and balanced advice for everyone. He was modest and unpretentious, and reluctant to share any part of the limelight, preferring to remain in the background. For the last twelve years of his life he was suffering intermittently from cancer, although he never knew that that was it: but he had to undergo some very unpleasant surgical treatment which he bore with immense patience. His wife was an author, writing adventure stories under the name of E. H. Clements; they were very good and they deserve to be republished. She had the hard task of keeping from Jim the nature of his illness, but she did so successfully until he died in 1971, shortly after he reached the age of seventy. His services to the *FT*, above all in making the atmosphere a happy one, cannot be exaggerated.

The other leading figure was Francis Matthew. He was in charge of the St Clements Press, which belonged to the *FT*, and which he had joined in 1936. For some years after the merger the *FT* continued to be run from its offices in Coleman Street in the City while it was printed at the premises of the St Clements Press two miles away in Portugal Street behind the London School of Economics. The *FT*'s offices were a pretty good rabbit warren, small and poky, but they had the advantage of being close to the Stock Exchange, which used to be regarded as obligatory. The printing works were stuffed with machinery, nearly all of it quite old. The St Clements Press before the war had been one of the leading firms of City printers, and at one time it was said to have had the printing of one out of every three new issue prospectuses. By a miracle it escaped bombing during the war. In 1940, when Speaights, an Eyre & Spottiswoode company in nearby Fetter Lane, was bombed, the St Clements Press at very short notice undertook the printing of *The Economist*, which remained with them until after the war. They printed a total of twenty-two publications including the *FT* and also a thirty-two page *Sunday Times*, as well as several French and Polish language dailies and weeklies. The total area occupied by the works was not enormous, a narrow triangle of land, and a great deal of ingenuity was clearly displayed to achieve so much with such moderate facilities. The man in charge was Francis Matthew. He was a member of a leading Roman Catholic family, with a very attractive wife, and a large number of children. I remember his pride when number ten came into the world, and I remember too his telling me that when he went to children's parties to collect his brood he was never quite sure which were his. He was a thoroughly unexpected person to find in charge of a large printing works, but he had a surprising technical knowledge. He also had a great gift of persuasion and of salesmanship, and it is obvious that he had something of the buccaneer in his make-up. A regular pleasure of his was a flutter or two on the day's racing. He went through the programme carefully, first thing in the morning, marked his fancies, placed his bets, and put the paper away, saying, 'That completes today's important business.' Whether he was a winner on balance is in some doubt. Brendan took an immense liking to him and saw him regularly. However, this was not for long. There came a moment when we decided something must be done about the muddled and archaic make-up of the *FT*. Stanley Morison, an ascetic figure dressed from top to toe in black, a garb he never changed, was the masterly designer of Times Roman type (*and* author of the *History of the Times*). He was a friend of Brendan and likewise of Beaverbrook, at whose house they met frequently. Brendan asked him to look at the *FT* make-up. He proposed a solution which we adopted and which basically involved the use of Times type throughout the *FT*. During the course of discussions with him on points of detail, it was necessary that the head of the *FT*'s printing works should see him quite often: and when the job of general manager of *The Times* fell vacant shortly afterwards, Francis found himself being offered it, going there in October 1948 and taking over nine months later. We had nothing comparable to offer him, and it was inevitable that he should accept. It was painful at the time, although we remained the best of friends.

Fortunately he had under him a forceful deputy with elements of a parade-ground manner, Geoffrey Hooper; and a remarkable works manager, A. J. Rampling, a small man with a large head, a cheeky-chappy grin, and an intensely cynical attitude towards the foibles of human nature. He had joined the company in 1920 at the age of fourteen, working his way up. He had collaborated extremely well with Francis Matthew, whom he nearly followed to *The Times*, finding it hard to accept the latter's succession by Geoffrey Hooper, with whom he could not blend. Rampling altogether had a tough time of it. After the war Matthew had suggested that St Clements Press should be relieved of pressure and expanded by the acquisition of the George Newnes printing works in North Kensington, where a number of popular Newnes publications, including good old *Tit-Bits*, were produced. Matthew had made friends with Herbert Tingay, who ran Newnes and who like Rampling had started work at the age of fourteen. He introduced him to Brendan, and despite their complete dissimilarity they greatly liked one another. Rampling was put in charge. He did a fine job in the face of many difficulties, not the least being the decision of Newnes after a shortish period gradually to transfer the printing of their various magazines away from the traditional letterpress method to which the North Kensington works were committed to the more economic method of gravure. When the works in North Kensington were finally closed down in 1958, he moved back to the *FT* as works manager: but he only remained for a few years more, retiring early and feeling, I fear, a certain justified sense of grievance.

Between them Geoffrey Hooper and Rampling had to supervise the move of the St Clements Press from its cramped conditions in Portugal Street into our new office building near to the junction of Cannon Street and Queen Victoria Street in the City; and much of the machinery was needed to produce the paper on the Friday night before being moved during the course of Saturday so as to be ready for use the following evening. It was a masterly exercise.

The new *FT* building was not in fact opened until after Brendan's death, although a decision to occupy new premises was taken some while before. Increasingly we had come to realize that as the paper grew in sale and in importance we could not continue with the fearful inconvenience, for a daily, of being edited and managed in one place and of being printed and distributed from another, not adjoining but two or three miles away. It was hopelessly unsatisfactory, and we were placed at a great disadvantage.

Brendan generally had a strong dislike of spending money. However, he was persuaded that the position could not persist unchanged. I did what I quite often did with success, which was to plant an idea in his mind and then when next I saw him I would refer to it as *his* suggestion. It was evident that we needed our own building, offices, printing works, the lot, all combined under one roof. The first initiative was taken I suppose in 1953 or 1954. We had to start by finding a suitable site, which was not then too difficult. Vast areas of the City had been flattened by incendiary and other Nazi bombs. After the end of the war the City Corporation acquired much freehold land, having decided that rebuilding and redevelopment would be greatly assisted if a number of key sites could be rented on long-term building leases to would-be developers. Together with two or three colleagues I studied the map, and visited several of the sites. One of these seemed to me by far the best. It was halfway between Fleet Street and the Stock Exchange, served by a number of bus routes and two underground railway lines, as well as being within easy walking distance of a main line station. On top of that, and of compelling importance, the site was only a short distance to the south-east of St Paul's Cathedral, and it was evident that any building erected there would have an uninterrupted and commanding view of London's greatest monument. This above all appealed to Brendan, who had a real love for the masterpieces of architecture.

The area of the site was one acre, sufficient for our needs with a margin to spare. Its proximity to St Paul's imposed justified restrictions upon the height to which we could build; but as our concern was largely with heavy printing presses and paper storage, both of which could go below ground level, we were not too distressed that we could only build a six-storey building, even though this would mean that we were not developing the site to its full potential. However, the rental for the one acre site was fixed by the City Corporation at £20,000 a year for a 99-year lease, without any nonsense about periodic rent reviews. The building we erected provided about 250,000 sq ft, including the basement areas. The cost of construction was under £1½ million, towards which we borrowed £1.3 million at 5½ per cent. It could therefore be said to have been a bargain.

When we first worked on the plans for the building it was anticipated that the *Observer* newspaper would become tenants and that our newspaper presses would be used to print it at weekends, thus giving seven-day working; but with their much larger circulation additional presses had to be ordered, and we had lengthy and detailed discussions with them over the method of financing this extra plant. In the event the discussions came to nothing, the fault being entirely Brendan's, and the *Observer* had every reason for major annoyance.

Initially, however, Brendan was extremely enthusiastic for the whole project, regarding the housing and printing of the *Observer* as an added justification. He decided that he knew exactly the right architect. Without proper consultation with the rest of us, he approached his good friend Professor Albert Richardson, and for better or for worse the die was cast. Professor Richardson was a man for whom I developed a true affection. He was something of an eccentric, who enjoyed making outrageous statements, which were usually rather reactionary in character. His home was near Woburn Abbey, and he was steeped in the knowledge of and lived spiritually in the eighteenth century. For the restoration of the architectural masterpieces of the past he had no equal. Whether he was the right person to design a building intended to house a newspaper and a large printing works is open to question. There is no doubt in my mind that he gave us a building of character, but there had to be too many compromises for there not to be some disappointment and criticism. The chief problem was how to deal with the printing works in an area which, although large was too constricted. Had we shown foresight, we should have realized then how much the space needed by the editorial and business staffs of the *FT* was going to grow. We should also have realized that general printing work in the heart of the City was certain to become quite uneconomic. As it turned out, quite soon after occupying the building the general printing was moved elsewhere and the staffs of the newspaper gradually came to spill over into virtually the whole of the works area. Had it been possible for Richardson to design from the start an exclusively office building, with provision at ground and basement level for the printing of the *FT*, I think he could have produced something more elegant, and there would have been extra office space that we could have leased out.

Although the works area presented the real technical problems, his main creative endeavour was concentrated upon the north block, which housed the staff of the *FT*. In his own view he was combining the best both of traditional and of modern styles, although to some the result was an uneasy compromise. A rather splendid feature was a large zodiacal clock above the front entrance, distinguished in two ways; first, no passer-by could quickly tell the time from it, and second, Winston Churchill's face smiled benignly from the centre of the hands. The clock looked particularly good at night because it contained a fair amount of brightly coloured glass which was illuminated from behind, so that it slightly resembled a stained-glass window.

A profound disappointment to me was the colour of the building. When we saw samples of the bricks and the stone intended to be used we judged wrongly. They seemed far paler than the final result. The bricks were specially made to the dimensions of those used in classical Rome. They were laid with immense care; but they were too dark. So was the stone, which came from the same quarry at Honiton that had supplied Coventry Cathedral. However, looking around at some of the neighbouring piles of concrete, only fit to be called characterless monstrosities, I regard the *FT* building as a thing of beauty. Whenever anyone was critical, Richardson would say, 'I build for posterity.' My contribution to the building was first of all, to insist that there should be a properly proportioned entrance hall, going up the height of two floors, despite some sacrifice of office accommodation; and secondly, to press strongly that a small cinema should be installed in the basement, a frivolous extra costing little but with a real goodwill value over the years. The interior decoration of the offices and of the canteen was largely placed by Brendan in the hands of Freda Casa Maury, and she made a very good job of it within the money and other constraints imposed on her.

One expensive mistake was made by Brendan in the later stages of planning. We had allowed for proper air conditioning throughout the building instead of simply in the basement. He panicked about the total cost, and insisted that the idea of full air conditioning should be dropped. Instead we installed a horrible thing called plenum ventilation, which warmed the air in winter, filling the offices with smuts in the process of its circulation, but failing to cool it in summer, and not cleaning it at all. Later we were obliged to install air conditioning into certain sections of the building, but it was piece-meal and costly; and resulted in some hideous metal excretions on the outside of the building, which Richardson would have loathed. Brendan died before we moved in. Had he lived, we should not have been able to name the building Bracken House. At one time he suggested naming it the Octagon, because of the peculiar shape of the central printing works area, but it would have conveyed little to the outside world, and our choice after his death was surely very much better.

Chapter 14

It is sad to relate that soon after the decision to put up a new building strains and stresses began to develop between Brendan and Oliver Crosthwaite-Eyre and I found myself in a fairly agonizing position in the middle. Brendan, who was to die in 1958, was surely already becoming ill. One symptom of which his colleagues were especially aware was an increasing caution. As Oliver's trustee this caution had unhappy consequences. Relatively to the rest of us, Oliver was wealthy, although it would be wrong to think of him as a very rich man. He was MP for the New Forest where Warrens, his family home, was situated. He loved Westminster, but he also loved country life. He farmed quite extensively, and he was constantly trying to improve the standards of his farm and the quality of his stock of cattle. High class cattle were not cheap, and improvements to farm buildings were costly. Reference had therefore to be made to the trustees for approval, which effectively meant reference to Brendan. His agreement was nearly always forthcoming, but only after questionings and procrastination; and he usually treated Oliver as a rather naughty schoolboy.

In the office there was constant bickering between them over the proposal to print the *Observer* in our new building. Oliver was chairman of the St Clements Press, and he had therefore been deeply involved in the discussions. Brendan's development of cold feet and his unreasoning reluctance to examine the figures dispassionately created an awkward and embarrassing situation all round. Had he said in the beginning that he would not countenance the *FT* doing the job on any terms, which was his true attitude, things would have been vastly easier. But he began by being enthusiastic, so that much time was wasted and feeling ran high. The real battle between them arose in relation to a famous property named Knoydart, situated on the west coast of Scotland; on the mainland, yet only approachable from the sea. This was something upon which Oliver had set his heart, and which he eventually acquired. The purchase price was considerable, but the property was unique for its situation and natural beauties. Brendan was terrified that in agreeing to the purchase he would be departing from his duty as a trustee. He thought it would be a bottomless pit, into which money would flow. The position became so difficult that Oliver's father, a good and kindly man who had emigrated to South Africa, in order to help his family more than for any other reason, personally delivered a letter by hand to Brendan in which he proposed that in the interests of their future friendship it would be sensible for Brendan to cease from being a trustee; asking him therefore in polite language to resign his position. Brendan had an intensely sentimental side to his nature, and he reacted as though he had been hit by a pole-axe. In the letter no reference had been made to Brendan's chairmanship of the *FT*, in which it must be remembered the Crosthwaite-Eyre family had the controlling stake, whereas Brendan had no stake at all. Brendan however made it clear that if he gave up being a trustee he would also give up the *FT*. In a mood of despair, he told me that he intended to sever all connection with the Eyres – which would mean resigning from the *FT*. I pleaded with him and urged him not to do so, writing in somewhat emotional terms:

B.,
   I am filled with gloom by what you said after lunch today. I know how trying your trusteeship has been to you, but that should surely cease now that you have ceased to be a trustee.
   The effect upon everyone here not to mention our shareholders of your ceasing to be chairman would be deplorable. I do beg you not to resign, and also not to announce your intention of resigning at the Annual Meeting. I need you, we all need you very much, you leadership was perhaps never more needed than now, and if you go I shall follow for my heart will no longer be in it.
                                                                     G.

But to no avail. I was therefore in no doubt that whatever chances I might be taking with my own future the only proper course open to me was to resign as well, since it was through Brendan that I had originally joined the organization more than twenty years before.

   This decision I conveyed to Oliver and his father. I do not think that either of them wanted or expected Brendan to give up the chairmanship, and therefore the question of what I might or might not do had not arisen. The prospect of losing the managing director as well as the chairman came as something of a shock. At this point Luke Meinertzhagen of Cazenove & Co., the company's stockbrokers, who had played a very helpful part at the time of the merger in 1945 between the *Financial Times* and the *Financial News* (acquired originally for the Eyre family by Brendan in 1928), came to the rescue. He was a close friend of Oliver from the war years, as well as being his (and the Eyre Trust's) financial adviser; and he had become a good friend of mine through our regular contacts in the City. He was therefore free to speak his mind. Also he had an elder brother, Daniel, who was then one of the principal managing directors of

Lazards, the merchant banking house controlled by S. Pearson & Son, over which Lord Cowdray reigned. Luke told Oliver emphatically that the effect upon City opinion of the *FT* simultaneously losing both its chairman and its managing director would be far from good, as well as being potentially hurtful to the newspaper. He also told him that he had too much capital tied up in this single investment, and he counselled him to dispose of it, which he believed he would be able to do for him for a profit satisfactory in relation to the original cost. Luke had a fairly clear indication through his brother that the Cowdray interests would welcome the opportunity of acquiring control of the *FT*, for it was known to be profitable and growing. The transactions leading to the actual transfer of control are not important, but as was obviously necessary they took place very swiftly and in secret, being concluded and announced in February 1957, when R. P. T. Gibson joined the *Financial Times* board.

Pat Gibson was high in the councils of the Pearson family. He was married to Dione, a sympathetic, attractive, and intelligent first cousin of John Cowdray, and he had played a large part in building up the successful provincial newspaper chain, Westminster Press Provincial Newspapers, into a very important asset of Pearsons. It was right that he should be the first new director to be appointed to the *FT* board and his arrival on the scene was for me most welcome. He had a wide-ranging knowledge of the newspaper business, and a wise, robust and balanced approach to problems which was most refreshing. It turned out too that he was a passionate lover of opera, being a member of the board of the Glyndebourne Opera Society, and also being a regular attender at Covent Garden, taking a helpfully critical interest in performances there. No one could have foretold it at the time, but some twelve years later he was destined to be appointed chairman of the Arts Council in succession to Arnold Goodman, an appointment which was imaginative and which worked out very well, although Pat struck a pretty terrible patch, for when he first started the job it was on the basis of an annual 10 per cent increase in real terms in the amount of Government money to be made available for the Arts, whereas by the end of his five-year term the prospect was at best a standstill.

On 24 September 1957 Oliver Poole, who at that time was joint managing director of Pearsons, was also appointed to represent the new controlling share-holder, and from my point of view, and I hope from theirs, a very satisfying relationship developed. Oliver was in fact already a friendly acquaintance of mine. We had sat together on the board of the Old Vic, although he was a member for a long while, between 1948 and 1963, while I only served for about five years from 1955. My own contribution was I fear very insignificant. However, I much enjoyed the jovial chairmanship of Sir Bronson Albery, a real grand old man of the theatre, and I was filled with admiration for the

artistic direction of Michael Benthall and the skilful management of Alfred
Francis who kept the Old Vic going by brilliant stratagems at a time when
Government support for the Arts was on a derisory scale. Without their efforts
there might well not be a National Theatre today, for in a sense they provided
the foundations. The same may emphatically be said of Oliver Lyttelton, whose
mother Dame Edith had dedicated herself to the cause of a National Theatre
from the early days of its conception; to honour her memory he made every
endeavour to make the dream a reality, becoming the first chairman in 1962.

Quite soon after his appointment to the board of the *FT* Oliver Poole had
to undergo the peculiarly unpleasant experience of the Bank Rate Tribunal.
This body was set up by the Home Secretary, R. A. Butler, in November 1957
to enquire into allegations that information about the raising of Bank Rate on
19 September from 5 per cent to 7 per cent (one of a series of measures the
purpose of which was to protect the value of the £ at $2.80!) had been
improperly disclosed to persons who had used the information for the purpose
of private gain. On 18 September the Chancellor of the Exchequer, Peter
Thorneycroft, had personally seen representatives of selected newspapers
(including myself from the *FT*, under the mistaken impression perhaps that I
was editor of the paper), and given a grim account of the pressures on the pound,
and of the need to restrict the supply of money and hold down the level of
Government expenditure, the kind of statement that would have been as relevant
in 1977 as it was in 1957, the only difference being that since then the value of
the pound had fallen by almost 40 per cent. At no point did he make any reference to the proposed increase in bank rate. Nor did he do so when he saw Oliver
Poole, who had just handed over the chairmanship of the Tory Party but who
remained deputy chairman, and who was regarded at the headquarters of the
party in power as an important point of reference on all economic and financial
matters. Representatives of the TUC and of the employers' organizations were
also seen, not by Thorneycroft but by two other Ministers.

The allegations about the misuse of information were vaguely hinted at by one
or two less responsible journalists, the implication being that someone or other
had profited by selling Government securities in the knowledge that they would
fall when the increase in bank rate was announced, after which they could be
bought back for a nice turn. On 9 October the Rt Hon. Harold Wilson MP
addressed a memorandum to the Lord Chancellor suggesting that 'misgivings
on this matter need to be allayed'; and less than two weeks later the Tribunal
consisting of Lord Justice Parker and two distinguished QCs was appointed.
They found unequivocally that there had been no improper disclosure of information, and no improper action of any kind, but between the first sitting of the
Tribunal and the issue of its report on 1 January 1958 anyone who had seen

Thorneycroft or the other two Ministers waited somewhat anxiously, not because of any sense of guilt but because of natural uncertainty. Above all, knowing the personalities chiefly involved, I was sickened that the finger of suspicion should be pointed at them in such a way.

To revert to the transfer of control of the *FT*, there was a clear risk that if a group controlling a leading merchant bank also controlled the only exclusively business-orientated newspaper, criticism could arise. It was therefore important that Pearsons should go out of their way not to interfere at all in the policy of the paper. They had given Brendan a categorical assurance to this effect, and I can say with absolute conviction that they never did so. Indeed, from a staff relations point of view it might be argued that they went too far in this respect, for John Cowdray himself was conspicuously absent. His determination not to interfere almost seemed to us in the office an attitude of aloofness. He seldom came near us, and this we regretted. It may have been his noted shyness, but I think it was more his desire not to be accused of interference. Fortunately for him, as well as for us, very soon after the take-over of control there was a major row relating to the affairs of the British Aluminium Company in which certain merchant banks were pitted against one another. On one side was Lazards. Mercifully the commentators of the *FT* took a point of view diametrically opposed to the Lazard position, but nothing was ever said to suggest that this was in any way regrettable. It was thus made clear from the start that the editorial independence of the *FT* would not be in jeopardy, and there was a great sense of relief. Most important though was the feeling of being less cramped and confined as a result of belonging to a very large group. The explanation for this should be self-evident. Essentially it was that the larger group was able to take a broader view since its risks were more widely spread. Also it needs to be said that both Pat Gibson and Oliver Poole are men of exceptional talent, and no one could have done more than they did to bolster my rather insecure sense of confidence in my own abilities.

There was one approach I received during the early months after the transfer of control of the *FT* to Pearsons, which it would be wrong of me not to record. One day, I forget the date, Siegmund Warburg asked to see me. I had come to know him in the course of my daily rounds, and I liked and admired him enormously. He had immense entrepreneurial flair, and he achieved marvels in overcoming the built-in resistance of established City institutions to a talented newcomer in their hallowed preserves. His approach was to ask me to become a managing director of his bank. The salary would at first be less than I was then receiving but the scope was clearly greater. I was sorely tempted and torn. In my heart of hearts I knew that I could not leave the *FT*, which had become such an integral part of my life, and for the future of which I felt a good deal happier following the transfer of control, although I also felt that I had a duty to see it safely through. I did however write to tell Brendan who at the time was away in South Africa on his last visit. This was his reply:

G.,

I have been in remote Swaziland and have only just seen your letter.

As you will understand it is hard to put aside affection and interest when asked for my advice about an offer which must end a partnership in work of a span exceeding a quarter of a century.

To get an offer which will bring you capital for your personal services in a time when Somerset House has ended almost all chances of capital accretion from ordinary 'gainful employment' is an opportunity which is indeed unlikely to recur.

Remembering all I owe to you and the happiness I've derived from our long partnership I must stifle very selfish feelings and advise you to seize this rare opportunity.

I know, too, how the offer of a roving commission now appeals to you. With a business novice* as Dearlove's successor in the general managership of the F.T. you as managing director would be more than ever bound to stick to the last in London.

Working for shareholders in a large public company will never enable you to create capital. The only way (it's hardly ever to be found) is to come across a rich, international enterpriser many of whose doings are outside Britain and the lawful jurisdiction of Somerset House.

By a coincidence in these Central Mining negotiations I've been dealing with the American capitalist Englehart who some years ago took a liking to one of its managers, Gordon Richdale, and offered him a job with a reward in capital. Richdale is now bird happy and his former senior colleagues greatly envy his lot.

If your merchant banker is Warburg he can surely do for you what Englehart has done for Richdale.

Warburg is set apart from the ruck of merchant bankers who pride themselves on hallowed but faded names and who for the most part stand upon their dignity and little else.

Warburg has a seeing eye, great ingenuity and resource plus an inheritance of honourable skill in money getting. He also cares for more civilised things than fortune making.

Your going from the F.T. must be a very sharp loss. No one can swiftly take your place and you will long be missed and will yourself miss things for which you care. But you have to think of the advantage to Joan and Derry of your getting that rare thing called capital – some of it, I hope, not in sterling.

Dear G. newspaper life will never be what it was before. I shall always miss you.

As our newly installed owner will want somebody of long experience of the F.T. to be steward of his fairly costly interest I shall give up the Union Corporation and look after the day to day affairs of the papers until a new managing-director can be found or trained. I shall then depart in the hope of peace and of living in London no more.

I wish I had your liking for travel. Three weeks of constant movings and frequent

* T. S. G. Hunter (see p. 138).

meetings with new acquaintances have tired me beyond all telling. Hence this inadequate letter written partly in the office here, and for the rest in a bumpy plane.

B.

That letter of course had the effect of confirming me in my deeply felt instinct that I could not move elsewhere. I must, I was sure, stay where I was until put out to grass, an eventuality to which since I was then only forty-seven I perhaps rather foolishly gave too little thought.

The idea of a total uprooting would really have been very hard to face up to. I not only had the *FT* to supervise, I also had to pay a good deal of attention to the various other constituent parts of the group brought together by Brendan, of most of which I had to act as chairman, and with each of which I had naturally developed strong personal ties. Pride of place in a sense went to our monthly *The Banker*, because it was his first venture into the field of financial journalism, from which everything else stemmed. Its sale was tiny, but it stood on its own feet. After the appointment of William Clarke as editor, it developed into an important and profitable magazine. (Clarke later became Director of the Committee on Invisible Exports, but continued as editorial consultant.) There was the *Investors Chronicle*, the appeal of which was also pretty specialized, and its profitability precarious until ten years later, in 1967, I successfully approached Cecil King about the possibility of a merger between it and its rival the *Stock Exchange Gazette*, then owned by IPC, whose chairman Cecil was, although his deposition, so vividly described by Hugh Cudlipp, was not far off. There was *The Practitioner*, the medical monthly, which was extremely well edited by Bill Thomson, a canny omniscient Scottish doctor, with an inexhaustible appetite for work, while Michael Fletcher, despite his frequent need for reassurance and encouragement, provided very capable management.

There was also *History Today*, a monthly magazine that we had started in 1950 by agreement with the Historical Association, whose president then was G. M. Trevelyan. This magazine was a great love of Brendan's because of his passionate addiction to history, especially the history of the English-speaking world, above all of the United States, where his knowledge was extraordinary. The joint editors of the magazine were Alan Hodge and Peter Quennell, that renowned man of letters, whose name I had strongly urged upon Brendan. For over twenty-five years they were to share a room together, complementing one another admirably and producing a most attractive if financially not very rewarding magazine, which achieved a monthly sale of over 30,000 without any yielding to the temptation to popularize its contents. A large part of the credit for the success of the magazine was in fact due to Robert Harling, now the editor of *House & Garden*, who designed the typography and layout for us, as well as helping with various *FT* typographical problems. He was a real original. For a while he and I became good friends, although we drifted apart when our excuse for meeting was gone. I well remember his most attractive wife with prematurely grey hair, whom he told me he had first seen on a bus, following her to her home after she had alighted, a true romance which really worked.

Finally there was *The Economist*, by far the most successful of the investments made by Brendan when he first formed his group, and it calls for a short digression. He had acquired a half share for £50,000, a figure which at the time seemed quite excessive; half a century later the annual profit was many times that figure. In 1928 the circulation was some 6,000. It advanced to 10,000 by 1938 when Geoffrey Crowther succeeded Walter Layton as editor. Geoffrey created *The Economist* as we know it today. Throughout the war years there was no scope for development. The real growth only became possible after the ending of paper rationing in 1949. I had been made Brendan's alternate on the board in 1938, becoming a full member in 1941 when he had to resign on being appointed Minister of Information; and I was to remain a member for over thirty-five years. I was therefore able to observe Geoffrey's brilliance and flair at close hand. Physically he was short and stocky. His head was large, with slightly oriental features, and he chuckled constantly. When he was an undergraduate at Cambridge he had been the star pupil of Professor Denis Robertson, and Maynard Keynes regarded him as being in a class apart for intellectual ability. Those who do not know the book would do well to glance at *An Outline of Money*, which Geoffrey mainly wrote during the phony war period, the first edition being published in late 1940. A revised edition appeared in 1948, taking into critical account the schemes evolved at the end of the war for dealing with international payments problems. There can be no better example of his gift for lucid exposition and analysis. The book is of course now largely out of date, but much of what he writes is still extremely relevant.

Apart from a short period in Government service during the war, Geoffrey edited *The Economist* for eighteen years. During that time the circulation rose to over 50,000. The quality of its editorials, many of them written by himself, gained respect: and some, like his famous 'The Carrot and the Stick', satirizing the British donkey, became in their way classics. He vastly broadened the coverage of the paper, particularly in its business section, and also in relation to the affairs of the overseas world, above all of the United States, with the result that the transatlantic sale of *The Economist* rose steeply; although, strangely, no American counterpart has ever been successfully established.

When Geoffrey handed over the editorship to Donald Tyerman in 1956, he became managing director, and then in 1963 he succeeded Walter Layton as chairman. Thanks to his imagination *The Economist*'s property development in

St James's Street was undertaken, and largely thanks to his ingenuity as well as that of Peter Dallas Smith, the then managing director, the necessary finance was found by judicious borrowing. No additional capital was sought from the shareholders, but the value of their equity was immensely enhanced through a scheme which no other weekly publication in Britain would ever have thought of undertaking, and which for sheer audacity, looking back on it, was extraordinary. Geoffrey and Peter were responsible for the choice of architects, Peter and Alison Smithson, who belonged to the group known, apparently as a complimentary term, as the New Brutalists: and to me the building, or rather the complex of three buildings, is one of the most ingenious and pleasing built in London since the war. Unlike Bracken House, the whole building is air conditioned; there is an underground car park: and the lifts work so rapidly that passengers hardly have time to get in and out. Furthermore the project was costed so that it was economically viable on the basis of an average rental of about £3 a square foot, which is about a quarter of the present going rent in the St James's Street area.

Geoffrey was also the inspiration behind the idea of setting up the Economist Intelligence Unit. As the circulation of *The Economist* grew, and as its influence developed, people increasingly tended to write in seeking information and advice. The editorial staff had quite enough to do filling the columns of the paper, yet to turn away enquiries was not congenial to Geoffrey. Hence the formation of the *EIU*, which had the advantage of association with *The Economist*, but was run quite separately. It was developed vigorously and a decision was taken to acquire the lease of Spencer House, overlooking St James's Park, a true nobleman's residence, one of the few still standing. For a while at the end of the war it accommodated the auctioneers, Christie's, and had then been adapted to office use by the British Oxygen Company. For the *EIU* to move into such imposing premises was a bold step, but it was proved fully justified by the growth, not invariably profitable, that was experienced. Many companies, as well as governmental and international agencies, turned to the *EIU* for advice, particularly on marketing prospects. Some of the fees earned were large, but so also were the costs incurred. A steady income was to be derived too from various specialized publications, notably a lengthy series of quarterly economic reports covering a wide range of foreign countries. In the marketing of these the connection with the name of *The Economist* was most valuable: and therefore, although the *EIU* was on its own, it was vital to ensure that the content and quality of the reports was such that *The Economist* could take pride in them.

The Economist itself also engaged in the production of books and newsletters. It was in the time of Geoffrey Crowther that the publication of the famous

Economist desk diary was started, soon to be followed by a very intelligently produced pocket diary. From this, under the guidance of Hugo Meynell, there developed a massive Weights and Measures Guide, and a remarkable compilation, the *World in Figures*, both of which in their different ways should become indispensable. As to newsletters, it was on Geoffrey's initiative that the celebrated, rather Sherlock Holmesian *Foreign Report* was launched. This consists of eight slim pages printed each week on blue paper, reporting behind the scenes happenings throughout the world, based on reliable information insufficiently authenticated for publication in *The Economist* itself. A high subscription rate (and sale by subscription only) helps the sense of exclusivity, not to mention the profit earned. In 1976 a *Financial Report* newsletter was introduced, and similar projects will follow.

Geoffrey played the major part in the establishment of The Economists' Bookshop, a company owned jointly by *The Economist* and the London School of Economics, and formed primarily to serve the specialized needs of the students of that eventful establishment, although thanks in the main to the initiative of Mrs Gerti Kvergic, the shop's first manager, an important mail order business was built up, serving both home and overseas markets.

Without Geoffrey, the probability is that *The Economist* would have remained a skilfully edited influential periodical. There is no reason for believing that the company would have developed so powerfully in other ways. This is not to say that all the credit is due to him. He was followed by two editors, who each served for nine years, Donald Tyerman and Alastair Burnet. Throughout their respective tenures the circulation of the paper continued its steady advance, most spectacularly under Alastair, who was the great popularizer, revolutionizing the cover of the magazine, and taking the sale from 75,000 in 1965 to 125,000 in 1974, when he was tempted away to edit the *Daily Express*, a somewhat short-lived honeymoon which ended with his return to the television work that he had first undertaken before he became editor of *The Economist*. Alastair was followed as editor by Andrew Knight, a brilliant young man who had previously represented the paper in Washington and Brussels. Although only thirty-four years old he was the candidate most strongly supported by the staff as a whole: and within three years of his appointment he had the agreeable distinction of seeing the sales top the 150,000 mark. Of these three editors I had known Donald Tyerman longest. I first met him early in the war, during my temporary release from the Army, when he had become acting editor of the paper on Geoffrey's relatively short-lived entry into Government service, and I had the task of keeping an eye on the affairs of the group after Brendan's appointment as Minister of Information. Above all he deserves an award of merit for physical courage. He had been struck by polio when a young boy, being forced to spend two or three years lying on his back, during which time he read his way through the *Encyclopaedia Britannica*, retaining a good deal of it in his capacious brain. When he regained the power to walk, he had to wear irons, and he needed the help of two sticks. But he never complained, always making light of his disability.

Of all those connected with *The Economist*, I have above all been conscious of the pervading influence of Roland Bird. He had been recruited in 1933 by Hargreaves Parkinson (who at that time was in charge of the Stock Exchange section), becoming deputy editor and business editor under Geoffrey, continuing in this dual capacity under Donald Tyerman. At a moment of crisis he became effectively managing director, with conspicuous success, until in 1971 at my suggestion Ian Trafford moved from Industrial & Trade Fairs to take over the management, when Roland became finance director. Roland was also obliged during a period involving complex personality problems at the Economist Intelligence Unit to take charge of that company as well. Therefore if Geoffrey was the real creative genius, Roland Bird was the man who more than any other helped to keep the company on a steady even keel in the later years of Geoffrey's life, and the debt to him cannot be exaggerated.

Brendan always had slight reservations about Geoffrey's motivation, while respecting and fearing his intellectual capacity. He had been provoked because soon after the war Geoffrey had accepted an invitation to join the board of the Commercial Union Assurance Company without having first sought consent. There is no doubt in my mind, in view of their very close association over the years, that Geoffrey was wrong about this, although technically he may have been within his rights. In any event Brendan took strong exception to being presented with a *fait accompli*. Geoffrey undoubtedly formed aspirations to turn into a tycoon. Through the introduction of Lewis Douglas (US Ambassador in London after the war) he became a director of Encyclopaedia Britannica, making regular visits to that company's headquarters in Chicago, until he resigned because he objected to the door to door selling methods they adopted. Later he joined the board of the Royal Bank of Canada. He also became chairman of Hazell Watson & Viney, an old established printing company, and through a series of complex steps was instrumental in bringing into existence the mammoth British Printing Corporation. He made friends with a budding young entrepreneur, Nigel Broackes, and introduced him to the Commercial Union, of which by this time Geoffrey was deputy chairman. As a result he joined the board of Broackes's company, Trafalgar House Investments, becoming chairman, a position he held for three or four years. Most surprisingly, through his friendship with Johnnie Miller of the World Bank, Geoffrey became a pioneer in the opening up of the Costa Smeralda. Miller was visiting Sardinia on behalf of the Bank. He was struck by its beauty, and together with Geoffrey he purchased some land on which they both built houses, Geoffrey, as he told me, financing the cost of his house by selling half his plot. A syndicate was formed for the redevelopment of the area, but the weaker spirits in it did not hold together; and only the 25-year-old Aga Khan, helped at first by his half brother Patrick Guinness, had the imagination and the courage to bring into existence an entirely new holiday district, now avidly sought after by the sun and sea loving élite of Europe.

Geoffrey's most important excursion into the world of big business had to do with hotels. In 1946 he was invited to join the board of the good staid old hotel business, Trust Houses, being elected chairman in 1959, after which he caused the company's hampering trust deed to be altered, and with his ever-eager quest for growth ('I believe in projects,' he used to say to me) he pushed the company into vigorous expansion, both at home and overseas. The culmination was a mammoth merger with the very large hotel and catering company built up by Charles Forte, bringing into existence one single huge catering, restaurant and hotel group, satisfying Geoffrey's desire to have under his control more hotel beds than anyone else. Forte and Crowther became the incompatible joint heads, a very unhappy story, for stresses and strains developed between them, ending in a painful contest from which Geoffrey emerged the loser.

During this strange period of his life, when he seemed to be consumed with a sort of power mania, Geoffrey also undertook the chairmanship of two Royal Commissions, both requiring the assimilation of massive documentation, and agreed to become Chancellor of the newly created Open University. The first Royal Commission was concerned with primary education, and arising from its report the school leaving age was extended by a year. The second was set up to examine nothing less than the Constitution itself; but he died in 1972 before the report was completed so that his personal views on the vexed subject of devolution are unknown. It is baffling that although Geoffrey's first love was always *The Economist*, in which he had also accumulated a substantial shareholding for himself and his family (whenever shares were offered for sale he would acquire them), he allowed its management to suffer through neglectful supervision on his part, and a moment came when in a mood of frustration some of my *FT* colleagues even talked of disposing of our group's 50 per cent shareholding, an attitude I passionately resisted, and which mercifully did not prevail. Indeed it was in these last years that the true importance of Roland Bird was fully revealed. Unhappily, the mental and emotional strains to which Geoffrey was subjecting himself became too much for his sturdily built frame, and he died quite suddenly, to the great distress of his colleagues. Fortunately Evelyn de Rothschild, whose family had had an interest in *The Economist* for nearly fifty years, agreed to become chairman in succession to Geoffrey, and he stimulated new thinking about the role of the company, showing much imagination in true Rothschild fashion, and guiding it more and more in the direction of an international newspaper produced in London but with two-thirds of its circulation and advertisement revenue arising outside the UK.

Chapter 15

Two other compelling reasons for my not making a break with the *FT* and its various associated interests appeared in the course of 1957. First was the illness of John Waverley, the chairman of the Royal Opera House. Throughout much of the year I had to take the chair at meetings, and as I hope I describe in Part Three this was by no means a sinecure. To uproot myself and start an entirely new business career at just the same time would have been very difficult.

Then in the autumn my father fell ill, and on 22 November he died. At the time I suffered seriously from a sense of guilt that I had not spent more time with him, and had not done more to ease the lonely state in which, since the death of my stepmother Olive, ten years previously, he had found himself. However, he had developed a very full life of his own as Chairman of Committes in the House of Lords, and he had also resumed many of his old friend-ships dating from before the time of his marriage to Olive, for during the twenty-five years that he was with her it was surprising how few people he wished to see despite his naturally gregarious nature. Yet perhaps my sense of guilt, an affliction from which for one reason or another I chronically suffer, was not as much justified as I then believed; for among my father's papers was a sealed envelope, addressed to me and marked to be opened after his death, containing a letter the text of which I reproduce, not in order to show myself as an exemplary son, because that I was not, but in order to show, in a way that no words of mine could do, what an exceptional father I possessed. This is the letter:

Dear Old Man,

When you get this letter I shall no longer be able to express appreciation. And so I just want to say what I should have found it difficult to say in my lifetime except to our mutual embarrassment – Thank you for having been such a very nice son to me. I fear that I have been an indifferent father but I have tried according to my lights, and I have loved you very much and been very proud of you.

My death will not – repeat 'not', as they say in the Civil Service – be an occasion for sorrow. Certainly not for me, for I shall be old and tired, and I am very lonely without Olive. I long to be with her again and, as I cannot be until I die, death holds no terrors for me but the possibility of great joy. I have been very lucky all my life and had twenty-five marvellously happy years, and now I am only marking time till I am told to pass along.

Only four things I want you to do for me. The first is to see that my funeral is absolutely private and that there is no memorial service for me. The second is to see that, if it is reasonably possible without great trouble and expense, my ashes are disposed of after my cremation in accordance with my wishes as expressed in a document which Walter, Burgis & Co. have. [His wish was that I should mingle his ashes with those of Olive, and distribute them around the roots of a large group of roses in Brookwood Cemetery]. The third is that you will look after Jenkins [his gardener–driver–manservant] and see that he is not turned out of the cottage here unless he wants to leave. And the fourth is that you will give Peg and Sandy [my stepbrother and stepsister] your advice and help if they ever need it. They have been very kind to me.

Thank you again old man. May you have many happy years on this strange earth. And may we meet again somewhere sometime.

Bless you.

> Daddy

After such a letter, any words of mine would seem meagre. Rather let me quote from Lord Home's tribute to my father in the House of Lords, and from a letter which Dingle Foot wrote to me. First of all the letter:

> I would like to say with what deep regret I read the news of your father's death. He and I worked very closely together for five years at the Ministry of Economic Warfare. It is an association on which I look back with the very greatest pleasure. What I chiefly remember is the genuinely friendly interest which he took in all the staff – extending even to the charwomen and messengers. I do not think that any Director-General can ever have been regarded with greater affection by the whole of his Department.

In his tribute Alec Home said:

> There have been many great Chairmen of Committees, but greatness alone does not necessarily guarantee that success in personal relations which Lord Drogheda had. I know of none who had that priceless gift of sympathy in such full measure as he: it allowed him to put himself in the other man's place before he gave advice or passed judgement upon him. It was one of the daily delights of this House to see him moving informally, happily and naturally amongst us, with a smile, a cheerful word and a pleasantry for everybody, and, of course, wise advice whenever it was asked. He knew full well, in the last two years, what it cost him in health as he drove himself to fulfil the duties of your Lordships' House. And so, my Lords, did we. But we also knew that it was useless to try to deflect him, because this frail figure, who was so familiar to us, had within him the spirit of a very gallant fighter. So it was that he carried on serving your Lordships' House to the very end of his strength and of his life.

For the first year or so after the transfer of control of the *FT* to Pearsons, Brendan continued to act as chairman, but the differences with the Crosthwaite-Eyre family, coupled with the grave deterioration in his health, had removed all his sparkle. He came less and less to the office. When he was there for lunch, he ate virtually nothing. Cancer had attacked his throat. He would ask for a poached egg, but even when it was scarcely cooked at all he would complain that it was too hard. By then he was living quite alone. For many years he had had a delightful couple named Beatrice and Costello, she English, he Irish, to look after him, but at the moment of his greatest need he insisted on pensioning them off. One day I told him that he should not be living quite by himself, and suggested asking the office cook, Mrs Norgren, a Swedish lady, who was devoted to Brendan, whether she would be willing to move into his house. To my surprise he agreed. When I spoke to her she reluctantly consented, but within a week she came to me and said that it was impossible for her to carry on. Brendan, she said, paced up and down the house all night long: she had no rest, and also found it impossible to communicate with him. I had to go to Brendan to tell him. He took it badly, and suggestions that I should try to find another companion were abruptly dismissed. He simply remained at the house all by himself until within a matter of weeks he was obliged, no, forced by his doctor to enter hospital.

A similar sense of everything coming to a halt revealed itself in relation to his car. He had had the same car, an old blue Bentley, since before the war, and the same driver, Aley. Aley achieved miracles to keep the car on the road. From time to time he told Brendan that it must be replaced, but to no avail. Brendan of course was right. After he went into hospital he was never to return home. His final weeks were spent in the Ford Motor Company's flat in Grosvenor House, the thoughtful suggestion that he should move there having been made to him by Pat Hennessy, Ford's UK chairman, a sympathetic and lovably sentimental Irishman who was a very devoted friend of Brendan and who could not bear to see his sad and solitary state in Westminster Hospital, where in any event further treatment would have been futile.

I went to see Brendan in Grosvenor House. The sight was tragic. His shock of red hair was grey. His hands resembled those of an El Greco saint. He had to be fed through a tube which passed from his right cheek through his nostril. And yet he was able to joke and smile; and he also talked of his intention to live in the country after he had recovered. He was reading the manuscript of Freddie Birkenhead's as yet unpublished life of Rudyard Kipling (a condition of publication was the consent of Kipling's sister, which she withheld), and he spoke of it enthusiastically. Then he took me by surprise by asking whether I would like him to leave me his Lord North Street house in his will. I could only express my deep appreciation, even though I had no wish for any such legacy, which as it transpired meant the last three or four years of a lease of a Queen Anne house in a serious state of disrepair: but his gesture, and his manner of telling me when he was so gravely suffering, conveyed to me more than anything else could have done that my place in his affections was real and true.

Brendan died on 8 August 1958. On the night of his death the main trunk of a fig tree in the small garden at the back of the house collapsed, and had to be sawn down almost to ground level, but mercifully the tree proved to be indestructible, and its constant vigour in a sunless corner is heartening.

For almost a week after Brendan's death Aley, his driver, stayed alone in the house, his task being to comply with the strict instruction he had received to destroy every letter and any other document which he might find there; and he sat solemnly in front of the fireplace consigning to the flames whatever papers he could find, and no one knows what secrets or what treasures disappeared. For his pains, Aley had bequeathed to him all the contents of the house, save for the books, which went to Sedbergh School, and some valuable Chippendale dining room furniture, which went to the Master's Lodge at Churchill College, Cambridge.

In preceding pages I have made many references to Brendan. I have tried to show what an unusual man he was. His virtues far outweighed his faults. He had immense loyalty and courage, real integrity, a vivid imagination, and a witty and lively mind of great capacity. He had a passionate belief in individual freedom, hating the onset of collectivist trends. Fundamentally, he was a very solitary man. He was an enigma in his sexual tastes. If they were ever in any way fulfilled, it was in complete obscurity. It is possible that he suffered from some deep-seated frustration which was the cause of his extreme moodiness. There were those who found him insupportable, but this was generally because he himself was out of sympathy with them. In such cases he simply could not disguise his feelings, and he was apt to be gruff and rude. He was terribly intolerant. This maddened me, although I loved his robust no-nonsense quality. No one could ever have been more generously treated than I was by him, and I constantly cherish his memory.

Brendan's death had the effect of lifting a heavy dark cloud from our heads, while in no way affecting the love and sense of gratitude which we felt towards him. The fact was that ever since the onset of his illness he had become morose, and realistic discussion with him of our various problems was hard if not impossible. Oliver Poole and Pat Gibson, the two directors appointed by our new controlling shareholder, went out of their way to be helpful. The extent of their interference was minimal. They had offered the chairmanship to Lionel Robbins who was quite coincidentally my colleague on the Covent Garden board; but he had first of all to clear his position with London University since he held a professorship at the London School of Economics, and the question was whether he would be permitted to do both jobs. This took over a year, and as a temporary measure Oliver was made chairman of the company, which he genuinely enjoyed, for he took great pride in the bright young men of the editorial staff. His period as chairman gave me the opportunity of frequent contact with him. Thus I could see in action at close quarters a very remarkable brain. Cant he could not abide. I have seldom known a greater realist or someone less ruled by his emotions or so little governed by preconceived ideas. His mind worked with astonishing rapidity, as it still does despite the damnable stroke he suffered in 1974; and once he had made a decision he was ruthless in seeing it executed. He could be kind and generous, and he had immense loyalty and affection for his colleagues; but he had a hard inner core which when it revealed itself through his sharp tongue and disconcerting eye was quite alarming. He asked nothing from his fellow men, and expected little, for he regarded human nature in the main with utter scepticism, and bad behaviour seldom took him by surprise. His influence was thoroughly salutary, and his all too brief period as chairman of the FT was for me a real pleasure.

Through my association with Oliver there entered into the life of Joan and myself someone who was to become our closest and most intimate woman friend. This was his beautiful wife Daphne, who gradually established a unique position in our affections. Her friendship with Joan was particularly strengthened when Joan had a heart attack at Covent Garden in 1964, and Daphne was constantly with her through the period of recuperation; and then after she and Oliver separated a year later Joan and she were in almost daily communication, and have remained so to this day. She visits us regularly, and is a keen and expert gardener. I could write much of her but will only say that she is devoid of vanity, the essence of goodness and unselfishness, and almost generous to a fault, without her innate virtue being in any way oppressive.

Before Lionel Robbins was able to join the board, Oliver Poole and Pat Gibson made another and very refreshing addition. This was John Smith, a member of an extensive and distinguished City family, a man with many interests, working in Coutts & Co. and an intimate friend of Pat's, with whom he used regularly to go ski-ing each winter. He brought to our board meetings a very original quality. He had a passion for canals, which he fought to preserve, and for steam engines. For a number of years he had participated actively in any organization that concerned itself with the protection of fine buildings or beautiful countryside. One of his great services was to form a private charity called the Landmark Trust, the purpose of which was to acquire small 'landmark' buildings, such as a watermill or a watchtower, worth saving because of their picturesque or architectural merit but too small for the National Trust, and then to convert them to residential use, renting them out, furnished, for short periods for holiday purposes. A few years after joining the board of the *FT* he became Conservative MP for Westminster, holding the seat from 1964 until 1970, when he decided that the job was too arduous, tedious and costly, so he resigned, being followed in the seat by Christopher Tugendhat,* who had been one of the bright young men recruited to the *FT* in 1960 by Gordon Newton. John Smith himself left the *FT* board at the beginning of 1968, because he wanted to devote himself to conservation matters.

Unexpectedly and rather idiotically, Lionel was not allowed both to hold professorial rank in the University of London and to be chairman of our company. He luckily opted for us: and in the event he also continued to lecture regularly at the LSE, where he was accorded the status of professor. In due course he also became chairman of the LSE, seeing it through an appallingly difficult time of student unrest, artificially stimulated from outside: and finally heading a highly successful appeal for funds to enable the School Library to move into Strand House. He succeeded Oliver as chairman of the *FT* at the end of 1960, holding the position until 1970, when he reached the age of seventy-two. One helpful consequence from my point of view was that we were able to consult almost daily about the affairs of Covent Garden, and his name appears often in the next section. It would be hard for me to exaggerate his help-fulness in giving me balanced and constructive advice. At the *FT* he felt very much in his element. As a leading economist who had spent many years of his life instructing the ablest students, first of all at Oxford and then at the London School of Economics, he took a tremendous interest in the younger members of the staff. He arranged a series of regular lunches to which he invited a large cross-section of those working on both the editorial and the business sides of the paper: and he took great delight in the talk, always saying that he found it as good as and more stimulating than that of most senior common rooms. He threw himself energetically into his job, counting himself fortunate to have embarked at the age of sixty-two on what for him was a new way of life. He derived particular pleasure from the fact that because of the group's 50 per cent interest in *The Economist* he became its deputy chairman and thus was able to witness a particularly interesting period in its development.

During his time as chairman of the *FT* we had three rather tiresome, awkward and costly problems to deal with. First was a company named Technical Information on Microfiche, or TIM for short. We were approached by Philip Zimmerman, a bright publisher whose father had come to Britain from America

* At the beginning of 1977, at the age of forty, Tugendhat was appointed one of the nine EEC Commissioners, and moved to Brussels.

and had founded the *Advertiser's Weekly*, from which the Mercury House Group of business publications had developed. Zimmerman suggested to me a joint company to exploit an idea for developing a service which was intended to be a kind of glorified version of the microfilm: and we were shown a very impressive piece of celluloid not much larger than a playing card on to which the entire Bible had been compressed. By positioning it correctly in a viewing box any desired page could be read with ease. The proposal was that a technical service on microfiches should be developed, each fiche covering one or more trade publications or catalogues. Misguidedly we believed the idea could be successfully exploited. The working capital had to be provided by the *FT*. We incurred a very substantial loss before we, so to speak, called it a day. The idea itself never, so far as I know, caught on.

Secondly, there was another disappointing although far less costly venture. We were asked to participate in a computer service business, and we made a modest investment, which was lost partly because though the idea was right it was premature, and partly because those in charge suffered from an excess of optimism.

Thirdly, there was a medical newspaper, a project proposed to us by Vere Sherren of the International Publishing Corporation, with whom we had first come into contact in connection with the exhibition organizing company that we had formed jointly with George Newnes (before it was part of IPC) and of which I tell in another chapter. Our group, it will be recalled, already had an interest in medical publishing through *The Practitioner*. Sherren suggested to us that a medical weekly concentrating on topical news would complement the service provided by *The Practitioner*, and, misguidedly as it turned out, we formed a joint company and launched *Medical News*. Sherren's son Graham was brought in to learn about medical advertising, working for some months in the offices of *The Practitioner*, and being introduced to all the large medical advertisers. Strenuous efforts were made to persuade doctors to become regular subscribers to *Medical News*, but, although the subscription rate was extremely low, they resisted, being already excessively bombarded with reading matter. Sherren urged that we should turn the paper into a free sheet, sending out copies gratis to every medical practice, but with our perhaps old-fashioned ideas and having before us the example of our own *Practitioner*, which was readily subscribed for by doctors, we were unwilling to agree, regarding free distribution as somehow unethical, and potentially hurtful to *The Practitioner*, which was highly regarded by the medical profession, and profitable, earning close on £100,000 a year. The upshot was that we acquired IPC's half shares in *Medical News*, so that we owned it entirely. Success eluded it, however, and we sold the company to an American group who wished to develop in the British market.

Their intention was to do what Sherren had proposed, but David Carrick, the editor of the paper, was unwilling to carry on under the new dispensation: and since we all liked him and admired him for his integrity, he was offered the post of medical adviser in Bracken House. This was to prove to be a very successful appointment, contributing much to the well-being of the staff. Sherren's son Graham must have benefited from his early introduction to the world of medical advertising. He launched out with a handsomely produced magazine called I think *World Medicine* which was distributed free to doctors, and did well. He clearly had green fingers when it came to money-making, for he now reigns over a prosperous publishing business known as Morgan-Grampian, a company with considerable overseas assets. In its most recent year it earned over £2 million, and towards the end of 1977 it was the subject of a take-over bid by Trafalgar House Investments for no less a sum than £20 million, Graham Sherren's share of this reportedly being some 11 per cent. Earlier in 1977 there had been a crowning irony, when *The Practitioner* (control of which had by then been transferred within the Pearson Longman group from the *FT* to Longmans) was sold to Graham Sherren's company for a mere £220,000, a particularly sad case of *sic transit*, and surely troubling to Brendan's spirit.

As to the *FT* itself, Lionel Robbins was always most assiduous in his attendance at the office, and was constantly ready with advice, although he left to me the basic responsibility for the day-to-day running of the paper. Early after the move into Bracken House I initiated a twice-monthly meeting of the various heads of departments at which problems of common interest could be discussed and differences resolved. We called this the Policy Committee, a name that deliberately made it sound more important than it was: and of course at the meetings there was never any question of even a whisper about editorial policy. Shortly afterwards, in the intervening weeks, we started to hold regular meetings devoted to the planning of the *FT*'s programme of surveys and special pages. For many years we had published supplements of one kind or another, but the programme was much smaller and was not methodically planned. It was only after our move that we deliberately planned to develop our surveys into a major factor in the advertisement revenue of the *FT*. As time went by, scarcely a day passed without the paper carrying, over and above its normal contents, a special survey or pages devoted to particular industries or countries. Readers used sometimes to complain to me that their patience was being tried. But many of the suggestions for surveys stemmed from the industry or country concerned, even though we made perfectly clear to them that they would have no say over the editorial content. I had no compunction about developing the programme ruthlessly and planning it for anything up to a year ahead. From the point of view of our advertisement staff they often gained admission to a com-

pany which otherwise kept the door shut, while a great deal of foreign revenue
was also earned.

At no point did we develop any kind of blueprint for the way in which we
wanted the paper to grow. Gordon Newton and I knew one another's minds
pretty well. We had occasional disagreements, and I am sure that I was the one
who usually made concessions, for Gordon had a commendably stubborn
nature. What is more, I never forgot Otto Clarke's observation about him that
he had a maddening habit of nearly always being right. In saying this Otto was
referring mainly to Gordon's judgement when it came to assessing the likely
course of political events or of movements in markets and exchange rates; and
he did indeed have a kind of sixth sense, which seldom deserted him. However,
he also had a remarkable skill in giving a lead to his editorial staff. If any copy
submitted to him did not meet with his approval, he would say, 'Take it away.
You know it's not right.' That and no more; yet when it reappeared it *was*
right. I never discovered the secret.

Both Gordon and I were very conscious that, since the *FT* was dealing with
the business interests of its readers, accuracy was of fundamental importance; a
mistake could do incalculable harm. Therefore we did not put scoops as our top
priority. To be right but late was better than to be early but wrong. And we
steered clear of what is loosely called investigative journalism, which well done
could be very costly, while spuriously done is contemptible, being not only
hurtful to the persons under scrutiny, but also undermines the credibility of the
rest of the paper, grouping it with the real gutter press, whose sanctimonious
relish in earning a steady income denigrating others, without a constructive
thought of their own, never ceases to startle me.

Next to accuracy, came completeness of coverage of our particular fields of
business and finance. We had to carry all the relevant political news, the news
of companies and of stock and commodity markets, of money markets, foreign
exchanges, business appointments and so on. Then there was industrial news, a
field to which we devoted more and more space. Since it was evident that the
subject of exports was becoming crucial, we decided to devote a regular daily
space to export news, giving stories of orders and contracts gained and also,
alas, sometimes lost. After some years the title of the feature was changed to
world trade news, mistakenly I thought, for export or die has to be the maxim
for the United Kingdom.

Most significant perhaps was the growth of our overseas coverage. We much
increased the number of editorial staff at home and abroad specializing in
political and economic foreign news, and of course in foreign company results.
Gordon and I were at one in believing that the *FT* must develop outwards, as
much for the sake of British industry and commerce as for ourselves. We were

determined to build up the overseas circulation. Leading industrialists in Europe were bombarded with promotional material. A powerful drive was made to swell the advertisement revenue from abroad; and it was very encouraging for us when a few years later we applied for the Queen's Award for Export, which is not lightly bestowed, and to our considerable surprise, we were awarded it.

Labour matters were steadily assuming growing importance, and the specialist staff in this field was greatly expanded. Technological developments were another area to which Gordon thought far more attention must be devoted than had been the case in the old days. At first he engaged a distinguished scientist, Sir Ronald Simon, *the* authority on a very abstruse subject, Absolute Zero, to contribute occasional articles to the paper. These aroused interest, and resulted in numerous enquiries: and it was not many years before the Technical page was born, appearing five days a week. The page contained news of new products and processes, contributed in the main by companies, British and foreign, whose developments were described, after being carefully vetted by Arthur Bennett and Ted Schoeters, who were appointed joint editors of the page from its beginning twelve years ago, and are still going strong. In 1967 David Fishlock was appointed full-time scientific correspondent, becoming a considerable asset to the *FT* thanks to his ability to describe developments in almost any branch of science in words intelligible to the layman; and Michael Donne, who had been on the staff for some years, learnt to fly and turned himself by sheer hard work into the most trusted of all air correspondents, believing passionately in the importance of the British aircraft industry. Defence matters generally also came within his purview. Then Gordon started a Building page regularly each Monday, giving news of important building and public works contracts at home and overseas; and this provided a very useful service not systematically attempted by other newspapers. He also recruited a splendid agricultural correspondent, John Cherrington, a large farmer in his own right, who appeared to enjoy the weekly discipline of writing, and who was most careful not to talk his own book, a master of imparting technical information in non-technical language.

There was another field in which the *FT* came to play an important part. This was the Arts. As with other sections of the paper, the development was not planned in any kind of advance detail. We had started with one very good theatre plus film critic, followed by an outstanding music critic. Their work was more and more taken notice of, and the pressures on them increased. Gordon had on his editorial staff a man of unusual ability, John Higgins, who had joined us in the summer of 1958, being shortly afterwards appointed features editor. He was asked as well to supervise the paper's coverage of the arts, until as the importance of the work grew he was in 1964 appointed the

FT's first full-time arts editor. Additional writers on the arts were engaged. The space allotted was increased to the best part of a page, and thanks above all to John Higgins, who always seemed to have seen, heard and read everything, and who had a keen sense of quality, the page assumed great significance in the history of the *FT*. Not much additional circulation was gained, but for the paper's prestige it mattered considerably. Also I do not think it far-fetched to suggest that our coverage of artistic matters really helped to modify the attitudes of businessmen towards what is loosely referred to as industrial patronage of the Arts.

Gordon was nearly always more than receptive whenever I spoke to him about any part of the paper, but he accepted it most readily and naturally in the case of the Arts page. There was not only my connection with Covent Garden. I had also been responsible for the *FT* acting as a sponsor of Peter Daubeny's World Theatre Season, and I became the first chairman of the City Arts Trust which was formed in 1962 to mount a biennial festival in the City of London, with the purpose of presenting a friendlier image of the City to the outside world.

I therefore had regular contact with John Higgins and his various con- tributors. One of these I had in fact been instrumental in introducing to the *FT* some years before John had been appointed arts editor and indeed while Brendan was still alive. It was on the advice of Kenneth Clark that we had approached Denys Sutton to write about the visual arts. He was an art scholar and historian with a wide-ranging knowledge and a very fluent pen. At the time he was acting as a saleroom correspondent for the *Daily Telegraph*, which hardly stretched his unusual abilities. Initially he wrote a regular article for the *FT*, but my colleague Pat Gibson was eager that we should have within our fold a serious art magazine: and when in January 1962 we bought for a modest though possibly excessive sum the magazine *Apollo*, which had a good title but a trifling sale, Denys became the editor and built it up into a most respected publication, in my view more distinguished in appearance and in content than any other in its field. His work on the editorial side was complemented by and indeed would not have been possible without the managerial talent of Victor Law, who joined us from the *Connoisseur* and whose understanding of the intricacies of the art dealing world was exceptional. Regrettably, it was not possible to achieve harmonious relations between these two gifted but utterly different men. I was constantly trying to act as a kind of go-between although their offices were only a few feet from one another. Fortunately, however, the magazine surmounted the tensions, and became a great credit to our group. At one moment the American tycoon Norton Simon showed a strong interest in acquiring *Apollo* for his art foundation. I took detailed figures with me to New

York and before letting him have them I asked him whether it was not really just a rich man's passing whim, to which of course he replied that it was not. But in less than a month he began to have delusions of political grandeur, and that was that. I also had a talk with the publisher of the *Connoisseur* to see whether some form of merger might be capable of achievement, but it was clear that no meaningful basis existed. Denys Sutton as well as editing *Apollo* continued to contribute his regular articles to the *FT*, adding distinction to the Arts page, and is still doing so as I write these words, following a miraculous recovery from a grave illness against which he most courageously fought.

For a while we had another invaluable contributor to the Arts page, Marina Vaizey, who wrote particularly about modern painting. Although she led a very full married life, she was indefatigable in her exploration of talent, and she always brought a most refreshing zeal to her work. Not surprisingly, when John Russell left the *Sunday Times* to go to America as art critic of the *New York Times*, Marina was offered the chance of succeeding to his position; and she had to accept, although she did so with regret for she enjoyed her time at Bracken House.

In the early days after the move of the *FT* into Bracken House Oliver Poole suggested that we should embark on a policy of acquiring pictures to adorn the offices, particularly the lengthy stretches of corridor. A ceiling of £2,000 a year was set, which in 1959 was a fair sum. Denys Sutton was asked to help with advice, and for a year or two he did so. I laid it down, in order to have some kind of guidelines, that any picture acquired must be by a living British artist, British being taken to include any foreigner who had made his home in the UK. Denys was most helpful at first, but then lost interest. As things evolved I found far more often than not that I made the choice of picture (although Pat Gibson was responsible for our acquiring a splendid painting by Anne Redpath and one or two others), and I got much pleasure from going around the art galleries, and selecting pictures as though I were a collector in my own right. With the increase in prices, it became more difficult, until one day a bright member of Gordon Newton's editorial staff, James Joll, who together with the formidable John Gardiner at that time wrote the Lex investment column, said, 'Why don't you go in for lithographs?', and sent me off to see a pioneering friend of his called Joe Studholme of Editions Alecto. A fresh world opened out, and a string of new names were added to the collection, many of them by now internationally famous. At that time it was still relatively rare for companies to decorate their offices in this way. Now it is more or less standard practice and it can be justly claimed that we gave a lead. In 1972 we showed a selection of our pictures at the Brod gallery in St James's Street. Marina Vaizey helped me make the choice. Grouped together they did not look at all bad. The

FT gave up making further acquisitions after I retired, I expect because there was no more wall space.

A curious feature of the circulation of the *FT* has always been that the Saturday issue sold far more copies than were sold on any other day of the week. At one time the difference was about 40 per cent. It arose for two reasons. First, there were people who had the paper delivered regularly each day to their offices, for purposes of record, but wanted a copy at home at the weekend. Second, there were those who only bought the paper once a week in order to keep in general touch with markets and who were specially catered for on Saturdays because we published a detailed record of the week's Stock Exchange dealings. To serve these people further, Gordon conceived the idea of giving the Saturday issue much more of a weekly magazine flavour. This development was viewed with some alarm by the staff of the *Investors Chronicle*, which was part of our group. However, their attitude could not be allowed to stand in the way.

Gordon's idea was to introduce a whole range of leisure features, and the development of his plans was much helped by his engagement of Sheila Black, a woman of exceptional talent, who had herself made the suggestion that she should be taken on to the staff to fill the position of woman's editor, something which in all the long years of its history the *FT* had never had. She proposed a weekly feature to appear on Saturdays designed to help people with their shopping. Gordon christened the feature 'How to Spend It'. The idea was splendid, and so was the execution. It was not long before Sheila's room became so full of samples of every sort that one could scarcely get in or out. But her talents went well beyond the shopping basket. She was really a pioneer in developing understanding between producers and consumers. There was no subject to which she could not turn her hand. She could both assimilate, and write. She also had enormous personal courage, proposing many weird assignments for herself, such as swimming the English Channel as part of a team. To the editorial staff she became a sort of sister-confessor: and for everyone she had helpful words, because she was both kind and infinitely resourceful. Her departure from the *FT* after Gordon retired from the editorship in 1973 was a particular blow.

As well as developing the Saturday paper, Gordon also introduced coverage of sporting events, although this in the main had to be on a very sporadic basis, because of the enormous cost. To do it on the massive scale of, for instance, the *Daily Telegraph*, would have cost us many thousands of pounds with no compensating return. Therefore it was a question of engaging a series of contributors to write regularly about cricket, football, golf and tennis, concentrating only upon major events and not attempting to be comprehensive. The one exception was racing for which Gordon introduced a daily commentary, with tips of course but without the detailed programmes, written at first by the admirably named Dare Wigan, who after a few years handed over to his knowledgeable son Dominic. Gordon effectively was his own sports editor. He was actively interested in golf and fishing, but took a general interest over the whole field. There was one less obvious sport he felt must not be ignored. This was sailing. He foresaw the immense growth in the ownership of private boats of all shapes and sizes, and he decided that there should be regular coverage of the subject. By a happy chance there was on the editorial staff an enthusiastic and intrepid yachtsman named David Prior-Palmer, a cousin of the famous Lucinda, who found us a very good yachting correspondent, Alec Beilby, but whose main achievement (in this field) was to enthuse me enough to persuade my colleagues on the board to authorize the spending of some £25,000 on the building of a trimaran yacht (christened *FT*) in which David could compete in the *Observer*'s singlehanded transatlantic sailing race. He was emphatic that he would win, and that this would be marvellous publicity for the *FT*; and, although he was not first overall, he was seventh, being first in his class as well as the first Briton to complete the course. David was one of the few members of the *FT* staff to have been at Eton, but he was always eager to play down his background, and he quickly dropped the Prior from his surname, becoming plain Palmer. He had astonishing determination, and he was a model of conscientiousness. When I retired from the *FT* in 1975 he was in charge of the news desk. He is now particularly concerned with plans for the Europeanization of the *FT*. He can go as far as his defiant nature permits him.

As well as covering outdoor sports, Gordon Newton did not neglect the tremendous interest in the indoor pastime of contract bridge; and with his usual talent for identifying gifted writers he persuaded E. P. C. Cotter, who wrote elsewhere as Pat Cotter, to join the ranks of *FT* contributors. His weekly bridge notes became a major Saturday *FT* draw, as they are to this day. For me they were just right, drawing sensible deductions from real play. The standard of my own bridge playing is best illustrated by a remark made to me by the late Iain Macleod, whose book *Bridge is an Easy Game* I had bought, full of expectant hope, but finding it very hard to follow; and then when I asked him how he had dared to give his book such a misleading title he replied, 'To make people like you buy it!' Later, chess notes were also added to the Saturday paper, but that I think was by Gordon's successor, Fredy Fisher, whose skill at both chess and bridge is considerable. However, his succession was still some years off.

Chapter 16

There is one aspect of my working life which emanated directly from my association with the *FT* and which deserves more than a passing mention. A year or so before Brendan's death Herbert Tingay, the chief executive of George Newnes, suggested that the *FT* might be interested in entering into partnership in the exhibition organizing business. Through a company named National Trade Press, Newnes owned a number of trade periodicals, which were at that time in the care of Vere Sherren, whom I mentioned a few pages back. Some of the periodicals were already associated with exhibitions concerned with their particular industries. From the point of view of the *FT*, Herbert Tingay's approach seemed to offer a valuable possibility of diversification, giving us access to a wider public, and helping our image as an industrial rather than a purely financial paper. Had it not been Tingay himself who made the proposal I doubt whether Brendan's reaction would have been so positive. But Tingay was a man for whom Brendan had developed great admiration and affection, as indeed did all of us who had dealings with him. One felt instinctively that he was fair-minded and wholly dependable. He had so to speak risen from the ranks, but he was very much a commanding officer. His appearance always put me in mind of a friendly hen. In character he was simple and unpretentious, with a quiet, calm, rather lethargic manner; but one knew that if he said that Newnes would take a given line of action, that was the end of the matter, and they would do so. In the periodical publishing business he was very much a father figure.

Fortunately, with their eyes always set on expansion, our new controlling shareholders favoured a positive response to Tingay's approach. It was agreed that I should be chairman of Industrial & Trade Fairs, as the new company was to be called; and at Herbert Tingay's suggestion we also invited in as partners Beck & Pollitzer, who acquired a 20 per cent stake in the company, while Newnes and the *FT* each took 40 per cent. Beck & Pollitzer was a sizable business engaged in every kind of movement of goods, as well as in exhibition standfitting. At that time it was owned by the Pollitzer family. They were represented on the board of ITF by the head of the family, George Pollitzer, and also by Stanley Bingham, who like everyone working for Pollitzer addressed

him and referred to him as 'Mr George'. Pollitzer's business had been founded
in Victorian times, but he did a lot to help it on its way. In appearance and
personality he resembled a successful financier with civic aspirations, florid in
the face and spruce in his dress. In about 1968 Beck & Pollitzer was acquired by
a large public company called Transport Development Group, which engaged
in road haulage on a huge scale, and had been built up by a very modest, very
able Congregationalist named Philip Henman, whom I met through 'Mr
George'. Henman was about as lacking in side as can be imagined. He had
achieved a substantial fortune, but spent very little on himself; however he
assisted many good causes, including three of concern to me, the World Theatre
Season, the Royal Ballet School, and the City of London Festival. The first of
these, the creation of Peter Daubeny, brought a wide range of leading theatrical
companies to London from all over the world for an eight-week season at the
Aldwych Theatre. It had been sponsored initially by the *Sunday Telegraph* since
the first season coincided with the courageous launching of that newspaper by
Michael Berry.* After a year or two they discontinued support and I suggested
to my *FT* colleagues that we should step into the breach, for I believed it to be
a very worthwhile enterprise, something with which association on our part
would help to show the breadth of our interests. Also I had enormous admiration
for Peter Daubeny for his vision, as well as for his courage and determination.
We felt obliged to limit our commitment, however, and it was thus that
Henman came in with significant help. (In parenthesis I should like to say that
I regard it as cause for great regret that there is no official body with funds
available to assist visits by leading foreign companies, a much-needed service not
embraced within the Charters of either the Arts Council or British Council.)
At the Royal Ballet School, the source of dancers for many companies besides
Covent Garden, there was need for finance to engage the services of a visiting
professor of male dancing. Again Henman helped to make it possible with an
annual grant which persisted for several years. As to the City of London
Festival, I had been asked in 1966 by the then Lord Mayor to become the first
chairman of this venture. Its purpose was to show the world that the City
was interested in the Arts as well as lucre. Ian Hunter, most ingenious deviser of
festivals, had originally proposed the idea to the City Corporation, finding a
welcome reception from that austere body. He thought that it would be good
to do for the violin what Leeds had done for the piano. Accordingly he suggested that the Carl Flesch violin competition should be internationalized and
given enhanced importance. This meant above all generous prizes, and here too
Henman helped to provide prize money, unobtrusively as was his wont. Thus
the approach by Herbert Tingay and the introduction of Beck & Pollitzer as our

* Created Lord Hartwell in 1968.

partners resulted in the conferment of unexpected benefits upon three most improbable recipients.

The involvement of the *FT* in the world of exhibition organizing also provided the occasion for the entry into our group of the man who fourteen years later was to succeed me in charge of it. This was Alan Hare. In 1961 his elder brother John*, a friend of mine since school days, who was married to a sister of our controlling shareholder and was a member of the parent company board, came to see me. He told me that Alan was planning to leave the Foreign Service, and he asked whether there might be a suitable opening for him with the *FT*. I explained that the staff on the management side was extremely small, a mere handful. I thought however that there might be scope with the exhibition company, which was growing. Alan came to see me. He was obviously very bright and he produced the most fascinating convoluted sentences, to which I had to pay close attention in order not to get lost. It was agreed that he should join ITF with the particular task of researching new projects. He buckled to with a will, but in fact he only stayed nine months with ITF, because an important vacancy arose at the *FT* where we required at short notice a new foreign manager: and it seemed to me that Alan with his wide-ranging acquaintance and cosmopolitan outlook would do very well despite his lack of newspaper experience. Thus he joined the *FT*, and did an excellent job building up the foreign department, recruiting skilfully, and doing much to swell our revenue from overseas sources, where it seemed to me that our opportunities for real growth must lie. When Jim Hunter, the general manager, retired in 1966, Alan took his place, following me in turn as managing director in 1971.

I served as chairman of ITF for twenty years. During that time the company grew by process of development and acquisition to be the leading exhibition organizing business in Britain; and, unlike many partnerships, at no point can I recall any kind of disharmony between the three partners. Vere Sherren had played an important part in getting the company into its stride, but after some five years he decided to devote himself exclusively to publishing. Fortunately we had anticipated the problem of succession. There was on the *FT* editorial staff an extremely able man named Ian Trafford, who held the position of industrial correspondent. He decided to abandon journalism for management. I was anxious that we should not lose his services, and I persuaded him to join the staff of ITF where we needed someone of his intellectual calibre and where I thought he might have interesting prospects. His decision was of crucial importance. He entered the exhibition world with eagerness. Through his experience as industrial correspondent of the *FT* he had acquired a wide knowledge of industry, and in his dealings with the various trade associations

* The Hon. John Hare, created Lord Blakenham in 1963.

he was able to speak to them on level terms. No one has ever been better at marshalling facts and setting them out in simple precise language with almost excessive thoroughness.

When he first became managing director it was jointly with Robert Boardman, a capable and agreeable man in charge of an exhibition company named F. W. Bridges which ITF acquired in 1961. Ian Trafford and Bob Boardman were joint managing directors from 1963 until 1967, but it was not easy for either of them since they did not blend temperamentally or intellectually, and when Boardman left to start his own business, Ian became the sole managing director. His time with ITF was marred by his unsuccessful struggle to persuade the various interested parties to commit themselves to the construction of a great new exhibition centre in the London area matching the facilities available on the Continent. He laboured heroically to bring the numerous interested parties, Government departments, local authorities, chambers of commerce, the Confederation of British Industry, as well as exhibition organizers and promoters, to reach the necessary agreements to make possible the construction of a splendid complex on the Crystal Palace site. There was plenty of goodwill but no money, everyone saying that it was someone else's responsibility. Then an ambitious contractor named Ronald Lyon worked out a plan and produced a superb model for a centre at Northolt in North West London. Again it was the same story, only more so, because by then the Birmingham Chamber of Commerce had shown real zeal for the National Exhibition Centre project; and the Labour Government was strongly attracted by the idea of moving the focal point for large-scale heavy industrial exhibitions away from London and agreed to give significant financial aid. This effectively killed all plans for a new centre in the London area. ITF was faced with the problem of its own office accommodation; and after much debate, with Gordon Newton the strongest advocate, we decided to move the offices of the company to the Birmingham area.

At about the same time, an urgent need arose for a new managing director of *The Economist*. I suggested to my colleagues that Ian would be just the right person. I felt that for him a change was important, and fortunately he had a very good deputy at ITF named Derek Lyons, a Methodist teetotaller from Northern Ireland, who was fully capable of succeeding him. Lyons had the unenviable task of supervising the move of the offices to Solihull, a dormitory town near Birmingham, where all the inhabitants seemed eminently respectable, house-proud, and well-to-do: and those members of the staff of ITF who agreed to move from London did not appear to regret their decision and would not wish to return.

As chairman of the company my role was to preside at the regular monthly meetings, and to make myself generally available for consultation and also for attendance at a strange assortment of functions. These in the main were not exactly exhilarating, and I never came to enjoy looking round the various exhibitions, finding it repetitious and fatiguing. There was the occasional light moment, as for instance at a dinner at the Mansion House before the opening of a huge printing machinery exhibition known for short as IPEX. Our guest of honour was Lord Gladwyn. He had been asked to make a speech in honour of 'The Printed Word'. After a perfunctory reference to Caxton, his lordship moved on to his favourite theme 'The Common Market', for which he fought so manfully; he spoke at considerable length. Gradually the audience became restless, until it became hard to hear what was being said. When he came to his peroration, he said, 'Finally, Mr Chairman . . .', and his voice was drowned by a chorus of *hear, hears*. I was sitting beside him, and when he sat down I said, 'Jolly well done, Gladwyn,' which was perhaps slightly exaggerated praise. His reply, though, was beautiful. 'Anyway, it will look alright in print,' as indeed, I must say, it did.

My most agreeable memories are of two visits abroad in connection with important exhibitions organized by our company overseas. The first was at Moscow in 1961 and the second at Peking in 1964. Both exhibitions had a strong pioneering element about them. The Americans had held the first ever foreign exhibition in Moscow. They had built two halls which were too small for our needs. The facilities were very poor, and we had to show them the way: and this included the provision of a detailed specification to enable the Moscow City Soviet to erect a further building capable of housing large engineering exhibits. Also we had to arrange for the movement and display, and subsequent sale of the exhibits themselves. Preparing the first exhibition was pretty nightmarish, but everything was ready in time for the opening. Then came the question who would be present at the opening ceremony; which member of the Praesidium would honour us? The night before, we were told that *no one* would come, and in the morning there was no word until suddenly, half an hour before the opening, a message was received telling us to expect pretty well the entire Central Committee of the Party. And sure enough dead on time a convoy of cars drove up containing Khrushchev, Mikoyan, Kosygin and others: twelve or more in all. We all sat on the dais erected in the open in front of the first building: speeches of conventional politeness were made, while cold sleet drove in our faces; and then Khrushchev commenced his tour, winning over all the exhibitors by his bluff and seemingly direct approach.

While in Moscow, I did not see a ballet performance because the Bolshoi Ballet company had only recently visited London, but I went twice to the Bolshoi Theatre, to see two opera productions, both with strangely dated costumes and decor, hardly surprising when producers and designers from abroad were so rigorously excluded; and apart from some fine basses it seemed to me that the singing was more memorable for vibrato than for beauty of tone. For me by far the best entertainment that I saw was the Armenian Circus, a series of acts of astonishing skill and fantasy, the most bizarre consisting of a hippopotamus which knelt down as a zebra ran round the ring, jumping over it, while a brilliantly coloured parrot carried on a running commentary. What stuck in my mind most was a short talk I had with Kosygin at a reception given for the Exhibition. He had been in besieged Leningrad during the war, when for nearly three years the city was encircled by the Germans. I asked if they could get fish from the Baltic. 'Of course not,' he said, 'it was frozen over.' 'What then did you eat?' I asked, to which he replied with one word, '*Wood*', leaving me completely silent.

The fact that ITF did a good job as organizer for the British Exhibition in Moscow confirmed our appointment to assist with the organization of a return exhibition in London a few months later which the Russians decided to hold. They were determined to put on a very lavish if predictable show, but in order to draw maximum attention to it we suggested that they should send over Yuri Gagarin, the first man in space, for the launching ceremony. As chairman of ITF I was deputed to meet him. Curiosity to see and greet him was intense. The time of his arrival was known in advance to the public, so that the route into London from Heathrow airport was thickly lined. I sat in the front seat of an open car, a Rolls-Royce specially numbered YG 1, while Gagarin stood behind me. Everyone wanted to show their admiration for this courageous man, loving his frank open face with its eager smile. Flowers were in season, so he was pelted; and in the front seat of the car I sat under a cascade. Afterwards, at a luncheon in his honour, I asked him why he had not brought his wife. He told me that they had had a child a few weeks before, and hence she was breast-feeding, a subject upon the importance of which he then treated me to a lecture. Having been undecided at first, Her Majesty's Government ended quite rightly by giving Gagarin a very full dose of official hospitality, including his being received by the Queen.

My other visit was to Peking, where our company was asked to mount an engineering exhibition. In fact I visited Peking before the exhibition opened. I went as a matter of courtesy, but more particularly as a matter of curiosity. I flew out via Singapore, spending a day there with the chief Far Eastern representative of Reuters, arriving just as the daily rainstorm had occurred, so that for a brief period the streets were rivers of mud. Beyond its strategic significance it was hard to see any obvious charm in Singapore. My chief memories are of a weird garden filled with hideously realistic models of animals and men, a kind of oriental Disneyland, created by the family that had made a fortune from a product named Tiger Balm, which was supposed to be a cure for all ailments; and then of a street in which on the one side were primitive shelters for the aged, with bunks ranged three tiers high, while across the street coffins were made, a number standing outside ready for instant use.

From there I flew to Hong Kong, where, thanks to the kindness of John Keswick, I was housed in an apartment used by the chairman of Jardine Matheson, a business trading on a huge scale in the Orient, of which John was very much the moving spirit, returning regularly to China despite the expropriation suffered by his company, for he had a passionate love of the country. I had arranged to meet him in Peking. He was chairman of the committee sponsoring the exhibition and was journeying out via the trans-Siberian railway, accompanied by his wife Clare, and the bold, very handsome Lady Alexandra Metcalfe, a daughter of Lord Curzon and the widow of 'Fruity' Metcalfe, the man who was so shamefully treated by King Edward VIII.* John had most kindly proposed that a young Chinese working for Jardines should accompany me as interpreter. To reach Peking from Hong Kong it was obligatory to travel via Canton. First, though, I spent a few days in Hong Kong, in many ways a credit but also a terrible discredit to Britain. With a population of well over 4 million, almost wholly Chinese, packed into 400 square miles, the evidence of overcrowding was alarming. The vast majority seemed to live packed together in old tenement houses, but there were also many tall blocks of flats standing like concrete sentinels. One of these I visited. It had no lifts because the building was *only* eight storeys high, latrines were primitive, flushed at twenty-minute intervals by sea water; and the living area of 120 square feet allowed to a family of four for all purposes was no larger than an average-sized bedroom at home. Social security scarcely existed. The hours of work were long and arduous, and the working week was six if not seven full days. It seemed a caricature of capitalism, with exploiter and exploited both Chinese. Communist China was much in evidence, owning several large stores selling its products, masterly examples of ancient skills; the Bank of China occupied what seemed by far the tallest building, and indeed Chinese trade through Hong Kong was on a colossal scale, China not only supplying the bulk of Hong Kong's food and materials and water, but also doing a massive entrepôt business, which they clearly wish to retain.

Before leaving for Canton, I met Fritz Koo, the young interpreter attached to me by Jardines. He had been named Fritz by his German foster-mother, who had cared for him when he had lost his parents in Shanghai. He was quite young, with a charming alert face, sensitive and perceptive, speaking several Chinese dialects, as well as perfect English. We set off together. At the frontier railway station, we were shown briefly into the waiting room, the chief feature of which

* The story is admirably told in Frances Donaldson's book, *Edward VIII*.

was a large table piled high with a range of freely available pamphlets, written in many languages, either extolling Chairman Mao, or denigrating the West, or, more gratifyingly, denouncing the Soviet Union, for it was not long after the withdrawal of thousands of Russian technicians, upon whom at the time China was seriously dependent.

The first stage of our journey was quite short. Arriving in Canton we were taken to a colossal hotel, with a lobby as big as a ballroom, containing not one single piece of furniture. The hotel only came alive for the Canton trade fair, which Fritz Koo was obliged to attend regularly for Jardines. At the time of our visit there was no fair, and only one corner of one floor of the hotel was open. It had a desolate feeling. The city itself, once the colourful opium-trafficking capital of the south, seemed lifeless, hot and smelly. We had to spend the night there. Before leaving Hong Kong I had been warned that we might be stuck in Canton for several days because at the time the Chinese were using obsolete Russian aircraft said to have rather primitive instruments, and at any hint of bad weather flights were cancelled. Sure enough we heard that the weather was bad, and that our flight was unlikely to go. There was a Frenchman heading for Peking to sell mining machinery, and he shared my wish to press on. I asked Fritz if we could go by train. This by dint of enormous efforts on his part was arranged. Thus the three of us found ourselves in a four-bunk compartment, the only foreigners in an immensely long jam-packed train, proceeding gently, stopping everywhere, a journey of over forty-eight hours. For miles the countryside seemed to consist of nothing but an unending vista of ricefields, tended by wide straw-hatted peasants, and irrigated by pedal-wheels which were operated by foot. At no point was there a trace of a vehicle of any kind. It seemed that it must have been just the same for thousands of years. Gradually as we moved towards the north the country changed, rice giving way to other crops. Whenever the train stopped, we walked on the platform. All the Chinese that we saw appeared to be constantly smiling, and they looked thoroughly contented. Everything would have been splendid, had it not been for the incessant propaganda talk and marching music, broadcast very loud, into every compartment in the train: and also had I not developed some kind of food poisoning, probably from a fish restaurant in Hong Kong, succumbing to a pretty agonizing pain, which was not helped by there being only one washroom cum toilet for the whole crowded carriage. Fritz felt personally responsible for me. He massaged my back and stomach in a very expert way and gave me some strange orange granules, a Chinese herbal preparation. It was to little purpose. I struggled with chopsticks but not even plain boiled rice could I eat. I developed a fever. Somehow Fritz must have sent a message to the Embassy, and when we arrived in Peking a grey-uniformed Queen Alexandra's nurse appeared, accompanied us to the hotel, and administered antibiotics. For the best part of two days I was in bed. Peking was very cold, with the wind blowing from the Gobi desert; although doors and windows were shut, a fine film of dust spread over everything in my room, and so I learnt why so often in pictures the Chinese were seen wearing white masks covering mouth and nose. John Keswick had arrived at the hotel, and after my recovery he took me with him to see various officials and to attend various formal meals. To the food I could not adapt myself, save for Mandarin duck, which I found delicious, nor to Chinese rice wine, which to be drinkable at all had to be kept warm. The only form of starch in the meal was a plain bowl of rice served at the end, but I was told that to eat it was rude since it suggested that one had lacked adequate nourishment. Even with an interpreter, conversation was very hard, and the best thing for me was that instantly the meals were over the Chinese all left for home.

I did my share of sightseeing, but the cold was too great for any real enjoyment. The charm of the people was well concealed. Men and women wore thickly padded uni-sex overalls and jackets, and when I was there any attempt at personal beautification was severely frowned upon. Most of the women wore their hair in short pigtails jutting out at right angles to their head. Socks seemed ostentatiously in need of darning. Drabness was obligatory.

Finally, despite much drinking of tea, we were never able to gain admittance to the building in which our exhibition was to take place. No clear-cut reason was given, but another exhibition was being held there, and it was evidently thought undesirable that we should see this. But we never knew why. My journey was thus made to seem pretty pointless, although I am very pleased that I made it. John stayed behind in China, to continue on his travels; I returned to Hong Kong with Fritz, fortunately by air this time. I was there for a couple more days, spending a most delightful evening with a young, glamorous high-class Chinese lady on the staff of Jardines, immensely bright, educated and elegant. We dined in the restaurant at the top of the Mandarin Hotel, with a view across the water to the crowded city, the bright gay lights obliterating the congestion and the squalor, curiously like those travel advertisements in which one never quite believes, an agreeable finale to a too brief visit.

On the return journey to London, I had arranged to stay at Kuala Lumpur with two good friends, Antony and Dot Head. He was then British High Commissioner to Malaysia, after a diversified career, having been a distinguished soldier, and having held senior ministerial office, regrettably from his point of view, at the time of Suez, the episode which always seemed to me the real climacteric in Britain's postwar decline. Before going to Malaysia, Antony had been High Commissioner in Nigeria at a critical time in that country's history. After he left Kuala Lumpur, he retired from public life when he was still too

25 Bracken House

26 St Paul's Cathedral at night – the view from Bracken House

27 My father at his desk at the Ministry of Economic Warfare

28 Oliver Lyttelton, created Viscount Chandos

29 Brendan Bracken in front of 10 Downing Street
after appointment as Minister of Information in July 1941

30 Sir Robert Sinclair, chief executive of the Ministry of
Production, created Lord Sinclair of Cleeve

31 Brendan Bracken in the early 1950s

32 Geoffrey Crowther

33 Lionel Robbins

34 Abram Games' *FT* poster design

35 Sidney Henschel with a client

36 Group photograph at dinner given by Esmond Rothermere in May 1962 on Lord Beaverbrook's eighty-third birthday. He sits between Winston Churchill and Harold Macmillan. Standing, left to right, are Michael Hartwell, Langton Iliffe, Cecil King, Alec Jeans, Geoffrey Harmsworth, Seymour Camrose, Max Aitken, Roy Thomson, myself, Harry Roseberry and Esmond Rothermere, whose face is hidden.

37 Alan Hare and myself arriving for a meeting at the TUC, June 1970

38 Gordon Newton, with his 1970 Granada Television Special award, flanked by Fredy Fisher, his successor as editor, together with myself

A few scenes from the *FT* 25,000 Issue Dinner held at the Hilton Hotel on 11 November 1969

39 Making my speech with Jennie Lee and Alfred Beit beside me

40 Jack Jones arriving

41 Jeremy Thorpe between Lords Camrose and Thomson. Arnold Goodman is in the foreground.

42 Denys Sutton (left) with Sir Thomas Monnington, then President of the Royal Academy

43 Richard Powell being received by Lionel Robbins

44 Alan Hare with Lord Cowdray

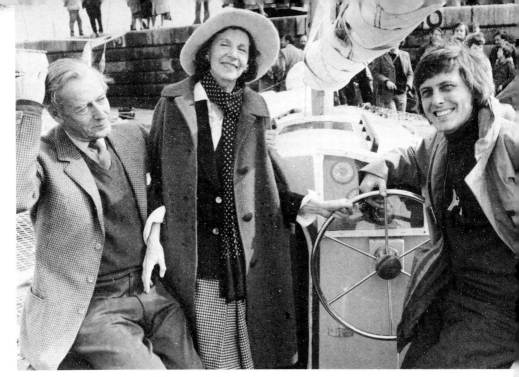

45 Joan and myself with David Palmer at the
launching of the trimaran *FT*

46 The *FT* garden at the Chelsea Flower Show,
1973

47 Joan with me at my farewell party in the *FT* canteen, March 1975. The card was a gift from my secretary Stevie Chisholm.

48 Arnold Goodman, Pat Gibson and myself before Pat's introduction to the House of Lords, 1975

young, accepting a peerage and withdrawing to the peace of Wiltshire, surrounded by birds and animals, with many charitable interests, but unable to
abide the hurly-burly. His disappearance from the scene is a real loss.

Arriving from the concrete of Hong Kong to the lush tropical green of
Malaysia was refreshing beyond words, all the more so because by chance a
fellow guest was the strikingly beautiful, venturesome Pamela Egremont,
whom I loved and admired. I had a brief but absorbing stay, seeing typical
examples of two important sources of advertisement revenue for the *Financial
Times*, a rubber plantation and a tin dredging property. (In the early days tin and
rubber companies were very numerous, and all used to advertise in the paper.)
While I was there a reception was given for the Prime Minister, Tunku Abdul
Rahman; and I was fascinated by the blend of different races, Malay, Chinese and
Tamil, although it was clear that their mutual animosities were fierce.

There was one minor drama concerning a parrot. It was customary for Dot
and Antony to lunch out of doors under a straw cupola. A perch with two or
three parrots on it was always placed beside Dot. Suddenly a deluge of rain
started. The perch was abruptly moved by Antony's ADC, and one of the parrots,
Dot's favourite grey bird, took fright and flew off. Parrots instinctively, it seems,
make for the highest branch of whatever tree they are in; Dot's parrot was no
exception. In a corner of the garden was a jungle-like valley in which the parrot
alighted, making its way to the top of a tree. Dot installed herself on a camp stool
underneath and tried to coax the bird down. The next morning the parrot was
spotted at the top of a very tall palm tree in a public garden nearby. Antony's
Chinese butler, slim and agile, courageously carried up a cage containing the
parrot's mate, left it there, with the door of the cage open, hoping that the parrot
would be lured inside. But this failed; and by the time I left, the bird had still not
been recovered. Eventually though he was, and he is now living happily with
Lord and Lady Head in Wiltshire; as also is the courageous Chinese butler.

From Kuala Lumpur I flew to Bangkok, where I was to change to a Qantas
flight for London. Beside me in the aeroplane was sitting a Japanese girl, not
beautiful but delightful in appearance. We fell into conversation. She told me
that she was the owner of three night clubs in Tokyo and that she had been to
Manila to visit a boyfriend, returning via Singapore, Bangkok and Hong Kong,
quite a round trip. I told her that I had to be in Bangkok for some hours, so we
arranged to go sightseeing together, temples, river market, kite-flying, displays
of dancing, a mixture of splendour and squalor, *and* of mosquitoes. In the afternoon when it was very hot, we took a room together in a hotel, where we had
an agreeably amorous siesta. I should have liked to stay a few hours more, but
I had to leave for the airport. Once there I learnt that the Qantas flight was
delayed, so the passengers joining in Bangkok were transported to the KLM

rest house, being escorted by an exquisitely pretty Thai air hostess, who told me that she had been in the Royal dancing troupe: and after she had disposed of the other passengers she came to my room and showed me some of the strange sinuous arm and body movements of which her style of dancing largely consisted: but another siesta was unfortunately not in prospect. From the moment of my departure from London until my return home, the whole trip to and from Peking had lasted only three weeks, although it seemed far longer, so much had I seen and experienced that was entirely new to me.

There were two other involvements which followed directly from my association with the *FT*. One of these was the Institute of Directors. At the time of the first Labour Government after the war, a group of the most ardent supporters of free enterprise became aware of the Institute's existence. It had been granted a Royal Charter in the early years of the century but had been allowed to sink into a comatose state, with a membership of only a few hundred, run from a single room near Portland Place by a secretary of impeccable character but lacking sufficient drive or incentive. The leaders of the group were Bob Renwick and Louis Spears. Renwick was a highly successful stockbroker. During the war he had played an important role at the Ministry of Aircraft Production, and although his upbringing had been non-technical he had developed an understanding of technical subjects which enabled him to hold his own with the experts. His father had been prominent in the electrical supply industry before it was nationalized. Bob had succeeded him as chairman of the County of London Company and conducted a passionate but unsuccessful fight against its nationalization with the result that his hostility towards state ownership was intense. Later he was the chief protagonist in the successful campaign for the introduction of commercial television, in due course becoming chairman of ATV and profiting considerably, although only after a lengthy period of losses. Spears was a friend of Winston Churchill and had played an important part in both wars. He had two particular claims to fame. He was a brilliant writer, and he spoke impeccable French, both textbook and *patois*. His hatred of socialism was violent, largely because of loyalty towards Churchill. He and Bob Renwick took the main initiative over the rebirth of the Institute of Directors. They were both friends of Oliver Lyttelton, whom they persuaded to become President. I suppose that it was at Oliver's suggestion that I was first approached to join the Council and the Policy Committee. It seemed to me that my joining would be helpful to the *FT*, a view shared by Brendan. Thus in 1948 I commenced an association with the Institute which was to continue with only a brief interruption until 1976. It gave me a good deal of interest and enjoyment, and it pleased me to be connected with a body which grew steadily from a membership of 500 to over 40,000.

Its true usefulness was impossible to judge, but that it became a significant force is certain. The chief credit for this is due to Richard Powell, a distinguished looking Old Etonian baronet who had won two Military Crosses during the war, and afterwards had been given employment by Bob Renwick in a company formed to raise funds to be used for the purpose of upholding the rights of free enterprise in industry and commerce; and since the chief political party supporting the ideals of free enterprise was the Tory Party they were the main beneficiaries from his endeavours. When the post of director-general of the Institute fell vacant in 1954 Bob made Richard available. This proved to be an inspired appointment. He had no great intellectual attainments, but he had imagination and enthusiasm, and a passionate belief in what he was doing, a sort of revivalist fervour coupled with an engaging naïveté which carried everyone along with him. Among the others who joined the Policy Committee when I did were several strong believers in free enterprise, Ronnie Weeks, the chairman of Vickers, John Reiss, the head of Associated Portland Cement, almost Buchmanite in his ardour, Harley Drayton, a self-made tycoon who had started work as a lift boy in the city at the age of fourteen, and Charles Stanley, a pugnacious Irishman who had founded Pye Radio, and continued as it grew to treat it almost as though it was his own child.

We were a strangely assorted group. At meetings I used to feel like the odd man out, regularly urging the moderate course, occasionally being thanked by Louis Spears for having exercised a restraining influence when he wished impulsively to rush into print or action. I remember once, I think it was in 1964, that Richard Powell and I had to persuade him that a bowler-hatted march of directors up Whitehall, with umbrellas at the slope, would not be helpful to the cause. Then in 1970 we had a fearful *contretemps* when the Policy Committee were discussing what criteria to apply in deciding whether a director of a nationalized industry was eligible for membership. I thought they should all be admitted. Louis was very reluctant to admit any. He then made a suggestion that we might use as a criterion the test that Hitler applied to decide whether someone was Aryan, namely, that they should be given the benefit of the doubt if they had only one Jewish grandparent, and thus directors not wholly engaged in nationalized industry might be acceptable. I told Louis at the meeting that I thought his parallel was most unfortunate. Afterwards he wrote me a furious letter saying that he had deeply resented my ill-mannered and aggressive attitude, going on to say:

I am sometimes tempted to compare your frequent waspish pronouncements of today with the submissive if not fawning posture you adopted towards your late employer, Brendan Bracken. You may perhaps reflect sometimes that the latter paid best.

I wrote him a soothing reply as follows:

Thank you for your letter. All I said at the meeting of our Policy Committee was that I thought your analogy of Hitler's method of deciding whether or not somebody was a Jew was a most unfortunate one for you to use in the particular context of the subject under discussion. I do not feel in the least contrite, and you must not think that because I was the person who spoke I was the only one who thought as I did.

You have always been extremely kind to me, and I like you very much, even after the offensive final paragraph of your letter, which must have given you infinite pleasure to compose. Of one thing I would assure you – that if I had fawned upon Brendan he would not have tolerated it for very long.

To this he replied:

Funnily enough your letter gave me pleasure for it threw a strong light on the fact that fundamentally I am very fond of you and that it has been given to me to know a genuine and therefore a fearless aristocrat.

Thus peace was restored and within two years directors of nationalized industries did become eligible to join.

Very early on I was instrumental in negotiating the purchase of the magazine *The Director* from a company which had no particular links with the Institute and who would have had no redress if the Institute chose to produce its own magazine, as it had to do if we were to grow. *The Director* was not profitable at the time. It had no more than potential nuisance value, but we thought it wise to pay £2,000 to acquire the title, retaining its excellent editor, Eric Foster, and David Dreebin, who was in charge of advertising. Gratifyingly, over the years *The Director* grew to be an integral part of the Institute, while Foster became the person upon whom Richard Powell mostly relied as a sounding board for his ideas, as well as supervising the various specialized leaflets produced as a service to members. With the growth in membership of the Institute, a move to new premises became necessary. The first move was to modest offices in Westminster and from there Richard proposed a bold move to the elegant district of Belgravia, carrying us all along with him as we acquired the lease of first one, then two, three and eventually four large houses on the north side of Belgrave Square, where the members were provided not only with offices, but also a language centre, conference rooms, and excellent club facilities. He also started a medical check-up unit under a lively doctor named Beric Wright which after some years was integrated into the new BUPA centre. His most spectacular initiative was to organize an annual Institute of Directors

Conference. The first conference was held in a room in a hotel, after which we moved to the Festival Hall, and finally very boldly to the Albert Hall, where despite its size Richard contrived always to fill its five thousand seats by persuading political, industrial and religious leaders as well also as Prince Philip and the Prince of Wales to come and address the membership. The expectations of the members were immediately aroused as they filed in before the start of the conference by the playing of stirring tunes on the organ; and then again after we had consumed our cardboard box luncheon and before the conference resumed for the afternoon session there was more organ music. It would be impossible to argue that the conference ever did much to alter the course of history, but it was always useful as a sounding board and it certainly helped to make the members feel that they belonged to a significant group the existence of which mattered, despite frequent political evidence to the contrary. There is no doubt that Richard Powell was a great showman, and he would really have been better employed promoting the best of Britain to the world at large. When he retired in 1974 much of the spark went out of the Institute. It saddened me that he left in a state of unhappiness. He had put so much of himself into the place that he could not picture things functioning when he was no longer there. His departure coincided with the real take-off of inflationary pressures, which like plenty of others he had failed to foresee; and therefore his successor had the gloomy task of putting up the Institute's subscription very sharply indeed twice in two years.

After the death of Bob Renwick in 1973 Louis Spears urged me to become chairman, but I was too committed elsewhere, and I declined. A couple of years later I agreed to become president, feeling that I had a certain duty in this regard; and so I presided at one conference in the Albert Hall, I hope with reasonable success. But without Richard as the impresario the hall was only half full. A few months afterwards I relinquished the presidency: I had under-taken various other tasks and I felt in any event that the Institute's new genera-tion could better work out their own solutions without a member of the old guard interfering.

A major break with the image of the past was to come with the decision to dispose of the Institute's Belgrave Square premises and to move into the building in Pall Mall formerly housing the United Services Club, a move which I wholeheartedly supported. Looking ahead, I think there is a strong case for there being some kind of joining together of the Institute of Directors and the British Institute of Management. There is inevitably an overlap between the services that the two bodies render, and the distinction between directors and managers is at many points blurred. If there were a close association or even merger, the services rendered could be improved, while in public statements the position of 'management' could be advanced with greater authority, and membership of various government bodies would be easier to justify. It would also be possible for there to be a very much stronger publication than now exists: and it must be said that the economy measures taken at the Institute of Directors had a most enfeebling effect on *The Director*, whereas *Management Today*, brilliantly edited by Robert Heller, in which both the *FT* and *The Economist* at one time had a quarter share until we were effectively frozen out, has succeeded in preserving its quality.

The other involvement stemming from the *FT* was my nomination in 1963 to the board of Reuters, and it was a direct consequence of my membership of the Newspaper Publishers Association. This remarkable news agency was founded in 1851 by a German Jew from Kassel, who changed his name from Josaphat to Reuter, became a Christian and settled in England. At the start he concentrated on the transmission of Stock Exchange prices between London and the Continent, Rothschilds being his first recorded customer. The business expanded and flourished until the start of the First World War, when it ceased being a family business, and its survival was secured by the purchase of its capital with the help of borrowed money by Roderick Jones, an ambitious reporter on the staff, and Mark Napier, the chairman of the company, who had been on the board for many years. Jones very probably saved Reuters from extinction, but he was far from popular. After the war he tried to persuade the British press as a whole to acquire the business. Only the provincial press, to whom Reuters' foreign news was a necessity, were at that time willing; and in 1925 the Press Association, which is owned collectively by the provincial press, became majority shareholders. The national press did not enter upon the Reuter scene until 1941, after Jones had resigned his position owing to a disagreement relating to the acceptance of Government aid necessary, as he saw it, to keep Reuters afloat during the Second World War when foreign revenue dried up. The board of the company, with William Haley, then of the *Manchester Guardian*, playing a leading role, believed that the agency's freedom would be imperilled. Jones was confident that he could preserve its independence, but his point of view was not upheld and he resigned. At that point the Newspaper Proprietors Association came into the discussions, and the upshot was that Reuters became jointly owned by both the national and the provincial press.

At the end of the war there was some thought of making Reuters a sort of Commonwealth agency. In 1946 the press of Australia and New Zealand acquired an interest, and in 1948 India followed, although the latter connection was short-lived because of disagreement over the extent of the Indians' say in relation to Reuters' activities in South East Asia. From the time that Reuters ceased being privately owned, it was agreed that it should trade on a non-profit-making basis, the various partners being 'assessed' for their respective shares of the cost of running the agency, the assessments being sufficient to enable the company to cover its costs but no more. This policy was acceptable so long as Reuters operated on a limited basis, but it became unrealistic as the growth in services to non-newspaper clients developed. Reuters had for many years provided a limited financial news service. The true growth came after the appointment of Gerald Long as general manager in 1963, and since this was only a few months before I joined the board I had the opportunity of observing the way in which his entrepreneurial skill transformed the business, taking Reuters into a commanding position as a supplier of economic and financial news, until by 1977 well over three-quarters of the turnover came from that source. The company's world-wide ramifications developed quite remarkably, and they are clearly still doing so. Gerry Long had the good luck to meet a highly inventive American named Robert Sinn who foresaw many of the new techniques which were going to revolutionize the transmission of news and the storage and retrieval of information. But had he not met Sinn I have little doubt that he would have met someone else working on similar lines, turning the encounter to equal advantage.

One thing that was self-evident was that these new techniques could not be had on the cheap. Capital would be needed, and this was not forthcoming from the shareholders. Outside borrowing would clearly be necessary but the board felt that it had to be kept to a minimum. Therefore Reuters, which in the past had not attempted to earn profits, must through its own trading generate as much cash as possible, and this meant that an entirely new attitude on the part of the board was necessary. In so far as possible, I gave Gerry all the support that I could in his determination to bring Reuters through into a new profit-conscious high-technology era, even backing him when he decided that we must attack the American market on its home ground. Enormous progress has been made. The company now has a turnover approaching £60 million a year, and is earning a seven-figure profit, all of which goes back into technical development: but I am convinced that it is only at the foothills.

During my fifteen years on the board there were only two chairmen, John Burgess from Cumberland, a courteous man without great cutting edge; and Bill Barnetson, a shrewd and canny Scot, who from being a radio and television commentator in Edinburgh and also editor of the *Edinburgh Evening News*, was persuaded by the afore-mentioned Harley Drayton to come to London; and has developed into being chairman of an important provincial newspaper group, chairman of the *Observer*, and a director of a large number of significant companies, adjusting himself to his ever expanding glory without a trace of difficulty. He was instrumental in my remaining on the Reuter board after I was retired from the *FT*. In general he has been a good friend, for which I am grateful to him; and therefore it pleased me when together with Arnold Goodman I was able to act as one of his sponsors when he first took his seat in the House of Lords.*

* Arnold and I also performed this service with considerable pleasure for Pat Gibson and Max Rayne.

Chapter 17

My major disappointment during the thirty years in which I was managing director or chief executive of the *FT* concerned the abortive attempt to effect a merger with *The Times*. The opportunity arose in the spring of 1966, an unhappy time for me because on 18 March my mother died very suddenly after an internal haemorrhage. Her neighbour Dr Jack Spira arranged for her immediate removal to St Mary's Hospital, Paddington, and then telephoned to me. Joan and I went to her bedside; but she did not recover consciousness and that same afternoon she died. It was a mercy that she died so quickly, for her life had become rather empty and she would have been a most difficult invalid. I experienced the same sense of guilt that I did when my father died, reproaching myself for not spending more time with her. I do not think that she herself felt neglected by me, for she knew that the newspaper and the opera house were both very demanding. She was a woman of great generosity of spirit, whose life was marred by her impulsiveness and her desperate inability to judge the character of others. By her express wish she was cremated, and her ashes were distributed from the air over the English Channel, in memory perhaps of her numerous friendships with aviators and her many experiences on the Continent. A few weeks after her death a group of white daffodils which she had given us the previous autumn flowered for the first time under a tall white cherry tree in the garden, and regularly each spring they return as a reminder and memorial.

While I was attending to her obsequies, I was also working very hard upon all aspects of the possible merger with *The Times*. It was widely known that the newspaper was making substantial losses, and that its circulation was wilting. The Labour Party had just won the General Election, and the business and financial communities were downcast. The prospects for revenue for those newspapers mainly dependent upon advertising, meaning above all *The Times* and *FT*, were not brilliant. However, unlike *The Times*, the *FT* was making good profits, and the outlook seemed reasonably fair – unless control of *The Times* were to pass into other hands which, with fresh resources and a new look, might then present a threat of unexpected competition. I realized that the *FT* had had a good run, having built itself a position that was basically extremely

strong, and having enjoyed a degree of success which far exceeded my expectations. However self-satisfaction was a mood which I constantly resisted, for I
was always fearful that something might happen to disturb our happy state.
Despite rumours about Lord Kemsley's intentions I was certain that no one would
have the hardihood to start up a rival business or financial newspaper, because
I knew the immense nightly effort which went into the production of the *FT*.
The supply of specialized journalistic and indeed advertising talent was simply
not available, and I was confident that our staff would not leave us for some new
and unproven venture. At the same time I was very much aware that because
of our specialized nature we were inescapably bound to remain a second newspaper. The *FT* certainly carried much general news, and the volume of foreign
news which we published was in terms of columnage higher than any other;
but when it came to sport, the law courts, social news and so on we did not
attempt to compete. To have done so on top of providing all our specialized
business news coverage would have crippled us financially. We should have
needed a limitless purse to draw readers away from *The Times* and the *Daily
Telegraph*, with no certainty of success after years of striving. It was our job to
try to produce the best possible business newspaper, interpreting the word
business as widely as possible, but we could never hope to give a complete
service. However, there was the constant possibility that following a change of
control *The Times* might greatly enlarge its business news coverage, and this in
times of difficulty could strike a hard blow at the *FT*. (A similar risk did not exist
in relation to the *Daily Telegraph*, because of its circulation of over one and a
quarter million, and the consequent cost to it in terms of paper and distribution
of adding several more business pages.)

   I was always apprehensive. Then one day I had a chance meeting with Kenneth
Keith, the head of Hill Samuel and financial adviser to Gavin Astor, who was
the proprietor of *The Times*. Kenneth hinted obliquely at the possibility of
acquiring control, and both he and I saw great attractions in the idea of bringing
two such leading papers together. Before speaking to any other colleagues I
spoke to Gordon Newton, our editor, and to Sidney Henschel, the advertisement director, whose judgements I respected as being far superior to my own
and above all whose support would be absolutely vital if the idea was to be
pursued. Both were enthusiastic. I then spoke to Lionel Robbins, the chairman
of the *FT*, who was sceptical because of his fear that we might be submerged
by the losses of *The Times*; and to Jim Hunter, the general manager, who surprised me by his somewhat irrational hostility to the proposal, while agreeing
that it must be examined. Next I saw Oliver Poole and Pat Gibson, both key
members of our board, Oliver being the managing director of our controlling
shareholder S. Pearson & Son, and Pat a powerful voice, especially important

because of his wide knowledge of the newspaper business. They agreed that talks should be opened.

William Haley, the editor of *The Times*, and George Pope, the general manager, had in the meantime been told of Kenneth Keith's talk with me, and both declared themselves to be strong supporters of the concept of a merger. During the ensuing weeks there were active discussions between those most closely concerned on both sides, the whole affair being treated for obvious reasons as highly confidential. Detailed estimates of revenue had to be prepared, and George Pope, Sidney Henschel and I worked together on these, being convinced as we went along that even on conservative assumptions a very significant total would be capable of achievement.

It was evident that if the two papers were to be merged there would only be a need for one production centre; and since the capacity of *The Times* plant was far greater than we had in Bracken House, and since also the *Observer* was printed on *The Times* presses, it was *prima facie* clear that production must be at Printing House Square. Besides this, I was increasingly concerned at the extravagantly high level of earnings of the *FT*'s compositors, which were an embarrassment in relation to the wages and salaries earned throughout the rest of the business. I believed that by moving the centre of production and merging the two production staffs significant economies would have been possible with only a few redundancies, and this view was shared by our head of printing, Alan Cox, who had extensive knowledge of the industry, and who, before he joined the *FT*, had been on the staff of *The Times* and therefore knew the principal personalities involved. Also the effect of moving production would have been to release for other use those areas of Bracken House required for printing. (At first I had hoped that our entire building would be freed, but *The Times* building was too small to absorb the whole of the *FT* staff.)

The estimates of costs which I worked out with George Pope of *The Times* and with the other members most closely concerned on both sides convinced me that, from the very start, the merged paper would be significantly more profitable than the *FT* alone, and I was confident that the shareholders would by no means suffer. I also believed that the new paper could achieve a degree of international importance which neither of the constituent parts could ever do on their own. In this view I was wholeheartedly backed by William Haley, who was at first extremely excited about the possibilities; a 'meeting of two equal partners' was a phrase he used – and he made this clear both to me, and also to Gordon Newton, with whom he had two or three meetings at which the shape of things to come, layout, disposition of contents and so on, was discussed in great detail. The key question to be decided was whether *The Times* and *FT* should each preserve their identity, the *FT* being printed as a separate section at the back of *The Times*: and we even explored the possibility of keeping its distinctive pink paper. This solution had to be discarded because although technically feasible it would have meant a too rigid control over the size of both sections and would have limited flexibility. Also, we foresaw nightly problems in deciding into which section stories of major economic importance should be placed. The two sections idea was clearly unworkable. The title to be preserved, all were agreed, must be *The Times*; but throughout its pages the paper would be strongly impregnated with the personality of the *FT*, and we of the *FT* increasingly came to feel that we would have to be the predominant force, while preserving and embodying the best features of *The Times*.

This change of emphasis undoubtedly lessened Haley's ardour. 'It's a take-over,' he said to Gordon Newton. Nevertheless he had meetings with Oliver Poole and agreed with him that in the event of a merger being achieved he (Haley) would become chairman of the company owning the paper, while Gordon Newton (editor of the *FT*) would become editor. I was to have been managing director.

The point came at which approval or otherwise of the board of S. Pearson & Son must be obtained if serious negotiations to determine acquisition values were to commence. A special meeting was held at the beginning of June 1966 to which I was invited. Lord Cowdray was in the chair. I deployed my case, not feeling that I was giving a very good account of myself. When I had finished, there was silence. Everyone waited for Lord Cowdray. After what seemed to me ages but was probably only a few seconds he said, 'I think it should be pursued.' And that was that, or rather that I hoped was that: at any rate if the lights were not at green, they were at least at amber, and we could move forward to the next stage.

One vital aspect which could not be overlooked concerned the Monopolies Commission. Under the regulations relating to the acquisition or merger of news-papers the transaction we were exploring was of such importance that it could certainly not have been achieved without the Commission's consent. It was therefore decided to seek assistance from Arnold Goodman. He came for a meeting with Oliver Poole and myself, and undertook that his services should be retained. 'We're on the rank,' was his agreeable expression. In the event no case could be submitted to the Commission because the merger terms offered to Gavin Astor were not accepted, but rightly or wrongly I did not feel that the Commission would be likely to withhold consent because no alternative proposal was then in sight and the closure of *The Times* seemed a real possibility.

The seriousness of Pearson's interest could at no point be doubted for in order to provide stability to the merged paper they proposed to form a new company into which their important provincial group, Westminster Press Provincial Newspapers, could be incorporated. Detailed valuations of assets were prepared and an elaborate scheme was worked out. Many hours were spent by the financial experts upon the numerous problems but the one overriding question was the valuation to be placed on *The Times* newspaper itself, because upon this depended the proportion to be held by Gavin Astor of the capital of the new company combining *The Times*, *FT* and Westminster Press: yet, beyond a valuation of the Printing House Square plant and buildings, which could be assessed, the value of the goodwill of *The Times* itself was something no one could scientifically measure. It was possible to argue that the figure should be a purely nominal one, or even negative, because of the losses *The Times* was incurring. An indication had been conveyed to us that if Gavin Astor were to be offered a $12\frac{1}{2}$ per cent or one-eighth interest in the combined group he would be willing to accept. However, the financial experts advising Pearsons suggested that his proportion should be no more than $8\frac{1}{4}$ per cent. I pleaded that this figure should be increased, because I was certain that it would not prove acceptable (in terms of assets as opposed to profits, figures suggested that one third of the assets of the new company would derive from *The Times*) and I felt that far more was at stake than a small percentage either way; but to no avail. The truth was that Pearsons were divided over their attitude towards the merger; otherwise I feel sure that the offer would have been improved. As it was, to the profound dismay of Gordon Newton, Sidney Henschel and myself the offer was duly and predictably declined. No increased figure was proposed and within a few weeks it was announced with a great flourish of trumpets that control of *The Times* had passed to Roy Thomson. I had had the strong impression that the Thomson solution would be *anathema* to William Haley, but he at once proclaimed that the joining together under one umbrella of *The Times* and the *Sunday Times* was something he had always desired: 'A Natural Marriage' was the title of his unctuous leading article on 1 October 1966. Gordon and I could not help feeling that this really was a bit uncalled for.

After the dashing of our hopes, my *FT* colleagues and I were fairly worried as to what might happen. Thomson announced that he was willing to spend umpteen million pounds to put *The Times* back on its feet, and it was not long before the blueprint was revealed. The plan evidently was to make a dead set at both the *FT* and the *Daily Telegraph*. These aims were of course incompatible. The business news was turned into a separate detachable section (back-set is the trade term), and a number of additional pages were added. They also started their own share index, and for a while stopped quoting the *FT* index which for years had been *the* stock market indicator. By trying to make the business section a newspaper within a newspaper two things happened. First, there was great uncertainty where to place certain items of news falling into the grey area which both those in charge of the main part of the paper and those in charge of the business section claimed as their responsibility. This as I said was a point we had already faced in our decision that if the merger had gone through we should only have had one paper. Secondly, there seemed to have been an instruction to get as many original news stories as possible, with the result that a number of non-scoops appeared, and in the early stages of the new regime the paper gained a reputation for inaccuracy which at the time was not undeserved.

The dead-set at the *Daily Telegraph* took the form of a massive circulation campaign. Immense sums of money were expended in a drive to build up the sale from the 250,000 at which it stood when control was acquired to a figure approaching 500,000. But the higher the sale was pushed the greater were the losses. Likewise, strenuous efforts were made to build up classified job advertising, which for many years had been a particular feature of the *Daily Telegraph* and one of its major strengths; but despite offers of attractive rates and a definite increase in the quantity of classified advertisements carried by *The Times* the attempt to make inroads into the *Telegraph*'s special preserves failed. After three or four years the separate Business News section was quietly discontinued: it was announced as being temporarily discontinued over one Christmas holiday period, but it never reappeared. At the same time the circulation was gradually allowed to fall back to a more realistic figure of between 300,000 and 350,000, the fall having been accelerated by fairly sharp selling price increases. And in its present format, without the separate section, without the non-scoops and the inaccuracies, with its impregnable correspondence and obituary columns, and with Bernard Levin, *The Times* is once more back on course.

The impact on the *FT* of the Thomson acquisition of *The Times* was in fact beneficial. It brought a fresh urge to the editorial staff, which Gordon Newton admitted was becoming too complacent. William Rees-Mogg, who had been appointed editor of *The Times* after the Thomson take-over, and in whose original introduction to Fleet Street I had played a part, seemed to Gordon and myself to go out of his way not to lure staff away from the *FT*; and this is one of many respects in which I feel I owe him a debt. The *FT*'s profits suffered for a while because additional promotional and other expenses were incurred, but the circulation and advertisement revenue figures advanced strongly during the ensuing six- or seven-year period, and the paper is obviously in a very healthy state. I doubt whether the merger talks will now ever be revived, and different solutions have been found. But I remain convinced that a great, indeed a unique, opportunity was missed by Pearson's.

Soon after the breakdown of our talks with *The Times*, I found myself, perhaps as a kind of consolation prize, becoming more closely concerned with the Newspaper Publishers Association, although only a masochist could find involvement with the NPA in any way consoling.

When the Association was initially set up in 1906, it was correctly called the Newspaper Proprietors Association, but the name was altered in 1968 to reflect the march of time. The first chairman was the Hon. Harry Lawson, later Viscount Lawson, whose family then owned the *Daily Telegraph*. It is the trade body of the so-called national newspapers printed in what is loosely termed the Fleet Street area. The essential and binding tie was that it regularly negotiated agreements on behalf of its members with the various printing unions, as well as with the journalists. This tie was significantly weakened after a meeting in February 1974 when the Daily Mirror Group (led on the occasion by Sir Don Ryder, later ennobled by Harold Wilson to become the first head of the National Enterprise Board) resigned in a somewhat dramatic way without having given any previous warning and to the general discomfiture of the other members. The *Mirror* had been having difficulties, and it seemed clear to those present that Don Ryder had come to the meeting with every intention of resigning. His pretext was that he did not wish to be responsible, at a time of national crisis, for seeking implementation of an important NPA agreement (no longer in existence) which provided that subject to a sufficient majority all members could be called on to stop production of their newspapers in support of a fellow member if his paper was the victim of improper union action. At the time his explanation struck me as pretty disingenuous; and this was confirmed when in a letter published in the *FT* on 4 August 1976, Edward Pickering, by then chairman of Mirror Group Newspapers, said that his company had left the NPA 'out of distrust of the Association's capacity to move forward rapidly and sensibly in tackling the industry's problems', which I fancy was much nearer the truth.

The usual custom was for each newspaper to be represented at meetings of the NPA by its chairman or chief executive, although the practice of sending alternates was usual. Only on occasions of the greatest crisis did all the leading figures appear, which was understandable but also regrettable, since the Association's authority was thereby weakened. Brendan Bracken was an offender in this regard. He hated committee meetings, and when he was chairman of the *FT* he virtually never attended meetings of the NPA. As managing director I attended regularly, continuing to do so when first Oliver Poole and then Lionel Robbins became chairman of our company. For the greater part of my time Lord Rothermere presided over the NPA. He first became chairman in 1934 and he held the position until 1961. Had he not felt obliged to resign because of concern over his state of health he might well be still in charge today, for whenever I see him he appears to be very robust. He was generally admirable at meetings, using the weapon of silence to powerful effect; and even at his most loquacious he wasted few words. His manner was bland and quietly humorous. He did not conceal his lack of interest in some of the duller items, although he often illuminated them with a joke. In union negotiations he was always both patient and firm: but years of experience had taught him that the interests of the various members frequently diverged, that harmony and mutual trust were often lacking, and that the NPA was usually only as strong as its weakest member.

The worst feature of Esmond Rothermere's chairmanship was the manner of his going. It happened on grounds of health, without warning and almost overnight. I have no doubt that he regarded his sudden departure as essential for his survival. It would however have saved much distress if plans for the succession had been the subject of prior discussion. The deputy chairman was Lord Burnham, Fred Lawson as he had been (the nephew of the Association's first chairman), who had continued to work for the *Daily Telegraph* after it was acquired from his family by Lord Camrose. At the meeting held to discuss the appointment of a new chairman, Fred as deputy chairman occupied the chairman's seat. He should not have done so. It was clear that he did not enjoy general support. However, no one said much until Cecil King, then chairman of the *Daily Mirror*, said sharply, 'I wish it to be clearly understood that I am not willing to agree that the affairs of the *Daily Mirror* should be placed in the hands of Lord Burnham', or some such words. Fred observed, 'Well, thanks very much', in a pained tone of voice, justifiably wounded for he had worked hard at NPA matters, particularly on the labour side, for over twenty-five years. The meeting broke up rather abruptly, and when it reassembled a few days later Cecil King himself was in the chair.

Cecil, like Esmond Rothermere, had Harmsworth blood. They were first cousins. In character they had similarities, but Cecil lacked Esmond's finesse and he always gave the impression of having a few chips on his shoulder. He was aggressively anti-Establishment (although by any normal definition he himself was an Establishment figure). He was very blunt, never being one for mincing his words. In appearance he was tall and imposing. Like Godolphin Horne, he held the human race in scorn: and with the passage of time he seemed to become more and more remote, believing that he was one of the few qualified to save the country from economic disaster – not that his belief was ever put to the test.

Fortunately my personal relations with him were always friendly, and it was indirectly because of this fact that I found myself succeeding him as chairman of the NPA. This is how it happened. Soon after Harold Wilson became Prime Minister in 1966, he was invited by the NPA to a luncheon at which there were only present editors and proprietors (as the members of the Association were all misleadingly called). For some reason Cecil was away, and the deputy chairman, Sir William Carr of the *News of the World*, acted as host. At the end of the lunch the PM said that he did not intend to make a speech, but preferred instead to answer questions. This would have been fine had Bill Carr not dropped off to sleep. The questions went on and on, and it was hard to see how the proceedings were to be brought to a close. I was sitting opposite him, but the table was too wide for me to be able to give him a gentle kick. There was however a waiter in the room. I attracted his attention, and whispered a request in his ear that he should go round the table and nudge Sir William, which he tactfully did. Bill awoke, realized what had happened, and brought the proceedings to an end with reasonable grace: but it was an embarrassing occasion.

A few days later I observed as much to Cecil. His response was to suggest that I should become deputy chairman with a view to following him as chairman. I replied that if Cecil so arranged matters with Bill and he agreed, I would be willing to become deputy chairman, but without any kind of commitment in relation to the chairmanship, which I did not want. Well and good, until some eighteen months later at the end of May 1968 Cecil's colleagues, headed by Hugh Cudlipp who for years was his right hand, decided that they must remove him from his position in control of the Daily Mirror Group because they thought that his head had got too high in the clouds; and this meant that he could not continue as chairman of the NPA, since he automatically ceased to be a member of it on being ejected from the Group that he represented.

His deposition occurred just after Joan and I had returned from America, where we had gone for the wedding of our son Derry, who having completed his military service was then working in New York. He had fallen in love with Eliza Lloyd, the daughter of Bunny and the stepdaughter of Paul Mellon, an attractive, impulsive girl whom we had met once before when passing through New York and liked very much. However, I could not help having grave doubts about the wisdom of a relative pauper marrying a wealthy heiress. With the sexes reversed it can work well, but for the man always to be at a disadvantage financially, particularly when the disparity is so vast, seems to me to be tempting providence. Our first slightly alarming meeting with Paul and Bunny Mellon took place at a lunch in New York where we were all thoroughly on our best behaviour, and it passed off well. In due course Joan and I set out for the wedding, I having hired a thin pearl-grey morning coat from Moss Bros. because I knew that in summertime Virginia I should stifle in my thick black worsted. The night before the wedding, Paul Mellon gave a party in his house in Washington, and I was placed beside one of Bunny's closest friends, Jackie Kennedy, with whom I could not find a common wavelength because her conversation was all the time so careful and *comme il faut*, perhaps not surprising after her terrible ordeal. Eliza looked lovely. She was possessed by a sort of frenzy, and danced wildly through the night. Then we were all transported to Upperville where Paul Mellon has his home, an unpretentious house resembling a series of cottages and surrounding on three sides a very pretty, immaculately kept garden, with a faultless planting of every type of cabbage in the pattern of a cartwheel as a main feature. The wedding took place in a nearby church, the sky being dull and overcast; and afterwards at the wedding reception the skies opened and torrential rain fell. Derry and Eliza left for their honeymoon, but after the guests had departed they reappeared at the house, where Bunny Mellon had decorated a bedroom especially for their *nuit de noces*.

To chart the subsequent course of the marriage would be in no way relevant or becoming. Let it suffice to say that my doubts proved justified, Derry becoming single once more less than three years afterwards, and developing into a talented professional photographer, although his divorce was saddening for Joan and myself because we loved Eliza, and were very fond of her mother Bunny Mellon and also her father, Stacey Lloyd, a splendid man who was obliged to live quietly in the Virgin Islands with his crippled second wife.

As to the NPA, the removal of Cecil King meant that a meeting had to be held to appoint a successor. This took place on 17 June 1968. I had already spoken to one or two members who would have been far more appropriate than myself, notably Max Aitken and Michael Berry, both major figures, pro-prietorial in a sense that I was not, and employing far greater numbers than we did at the specialized *FT*: but neither was willing to be a candidate. Arriving at the meeting in the gloomy council room with its large oval table I remembered the painful experience of Fred Burnham, whose portrait by then, together with that of Esmond Rothermere, looked down on us sardonically from the walls; and so I was careful not to sit in the chairman's seat. I think it was Hugh Cudlipp who proposed my election, and Max Aitken who seconded, and thus I was elected. All along I had tried to make it clear that I was not in the least eager for the job. Apart from my position as managing director of the *FT* I was also chairman of Covent Garden, which took up a good deal of time: and I knew all too well what unpredictable troubles could arise at short notice, demanding immediate attention. However, I realized that as deputy chairman I had little alternative and that I could not refuse election.

In accepting the appointment, I requested my NPA colleagues to agree that Frank Rogers of the Daily Mirror Group should be elected deputy chairman. He had become a good friend of mine through our regular contacts at meetings. I liked his manner and his voice, and I knew that he had a far greater under-standing than myself of production and labour relations matters. The full-time director of the NPA, the one who really had to bear the heat and burden of the day, and often of the night, was Neville Hopwood, a man both able and tenacious. His knowledge of the various personalities and problems of the industry was quite invaluable; and it was an unhappy moment when in the final months of my time as chairman he was tempted away to a better rewarded and less frustrating job. (Later Frank Rogers was himself for a while to become the director, having the discomfiture of being in that position when his old Daily Mirror Group staged their dramatic resignation.)

By far the greatest part of the time at NPA meetings was devoted to labour matters. Their discussion was seldom easy or harmonious. There were many reasons for this. First of all, it was rare for employers and employees to be pulling in the same direction, with a common purpose and objective. While everyone paid lip service to the various threats to the survival of the industry, few were willing to subordinate their own narrow and immediate interest. If awareness was greater on the part of the employers, there were equally plenty of occasions when one or other group was not above taking advantage of the discomfort of a competitor, while shamelessly claiming to be completely in step. On the employees' side, the most unsatisfactory feature was the number of different unions with which it was necessary to negotiate, frequently members of different unions working side by side doing basically similar or complementary jobs. This almost always tended to prolong negotiations and make them far more difficult than they should have been. There was a fearful irresponsibility about the actions of certain union officials, who seemed to delight in flexing their muscles and exerting their power, without any regard, beyond a few crocodile tears, to the hurt they caused, and if a lot was heard about their rights, precious little was ever heard about their duties. It was cold comfort to reflect that the state of disorder was one which bedevilled other sections of British industry, being rooted in the past history of British trade unionism, and appearing to be almost unique in the whole world. (It is ironical that the logical, sensible system adopted in Germany – one union for each industry – should have been imposed on the Germans by Britain after the war.)

The NPA aimed as far as possible to negotiate rates of pay on behalf of all its members, but separate negotiations also took place in each office, with the result that the pattern of earnings resembled a ridiculous patchwork, known by everyone to be indefensible but also incapable of alteration without major upheavals and stoppages.

At the *FT* the most extreme example of the problem arose in the composing room. Compositors were paid by reference to a piecework scale, known as the London scale, which dated back for many years to the days when much setting had to be done by hand, and it was absurdly out of date. It bore particularly hardly on the *FT* where a great deal of the setting was of figures and of tabular matter in small type, for which the scale charges were very costly. One real absurdity was that men working in the composing room had to be paid for advertisements appearing in the paper as though they had themselves set them, even when the advertisements had come in to the paper as fully prepared blocks ready for insertion; and the rate of payment was fixed on the assumption that the whole space occupied by the advertisement had been set in the smallest size type appearing anywhere in the advertisement, even if it only contained a few words of text.

There was a time, nearly twenty years ago now, when the average weekly earnings of the compositors at the *FT* were some £45 a week. I was sorely tempted to propose an annual salary basis of £3,000 a year and the total elimination of the piecework scale, but the arguments against were too strong. There was no doubt that the piecework scale gave a real incentive to high output. Aside from that there was the problem of the repercussions on other sections of an annual salary to compositors of over £3,000 a year, when the average pay of journalists was perhaps under £2,000 a year. So nothing was done, and the compositors' earnings continued steadily upwards until they came to a figure well over £250 a week, indefensible by any rational yardstick, but inescapable without a major renegotiation, accompanied almost certainly by a major stoppage of the *FT* in isolation, for other newspapers would surely not have been willing to shut down in sympathy at immense cost to themselves, when they were not in dispute, and when what was at issue was an agreement freely entered into.

The *FT* was of course not the only publication with high earnings in the composing room or elsewhere; and in other newspaper offices there were enormously high payments in different departments. Every newspaper in one way or another was saddled with rates of pay entered into in the palmy days of the past, but which with the growth of inflation had become increasingly hard to defend.

There were times when the national press as a whole were willing to stop production in support of some major issue of principle, for instance an effort to interfere with the editorial content of a newspaper. In the main, though, stoppages were detested. As well as being very costly, there was the sense of duty in providing a service essential to the life of the community. Unlike an ordinary factory, a day's production of a newspaper could never be retrieved. A prolonged stoppage could mean a permanent loss of readers to a competitor. Therefore there was a strong incentive for solidarity among the various employers, but the scope for this was gravely diminished when Don Ryder took the Daily Mirror Group out of the NPA, and news of labour difficulties in the *Mirror* office always thereafter aroused a certain feeling of *schadenfreude*.*

The need for a new wage structure for the industry was generally recognized, and during my period as chairman Neville Hopwood devoted much time to exploring the possibilities; but while certain unions were willing to enter into discussions, others were not, and, since it had to be a case of all or none, nothing effectively happened. There was a built-in resistance to change, and past experience had shown that the introduction of improved methods as likely as not resulted in demands for increases in pay on a scale so great as to nullify the financial benefits which the new methods might yield.

While I was chairman of the NPA the most senseless burden imposed on newspapers by union action arose from certain so-called 'political' stoppages, usually for only twenty-four hours, which were aimed not at employers but at some aspect of Government policy. These were brought about by a relative handful of men withholding their labour, thereby making production impossible, with consequent loss of revenue, while all wage and other payments, except to the actual offenders, had to continue. On 29 April 1969 we felt obliged to issue a press statement apologizing to readers for the unaccountable action of the union known as SOGAT† in holding up production for political reasons. The statement (issued in advance of the threatened stoppage, which needless to say still took place) was as follows:

The threatened stoppage is wholly political and is not in any way directed at employers. This will be the third time in the last three weeks and the fourth time in twelve months that national newspapers have suffered in this way. This is putting the industry in an intolerable position. Certain papers are known to have considerable financial problems. All papers will be severely damaged by the proposed action.

We accept the right of employees to demonstrate in their own time against the Government proposals. It is a completely different matter when demonstrations are designed to cause serious loss to the industry and to those employed in it.

It is a matter of the greatest regret that the printing unions have apparently not been able to take any effective action to prevent the threatened stoppage. Even worse, S.O.G.A.T. have not been prepared to meet the N.P.A. to discuss the situation, despite repeated requests for such a meeting over the last three weeks.

The General Secretary of SOGAT at the time was R. W. Briginshaw, who was made Lord Briginshaw by Harold Wilson in 1975. I used to see him quite often, and we got on well enough together, but at meetings he could be really insupportable. He was very good at going to ground when one most needed to see him. He had a great talent for conveying the impression of unawareness of

---

* Pleasure at the misfortunes of others.
† Society of Graphical and Allied Trades.

the actions of his members, although it was hard to believe that he was not well informed.

The other leading union figure in my day was John Bonfield of the National Graphical Association, the union of the compositors and machine managers, who was personally a delightful man. But he had his own brand of pigheadedness; and the fact that his union had its headquarters in Bedford, fifty miles from London, did not help.

There are now new personalities at the head of these two leading unions. Whether this will make any difference I should hate to predict. Nor would I predict when the new production methods, from which so much is expected, are likely to be introduced. They are essential for the survival of Fleet Street, but they need the consent not only of the two big unions but also SLADE;* and, most importantly, of the union membership, amongst whom at times there really does seem to be a kind of collective death-wish.

I gave up being chairman of the NPA in June 1970, one of my last acts being to persuade my fellow members that the NPA should belong to the CBI, this having always previously been resisted on the erroneous view that membership would in some way inhibit editorial comment about the activities of the CBI, which needless to say it never did. I attended the CBI meetings regularly as the representative of the NPA, continuing to do so after I had handed over the chairmanship, making fairly frequent interjections, especially if the Press was attacked; but except on rare occasions the full council was too large a body to do much more than endorse the recommendations from the chair. With a Labour Government in power one felt that the CBI was strangely helpless, because doctrinaire views nearly always prevailed over common sense, especially in any matter bearing upon the unions or upon taxation policy. The CBI are now trying to vie with the TUC in holding a public conference which, if successful, will become annual. And since they have an eminently sensible director-general in John Methven advantage should be gained from a rather bold step.

Already several months before giving up the chairmanship of the NPA I had told the other members that I wished to be released. It was wholly fortuitous that I was in the chair. Covent Garden imposed on me a need for regular attendance, while at the NPA sudden squalls would blow up out of a clear blue sky. However, handing over was not a simple matter. None of the existing members, at any rate none who would have been acceptable to the rest, was willing to serve.

In the eyes of many, M. H. Hussey, known as Dukie, would have made an excellent choice. He had followed Frank Rogers as my deputy chairman at the beginning of 1970. He knew the industry through and through, and he was

* Society of Lithographic Artists, Designers, Engravers and Process Workers.

widely liked and trusted; but he had just left the Daily Mail group to go as managing director of *The Times*, and there were still some scars. Later, when the possibility arose again, his colleagues at *The Times* would not agree that he should become chairman of the NPA whilst also running *The Times*, although their attitude was hard to understand, for they allowed him to carry on as the NPA's deputy chairman and also to act as co-chairman of the joint board for the re-equipment of the industry. Another possibility might have been Peter Gibbings, of *The Guardian*, a wise, balanced and sympathetic man, but he had too many problems, and he had to spend much of his time in Manchester.

Then a brainwave occurred to Max Aitken. Some eighteen months before, he had accompanied Arnold Goodman on a fact-finding peace mission to Rhodesia, and a close friendship had developed between the two men. Max conceived the idea that Arnold would be an ideal chairman of the NPA, attaching for the first time a modest element of remuneration to the post. He had strong support from Rupert Murdoch, the publisher of the *News of the World* and *Sun*, in whose office building Arnold's law firm was then a tenant. Since Max and Rupert, for all their attractive qualities, were the most capricious personalities, and most apt to adopt an individual stance, it was vital that the chairman should be someone who had their complete confidence, and whose word they would heed. I strongly supported the proposal, and I did what I could to bring it to fruition.

I knew Arnold well because, in his capacity as chairman of the Arts Council, I had frequent cause to see him about the affairs of Covent Garden, as I shall relate, and he had won my heart. He had numerous Fleet Street links, being in particular chairman of the trustees of the *Observer*. His appointment did however mean a departure from previous practice as the chairman of the NPA had hitherto been someone working full time in a particular newspaper office. But there was a powerful case for change in view of the increasing demands made upon the chairman, above all in terms of time.

For seven years Arnold fought nobly on behalf of the national press, his task becoming infinitely harder when the Daily Mirror Group abruptly withdrew from membership of the Association. Despite having countless other interests, his ready availability at short notice and his patience and good humour in the face of obstinacy and unreason, by no means confined to union leaders, won the admiration of all. He had a habit of arriving late at meetings ('the late Lord Goodman' was Jennie Lee's nickname for him), but I am sure that as often as not his lateness was carefully premeditated: and he had the knack of arriving when a lot of the verbiage had been cleared away. The entry into the council room of his imposing presence, his calm walk round the room to his chair, the speed with which he picked up the essentials of the discussion, even when he had not read his papers, and the lightness of his touch always had a comforting and reassuring effect upon those present. It cannot be said that he succeeded in finding solutions to every problem. Often, the problems were too intractable, and the interests of the members too disparate. Fleet Street was assailed by outside forces of great strength. The seeping away of advertising revenue to other media, and the fall in circulations were forces that seriously threatened survival. We were all aware of the new techniques being developed and introduced outside of London, which clearly had the effect of reducing costs in a very material way: but the built-in resistance to change, the vested interest in the *status quo*, meant that many union members preferred to risk the death of titles to the sacrifice of highly paid jobs. The scope for argument was endless. No one could have achieved more than Arnold did; and he was a marvellous spokesman for the industry. It is a tribute to his sense of loyalty that he stood it all for so long. He must have found his appointment as Master of University College a splendid opportunity for release from his bondage.

During the latter part of his time as chairman, he had occasion to wage a mighty battle on behalf of the cause of the freedom of the press, nearly precipitating a major Lords versus Commons crisis, with the House of Lords challenging the will of the Government majority in the House of Commons. The occasion arose from the decision of the Government soon after they had been returned to power in the autumn of 1974 to introduce a Bill drastically amending the Trade Union and Labour Relations Act which they themselves had presented to Parliament during their brief period of minority government a few months earlier but which had been radically altered during the Committee stage of the debate when they had no true parliamentary majority.* The purpose of their Act had been to scrap the guts of the Tories' Industrial Relations Act of 1971, a measure aimed at making the closed shop illegal and generally imposing

---

* It may be helpful to explain briefly the laborious parliamentary processes necessary before any intended piece of legislation can become law. After the formal introduction of a Bill into the House of Commons, a second reading debate follows, which is solely concerned with the broad issues of principle involved. Detailed discussion of the Bill's individual clauses takes place a few days later at the committee stage, when drafting amendments can be moved. There follows the so-called report stage, which in essence resembles a further committee stage debate, and amendments can again be moved. Finally comes the third reading, when as at the second reading only the broad principles of the bill can be discussed and called in question by means of an adverse vote.

The Bill then goes to the House of Lords, where exactly the same stages have to be gone through, after which if there are no amendments the Bill is ready for the Royal Assent, and it becomes a legal Act of Parliament. However, if the Lords amend the Bill it must return to the Commons for further debate; and if the amendments are acceptable to the Government, the Bill will then become law. If they are not, the amendments are likely to be removed, and the Bill is returned once more to the Lords, where the amendments can be reinstated, and returned to the Commons, until eventually if the Lords remain adamant the Government may override them by invoking the Parliament Act of 1949, which gives an ultimate sanction to the political party in power. (Bills can also originate in the House of Lords, when the foregoing procedure is followed in reverse.)

badly needed restraints upon the powers of trades unions, but at the time their majority was insufficient for this to be possible. After the election in October 1974, when they were returned to power with a majority of five, they immediately proceeded to set their purpose in train, thereby, after the passage of legislation, effectively removing any kind of legal sanction against reckless strike action by employees. Arnold Goodman's particular concern, however, was with the legalization of the closed shop as it affected journalists. For many years almost all newspaper offices had accepted the principle of a closed shop among production workers, and indeed welcomed it because it simplified wage negotiation. In the case of journalists there was no objection to collective negotiation in relation to basic rates of pay. However, Arnold, and many others besides, felt deeply and strongly that to allow one union the power to determine who might or might not write for the press, which could conceivably be extended to *what* they should say, was potentially a grave threat to democratic freedom: and signs of real militancy among those influencing the decisions of the National Union of Journalists constrained him to go into battle with the object of having journalism excluded from the scope of the Labour Government's amending Bill. When the legislation came to the House of Lords in 1975, it was evident that there was a powerful feeling among members of all parties that something should be done to safeguard the position of the press. A Labour peer, Lord Houghton, moved an amendment providing for a press charter which offered a degree of protection, but also stipulated that if the various interested parties could not agree upon the terms of a charter, the Secretary of State for Employment (which then meant the passionately doctrinaire Michael Foot) would be charged with the duty of imposing one. Arnold was emphatic that there must be written into the Bill specific protection for the position of editors and their deputies, an assurance of access to the press by contributors, *and* freedom for journalists to join what was phrased as the union of their choice (there being in fact two journalists' unions, the NUJ, and the much smaller but respected Institute of Journalists). He therefore tabled an amendment to Lord Houghton's amendment, and by agreement with him I joined my name with his. I then told Pat Gibson what I had done, and he asked if he too could append his name. We had to establish whether this would be in order as Pat had not yet made a maiden speech. In the event the amendment appeared in our three names. Pat and I did what we could to help. I attended the debates regularly, intervening when I could. I regarded myself, as I told Arnold, as his lieutenant, acting as a go-between between various Tory, Liberal and Cross Bench peers. The outcome was that our amendment, which was also supported by several Labour peers, was overwhelmingly carried. The Government, predictably, refused to accept the verdict of the House of Lords, and invoked the Parliament Act, but they broke with precedent because when

the Bill returned to the House of Commons, out of deference to the strong feelings of many of their own supporters, they incorporated into it the Houghton
amendment providing for a press charter, although of course lacking the specific
safeguards for which we had pressed. The Commons approved the amendment,
and it was in this form that the Bill returned once more to the House of Lords at
the beginning of 1976. The effect of the Government's action was that it rested
with the Lords whether or not there should be any press charter. A negative vote
would have meant that the closed shop legislation would pass without any
mitigation. Feelings were somewhat divided. I was among those who thought
that some form of charter was crucial to furnish minimum protection for editors.
Arnold had come to believe that it would be better to have no charter than one
imposed by a Cabinet Minister, possibly containing various restrictions which
might for years bedevil newspaper offices. He still hoped, however, that his
desiderata would be met by the Government. He was ill and could not be present
when the House of Lords held its second reading debate on the amended Bill on
10 February, although had he been there he would not have forced a division
because of his continuing hope of persuading the Government to reconsider
before it was too late. During the course of the debate I tried to voice his feelings
in a short speech, but without obtaining any sign of a change of heart.

Two weeks later, when the Committee stage was reached, there was a surprise development. Quintin Hailsham, a former Lord Chancellor, who is a man
of passionate sincerity with formidable debating powers, decided to introduce
an entirely new concept by moving an amendment, of general application and
not related to the press charter, stipulating that 'sincerely held personal conscientious conviction' should provide grounds for non-membership of a trade
union; and he rallied enough Tory support to have his amendment carried by
128 to 91 votes. (It was of course later annulled by the Commons.) After this
vote, the debate proceeded, and Arnold made a further plea to the Government,
making it clear that otherwise he would ask the House to reject the proposal for
a press charter. I was abroad at the time, which I did not regret, because I was
against eliminating all provision for a charter, even one drawn up by a Minister
as an Order in Council, for it could not have the force of law until it had been
tabled and approved by Parliament, so that had it been in any way obnoxious it
could have been prayed against and another vote taken, which certainly in the
Lords would have been successful.

At the report stage of the debate on 2 March I was still abroad. Arnold had
failed to make further progress, and so although he had fought for a charter in the
beginning he went ahead with his announced intention. To achieve his purpose
he needed the support of the Tory peers. He took a deputation to see Margaret
Thatcher, and largely through her intervention, as he told me, a free vote was

conceded. He did not have time, however, to rally sufficient votes; and despite a powerful speech by Lord Windlesham, a much respected Tory and former Leader of the House, the division was lost by 109 to 71 votes.

After the passage of the Bill, talks had to be held between the various interested groups in order to see whether agreement could be reached over the terms of a voluntary press charter. It was a virtual certainty that these would fail, as they duly did. And now, under the terms of the Act, the Secretary of State for Employment has the task of drawing up a charter, which Parliament can approve or otherwise. The test will be whether he has the courage *not* to impose a closed shop for journalists, but I fear that the likelihood of a display of such bravery with a Labour Government in power is remote, however much individual Labour members of Parliament, including members of the Government, may dislike signs of aggressive behaviour by the NUJ. It may well be that nothing at all will happen until after the next General Election. In any event, the importance of Arnold's *démarche* was that it forced everyone to reflect upon the potential threats to editorial freedom; and the value of this is hard to exaggerate.

Chapter 18

While I was chairman of the NPA significant changes were taking place in the composition of the holding company which controlled the *FT*. Initially when the *FT* was brought together with the Westminster Press Provincial News-papers in 1967 the name given to the holding company was Financial and Provincial Publishing Company Limited, accurate enough but scarcely alluring, and shortly afterwards it was changed to S. Pearson Publishers, which at least established more clearly in people's minds that we were part of the Pearson group. Then in 1968 a great prize appeared in the shape of Longmans, Green, perhaps the most illustrious educational publishing business of all, which had been effectively controlled for many years by Mark Longman's family and where the need arose to sell a substantial shareholding. Longman had always been close to Lazards, his financial advisers, and Daniel Meinertzhagen was on the board. Assimilation therefore into the publishing side of the Pearson Group could be effected naturally and easily; and it was thought desirable to incor-porate the name of Longmans into that of the holding company, which accordingly became Pearson Longman.

No further change of title was regarded as necessary when the possibility arose two years later of acquiring another very great publishing company, Sir Allen Lane's Penguin Books, a name possessing perhaps more magic than all the rest, the pioneer of the paperback, a business respected throughout the world, and one which curiously enough while Allen Lane was still alive was nearly sold by him to *The Economist* during Geoffrey Crowther's regime, and probably would have been had Geoffrey not miscalculated the price asked through over-looking a scrip issue that substantially increased the number of shares to be bought. The acquisition of control of Penguin made Pearson Longman a com-pany of immensely wide influence and ramifications overseas as much as at home; but Pat Gibson, the chairman, grew in stature as the company grew in size, managing to take it all in his stride, knowing exactly how far and how far not to intervene in the affairs of each part of Lord Cowdray's extensive empire.

Fortunately the *FT* was doing reasonably well and markets were enjoying a period of euphoria. The Tories were returned to power in June 1970. They celebrated their arrival by adopting a doctrinaire policy of the survival of the fittest in industry, and by scrapping the Prices and Incomes Board which Labour had created in an effort to preserve some sort of balance between the two competing forces. After a few months, taking fright at the level of unemployment, they embarked, most misguidedly as it turned out, on a policy of spending, believing that thereby they would enable the country to break through a kind of sound barrier into a new era of prosperity. They showed wisdom in passing much-needed legislation designed to curb some of the recklessness of the trade unions. Against this, however, when they realized that their financial policy was not succeeding, they showed tactical folly because, instead of reintroducing the Prices and Incomes Board as they should have done, they decided, in order to appear different, to create two separate bodies, one designed to keep prices down and the other to restrain rises in income. The foreseeable and calamitous result was that when Labour was returned to office in 1974 they retained the Prices Commission but abolished anything exercising a restraining influence on incomes. The Tories' spending resulted in what turned out to be a pretty phony boom, and markets boiled over. A number of large financial and property companies built up on borrowed money were unable to fulfil their obligations and failed, dragging one another down. Tight wage controls were introduced, and organized labour grew increasingly restive. In the autumn of 1973, following the Middle East war, there came massive oil price increases; and these tremendously strengthened the position of the miners. They pressed large wage demands, and Heath revealed his lack of flexibility by refusing to accept the assurances given him by the TUC that a generous settlement with the miners would not result in a chain reaction. He decided instead upon confrontation, and was predictably unsuccessful. Then, lamentably, he called a General Election, and suffered defeat, admittedly by a very small majority but defeat it was. In came Labour, with Harold Wilson again in the saddle, and all the legislation of the Tories aimed at union excesses was repealed, with disastrous and far-reaching consequences. It was a supreme example of the all too frequent reversal of governmental policy as the party in power has changed, thereby gravely shaking business confidence and therefore limiting capital investment.

Throughout the period of the Tory regime the *FT* was decidedly sceptical. The scepticism was not confined to the leading articles. There were three particular weekly columnists whose renown steadily increased, Sam Brittan, Joe Rogaly and David Watt. Sam Brittan has for a number of years written a weekly column, 'Economic Viewpoint', which is entirely personal. There was always an argument whether he or Peter Jay of *The Times* was the more brilliant, but now with the posting of Jay to Washington as British Ambassador Sam has

the field to himself. He was recruited by Gordon Newton straight from
university. He left for a while to join the staff of the *Observer* newspaper, and
from there he went to George Brown's ill-fated Department of Economic
Affairs. But it was not long before he was telling Gordon that he would be
happy to return to our fold where since 1966 he has fortunately remained.
To the *cognoscenti*, Sam is outstanding. He has no fixed political stance, but he
inclines towards a liberal position, because of his strong belief in a market
economy, with central control over the money supply, but over as little else as
possible. Like many economists and statisticians he is a passionate lover of music,
and goes to concerts whenever he can. It would be grand to see him leading a
bride to the altar, but I cannot visualize him overcoming his shyness sufficiently
to put the question: and if he did succeed he would probably mislay the
engagement ring.

Joe Rogaly happened by pure coincidence to be married to the daughter of
my old schoolmate, Francis Baring. He is as engaging a character as one could
wish to meet. For a time he wrote the 'Men and Matters' column in the *FT*, and
then was our correspondent in New York; but since 1969 he has contributed a
weekly column labelled 'Society Today', roaming far and wide over the social
and politico-economic problems of these troubled times. He could fairly be
called a man with a load of conscience, mercifully relieved by a considerable
sense of humour. Politically he is to the left of centre, but he is essentially
moderate, and usually realistic and objective in what he writes. If he could have
his way he would edit a magazine on behalf of a philanthropist whose concern
was more for the product than with the profit and loss account, and if any such
person should read these words, Joe is the man for him.

David Watt already had an established reputation when he joined us. He was
the most perceptive of all political correspondents, and there were few politicians
upon whom he did not cast a jaundiced eye. His own stance was also a shade left
of centre, but he was essentially a man of reason and goodwill, and 'a plague on
both your houses' could well have been his motto. For a while, in order to
widen his experience, he was placed by Gordon in charge of the editorial planning of the surveys department, continuing all the time with his regular political
articles. During the years that he was at the *FT* while I was there, he perhaps
gave me more encouragement than any other member of the editorial staff,
praising me for what he used to call my qualities as an impresario, not that I ever
saw myself at all in that light. There was always a fear that David might be
lured away to some tempting job, and he was away for a year as a Visiting
Fellow of All Souls, but happily for the *FT* he remained on the staff for a long
time until in 1977 he was offered and accepted the post of director of the Royal
Institute of International Affairs where he followed Andrew Shonfield (another

very able product of the *FT*), and where his experience and contacts in Westminster will be invaluable.

All the time the *FT* was of course evolving and becoming less and less the specialist newspaper, and broadening the scope of its coverage. The change in the general attitude towards us was gradual and almost imperceptible to those working regularly in the office; but it was taking place, and the fact was clearly evidenced by a slow but steady increase in our circulation. It is arguable that we could have promoted the increase more vigorously had we not so steadily advanced the selling price. We had established ourselves as the most expensive daily newspaper, and in those days we took the lead in price increases, with *The Times* following along behind although by 1977 the initiative in this regard became theirs, the *FT* proceeding more cautiously.

One change that was gradually happening was the growing habit for members of the editorial staff to sign their contributions. I could not help feeling that this was being allowed to be overdone, even quite trivial news items being signed, but Gordon Newton assured me that it was necessary in order to retain his staff, and certainly there was a similar trend at *The Times* and elsewhere. The one publication which has so far adhered rigidly to the rule of anonymity is *The Economist*, and in my view this helps to give great authority to the paper. However, I realize that I am in a minority, and it is certain that the trend will not be reversed. There was one major alteration in the make-up of the paper which I pressed for, and which we implemented after the failure of our talks with *The Times*. This was the removal of Stock Exchange share prices from the back page in order to make way for news. The prices had always appeared there, and to remove them inside the paper seemed to some almost as hazardous a development as the removal of the so-called agony column (meaning the personal classified advertisements) from the front to the back page of *The Times*. Had the *FT* quotations been confined to a single page the scope for argument would have been greater; but share prices already appeared on an inside page as well as on the back. It was therefore possible to argue convincingly that a double page spread of prices across the penultimate two pages would be a service to readers as well as to the companies whose shares were quoted. The change-over took place at the end of 1968. Unfortunately Gordon did not plan the disposition of the contents of the new back page as I wished. I wanted it to be a sort of mini front page, with the daily investment notes Lex feature transferred there to make more room for news on page 1. This did indeed happen, but it was done in a typographically displeasing way, with the feature run horizontally across the top of the page instead of vertically in the right hand columns, thus sacrificing the scope for news story headings. The space available for news was further reduced because Gordon elected to include on one side of the page a detailed weather report, and on the other, so as to give a balanced appearance, he introduced the daily Lombard feature, which since it was first started many years before had always appeared on an inside page, where it properly belonged.

The Lombard column was something inherited from the *FN*, where until the merger in 1945 it had been written by the indefatigable Paul Einzig, who was rarely objective in his contributions. For a while, when Einzig became lobby correspondent of the *FT*, the column was written in anodyne fashion by an agreeable old pro named Grahame Parker, who had spent all his journalistic life in and around Lombard Street, as the money market is colloquially referred to in the City. Parker was succeeded by a faithful servant of the *FN*, C. Gordon Tether, who had Einzig's industry as well as his campaigning spirit. With the passage of time Tether became more and more concerned with the harm, as he saw it, that would be done to Britain by membership of the Common Market. He felt obliged to devote the column with great frequency to this theme, which was tedious for some readers of the paper and also a bit confusing, because the editorial stance of the paper under both Gordon Newton and his successor Fredy Fisher was strongly pro-European. During approximately the same period, an increasing effort was being made to induce more readers to write letters to the editor, a field in which we had always inevitably lagged very far behind *The Times*; supervision of the letters had been entrusted to Joe Rogaly, who took it on while continuing his weekly 'Society Today' article. I pointed out that with our 'Letters to the Editor' tucked away on page 2, as they then were, the inducement for anyone to write was not great. Why not, I suggested, move the feature to the page facing the Leader page, right in the centre of the paper? To fill the vacuum thereby created on page 2 I urged that we should place some of our regular sports contributions there; and also restore Tether's Lombard column to an inside position so that the back page could assume the layout I had hoped for, with the Lex investment column on the right hand side, and the page becoming much more the news page that I had wanted it to be. The change was finally effected in January 1975, shortly before my retirement. It was visually an improvement, while the shift of 'Letters to the Editor' gave them more prominence, and certainly encouraged more people in positions of authority to write.

The change took place quite early in the regime of Fredy Fisher as editor. So far I have scarcely mentioned his name, although he had in fact been a member of the staff since 1957, during which time he had filled a number of important editorial posts. His succession took place at the end of 1972, when Gordon Newton retired on reaching his sixty-fifth birthday, while remaining a member of our holding company board. Just as the name of Gordon Newton as editor had been strongly backed by his predecessor Hargreaves Parkinson, so Gordon indicated that in his view Fredy was the right man to follow him, a view shared by most other members of the staff. We had indeed appointed Fredy deputy editor some months before the date of Gordon's retirement, thus making it clear that we thought the right of succession was his: and when his appointment as editor was announced there was no sign of dissent, and only one departure from the editorial staff, which was purely coincidental. The columnists continued writing their columns; various consequential changes were made to the posts occupied by a handful of individuals, but otherwise life continued on its way as calmly as external circumstances allowed. These were, of course, generally dreadful. Fredy took over at the height of the phony Tory boom. Within a short space of time he was having to contend with the collapse of one insecurely based financial empire after another, Heath's disastrously misjudged confrontation with the unions and his fall from power, and the final stages of Britain's struggle to join the Common Market, a cause to which Fredy had been wholeheartedly committed from the start of negotiations several years before, and from which Harold Wilson to his credit did not deviate despite the passionate opposition of his left-wing.

For Fredy it really was a case of getting in at the deep end, but this presented him with no problem. Not only is he a highly experienced journalist, but he has a balanced approach to life which at all times seems to stand him in very good stead. Like Claus Moser, my successor as chairman of Covent Garden, Fredy comes from a German Jewish background, and is a distinguished representative of the rare breed that Britain owes to Hitler. His father was a well-known lawyer, and an intimate friend of Otto Klemperer and Artur Schnabel. Fredy himself is intensely musical, enjoys playing the piano, and has a wide knowledge of the basic classical repertoire. Bridge and chess are two of his other forms of recreation, which he plays well, and golf, not I imagine up to the standard of Gordon Newton. He is an enviably well-integrated person, with a sympathetic Australian wife, who is a talented sculptor, and two exemplary children. If he has any political stance he has always kept it strictly to himself, being as coolly objective as Gordon Newton; and when the story of his editorship comes to be written I believe that his main contribution will be found to have been to push the *FT* significantly in the European direction, and for this the owners of the paper will be grateful. He is extremely wise, and I know from personal experience that no one has a more kind or considerate nature.

It was not at all surprising that when he took over as editor in 1972, he retained the loyalty of his staff. He would be the first to agree that this loyalty was also in large measure to the *FT* itself, a constant and most gratifying factor during the thirty years that I was working there, for which I can offer no explanation except that we *were* different, a difference emphasized by the pink colour of our newsprint. The nearest comparison is with the *Wall Street Journal* in the United States, an absolutely brilliant production job, but far more parochial as a newspaper than the *FT*, scarcely recognizing the existence of abroad, and infinitely less complete in its overseas news coverage. People did of course leave our staff, not in the main to work on other newspapers, but to go to jobs in commerce or finance; and Gordon Newton used to say that he would be distinctly worried if none of his editorial staff were ever offered outside jobs, regarding it as a reflection on himself as much as on them. There were in fact three or four who left us only to return like homing pigeons a few years later, for instance Sam Brittan, and another able economic journalist named Tony Harris; and these reappearances always pleased me greatly.

Such departures as there were tended to be confined to the editorial staff of the paper. The business staff were remarkably constant. This was in part because their work was so specialized, and they believed, quite rightly, that in its particular field the *FT* led. The figurehead for most of the time was Sidney Henschel. Although he retired from the position of advertisement director in 1969 when he reached the age of seventy-six, handing over to Wilfred Gabriel who had joined us from the defunct *News Chronicle*, Sidney continued to come to the office pretty regularly until he was over eighty, and for countless matters he remained the point of reference because of his experience and his rare judgement. Wilfred was followed by Peter Yeo, an attractive, highly strung individual, who had grown up in the office and was one of Sidney's protégés. Alongside him was Richard McClean, the able son of Stuart McClean whose tragic death while still very young was much mourned in Fleet Street, where he was a pillar of the pre-tabloid *Daily Mail*; and Richard in fact succeeded to the top advertisement position quite soon after my retirement, being elected, unlike his predecessors, to the board of directors.

Financial advertising was in the hands of Robert Piper, a bright cheerful young man, with silver-grey hair with which I used to say he must have been born. He came under the advertisement director, but he had a large degree of independence and his department was responsible for a large volume of revenue. Its nature was constantly shifting, and the type of financial advertising common in my early days, solid wodges of type containing rather smug chairmen's speeches, was giving way to advertisements which more nearly approached to a display style, and which could be misleading because often they simply consisted of a number of boastful headlines, such as 'record turnover and profits', without any attempt to qualify or explain. They were also tiresome because they tended to result in no advertising if the figures were not good: and this we had to do everything possible to resist. In the old days it was not necessary for companies to publish profit figures more than once a year, but in

1965 the Stock Exchange made the publication of half-yearly profit figures obligatory, accepting in principle that an advertisement in two national daily newspapers would serve as an alternative to circularizing shareholders. I urged our advertisement staff to do all they could to promote this potentially valuable new source of revenue, and we worked hard to persuade advertising agents and their clients of the wisdom of booking space rather than leaving publication to editorial whim.

There were bonanza years when there was a new issue boom in the City. These were welcome not only because new issue advertising was charged for at a specially high rate, but also because they brought fresh companies into the advertisement department's scope. However, they had the disadvantage in the old days that publishing a financial newspaper tended to be a feast or famine business. Because of this our aim at all times was to diversify as far as we could the sources of our advertisement revenue, upon which, despite regular increases in the selling price of the paper, we were always dependent for well over 80 per cent of our total income.

One of the most gratifying aspects of our attempts at diversification was the steady growth in foreign advertising in the paper; and this came not only from special surveys but also from financial and display sources, to the extent that we received the Queen's Award for Export not only in 1971 but again in 1975. In charge of the Foreign department was Adrian Secker, who had succeeded Alan Hare when Alan became general manager in 1966. Adrian had the advantage of a journalistic background, having previously been a member of the editorial staff of the *Daily Telegraph*. He had an agreeably vague manner which concealed a very shrewd judgement, and he did much to promote the development of the department along lines already well and truly established by his predecessor.

I did everything in my power to stimulate the various sources of our advertising revenue. I exerted constant pressure on the business department staff, and I was always willing to intervene personally if trouble was being experienced with a recalcitrant advertiser. If it was known that the *FT* was being excluded from an important campaign I was always angry at not being told while there was time to make representations. I used to make a thorough nuisance of myself pursuing certain tycoons who were reluctant spenders, and my chief argument, if a direct benefit could not be proved, was that the *FT* rendered a vital service to businessmen, and this was only possible because of the income we derived from advertising. It was a simple argument but a perfectly valid one; and in the main it was effective.

All my life I have tended to work too much on impulse. I was never one for management techniques. I used to read the books, but instinct always guided me. My ways were thoroughly unorthodox, something which I inherited I suppose

less from my father than from my mother, who was always fearfully impulsive.
I had a habit of wandering round the office, and dropping in on people in a
completely haphazard way, trying quietly to sense the atmosphere. From these
chance encounters developed chance ideas, and as often as not they proved
fruitful.

It was rare for me to engage anyone for the staff, although quite often I saw
possibilities for people once they were there. There was, however, one example
of a curiously haphazard engagement which worked out well. Some years ago
I was flying back from New York in a BOAC aircraft. Among the few advantages of travelling first class is the provision of free drinks. A group of four
American businessmen was taking full advantage of the facility, and as a result
they became extremely fresh and familiar with the air hostess, a tall personable
young lady who contrived to keep them under control without in any way
giving offence, despite great provocation. I was very impressed by her demeanour,
and I thought that someone so capable might make a useful recruit for the
FT's business staff (the only area in which any kind of freedom of recruitment
existed). After a while I scribbled on a piece of paper, 'If you want to make a
change of job let me know,' handing it to her as she walked past me. A few
minutes later she slipped me a note simply saying, 'Thank you very much,' and
giving her telephone number. When I went to the office next day I saw Sidney
Henschel, who was slightly taken aback because he had no vacancy, but who
was always ready to help. The upshot was that this young lady joined us as a
trainee, taking a substantial cut in salary compared with what she had been
earning as an air hostess. Some months later a girl who had been found for
Covent Garden by Sidney Henschel to obtain advertising for their nightly programmes left in order to be married. Sidney suggested that my protégée should
succeed her, promising to give her what assistance he could. John Tooley
approved, and the transfer was effected. Now, seven years later, her name is still
listed in the nightly programme among the administrative staff and she performs
her job with professional skill and without any sense that I did her a disservice
when I scribbled that note in the aeroplane.

There was one particular division of the *FT* which I was instrumental in
launching. This was what we called the Business Enterprises division. Its purpose
was to bring together under one central point of control certain miscellaneous
activities which were actual or potential sources of revenue. The chief of these
were conferences and syndication, but there were others as well; and the scope
for profitable use of the name and good reputation of the *FT* was clearly considerable. What was needed was someone to pull these various activities together and give them a greater sense of purpose and direction than they had
hitherto enjoyed. To head the new division I suggested Christopher Johnson

who had joined the editorial staff of the *FT* in 1960, becoming our chief editorial representative in Paris where he was stationed at the time as No. 2 man in the *Times* office. From Paris he came to our London office, becoming in turn diplomatic correspondent, foreign editor and managing editor, the post he occupied when I suggested his translation to the business staff. In doing this I had in mind the fact that he was unlikely to be offered the No. 1 editorial position, while I remembered the successful move of Jim Hunter from the post of deputy editor to become general manager. Christopher had enormous industry, and he was shiningly eager and enthusiastic. His fault was excess of zeal. He ceaselessly generated new ideas, and I found that I spent a good deal of time trying to restrain him; but I could not always do so, and sometimes I was fearful that my scepticism would have a discouraging effect, and therefore I tended to give him the benefit of the doubt. Christopher was a perfect example of someone whose geese tended to be swans. But the overall profitability of the division he left behind when he went to become chief economic adviser to Lloyds Bank was considerable. Much the most extensive work of his division was concerned with the organization of conferences, both at home and abroad. This called for considerable flair and judgement in the choice of subjects – and of speakers, where Christopher's editorial experience was very valuable. The work also required the qualities of an impresario, and in this regard he had plenty to teach me.

My own principal effort as an impresario was a mammoth dinner which we held at the Hilton Hotel on 11 November 1969 to celebrate publication of the 25,000th issue of the *Financial Times*. One day, about a year before, I noticed that we had published some 24,700 issues, and I thought '25,000 is a good round figure. Why not have a party to celebrate it?' At the next meeting of our policy committee I sought the views of our various heads of department, who understandably were all in favour. So, fortunately, were my colleagues on the board of directors. They agreed that if we were to do anything it must be in style, making sure as far as we could that no one who could reasonably claim to have a right to be invited should be overlooked. So we set about making a list including the key members of the Cabinet, headed then by Harold Wilson, leaders of the other political parties in both Houses of Parliament, the chief diplomatic figures stationed in London, the captains of industry, commerce and finance, the chairmen and chief executives of the national press, the leading personalities of the TUC and of all the printing trades unions, representatives of every division of the *FT* and of most of the companies in the group to which the *FT* belonged; then of course the Arts, in conformity with the image that we had consistently been seeking to establish for the *FT*. Jennie Lee and Arnold Goodman naturally headed this last contingent, and I was at pains to place her beside me, while the Prime Minister sat beside our chairman, Lionel Robbins; and as so many of the guests were illustrious, we divided the room up into seventy-six tables of ten or twelve, with a member of the *FT* board or a senior staff member of our group at the head of each table. Since the total who were to attend came to some eight hundred people there was little choice of suitable venue, and in the event we had to use the banqueting room of the Hilton, a room which struck me as particularly ugly but which by the masking of lights and with the help of candles we managed to transform, introducing our *FT* pink colour as far as we could into the decoration scheme, with all the guests being given pale pink carnations for their buttonholes. The Hilton people were delighted to have been chosen, making a major effort to give satisfaction. On the question of drink there could, I felt sure, be no argument: it must be Château Latour in view of the fact that this great vineyard was owned by our controlling share-holder, S. Pearson & Son. By good fortune we were able to acquire, at reason-able but commercial prices, some sixty cases of the 1963 vintage, cheap because it was fast maturing and said to lack staying power. In order that the guests should be able to enjoy this delicious wine to the full I thought that we should give them cheese instead of pudding: so we had seventy-six large Brie cheeses, one for each table; the waiters had orders to see that no glass was left empty; and I can truthfully claim that a good time was had by all. How far the occasion benefited the *FT* is impossible to say, but it certainly lingered for a long while in people's memories.

There was another dinner that I initiated. This was to honour Vic Feather on the occasion of his retirement in 1973 from the post of Secretary-General of the TUC. He had always been kind and helpful to me, particularly during my time as chairman of the NPA, when I had several opportunities of realizing that he was essentially a man of peace and goodwill occupying one of the most difficult positions in the country, a perfect example of responsibility without power. The dinner was held in the Skinners' Company Hall. It was on a much smaller scale than our Hilton jamboree, but it was attended by senior Ministers and Opposition leaders, top civil servants, union officials like Len Murray, Jack Jones and Hugh Scanlon, the chief figures of the CBI, the Governor of the Bank of England, The Queen's principal private secretary, and – because of Vic's love of painting – the President of the Royal Academy. It was a happy and satisfying occasion, for Vic was a lovable person whose chief fault was an exaggerated *bonhomie*.

The promotional activities of the *FT* were largely under the care and super-vision of John Geddes, a member of the noted Geddes family which by instinct and upbringing has always been dedicated to public service. One particular responsibility of his was a competition known as the National Management

Game. This was jointly sponsored by International Computers and the *FT*. Teams from a large number of companies competed regularly each year, arriving by process of knockout to finals where the winning team received a modest award but much kudos. The competitors were required to react to a series of supposed situations bearing on the profitability of an imagined company which they were managing. The computer checked their results; and the team earning the highest theoretical profit won the prize. To me it was gobbledegook, but it was certainly popular, and very good publicity for the *FT*. Another valuable promotion was the *FT* Industrial Architecture Award. For years we had run regular architectural pages in the *FT*. These went back to the days of Brendan Bracken, who was passionately interested in architecture. They were partly designed to raise revenue, but also to raise standards. We had on the editorial staff an architectural correspondent named Harold Brockman, who was himself a qualified architect. Alan Hare suggested to him that we should give an annual award for the best building used for productive purposes, in other words excluding office or domestic buildings. The judges were two architects nominated by the RIBA and an 'industrial assessor' who regularly until 1977 was Colin Anderson, a colleague of mine on the Covent Garden board, whose aesthetic sensibility and judgement were widely respected. The award was presented each year at a luncheon organized by John Geddes at one of the livery company halls, and it became an important event in the RIBA's calendar.

In 1971 I initiated a somewhat off-beat form of promotion. We had, rather exceptionally, two very good gardening correspondents writing regularly for the paper, Arthur Hellyer and Robin Lane Fox. Hellyer was the doyen among writers on gardening subjects, and author of numerous books, and Robin a very brilliant young historian who had been introduced to the *FT* by Pat Gibson and whose weekly articles about what essentially was his hobby were a delight. I thought that it would be helpful for the *FT* to draw wider attention to their contributions and be useful in emphasizing the breadth of our interests if we were to have an *FT* garden at the Chelsea Flower Show. A garden landscape expert named John Brooks was asked to submit designs which we discussed with the two correspondents, and a garden construction firm run by a Mr Chalk was engaged. The garden which resulted was too architectural for my taste, but it was found generally pleasing, and when the judges made their rounds of inspection on the opening day we were awarded a gold medal. Unfortunately the weather in 1971 was atrocious, and all the surround of the garden was turned by viewers into a sea of mud. We were, however, sufficiently encouraged to repeat the effort a year later, and again in 1973, each year with a different design but always using the same team, although in 1973 I also asked Eddy de Rothschild, the owner of the famous Exbury Gardens, whether he would be willing to help with the supply of some of the trees and shrubs, and he very kindly did so. Three years in a row we were awarded a gold medal, but after the third endeavour we thought that it would be tempting providence to go on, and therefore decided to rest on our laurels.

From a promotional point of view one of the chief assets of Bracken House was the dining room on the sixth floor, sited at the north-western corner of the building, with a splendid diagonal view of the south side of St Paul's Cathedral. After we had moved in, I realized as I sat there one day that the view could be greatly improved by enlarging the window, widening and deepening it. I knew that Albert Richardson, the architect, would have resisted any change, even though the appearance of the building from the street would not be significantly affected; but he was dead, and we made the alteration with a clear conscience.

It was our usual practice in the dining room to have just one guest at a time, inviting the appropriate members of the editorial and business staff to be present. This seemed to me fairer to the guest, and much more fruitful for the staff. The method pursued in certain other offices, notably the *ancien régime Times*, of having a lot of guests at once, drawn from various unrelated walks of life, struck me as a great waste of time. It may have flattered them, but it was apt to have an inhibiting effect upon the talk. We always told our guests that anything said would be treated in strict confidence and would not be used (without specific consent) to make a story in the *FT*, at the same time pointing out that by speaking freely they might prevent errors from appearing in the paper. A minor diversion for them was a betting book which I introduced and which encouraged them to commit themselves about the likely course of such things as the rate of exchange or the level of markets, election prospects, and so on.

The single guest was always placed in the seat with the commanding view, and only those most insensitive to their surroundings failed to catch their breath with delighted surprise. During the course of a year we entertained quite a lot of people, politicians, civil servants, diplomats, businessmen, trades union leaders and so on, a real cross-section, not overlooking that most important group, the advertising agents. The best guest that I can recall is Geoffroi de Courcel, the newly appointed French ambassador, whose first visit to us almost coincided with de Gaulle's devastating 'Non' to Britain's application to join the Common Market. Since the *FT* was a passionate supporter of British membership, we were very downcast; but Geoffroi's defence of the General was so brilliant that we were almost forced to agree that he had been right at the time to deny us entry. The worst guests were usually the politicians, notably Ted Heath, who had a remarkable talent for sulking if something had appeared in the paper which displeased him.

As well as the sixth floor dining room, we also provided three private dining rooms in the (air conditioned) basement. These were made available on a rota basis to the editorial and business sections of the staff for them to do such entertaining as they wished, for there was no doubt that people far preferred to be entertained in the *FT* building than outside in a costly restaurant. There is no doubt too that entertaining is a necessary and inescapable part of business life; and here my Covent Garden connection was unquestionably helpful, for to be able to offer entertainment at the Royal Opera House to business acquaintances had obvious appeal, while from the point of view of Covent Garden the development of interest among the business community helped to build up a valuable body of support for the work of the theatre.

Without the broadmindedness of my *FT* colleagues in allowing me to take off the large amount of time that my chairmanship of Covent Garden called for I should never have been able to perform my functions there to anyone's satisfaction. No less than to them am I grateful to the various secretaries who worked for me at Bracken House and who spent many hours in the unpaid service of Covent Garden. Mercifully I was always tremendously fortunate in the choice of delightful young ladies who were willing to cast in their business lot with mine. In absolute terms none of them could stay very long, because marriage and motherhood claimed them; but while they were with me almost without exception we seemed to develop an intimate relationship, best summarized in the words of one of them as, 'like being married without the sex'. Over a period of thirty years inevitably there were many comings and goings, and to Joyce, Gill, Beverley, Phyllis, Dorothy, Elaine, Stevie, Diana, Muriel, Sheila, Maureen and Pam, I can say no more than a collective thank you. Each in her turn meant much to me.

PART THREE

Covent Garden

Chapter 19

In the summer of 1951 the posting to Washington of a senior civil servant was to result quite fortuitously in my association with the Royal Opera House. Before I relate how this came about, I should give some background. During the war Covent Garden had been rented and used as a dance hall, and when the war ended there was a real chance that that might be its permanent fate. The deplorable prospect was prevented from becoming reality through the initiative of Leslie Boosey and Ralph Hawkes, who were the two chief partners in the important music publishing business which bore their names. They were strongly encouraged by Kenneth Clark, who was acting as chairman of CEMA (the Council for the Encouragement of Music and the Arts)★ during the absence in America of Maynard Keynes. They received a promise of financial backing from the Treasury, and took a short lease of the building, while, behind the scenes, negotiations were going on which resulted in the Government acquiring a fifty-year lease of the property and renting it to a newly created Covent Garden Opera Trust, of which Keynes was chairman and Kenneth Clark a prominent member. (In 1950 the Trust was, for convenience, converted into a non-profit-making limited liability company, the Royal Opera House, Covent Garden Limited.)

Before the formal registration of the Trust in February 1946 it had already been agreed that David Webster should be appointed general administrator. The original suggestion of his name came from Kenneth Clark. He had met David in Liverpool and had been impressed by his running of the Liverpool Philharmonic. They had talked at length about opera, and K had concluded that he would be a suitable person to run a national opera at Covent Garden. The impresario Harold Holt had also urged his name, but it was above all the recommendation of Kenneth Clark which mattered, for in Boosey's words, 'Everyone listened to him.' The actual approach was made by Anthony Gishford, who was a cousin of Hawkes and an acquaintance of David. Conditions for his employment were quickly agreed, despite the fact that he had already

★ CEMA wisely changed its name to Arts Council at the end of 1945. A Royal Charter was granted on 9 August 1946, and Sir Ernest Pooley was appointed the first chairman, serving from 1946 to 1953.

signed a contract to join the staff of the Metal Box Company, from which he was released.

The plan of the new Trust was to present opera and ballet on an all-the-year-round basis. In order to get things off to a flying start the Sadler's Wells Ballet Company was moved into Covent Garden as its permanent home, with a handsome new Oliver Messel production of *Sleeping Beauty* on 20 February 1946, a performance scarcely witnessed by Keynes because as the curtain rose he was taken ill.

It has never been clear to me whether the question of the Sadler's Wells Opera Company also being transferred to Covent Garden was raised, or, if it was, why it was not pursued. They gave the première of Benjamin Britten's great operatic masterpiece *Peter Grimes* in 1945 with immense success. The Company contained Joan Cross and Peter Pears, and they had a degree of professionalism lacking elsewhere. Much time could have been saved, and many subsequent difficulties avoided, had Sadler's Wells Opera also been included in the plan.

It had been Keynes's hope to raise substantial sums for the support of the Opera House from wealthy individuals who, until the budget of 1946, had been able, providing they covenanted for seven years, to set off charitable donations against their income before being assessed for tax. Since tax on the top slice of a rich person's income was levied at a rate of $97\frac{1}{2}$ per cent, the true cost to those in the highest tax bracket of an annual donation of for instance £1,000 was no more than £25. The prospect of being able to raise large sums of money by this means was therefore very real, but not for long. Hugh Dalton's 1946 budget, introduced on 19 April, withdrew the concession in so far as it related to surtax. He did this partly through fear of the possible heavy loss of revenue to the Exchequer, if substantial donations to charitable causes by wealthy people could be offset against their surtax liability; but partly also, I am sure, because Dalton thought it might be regarded as morally offensive that the rich should be able to wear a halo of righteousness at so little real cost to themselves.

The practical result was that the true cost to the taxpayer of giving £1,000 instead of being a mere £25 would be more than £500. Thus the possibility of large private donations vanished, and Keynes's hopes were dashed. What he would have done, what his ingenuity might have devised, can never be known for he died on 21 April, only two days after Dalton's announcement; and Covent Garden was faced with the first of many financial crises.

There was a surprisingly long delay between the death of Keynes and the appointment of his successor. After careful thought the choice fell upon Sir John Anderson, who had not only been a distinguished civil servant, but also Chancellor of the Exchequer, Home Secretary and Lord President of the Council for a long period during the war; and it was thought quite rightly that he would be pretty good at finding his way through the Whitehall maze. Sir John took his time before replying, insisting above all on obtaining some kind of undertaking from the Chancellor of the Exchequer. The figures by comparison with those of today are trifling, but then they meant the difference between starvation and survival; and an undertaking was obtained. It was contained in a letter from Hugh Dalton which John Anderson used always to carry about with him in his pocket, taking it out and brandishing it when the need arose. The somewhat vague wording of the pledge was to the effect that if Covent Garden played its part the Government would not let Covent Garden down; and like a good public servant he held it to be morally binding on all future Chancellors until formally withdrawn or annulled.

Sir John became chairman in August 1946. As soon as he had been appointed he stipulated that since the Royal Opera House was in receipt of public funds a proper record must be kept of the proceedings of the board of directors. He was not content that this should be left to the company secretary. Minutes must be prepared, as they were in Whitehall, and for this purpose a qualified civil servant must be made available, although he would of course not be paid for the work and he would have to do it in addition to his official duties. He offered the position to Denis Rickett who had worked extremely closely with Sir John during the war on highly secret matters relating to the atom bomb and with whom I had myself for a while shared a room at the Ministry of Production. He was an ideal choice as secretary to the board because he was centrally placed in the Treasury as well as being both an impeccable draftsman and intensely musical. Sir John had complete trust in him. The arrangement worked well for some five years until Denis was appointed Treasury Representative and Minister Economic at the British Embassy in Washington; and this was the moment when I entered the scene.

The actual suggestion that I should take over the job of secretary to the board was made by Kenneth Clark, with strong encouragement from his wife, Jane. The idea was put to Sir John, and because I had worked for a longish spell in Whitehall during the war, having gained much experience of minute taking and knowing my way around a little, he approved. Accordingly I saw Denis, in order to ask whether he was content. He said, 'Naturally, so long as you let me have the job back after my return from Washington.' I told him that I regarded myself purely as his *locum tenens*; and indeed I was very conscious of my good fortune, without any expectation that I might be asked to carry on after his return from Washington in two or three years' time.

My enthusiasm for opera as an art form went back many years. At its best it seemed to offer a combination of musical, dramatic and visual delights which placed it in a class of its own. The challenge was that there were so many different elements, singing, acting, conducting and playing, design and production, all of which had to blend for a perfect result to be achieved. The same held true in the case of ballet, although looking at the repertoire as a whole the scale of demands was less exacting. With so much at risk in performances of both opera and ballet, frequent disappointments were inescapable; but with so many supreme masterpieces to perform I felt that the effort to achieve success was tremendously worth making. Above all I believed this to be true in Covent Garden, with its extraordinary acoustics and beautiful auditorium, possessing the perfect degree of intimacy, giving a sense of involvement even to those sitting in the remotest part of the amphitheatre. Therefore when I was offered the opportunity of an association with the theatre, if only for a limited period, I seized it eagerly.

The first meeting I attended was on 19 September 1951. The board were a distinguished group. Besides Sir John, Kenneth Clark and Leslie Boosey, the other members were: Professor E. J. Dent, Sir George Dyson, Lord Harewood, Sir Barry Jackson, The Hon. E. J. Sackville-West, The Hon. James Smith, Lord Wakehurst and Sir William Walton.

Professor Dent, Willian Walton and Jimmy Smith had all three joined the Covent Garden Opera Trust in 1946. Dent, who had been Professor of Music at Cambridge, had established himself as the source of authoritative English trans-lations of many opera libretti. He was on the board of Sadler's Wells, as well as of Covent Garden, and he had played a prominent part in the early postwar history of opera in London. By the time I appeared he was very deaf, with an ear trumpet of Beethovenesque size, and he seldom took part in the discussion. Willie Walton, whom I had known from Wimborne House days, had, I sup-pose, been brought on to the Trust by Kenneth Clark, for they were closely acquainted. Unfortunately he only attended one meeting after my appointment, being then given nine months' leave of absence in order to compose, and he was not to return except as the composer of *Troilus and Cressida*. I regretted his decision for I knew I should miss his sardonic manner and his puckish and astringent sense of humour; but as a creative artist he was wasting his time at the boardroom table. Jimmy Smith had been involved in London musical life for many years. He had been a member of the syndicate which promoted opera at Covent Garden before the war. He was a governor of the Sadler's Wells Foundation, and in May 1948 was elected chairman, a position he held until December 1961 and in which he did much to assist good relations between the two theatres. His influence in operatic circles extended over many years (he was in fact on the Covent Garden board from 1950 until 1961) and was wholly beneficent. No better example could be found to justify a leisured class.

Sir George Dyson, Sir Barry Jackson, Eddy Sackville-West and Lord

Wakehurst had joined the Trust in 1949. Dyson preceded Jimmy Smith as chairman of the Sadler's Wells Foundation. He had been Principal of the Royal College of Music. He composed church music and in general was very much part of the traditional British musical establishment. Sir Barry Jackson was a friend of David Webster, and during the six years in which he was associated with Covent Garden, he gave David plenty of support, subject to the fact that as he was in charge of the Birmingham Repertory Theatre his base was some way from London and therefore regular attendance at performances was not easy for him.

Eddy Sackville-West was wide-ranging in his knowledge and a very refreshing companion. At Eton he had been the star pupil of the pianist Irene Scharrer, whose husband was Eddy's house-master. Together with Desmond Shawe-Taylor he compiled a very useful *Classical Record Guide*, which should have become an annual; but I suppose it was swamped by the weight of material. He suffered from delicate health and during the winter months he was often absent from meetings, but whenever he was present he aired his views forcefully and made a very valuable if rather prejudiced contribution. John Wakehurst was a Tory politician, who was made a director by Sir John. His lack of musical knowledge made him far less qualified than the others, but he had a great passion for the ballet, which was short of champions on the board, and therefore he played a useful role.

George Harewood joined the board in 1951, shortly before I became secretary. He had a more extensive knowledge of the operatic repertoire (and of much other music besides) than anyone else on the board and probably also on the staff. His love of opera was a real passion, and in 1950 he had founded a very useful monthly magazine, *Opera*, which was edited by Harold Rosenthal. George was taken prisoner in Italy in 1944, and his chief reading during his year of captivity was Grove's nine volume *Dictionary of Music*. Both his mother, the Princess Royal, and his father were musical, so that his love of music was inherited. He left the board after only two years in order to become a member of the Covent Garden staff, where he gave valuable service for about seven years, until he left in 1960 to go to Edinburgh as the director of the Festival. It was certainly true that he played a more important part in the operatic side of the work of Covent Garden than any other single individual. He established links with several of the leading conductors, notably Klemperer, Giulini, and Kempe, who were to do much for the evolution of Covent Garden. There is little doubt that David Webster leant on him heavily, although not always giving credit where it was due. Ironically, George was only given his title, Controller of Opera Planning, and only had his duties formally spelt out in his last year of working at the Royal Opera House.

My immediate impression at my first meeting was that the chairman, Sir John, had a somewhat inhibiting effect upon the discussion, and nothing which happened at subsequent meetings caused me to change that view. He had a remarkable brain; and he was among the great administrators of the century, speaking with years of experience and high authority behind him. He was indeed one of the real war-winners, having done more than anyone to lighten Churchill's load, acting as general economic co-ordinator. In a crisis he was splendid, for he was strong and rock-like, but as a rule he did not make people feel at ease. He was not noticeably tall, but he had a large torso and fine powerful head, so that when seated he looked especially formidable. Whenever he spoke it was firmly, and to the point. He seldom laughed, and when he smiled, which was not often, it was with a slightly deprecating air. His knowledge of opera and ballet was minimal, and he did not pretend otherwise. His wife Ava had somewhat greater pretensions in this regard. She was certainly a considerable help to him. Through her, his staid and solemn manner was much lightened, for she had a very sharp wit, and could be extremely amusing. She had been largely educated in France and she had a more cosmopolitan outlook. Many of the leading diplomats were her friends, as well as several of the most prominent British politicians. She was an indefatigable letter writer, very persistent in attaining her ends. I knew her well, and was fond of her despite her somewhat transparent machinations. Occasionally at performances I used to hear her venture a criticism, and he was apt to rebuke her, saying, 'Now, now, Ava, you must remember that they are doing their best.' His experience in Whitehall had taught him that his senior officials must always be upheld, which would have been well enough if his public support had been combined with a measure of criticism in private; but he regarded his main purpose as being to keep Covent Garden on an even keel, and to see that the pledge which he had had from Hugh Dalton was not broken by succeeding Chancellors.

Turning up the minutes of my initial meeting, two items particularly struck me. First, David Webster informed the board that the title role of *Billy Budd* had not yet been cast, although the world première of this new opera by Benjamin Britten was due to take place in about two months' time. (It must be said that the casting actually achieved was excellent, but only as a result of a lightning trip to New York by David accompanied by Leslie Boosey, and then more by good luck than by good management.) Secondly, a certain member of the board suggested that it might be a help if a record were made of the conclusions reached (not, be it noted, of the discussion) at meetings of the opera and ballet committees.

These two items between them gave a foretaste of frustrations in store. In the conditions as they later developed it would have been unthinkable that leading roles in new productions, let alone indeed in revivals, could have been left so completely to chance. It became almost obligatory for repertoire and casting to be planned in detail for at least two years ahead, no other way being possible except with a repertory company (as in the theatre) where the artists are engaged full time without the right to accept outside engagements, a condition to which artists of the standard expected at Covent Garden are in the main unlikely to agree.

As to the suggestion meekly put forward by one of the board members that a record should be made not of the discussion but of the *conclusions* reached at the meetings of the two committees concerned with detailed opera and ballet matters, it is very strange and quite out of character that Sir John had not himself insisted upon it from the beginning of his chairmanship, particularly because he must have observed that David Webster tended to prefer a large degree of secrecy.

In my early stages as secretary I was in frequent touch with the chairman, normally seeing him at his office at the Port of London Authority, of which he was chairman. (At election times he used sometimes to attend meetings in the docks area, camouflaged in a cloth cap and tweed jacket.) He was given a peerage in 1952, becoming Lord Waverley, although to me he always remained Sir John. At the time one matter particularly caused him concern, the circulation of a number of anonymous communications highly critical of the Administration, implying that homosexuality was rife and almost necessary for hope of advancement. This allegation was nonsense. Sir John however felt it necessary to see David Webster and assure him of his full support, while at the same time warning him to beware of any action substantiating the allegations, for he did not wish Covent Garden to be a centre of scandal. David's leanings were not in doubt and were accepted as part of the natural order of things by all reasonable people, but the law legalizing sexual relations between consenting males, a remarkable achievement, due entirely to the determination of Lord Arran, who himself had nothing to gain thereby, had yet to be passed; and therefore anyone in a prominent position was liable both to be prosecuted by the police, and to be blackmailed by scoundrels.

From the beginning of my attachment to Covent Garden I used to see David regularly. Our relationship extended over a long period of years and I grew to know him well. His family came from Dundee in Scotland, where he was born; but while he was still young they moved to Liverpool, his father having been appointed area manager for the famous old business of Reckitt's, and there David was educated, first of all at the Holt School, and then at the University. He studied economics, but from an early age he was involved with amateur dramatics, both as producer and actor. He was chairman of the University

Dramatic Society, as well as being president of the University Guild, and he became the moving spirit of an amateur theatrical group, producing a number of plays, including *Macbeth*, *Murder in the Cathedral*, and Hugh Walpole's *The Portrait of a Man with Red Hair*, in each of which he played the leading role, to very good effect. He also fancied himself in cabaret, and I can well suppose that he was extremely droll.

After he left the University in 1924, he joined Lewis's of Liverpool, a large department store group; and it was not long before he found himself manager of their Bon Marché store. He came frequently to London because he was fascinated by the theatre. On one of his visits, I think in 1931, he met a young man called Jimmy Cleveland-Belle, whom he induced to leave his job with Shell-Mex and move to Liverpool to join the staff of the Bon Marché, from which time for forty years they became constant companions, sharing a house together from the moment David came to London to take over the running of Covent Garden. During the greater part of the war, David was attached to the Ministry of Supply, his job being to act as a kind of productivity expert and progress chaser at several large munitions factories; and report has it that he was successful in his efforts. He was also, from 1940 to 1945, chairman of the Liverpool Philharmonic Orchestra.

Today the informal method of his selection to be the head of a major public institution would be unacceptable. His lack of previous relevant experience would have ruled against him, and I think it unlikely that he would have been chosen, but this is a criticism of the system rather than of him, for despite his faults he was a substantial personality with a considerable flair for showmanship. In the main he earned the loyalty of his staff for he brought great dedication to his job and he had a generous nature, although he found it almost impossible to go backstage after a performance to say, 'Well done'. Why this was, I never discovered. He was, as a rule, good at sensing the atmosphere and judging people. He had undoubted authority, and his presence was felt whenever he entered the theatre. He spoke fluently, and he expressed himself well on paper, despite almost indecipherable handwriting. His visual taste was very capricious and occasionally a slight streak of vulgarity obtruded, while at times his attempts at humour failed lamentably.

Physically, he was rather short, plump and soft-featured, with a bald shiny head; and one felt that he had never seemed young. He had a maddening habit of drumming his fingers on the table if he was put out about something, and he tended to whistle a tune *sotto voce* if there was a lull in the conversation and he felt ill at ease. He was usually simply dressed in a dark blue suit, although he was attached to a lightweight check overcoat and a floppy black hat, which he wore on the side of his head so that when walking in the street he resembled an on-course bookmaker rather than the general administrator of the Royal Opera House. His favourite tunes tended to be the most sentimental, for example the love duets in *Boris Godunov* and *Turandot*. His chief virtue was his calmness and unflappability, and his ability to cope with crises, many of which it must be said arose from his own lethargy. He could be terribly dilatory in answering letters. To several of my colleagues on the board he was known as the arch-procrastinator, or A.P. for short. He undoubtedly found the board in general, and especially myself, something of an encumbrance. He liked to keep things to himself, and it was not unusual for him to commit us to a particular course of action without proper consultation, and this at times caused much annoyance, since the ultimate responsibility was ours. Ideally he would have liked to be a great impresario, a sort of Diaghilev and Hurok rolled into one, answerable to nobody but himself. He never earned much money, but he loved celebrities and he was positively sybaritic and a real *bon viveur*, measuring his visits abroad by the number of 'main meals' he would consume. The operatic policy to which Covent Garden was committed after the war, opera in English by English artists, was not the one best suited to David's tastes and proclivities, for he was far happiest operating on the international scene.

However, in 1951, and indeed for some years to come, the opera in English policy was pretty rigidly observed. The first rather timid suggestion of a departure from it came towards the end of 1952, when it was agreed that if sufficient leading artists could be engaged for the leading roles two operas during the course of the season might be performed in their original languages, the operas specifically mentioned being *Aida* and *Meistersinger*. In the summer of 1953 a season of Italian opera sung in Italian was given at the Stoll theatre. This had been well attended, and the Covent Garden board had an interesting dis-cussion about the whole question of language policy, but basically the view still was that the original objective must be adhered to, despite the extremely un-satisfactory compromises and very poor attendance figures to which it all too often gave rise. For me the most objectionable aspect was the not uncommon need to perform operas in more than one language on the same night. This arose quite simply because of a last minute case of withdrawal on account of sickness or for some other reason, with the only available replacement having to be brought over at short notice from the Continent, and the virtual certainty that the singer coming to the rescue would not know the role in English.

Whenever the question arose in discussion I threw my weight vehemently into the opera in the original language camp in so far as concerned the basic German and Italian repertoire (including as Italian the operas of Mozart other than *Magic Flute* and *Seraglio*). For Russian operas it seemed to me that a flexible approach was necessary. The thing I could not abide was a mixed language performance. For Czech opera, which meant Janacek and Smetana, there could obviously be no argument: it had to be English. Difficulties always arose over French opera, notably of course *Carmen*, a work which at Covent Garden more or less has to be a star vehicle. It is arguable that the perfect Carmen simply does not exist, since it is impossible to find a universal prototype *femme fatale*, above all one that can sing. But nevertheless the probability was that at Covent Garden the title role in *Carmen* had to be cast from overseas, and that almost certainly meant that the lady would only know the part in French. Therefore if Covent Garden was to give this most popular of all operas, which clearly it must, the language had to be French, despite the amount of spoken dialogue (or recitative, depending upon the version used), and despite the embarrassing inability of many of our singers to disguise the fact that they were British, notwithstanding the improvement in the quality of foreign language coaching. Another French opera about which curiously there was never any argument was *Pelléas et Melisande*, this presumably because of Maeterlinck's verse: although if the literary quality of the libretto is to be the determining factor, then surely von Hofmannsthal's *Rosenkavalier* (and indeed *Arabella* and others) ranks at least as high. For modern opera, meaning opera in the modern idiom, with fairly elaborate and probably cerebral librettos, translation was essential, and in no way in dispute.

At Covent Garden, as the opera in English policy was departed from, so the quality of performances tended steadily to improve, and with it the attitude of the music critics, who in the earlier days had castigated the Royal Opera House with terrible consistency. My own attitude was based upon both artistic and pragmatic grounds. I wanted to hear works given as the composer originally intended: I mean the actual vowel and consonant sounds, or as near to them as we could get. Italian and German, *and* French and Russian, are all very musical languages, and to hear them beautifully sung adds immensely to the pleasure of listening. Furthermore, in translation fearfully contorted English phrases are often used and even changes in meaning to make the syllables fit the music, giving rise to smiles or worse at moments of drama or tragedy. Then, from the point of view of British singers, the opportunity of learning basic repertory works in the original language added greatly to their ability to obtain engagements overseas. The policy also meant that famous foreign singers would come to London to appear at Covent Garden, which otherwise they would not have done. One used always to be told that after the war the glorious Flagstad and Schwarzkopf and Hotter came and sang many roles in English; but that was over twenty-five years ago, and their successors would certainly not, except for some very special reason, spend the extra time needed to learn parts in English, knowing that the effort would be useless to them elsewhere. There was a minor consideration which to me seemed important. When operas were performed in English, Equity, who in any event tried whenever they could to promote the claims of British singers, however unsuited to the role under discussion, were a good deal more likely to try to prevent the engagement of a foreign artist, quite overlooking the growing employment overseas of British singers.

At Covent Garden there were endless and sometimes bitter arguments upon the subject. More than once I was rebuked by the Arts Council and indeed when David Webster and I appeared before their music panel we were made to feel slightly like criminals in the dock. His own position about language was never clearly stated, but I feel pretty certain that he shared my point of view, although more cautious because of the supposed 'political' implications.

The change in policy was finally vindicated in 1968 when the Sadler's Wells Opera Company was installed in the vast spaces of the Coliseum, so large that it made Covent Garden seem the intimate theatre: and the company was subsequently renamed the English National Opera, so that Covent Garden's role must be as an international house following the original language policy now in fact largely pursued by most of the leading international opera houses throughout the Western world.

Perhaps the major problem exercising the board when I became secretary related to the post of musical director. The position had fallen vacant through the non-renewal of Karl Rankl's contract. Rankl had held the post from April 1946. David Webster's choice of him was surprising, for the names of Bruno Walter and Eugene Goossens among others were, it seems, previously discussed. Either would have made a greater public impact than Rankl, but neither was strongly pressed to accept the job. Rankl had had considerable operatic experience before the war, although not in a leading post, and he had come to Britain in 1939 as a refugee from Hitler. He did a good deal to build up the Covent Garden orchestra and chorus from nothing, but I cannot help wondering whether other and more distinguished persons could not have done as much, while at the same time giving a higher standard of performance than Rankl usually achieved: and it must be said that the critical reviews in the early years were often very poor. Be that as it may, Rankl was, so far as I can judge without having had any personal contact, pretty shamefully treated. For the last year of his employment at Covent Garden, which was the first year in which I acted as secretary, his title as musical director was dropped: and then in the 1953 Coronation Gala Performance book which included a history of the Royal Opera House, no reference whatsoever was made to the part Rankl had played. There was also the introduction of Peter Brook as director of productions, a highly gifted *enfant terrible* with whom Rankl did not mix at all well. There was the engagement of the great maestro Erich Kleiber as principal guest conductor, upon whom favours were lavished in a way they never were upon Rankl, a crowning disappointment being when Kleiber and not Rankl was given the conducting of the London première of *Wozzeck* in January 1952.

It was in any event clear that Rankl's continued employment was in doubt. Kleiber, while agreeing to conduct regularly as a guest, would not commit himself to the rigours of a substantially whole-time appointment, and a search had to be made elsewhere. When I appeared as secretary, discussion centred around the name of John Barbirolli, who was in charge of the Hallé orchestra. Talks with him persisted on and off for the best part of two years, and I myself always felt that he had no ultimate intention of accepting, for his heart was with the Hallé; but it would have saved everyone much trouble if he had said this unequivocally at the beginning. After his final turn-down of an offer, the best part of three years elapsed before a new musical director was appointed. The choice was to fall upon Rafael Kubelik, distinguished son of a distinguished father, whose homeland, Czechoslovakia, had been engulfed.

Well before I commenced my association with the theatre, there had been a good deal of concern among members of the board arising out of the constant press criticisms levelled at Covent Garden. A special committee of the board recommended the appointment of an artistic director. David was a member of this committee, although it is hard to believe that he strongly supported the recommendation: and the upshot was that instead of an artistic director a deputy general administrator was appointed to relieve David of some of his load. The man appointed was Sir Steuart Wilson, who was on the Covent Garden board and a member of the special committee. He was at the time Head of Music at the BBC, having before that been in charge of the music department of the Arts Council, but he had made it clear to his colleagues on the committee that he would welcome appointment to the opera house staff. The choice was not exactly a happy one. A powerful antipathy developed between David and himself, and quite soon after his appointment he saw the chairman, John Waverley, and made various criticisms about the running of the theatre. Relations evidently worsened, because two years later he circulated a highly critical memorandum to members of the board, asking to meet them in order to elaborate his views and threatening otherwise to make his criticisms public. The chairman was not going to tolerate this sort of behaviour. He said that when he had seen Wilson two years previously and listened to his complaints, he had believed him to be satisfied: in any event it was not proper for an employee to appear before the board in order to criticize the administration. I was deputed to tell Wilson that his request could not be granted, but that if he wrote to the chairman asking for an interview Lord Waverley would agree to see him together with one or two other colleagues. To the best of my knowledge no further letter was written and no interview took place: and shortly afterwards Wilson left the staff, celebrating his departure by giving a wholly offensive interview on 24 July 1955 to the Sunday newspaper, *The People*, in which he announced his intention of launching a campaign against homosexuality in British music in general and Covent Garden in particular, although subsequent evidence of the campaign was strangely lacking.

The disappearance of Steuart Wilson conferred one notable blessing upon Covent Garden. The knowledge that his contract was ending in June 1955 meant that a successor must be found. Edric Cundell, the head of the Guildhall School of Music, who had joined the board in 1953, made a major sacrifice. He suggested that the secretary of his school might be a suitable replacement. The man in question was John Tooley. It was agreed that first David should see him, and that then I should (why me at that point of time, I cannot imagine). We both reported favourably. He then had to see John Waverley who likewise was impressed. The result was that at the board meeting in April 1955 John Tooley's appointment was confirmed, not be it noted as assistant general administrator, but as assistant *to* the general administrator, a title with which he was forced to content himself for nearly five years, because, following the bitter experience with Wilson, David was very chary about committing himself to another deputy. I suppose too, looking back on it, that the presence of George Harewood on the staff with obvious possible claims as a number two had an inhibiting effect upon David, a situation which was only resolved when George left to go to Edinburgh.

During the years that I was secretary, just as in the years before, and in the years after, finance was the dominant subject. In spite of the pledge Sir John had obtained from Dalton we were nearly always fighting to secure our future. There were brief periods when we were given a kind of sense of security, but they were very much the exception: and although we felt that in the last analysis we *should* be all right, it could never be taken for granted, and we had a sizable sense of gratitude to our bankers Coutts & Co. for more than once seeing us through. In 1952 the Covent Garden grant was under £200,000 compared with over £5 million in 1978/9: and we were debating whether we dared risk putting up the price of stalls from 17s. 6d. to 19s.; but that was in pre-inflationary days, when the chorus rate of pay was £9 a week, and in negotiations for an increase the settlement was for an additional £1, to take effect from September 1952, the pay of ballet dancers being roughly on a par.

It was largely the ballet that helped to keep Covent Garden in a state of financial equilibrium during the first decade after the war. This was for several reasons. First of all, the company, then still called the Sadler's Wells Ballet, already had international renown. Secondly, ballet was less costly to present and in the main drew larger audiences. Thirdly, David Webster had established very good relations with the famous American impresario, Sol Hurok, of Russian Jewish extraction, who starting I think in 1949 had taken the ballet company regularly every other year to tour the United States for a period of three months or more, an arrangement which brought significant revenue to Covent Garden and augmented earnings for the dancers, and which did a good deal for Britain's general standing in transatlantic eyes. Hurok was extremely tough, but he took a genuine interest in the careers and the well-being of the artists he presented. Whenever I saw him I told him that for all he owed her the least he should give Ninette de Valois was a fur tippet, but he never complied.

Despite the valuable, indeed vital part played by the ballet in the affairs of Covent Garden the members of the company always had the feeling that they were being treated like poor relations. They believed that without their exertions Covent Garden's state would be extremely parlous. And yet when it came to the use of the orchestra and the stage for rehearsals, consideration of their needs always came second. In early 1953 Ninette de Valois felt constrained to make representations to the chairman, including a complaint that she was never allowed promptly to see extracts from board minutes bearing on ballet company affairs. As a result it was inadequately agreed that she should be invited to meetings of the board 'possibly once a quarter', which struck me as being far too much an arm's length relationship, and one which was eventually righted, when I established that the head of ballet and the musical director should both be entitled as of right to attend board meetings regularly except when their own personal position was under discussion.

During the course of 1953 a lot of time was devoted to the title of the ballet company. When Covent Garden opened after the war, the Sadler's Wells Ballet company, which had been taken over by the Royal Opera House, retained its original name, because of the goodwill attaching to it; but before long Sadler's Wells theatre decided to form a new ballet company to ease the strain on their opera side. This new company was named the Sadler's Wells Theatre Ballet, and Ninette de Valois became its director, while retaining the direction of the company based on Covent Garden. There was thus a fair amount of confusion, which was enhanced by the existence of a ballet school, also founded by Ninette and also named after Sadler's Wells. The problem was discussed at length, without any clear solution in sight, until in December 1953 Ninette herself suggested the possibility of a Royal Charter embracing the two ballet companies which would then be closely integrated with the school, with the title Royal being conferred upon all three entities. She was eager for the Charter not so much for the title as to provide some ultimate protection if Covent Garden were to fail in its responsibilities; and in any event Covent

Garden was only required to present ballet, not simply one particular company.

In April 1954 a solicitor was appointed to frame a new constitution for the ballet organization. His name was Mr Arnold Goodman, and so far as I and many others were concerned this was the first moment at which a most remarkable personality emerged and came as time went by to play a major role in all our lives. He had only recently set up his own law firm, having previously been working in the offices of Rubinstein, Nash, who for all routine business were solicitors to the Royal Opera House. He was then scarcely at the foothills of his astonishing rise to fame. None of us would have foretold that within fifteen years he was destined to become chairman of the Arts Council, and then chairman of the Newspaper Publishers Association (of his connection with which I wrote in an earlier chapter), as well as being the Prime Minister's legal adviser and the confidant of many of the tycoons and political leaders in the land, sought after on all sides for his wise counsel, his kindness and his witty discourse. The new constitution was debated for a long time, and it was over two years before the Charter was granted and the change of names took place.

Another important event in the history of the Royal Ballet during my time as secretary was the conferment upon Frederick Ashton of the title of associate director of the company, the purpose being to make it clear to all that the right of succession to Ninette when she retired was his: not that there was much doubt in people's mind about this for he stood head and shoulders above others in creative genius, being a master of significant understatement, and having unerring artistic judgement and understanding. In those days his extraordinary collaboration with Margot Fonteyn was at its peak; each inspired the other, and together they inspired the whole company.

By comparison with the ballet the opera side of Covent Garden life was still feeling its way ahead. One major disappointment was experienced. The coronation of Queen Elizabeth II was to take place in 1953, and plans were made for what it was hoped would be a suitable celebration at the Royal Opera House. With George Harewood as the catalyst, Benjamin Britten's enthusiasm was fired for the composition of an opera especially for the occasion, based upon the private life of Queen Elizabeth I, and John Piper was commissioned to do the decor. Her Majesty agreed to the proposal that she should attend a special gala performance at which Britten's new opera, named *Gloriana*, should have its world première. The leaders in all walks of life, including the principal diplomats stationed in London, were invited to attend what promised to be the great artistic event of the year, a white tie and decorations occasion which would long be remembered for its splendour. Long remembered it was, but as a fiasco. The music was not remotely difficult to music-lovers, but much of the audience were not in the habit of attending opera at all. *Gloriana* was quite long, the evening was warm, the intervals seemed endless, stick-up collars grew limp, and well before the end a restlessness set in. 'Boriana' was on everyone's lips. Most distressing was that in one scene the elderly Queen Elizabeth I removed her wig from her head and was revealed as almost bald: and this was taken, for no good reason at all, as being in bad taste, given the particular nature of the audience. A number of years went by before the opera was given again, and then it was not at Covent Garden but at Sadler's Wells and later at the Coliseum, where the serious and moving nature of the work was revealed.

I do not know whether it was before or after the *Gloriana* gala that Sir Arthur Bliss was made Master of the Queen's Musick. However, he celebrated his appointment by conveying to Sir John that he had a prescriptive right to be a member of the Covent Garden board. There was no precedent to go by, and Sir John was somewhat taken aback. The proposal was debated by the board and views were divided. His opera *The Olympians*, with a libretto by J. B. Priestley, had been given its première at Covent Garden some five hears previously, but it had not succeeded either with the intellectuals or the average opera-goer, and it was certainly not a recommendation. Sir Arthur, though, was known to be an agreeable and clubbable man, even if slightly self-assertive, and an invitation was issued to him in March 1954. He remained a member of the board for three and a half years, enlivening such meetings as he attended, although I do not think that his interest was ever seriously engaged. There were two other board changes while I was secretary. In April 1953 Sir John invited a friend of his, a retired diplomat named Sir Philip Nichols, to join. He was a delightful man, but I am not sure that he made a significant contribution to our deliberations, and living in the country he was not a great attender. More importantly, in 1952 Kenneth Clark, that extraordinary polymath, who had first introduced me to the scene, had been offered the position of chairman of the Arts Council, which he very rightly accepted. But the consequence obviously was that he could not remain a member of the Covent Garden board, although for the opera house it was extremely valuable to have at the helm of the Government's disbursing agency for the Arts someone who had first-hand experience of some of the problems.

Finally, in August 1954 I myself was elected a member of the board, and thus I was no longer obliged to be simply a silent taker of minutes.

In early 1955 Sir John added two formidable characters to our ranks. These were Isaiah Berlin and Oliver Franks. Isaiah Berlin, a world-renowned figure, is unique. He is mercurial, hypersensitive, with antennae stretching out far in every direction, omniscient, prejudiced, funny, human and lovable. His association with Covent Garden was to extend over a far longer period than Oliver's. He had to leave the board in 1965 when he went to apply himself to the problems of building Wolfson College, Oxford, literally from the grass-roots upwards, but he continued to serve as a member of the opera committee, and he resumed full membership of the board in April 1974, being present therefore when I retired from the chairmanship in July of that year. Throughout his term as a director, Isaiah was intimately associated with many of the inner artistic personality and policy problems which emerged; and at all times he made himself indispensable, outstandingly so to myself.

Oliver I had known slightly during the war when he was second secretary (Raw Materials) at the Ministry of Supply. He was very tall, with aquiline features, and whenever he entered a room his authority immediately asserted itself. It was clear that he had an astonishing gift for assimilating the essentials of any situation or problem. In disputes at a meeting he tended to stay quiet while argument raged, and then at the critical moment he would speak. 'Aren't you trying to say this?' he would ask, followed by a brilliant résumé, coupled with a formula which in some mysterious way would commend itself to the rival factions as being exactly what they had both wished to suggest. I cannot remember any specific examples of this power to mediate, but it is certainly true. And if he himself was ever in disagreement with people, and they were floundering helplessly in the face of his powerful intellect, he would go out of his way to help his opponents by rephrasing their arguments for them. With the ordinary routine stuff which came before the Covent Garden board he was never greatly concerned, and I do not think that he had a very extensive knowledge of opera or ballet: but whenever a critical matter arose he was superb. He was much missed when he retired from the board in October 1960.

A year later, in January 1956, Lionel Robbins was elected to the board. I suggested his name to Sir John, and he was clearly upset that he had not himself had the idea, for it was undoubtedly a good one. Lionel is among the most distinguished men of the century. He was born in 1898, but he had and still has the gusto and vitality of someone less than half his age. By profession he was an economist, although his interests extended far further than this would imply. He rendered immense services in a wide variety of fields. At no point was he activated by any self-seeking motive. His one concern always was to serve the public good as he saw it, seeking no personal advantage and no monetary gain. He lived simply and modestly, and he always went out of his way to give credit to others, however little it might be their due. Whenever there was a tough assignment, he was the first to step forward. He was no plaster saint, and he had one or two *bêtes noires* who could do no right in his eyes, but he was essentially the embodiment of goodness, and one to whom we should all feel indebted. At Covent Garden he served for many years as chairman of the all-important finance committee, a committee which curiously enough Sir John would not bring into being, on the doubtful argument that finance was so important that it was a matter for the whole board, with the result that discussion of financial matters tended to be cursory and superficial. It was only towards the end of his life that he was persuaded by Lionel to change his mind.

Lionel was also the first person to urge upon Sir John that Covent Garden had a duty to produce a full and detailed annual account of its activities, and our yearly press conferences, of which in fact Sir John held only one, developed into significant and worthwhile occasions. It did however take an appallingly long time to get the first report into final shape. The preparation of this was in fact proposed before Lionel came on to the board, and when it appeared it was a somewhat inadequate self-laudatory document covering in a slightly smug way the ten years from 1946 until 1956, glossing rather ludicrously over the various failures and mistakes. The regular annual report came two years after the first ten year review. The important introductory section was drafted by Lionel himself, in his Augustan style, and when I became chairman of the board he was always present with me at the press conferences held when the annual report was issued.

The first of these gatherings took place on 8 January 1959. They were usually amicable occasions. The normal procedure was for me to make a short opening statement, directing attention to salient points in the report, and then I would invite questions. Since we instituted two other annual press conferences each year, at which the musical director of the Royal Opera and the artistic director of the Royal Ballet would announce their respective plans for the coming season, my press conferences were intended to cover the broader issues, such for instance as the balance of performances between opera and ballet, policy relating to pricing, language, training, touring, redevelopment, guest artists and so on. The press representatives who attended sometimes made me feel as though I was in the witness box, but at heart they were almost invariably well disposed, and recognized that our chief problem, particularly in the earlier stages, was to be assured of an adequate annual grant. They took pride in Covent Garden as an institution, wanting to see it flourish.

There was a certain duality about my position. As managing director of the FT I identified myself with the representatives of the press. As a director of Covent Garden I wanted the maximum sympathy and support for our work. There were occasions in most years when I had brushes with individuals, but I do not think that I ever questioned a critical opinion as such. I was admittedly always quick to correct a definite misstatement of fact; I hated it when criticism became carping, and I sometimes took strong exception to needlessly vehement language, or to words written with a lack of humility and an assurance of infallibility, because I saw plenty of instances of the pain caused. I was also aware of the possible effect upon foreign artists whose services we required and who were very fearful of the London critics: and if I ever said to a singer, 'But think of that marvellous applause!' I would be told, 'I can't take that away with me. All I can take are my notices.' There were two things to which I deeply objected: first, anything which smacked of a vendetta against a particular individual, and second, the maddening habit of sub-editors of singling out one offensive phrase in a perfectly objective notice and making it the heading, thus encouraging people to regard the reading of the notice as unnecessary, and quite possibly doing great harm to box office attendances. Despite my eagerness to rush to the aid of Covent Garden and of the artists appearing there, despite my occasional brushes with one or two individuals, the Critics' Circle were kind enough to give me a farewell luncheon, and present me with a parting gift; and this particularly warmed my heart, for with many I had developed a true friendship, and for all I had a sincere respect for their conscientiousness and their integrity.

However, returning to the sequence of events, 1956 was a year which had more than its fair share of pleasure and of pain. On the ballet side a major cause of satisfaction was the first visit to London by the Bolshoi Ballet Company for a seven-week season, a great triumph for David. There was intense excitement in advance of the company's arrival, and the reception the dancers received must have more than matched their anticipation. Most people agreed that visually the productions were dated in style, jejune and pretty unimaginative: and the costumes sometimes bordered on the ludicrous. The men were required to wear shorts over their tights, for the sake of decency one presumed: although mercifully on a later visit this inartistic habit had been discontinued. But the technical skills displayed, the poetry of movement revealed by the pure classical dancing, the strength and virility of the men of the company, were a revelation to the ballet-going public and acted as a tremendous challenge and stimulus to our own dancers. There was no nonsense about 'pansies in pink tights', a phrase used by Cecil King when I once invited him to the ballet. It was for the development of ballet in Britain a major turning point. The individual triumph went to Galina Ulanova, who occupied the kind of pinnacle achieved by Margot Fonteyn here. Thanks to David's insistence, she danced two or three times each week; and Ava Waverley practically adopted her during her stay, although their means of communication were very sketchy. At the suggestion of one of us the board members and David Webster clubbed together to give Ulanova a leaving present, and I was asked to make a choice. There was £65 to spend. I found three handsome Revelation suitcases of differing sizes, and two excellent handbags, one for travel and one for the evening; and that surely was bargain shopping.

The Bolshoi visit was a real help in relation to Covent Garden's finances in the 1956/7 year. It was the forerunner of several more Russian visits, two by the Bolshoi, and two by the Kirov from Leningrad. The Royal Ballet should have made a reciprocal appearance in Moscow shortly after the Bolshoi's first visit, but the plan was abruptly cancelled because of the Soviet Union's callous display of military might in Hungary. It did not finally take place until the summer of 1961, when the company visited both Moscow and Leningrad. The visit was hugely successful, Frederick Ashton's *Fille mal Gardée* in particular.

On the operatic front there were a number of excellent performances, and some frankly less so. Rafael Kubelik had embarked upon his three years as musical director towards the end of 1955, starting with an impressive *Otello*, sung in Italian, and a splendid production of the ebullient Francis Poulenc's *Dialogues des Carmélites*, sung in English, and incidentally with the then little-known Joan Sutherland in a leading role. Both of these productions were designed by Georges Wakhevitch who in those days was responsible for a number of sound, economical and workmanlike additions to the repertoire, devoid of tricks and always presentable (*Boris Godunov* and *Carmen* were others). Kubelik's engagement was, I am sure, as much the inspiration of George Harewood as of David Webster. He was a fine conductor, and a kind and sensitive man, too highly strung for the strains to which he was to be subjected. These arose obliquely as a result of the issue of the 1946–56 ten-year report, which was published in June 1956, being introduced at the only press conference held by my distinguished predecessor. Its publication touched off a whole stream of criticism aimed at Covent Garden, in which a good friend of mine, Martin Cooper, chief music critic of the *Daily Telegraph*, played a leading part. Rafael Kubelik could not restrain himself. He produced a draft letter to send to the *Daily Telegraph*, but Sir John saw him, told him that it was far too long, and persuaded him instead to send a *short* letter to *The Times*. Unfortunately Kubelik did not show his re-drafted letter to anyone. It was largely based on his earlier draft and it was published on 23 June. In it he complained of the most unfair disparagement of British singers. He said that they did not have small voices, and only suffered from the characteristic British inferiority complex, from which it was the job of critics to free them. His letter went on somewhat sententiously (goodness knows who helped him with the drafting):

We should all strive for a British national opera, supported by critics who must ignore the snobs and instead fight for communion between the British public and British composers and singers.

And so on. This of course provoked Martin Cooper himself to write a fairly devastating letter to *The Times* which appeared two days later, assuring Kubelik of his willingness to ignore snobs and to fight for communion, etc., but, said he,

. . . these singers must be worth communing with, and it is on this point that some of us have questioned the present Covent Garden inability first to find the best voices and then to train them. If Mr. Kubelik is right about the inhibitions of the average British singer, what has Covent Garden been doing to overcome these? I hope that he is not proposing the appointment of a house psychiatrist to be attached to the Royal Opera House; but what about an opera school?

Then into the fray stepped Sir Thomas Beecham, a conductor of undoubted genius, who had steadily smarted under the fact that he himself had not been invited to take over the running of the opera side of Covent Garden when the theatre reopened after the war. His long and disgraceful letter appeared on 27 June. In it he animadverted upon the earlier appointment of Karl Rankl ('In defiance of all common sense they engaged as musical director a foreigner, and let him loose upon the unhappy creatures who had been led to expect beneficial results from this monumental stroke of stupidity') and then continued,

After the departure of this gentleman from the London scene there followed a period of interregnum during which the misguided directors had plenty of time and opportunity to select some Englishman of musical attainment and general culture to meet this supreme need. Now we have another foreigner in charge. But does he possess any of the quali-fications essential for the creation of a truly national organisation? It is not a question only of conducting; the modern world positively teems with conductors of every nationality and nearly all of them are highly praised by the press.

What we have all got to realise is that Covent Garden has neither accomplished the purpose for which it was established, nor is it likely ever to do so while it remains in the hands of those who are now in charge of it. The time has come for a full and enlightened inquiry into every branch of its activities, and this should be undertaken by an independ-ent body, not one of whom has any association with it, or who has an axe to grind of a material kind.

Kubelik not being British and not knowing what Beecham could be like, was offended, and affronted. That same day he wrote to the chairman in the following terms:

Through the recent attacks on the policy of the administration of Covent Garden I learned that my status as a foreigner might be regarded as a handicap to creating a British national opera. Feeling that my person could be a serious obstacle to the successful achievement of this noble goal I prefer to resign as musical director as from the beginning of the coming season.

I can assure you that it is my love for the work I have started at Covent Garden which brought me to this decision. I admire British musicians and their friends in administration

who are striving for a better future in the opera field in Great Britain. I hope that sooner
or later they will unanimously find a way to work together with goodwill towards new
operatic horizons which some other nations have already attained.

My sincerest wishes are with them and also my gratitude to all who gave me the
privilege of working with them for a short period on the same lines.

To the editor of *The Times* he wrote:

In his letter of 25th June Sir Thomas Beecham doubts whether I as a foreigner 'possess
any of the qualifications essential for the creation of a truly national organisation.'
Having great respect for his 54 years' association with the lyric theatre and 46 of them as
impresario, manager, and musical director, I can assure him that I came to his country
for the sole purpose of helping with the development of something which I thought the
majority of the British opera-loving public longed to possess: a British national opera.

Since I see now that the British have not settled among themselves the problem of
whether or not they want to have such a noble institution, and since I do not want to be
in the way as a foreigner, I can set Sir Thomas Beecham's mind at rest: I have submitted
to the Chairman of the Board of Directors my resignation as Musical Director of Covent
Garden.

I was asked to see Kubelik as a matter of urgency, and prevail upon him to
hold up his letter to *The Times*. I succeeded in persuading him to do this for a
period of twenty-four hours, but as he had already sent his letter round by hand
I had to make him ring up and request *The Times* not to publish it that same
night. I reported to the chairman as follows:

I have just returned here from the Opera House where I have been prevailing upon
Kubelik to hold up his letter to The Times. This he has agreed to do, anyway for twenty-
four hours, and he has personally asked The Times not to print it tonight. I feel that you
yourself may have to write a letter to the editor saying that Kubelik has offered his
resignation, which we have refused to accept, and that we have the fullest confidence in
him. What has really upset him is being stigmatised as a foreigner. But what Englishman
could hold the job, other of course than Sir Thomas Beecham!

I told Kubelik that if he wished to resign he must do it to the board, and not to The
Times newspaper: and that he would do his reputation incalculable harm if two days
after publishing his declaration of faith he were to throw his hand in. I believe that he
will stay, but we shall have to uphold him strongly.

An urgent board meeting was summoned for the following afternoon. Lord
Waverley drafted out a brief letter to be delivered immediately to the editor of
The Times. The letter simply said:

My colleagues and I on the board of the Royal Opera House, Covent Garden, think it
right that the public should know that, after reading the strictures contained in the letter

from Sir Thomas Beecham, published in The Times yesterday, Mr. Rafael Kubelik formally tendered his resignation on the ground that it appeared that his status as a foreigner might be regarded as an obstacle to the development of a British national opera.

The board have informed Mr. Kubelik that they are unwilling to accept his resignation. They have assured him that he has their entire confidence and that he can rely on their unstinted support in pursuit of the policy he has outlined during his tenure of his present office.

Kubelik was summoned to the board room, and the letter was read to him. His face was a mixture of smiles and tears. He flung his arms wide apart, said dramatically, 'It is finished,' and then embraced the chairman. His resignation was at once withdrawn. He left the meeting, and wrote the following heartfelt note of thanks to Sir John:

Please accept these few lines of gratitude which I deeply owe to you.

The solution which you and the other Directors have found for my difficult position strengthened my faith that goodwill, trust and real understanding among people alone can bring happiness and success, and out of this we shall, let us hope, achieve what we are all striving for: a British national opera which would challenge the world!

It only remained for me to make sure that Kubelik's original letter to The Times was not published by mistake.

The storm which had been raised did not of course instantly die down. John Christie of Glyndebourne felt constrained to write a letter with which I was in sympathy, about the illogicalities of Covent Garden's language policy. Steuart Wilson, whose behaviour had already been pretty outrageous when he was on the staff, tried to stir the embers, but without success. And Beecham himself wrote another letter, retracting little, but attempting to make amends for his personal attack on Kubelik. John Waverley himself spoke to the editor of The Times, and gave him some background to the affair. The offer was made of a general piece by The Times' chief music critic. This was published on 6 July 1956, and although it did not say much it helped to comfort Kubelik. More helpful was an article entitled 'The Breeze at Covent Garden' by Desmond Shawe-Taylor which was published in the New Statesman on 7 July 1956. This set out the issues and problems very clearly, putting Sir Thomas well and truly in his place.

However, despite Kubelik's withdrawal of his resignation, he had clearly been deeply wounded. His period as musical director was important, and left a number of landmarks in the history of Covent Garden. He was offered an extension of his three-year contract, but he did not wish to renew it, although he returned in the season after his departure to give some more performances of the *Trojans*; and also a splendid revival of *Boris Godunov*, sung in Russian with Christoff in the title role, the original language being used because Christoff would not sing it in English, and we were unwilling to have any more mixed-language performances.

All those who knew Kubelik remembered him with great affection. The injustice of the attack upon him seemed to be enhanced by the personal distress which he suffered through the chronic ill health of his wife, a charming and attractive violinist who had been permanently injured through being thrown out of a window by a mad maid in Prague, having as a result to undergo many operations and being in fairly constant pain. Kubelik was a splendid musician: but even without the added worries imposed on him I do not think that he was suited to the cares of overall musical responsibility. I was indeed surprised when a number of years after he had left Covent Garden he accepted a similar post at the Metropolitan Opera in New York; and so it did not surprise me in the least that after a very short period he asked to be released from his contract there.

I suppose that the musical highlight of Kubelik's three years at Covent Garden was really the *Trojans*. Eddy Sackville-West, who was a colleague on the board until the end of 1955, and George Harewood, who was on the staff, both played an important part in encouraging what seemed at the time a rather risky and costly production. It was virtually the first performance ever of the two parts of Berlioz's great masterpiece given together on the same evening. The production enabled Jon Vickers in the role of Aeneas to have a major triumph on his way to stardom. Vickers was then a young Canadian tenor in whom David Webster took a justified pride as his 'discovery', although it would be wrong to suppose that with such a rare voice and with such passionate intensity in all that he did, he would have remained for long undiscovered. It was also memorable for Amy Shuard's menacing Cassandra, for the moving appearance of the classically beautiful Diana Wynyard in the silent role of Andromache, and for the striking *coup de théâtre* of Blanche Thebom, the handsome American who sang the part of Dido, and who before the final immolation scene unpinned her long dark tresses, her very own, allowing them to cascade literally to her ankles. For me there was one great disappointment, that John Gielgud, the producer, did not accept as designer Robin Ironside, a gifted artist with theatrical experience, who had done much work on the *Trojans*, and whose claims I had strongly urged upon David. David's reaction when faced with a proposal to which he did not himself respond was to do nothing, and I do not think that he pressed Ironside's claims to Gielgud. The designer chosen was named Mariano Andreu. What other work he had done I do not know, but his designs for the *Trojans* were not distinguished, and this made the production a less than total triumph. Ironside himself was deeply disappointed not to have been chosen.

The choice of the other designer was not reported by David to either the opera committee or the board until after the commitment had been made. As chairman of the former I took strong exception to the lack of any prior intimation, and I sent a note to John Waverley saying that if this sort of thing was to be allowed to happen the committee was placed in a ridiculous position, and I would prefer not to go on acting as its chairman. Sir John sympathized with my point of view. David was asked to produce a note for the board explaining how he saw the functions of the opera and ballet committees. I found it neither convincing nor satisfactory. The gist of the note was contained in its first sentence, which said that the committees' duties were 'mainly advisory and consultative', a point of view with which I did not quarrel, so long as they *were* asked to advise and *were* consulted with: if advice was only to be sought when it suited the general administrator the committees would be wasting their time. I circulated a memorandum to the board of which the last two paragraphs read as follows:

In my view, if the Opera Sub-Committee is to fulfil its duties satisfactorily, all major decisions relating to the employment of artists should be discussed by the Sub-Committee before action is taken by the Executive. The minutes of the Opera Sub-Committee (but not of the Ballet Sub-Committee) are always circulated each month in time for the Board's monthly meeting, so that any proposal can be questioned if any member of the Board so wishes. This cannot be so if decisions are taken by the Executive without reference to the Sub-Committee. I fully recognise that there are occasions when a swift decision is necessary, but on such occasions it should be possible for the Executive to refer to the Chairman of the Sub-Committee, particularly when the decision proposed is contrary to the sense of the Sub-Committee's discussion on the matter in question.

The last thing I wish to suggest is that either Sub-Committee should undertake the functions of the Executive. My only concern is that they should be in a position to discharge the duties which I believe should be laid upon them by the Board, who bear the ultimate responsibility for success or failure.

My point of view was upheld by the board. But for a long time there were still occasions when the request was not adhered to. The trouble was David's ineradicable desire for secrecy, which was so stupid since we were all working together, and he had himself in his own note volunteered the view that the board's responsibility was paramount.

One of the stalwarts whom I recall from those early days was Michael Wood. He had been appointed press officer in 1946 before the theatre actually reopened, and he did a very good job for Covent Garden at a time when standards of performance were uneven to say the least. After some years, in 1958 I think, he became ballet company manager, one of the few people in the ballet hierarchy who had not been a dancer, and this was a positive advantage to him in his work. In 1966 he succeeded Arnold Haskell as director of the Royal Ballet School, a post he held until he retired at the end of 1977. He was thus just about the longest serving member of the staff. During the war he had served in the Brigade of Guards. In appearance he was very much a suave guardee, but his languid manner concealed real toughness of character; and it should be recorded that for over thirty years he rendered considerable service to Covent Garden.

Towards the end of 1956, and continuing through a large part of 1957, there were long talks about the possibility of closer working between Covent Garden and Sadler's Wells, and even of the actual integration of the two organizations. The initiative came through the Arts Council from the Treasury, who were concerned not with the artistic aspects, but with the financial savings which might be achieved. As I have never been among those congenitally opposed to mergers, I was all in favour of a study being carried out. Before the talks were under way, one important problem was resolved since Sadler's Wells decided as an economy measure to disband their ballet company, by then known as the Royal Ballet at Sadler's Wells and also, like the Royal Ballet at Covent Garden, under the artistic direction of Ninette de Valois. The disbandment of this smaller, well-regarded company was quite rightly not acceptable to the Arts Council, and we were asked to take it over and run it from Covent Garden. Since the company spent a large part of its time touring, a co-ordinated plan could be worked out. We made it clear as a condition that we must be relieved of any additional financial burden, to which the Arts Council readily agreed: and responsibility for the company was assumed by Covent Garden in the summer of 1957.

The wider problem of the integration of the two opera houses was pursued in some detail and an estimate of possible economies was made. The resulting figure was relatively insignificant, but the Arts Council still seemed eager to pursue the idea, and, I supposed, foresaw artistic advantages. We came close to the point of agreeing upon the composition of a merged board of directors, when rather abruptly a halt was called to the talks, and the next thing we heard was that an old proposal had been revived, that Sadler's Wells should take over the Carl Rosa Opera Company, a nomad group of long standing which was without a permanent home and which was clearly something of a headache to the Arts Council, who I suppose decided to push it in the direction of Sadler's Wells. By then no one connected with Covent Garden very much minded the wasted hours of talks. The Carl Rosa/Sadler's Wells merger was likewise not achieved, although several of the Carl Rosa singers were formed into Touring Opera 1958, which was placed under Humphrey Proctor-Gregg who, poor man, was later asked to take on the running of the London Opera Centre. Touring Opera 1958 was absorbed into the Sadler's Wells organization, and the Arts Council decided to withdraw all support from the Carl Rosa company. This resulted in a rather vociferous storm. It welled up during a debate on the Arts in the House of Lords some months after I had taken my seat, giving me the occasion to make a maiden speech in which I spoke of Covent Garden's role and its financial problems. Dame Irene Ward, a Tory MP, and a governor of the Carl Rosa Company, was aware that the debate was taking place. Irked by the withdrawal of support by the Arts Council, she was in a state of high dudgeon. She stood behind the Bar in the House of Lords, listening, and making comments which gradually became more and more audible, until eventually Sir Brian Horrocks, who was Black Rod, went quietly over to Dame Irene's side, and said in his most courteous manner, 'You must remember that you are not in the House of Commons now.' Silence ensued, and the debate continued without further interruption.

Although a good deal of our time at Covent Garden meetings had been taken up with the discussion of the possible merger with Sadler's Wells, we had to proceed on the assumption that we should continue with our independent existence, as in fact we did. An important question was what was to happen about the musical directorship after Kubelik's departure which was due in the summer of 1958. David Webster had high hopes that Rudolf Kempe might be persuaded. He was a brilliantly versatile German conductor possessing remarkable powers with the orchestra, who loved him, and great sympathy and understanding for singers. He was already conducting quite often at Covent Garden, where he clearly enjoyed working. His debut was in 1955 with a gloomy production of *Tannhäuser*, although he himself made his mark. His first real success was with *Elektra*, an occasion when George Harewood saved the day for us with an inspired piece of emergency casting. Christl Goltz, who should have sung the title role, had fallen ill. George had recalled a notice in the magazine *Opera* of a performance by a little-known German singer named Gerda Lammers, who happened to be in London to give a song recital. She sang four performances of *Elektra* at Covent Garden. The house was half empty, but those there had an unforgettable experience. Then in the autumn of 1957 Kempe conducted two cycles of the *Ring*, most memorably, with as fine an international cast as could be found anywhere at that time.

David's hopes were generally shared; but unfortunately Kempe, although willing to conduct regularly at the Royal Opera House, was not willing to commit himself to the overall responsibility. It was naturally discussed whether there was any British conductor with the required experience and personality. No name however commended itself at that time. It was also already known that in the following season a rising and highly gifted Italian conductor, Carlo Maria Giulini, would be making his debut with us, but in 1957 the thought that he might be approached to be musical director entered nobody's head. The view was clearly held and stated that we should do better to proceed with no one in the position than to make the wrong appointment. Accordingly we accepted that when Kubelik left in the summer of 1958 our correct course was to go ahead without a successor to him, relying upon Kempe and, we hoped, Giulini as distinguished guests, together with our resident conductors, until in the fullness of time someone suitable emerged.

During the course of 1957 there were two additions to the board, Bill Coldstream and Burnet Pavitt. Coldstream was a distinguished artist, and the head of the Slade School of Art. He was also a trustee of the National Gallery, and a member of the Arts Council and chairman of its Arts Panel. It was anticipated that he would be able to help with the choice of designers, but he found the way in which he was usually presented with a *fait accompli* in the selection very hard to bear. He was an exceptionally talented portrait painter, though I cannot believe that he ever earned much money through his labours, for he seldom finished a portrait in less than eighty sittings. He was a most agreeable colleague, and he had my fullest sympathy in his sense of frustration.

Burnet Pavitt was someone I had known for a number of years. It was at my urging that he was elected. My wife had first met him in the early stages of the war when he was living in Paris, and she was over there attached to the Red Cross. They were kindred spirits, with music making, often on two pianos, only one of their many bonds. However, it was not until after the war that our friendship developed, because quite early he was posted to the Middle East and we had no opportunities for meeting. At the end of the war he met a certain Dr Barell, who was head of the giant Swiss pharmaceutical business, Hoffmann La Roche. Barell was impressed with Burnet's personality and boldly offered him the post of managing director of the British subsidiary, Roche Products, although he was without qualification as a businessman, let alone as a pharmacist. The doctor was right in his judgement. Burnet continued as managing director for over twenty-five years, seeing the company through a great period of growth and becoming a leading figure in the British pharmaceutical industry. I was sure that he would make a valuable addition to the Covent Garden board. He had a passionate love of opera and was intensely musical. He was also very humorous. He was able to speak French, German and Italian fluently, having a wide-ranging acquaintance throughout the Continent. Most important, unlike myself, he was a model of diplomacy. He was liked by all those whom he met.

His only fault was an excessive modesty, because of which, except in the eyes of his friends, he never received the recognition he deserved. On the opera house board he was an invaluable colleague with good musical taste and judgement, serving for a number of years as chairman of the opera committee, always in his quiet way making his presence felt.

Chapter 20

In the second half of 1957 John Waverley fell ill. The last meeting he attended was in July. I was asked to act as chairman in his absence. During the closing months of the year he was in St Thomas's Hospital, where I visited him regularly, having also lent him a portable TV set, the first he had ever seen. There was one thing that particularly concerned him, that he had not in time taken steps to recommend that David should be knighted, and this was his departing injunction to me. I did what I could to comply, for I shared his feelings. Yet it was curious to see how doubts persisted in official quarters: and I was virtually required to give a firm personal pledge regarding his future conduct, which I readily did, for I knew that David was not a fool and had plenty of sound Scottish common sense.

On the morning of Saturday, 4 January 1958 I telephoned to Ava to enquire about Sir John. There was a long delay before she came to the telephone, and then she told me in a frail voice, 'He died this morning at 5 o'clock.' 'How awful,' I said. 'I am so terribly sorry,' followed by, 'Could I come and see him?', as though she had said he was feeling rather better, only realizing afterwards what I had suggested. A silence ensued, until she replied, 'I don't know. I must find out. Ring me up again in half an hour.' I did as she asked. She then told me that on Monday morning she would be taking John down to their home in Sussex where he was to be buried. Therefore would I please come for her at 10 o'clock the following evening, and we could go together to St Thomas's Hospital where he would be lying in the Chapel of Rest. Thus it happened that we entered this silent place hand in hand, and saw him peacefully reposing with a Sister of Mercy by his side, and four tall candles at the corners of the bier. We stayed together for a few minutes, and then I tiptoed quietly out, leaving them alone together. Afterwards she thanked me for having made what I knew to be a suggestion inadvertent at any rate to my conscious mind, saying that by herself she could never have gone and there was no one else she could have asked to accompany her.

Soon after Sir John's death my colleagues on the board elected me chairman, and the appointment was approved by the Arts Council, and by the Treasury, which was the responsible Ministry at the time. (It was to be another eight or nine years before Harold Wilson appointed Jennie Lee to be the first Minister for the Arts.) I had been on the board slightly longer than any of my other colleagues, and I had certainly been the most active and interfering in the running of the theatre. I was also I suppose the member of the board to whom Sir John most frequently turned, having already established a close working relationship with him when I was secretary of the board. In addition my regular proximity to Covent Garden as managing director of the *FT*, and the willingness of my *FT* colleagues to allow me the necessary secretarial and other facilities, above all time, were quite invaluable. Indeed, without the help I received, I could not have done the job to anyone's satisfaction. I should like to think that on balance neither Covent Garden nor the *FT* lost by my double connection.

Brendan himself had given me every encouragement when I first asked to be associated with Covent Garden. He was pretty well tone-deaf and he never went to any kind of musical function (although boasting of the attention given to music by his old school, Sedbergh). In any event, my appointment as chairman of the Royal Opera House in January 1958 only a few months before his death gave him considerable satisfaction, and I remember him saying, 'How pleased your father would have been.'

I attended my first meeting as chairman on 21 January 1958. There were one or two changes which I wished to effect at once. First of all, I was unhappy about the rule in the articles of association which required that each year at the annual meeting the two directors who had served longest on the board should retire and would not be eligible for re-election for twelve months. Since there were at the time only eight directors the rule meant that no one could expect to serve for more than four years, and the period might in practice be even less because of disappearances through death or other causes. My experience had been that directors could only be expected to make a valuable contribution to discussions after they had served on the board for a good year, and then at the moment that their interest and their involvement, and therefore their usefulness, was at its greatest, they were forced to vanish from the scene: in commercial life the idea of directors being forced to stay away for a year would have been regarded as absurd; and Covent Garden was in a very real sense a commercial enterprise, even if by its nature unprofitable. An absence of a year often meant an absence for good, acceptable in the case of those not pulling their weight, but otherwise most unsatisfactory. I knew that to propose any dramatic alteration would be ill-received by the Arts Council, and I therefore suggested a simple change to the company's articles, still requiring two directors to retire at the annual general meeting but also providing that they could be re-elected after the first of January; and since the annual meeting was always held only a few weeks before, at the end of November, continuity was ensured. This did not mean perpetuating the presence of every director. It was still perfectly possible not to invite them to serve for a further term; and in any event all proposals for election or re-election (thank goodness the choice of names rested with us) had to be approved by the Arts Council and by the responsible Minister as well: but it did mean that the services of those of most help would not be lost.

A few years later, there was another change to the articles of association which I effected bearing on the attendances at meetings by the members of the board. In the main their regularity of attendance was exemplary, but there were one or two of whom this was not so. I therefore caused an amendment to be introduced whereby if a director had, without leave of absence, missed three consecutive meetings he automatically ceased being a director. No one demurred from this. In practice the new article was never invoked. In addition I regularly received from the box office a note of the board's attendances at performances each month, because I thought it imperative that they should as often as possible observe the quality of the work of the house.

Most importantly there was also the question of the chairman's term of office. It had always seemed to me wrong that the article relating to the retirement of directors specifically excluded the chairman from its provisions. The chairman was therefore effectively there for life, which was indefensible. I proposed and it was agreed that the article should instead provide that the chairman was elected for five years, but that he could then again be re-elected, if, that is, his colleagues wanted him to go on, and the Arts Council and the responsible Minister approved.

Then came the use of the so-called Royal Box. It had been accepted practice that unless the box was requested by a member of the Royal Family or was required for Government entertaining it was the chairman's prerogative to use it as he wished. The result was that all too often the box was empty. This created a bad impression at a time when we were desperately anxious to obtain better houses. I therefore proposed that it should be available for use by all members of the board, it being understood among my colleagues that the chairman would have first call on the box for first nights, but otherwise it would be a question of first come, first served: a list of box bookings was circulated regularly each week to the directors so that they could see what gaps there were and thus the box was pretty regularly filled, even for unappetising programmes. There were of course occasional lapses. My colleague Isaiah Berlin once received a complaint from an Oxford colleague of his that the box had been empty when the rest of the house was full, and he wrote to me suggesting that, if seats in the box could not be sold and members of the staff could not use it, 'perhaps waxwork figures of the directors, or at any rate the relevant portions of them, could be made (and also of the guests, of either sex, whom they are likely to invite) and an ever-varying selection of these be presented from the box, in characteristic attitudes.' This lovely proposal, however, never had to be resorted to.

It was a dominant thought in my mind to see a full house every night. During my time as secretary to the board, the question of selling seats to business houses on an all the year basis had already been raised, but it had not been pursued. One of my earliest steps as chairman was to reopen the subject. The popular operas never presented a real problem, however indifferent the performances might be. But with anything off the well-beaten track it was another matter. I knew that many companies liked to use Covent Garden for business entertainment. It was obviously much easier for them to take visitors from abroad to the ballet, and also to the opera even when sung in English, rather than to take them to the theatre. It also seemed to me desirable that leading companies should develop a measure of involvement with the Royal Opera House: the more their sympathies were engaged, the more they used Covent Garden to entertain foreigners, the better the case I could develop to the Government, whatever the party in power, for continuing public support. We decided therefore to launch what I named the Premium Stalls Scheme. The title arose through a calculation of the amount of money earned during the course of a year for a single stall on the basis average of occupancy and average price, and then rounding up the resulting figure by a *premium* charge, for the facility offered, of some 15 per cent. It was agreed initially to set a target of 40 seats, out of a total number of some 600 stalls (and total seating in the house of 2,100); and also to try to sell all the available boxes on the same basis, since the casual demand for boxes, which are uncomfortable and give a poor view, was always small, even for box office favourites. The scheme was well received, and our target was achieved. As time went by, the number was allowed to grow, until by 1975 the number of seats sold each night in this way was in the region of 140, most companies having their seats on a two or three nights a week basis. When Jennie Lee first became Minister for the Arts she questioned whether it was right that those in a position to make out a large cheque should be privileged to pre-empt seats. Had the scheme not already existed before her appointment she might have asked us not to introduce it. She did however recognize that the scheme was not without merit, and she accepted it as a *fait accompli*. It has without question been proved most valuable to the theatre, particularly as inflation has forced up the level of seat prices, making it harder and harder for heavily taxed private individuals to find the wherewithal to pay. And to have enlisted the support of many of the greatest businesses in the land is surely of immense benefit.

I had another wish. This was to effect a small but important improvement in the appearance of the auditorium. For some unexplained reason a part of Edward Barry's original design had not been carried out when the theatre was built in 1858. He had planned a series of decorative figures on the three-tier fronts depicting the Three Ages of Woman. The white moulded figures were to be illuminated by three rows of candelabra lit by gas, but the top row, representing Woman as a Child, was never installed. When I first became conscious of the omission, no one had any explanation to offer. Everyone to whom I spoke agreed that it should be repaired. I asked David Webster to obtain a quotation for making thirty-five replica wall brackets and for having the work of wiring and installation carried out. The total estimate amounted to £2,670. The first person to send me a contribution was Colin Anderson, who was not at that time a member of the board although he was to become one two years later. He had been to the première of Zeffirelli's *Lucia di Lammermoor* with us and I had pointed out what I wanted without any thought of asking for money, but the following day I received a generous cheque from him with a note saying that he had just won a premium bond prize and hoped I would allow him, as he said, to 'satisfy my whim'. A few days later the Queen Mother was with us at a performance. I told her what I wished to bring about, and what Colin had done; and she very sweetly and generously said that she too would like to satisfy *her* whim, for she had a great love of the Covent Garden auditorium and saw what an improvement there would be. Thus I knew I was well and truly started. I approached Sir Brian Mountain, chairman of Covent Garden Properties Limited, the ground landlords, and he agreed that the company should give the cost of two candelabra. Several members of the board contributed. Aline Berlin, wife of Isaiah and dearest of friends, gave me a handsome cheque. So did Lewis Douglas, erstwhile American Ambassador to Britain, and Alfred Beit, Nin Ryan, Leo de Rothschild and Dorothy, the wife of old Sir Robert Mayer. Then Sol Hurok, the impresario through whose auspices the Ballet had made many visits to the United States, came to the theatre one evening, and I had no sense of shame in asking him to weigh in. 'I give you a t'ousand bucks,' he said, which at that time was worth £353. I was still £1,000 short, so I asked the Arts Council for permission to include in our annual budget the balance still needed, but of course they said this would be out of the question. Then one evening Simon Marks, the head of Marks and Spencer, the great business which perhaps more than any other has helped to improve living standards in Britain, came to a ballet performance. I told him my tale. 'How much do you need?' he asked. '£1,000,' I replied. 'You can count on me,' he replied. We in fact ended with a small surplus which I arranged should be used for the purchase of a stereo gramophone for David Webster.

At the beginning of 1958 there were several vacancies on the board, Edric Cundell, Arthur Bliss and Phil Nichols having retired in 1957, and these I decided should be filled. First of all, it was desirable that the world of academic musical life should be well represented, as it no longer was following the retirement of Edric Cundell. Being ignorant of that world, I sought advice. I found a consensus that Dr Thomas Armstrong, the principal of the Royal Academy of Music, would be a most popular choice. He had been organist at Exeter Cathedral, and then from 1933 until 1955, at Christ Church, Oxford, where he had formed a wide-ranging acquaintance; and all those whom I consulted spoke of him warmly. I approached him and found him receptive and interested. He had a strongly developed sense of public duty, and he clearly thought that the well-being of Covent Garden mattered, and he was eager to make a contribution. Meeting him, I felt certain that he would be a most conscientious colleague, in a position to act as a helpful sounding board of musical opinion and to give good advice from a professional standpoint.

My other two choices were strongly contrasted. The first to accept an invitation was Mark Bonham-Carter, by no means then an addict of opera, but an enthusiast for the ballet, which represented a good half of Covent Garden's endeavour, although short of spokesmen on the board. He was at the time working as a director in the publishing firm of William Collins, where he seemed set for a splendid career, brought to a premature end because of his incursion into active politics. There were plenty of others who might with justice claim that their knowledge of ballet greatly exceeded Mark's. I wanted him more particularly because of his very acute mind, his sharp astringent wit and because he was a fighter for what he believed in and a splendid debunker of nonsense. I had known him, not well, for a number of years, and, to use a nautical expression, I liked the cut of his jib. He had two other claims. First, he was a good friend of Princess Margaret, who was the President of the Royal Ballet, and who participated actively in the work of the company, knowing personally many of its members. Secondly, he was closely identified with the Liberal Party; and although the establishment of links with political parties had never been an objective in the choice of individuals to serve on the Covent Garden board, to have among one's colleagues some who were or who had access to those who were politically motivated seemed to me sensible at a time when Covent Garden was requiring steadily increasing sums from public funds, a process which could move in only one direction – upwards.

The third invitation was to Jack Donaldson, a tried and trusted friend of almost thirty years' standing with complementary tastes and reactions to mine, with whom in 1932 I had started the Quartet Society in London and who ever since then together with his wife Frankie had played an important part in my life. He likewise had links with a political party, although in 1958 he would certainly have denied hotly that he was destined to become a Minister; and when in 1976 he was made Minister of the Arts it was indeed a turn-up for the book. However, he was on friendly terms with many of those at the heart of Labour Party politics, the moderate, mixed economy, pro-Europe members, who later came to be in charge of some of the great Offices of State. I knew that he would be a staunch supporter of the cause of Covent Garden, for he had a great love of opera, and any cause he believed in he would embrace whole-heartedly, throwing his active and enquiring mind into the proceedings with zest.

In the early months of 1958 there was plenty to worry about on both ballet and opera fronts. Finance was of course a constant problem, but we were sympathetically regarded in the Treasury at the time, and in those days, before the appointment of a separate Minister for the Arts, when Covent Garden took such a high proportion of the total Arts Council grant, it was possible for us to argue our case directly with the Treasury, although the Arts Council were invariably associated with any representations we made. What most immediately imposed itself on my attention was the sense of strain felt by those in charge of the ballet. About a month after becoming chairman I received a letter from Ninette de Valois enclosing a copy of a memorandum headed 'Points to Discuss', which explained very clearly her causes of dissatisfaction. The purpose of the note was to bring home to me the difficulties with which she was having to contend. She recognized that the problem sprang from there being two big companies in the same theatre, each run on a different basis, since the ballet company was basically self-contained, whereas the opera side was in large part international. There was inevitable competition for inadequate rehearsal facilities, above all stage rehearsal time: and in this competition the ballet usually came off worst, despite the large amount of work it had to undertake. And it rankled, it must be said, with all the ballet people that they had least consideration and yet were far less burdensome financially to Covent Garden. Ninette complained about the unsatisfactory arrangements for planning, about approaches from Equity regarding rates of pay of which she had been kept in the dark, the short notice she was given of coming opera schedules, the little time that she therefore had to plan her own schedules, and the lack of a stage director with overall authority to plan the use of the stage, this job being left to the production manager who had plenty else to do besides. The picture painted was very depressing, and if exaggerated was not greatly so.

The ballet committee met in March under its then chairman, Lionel Robbins, and assurances were given which soothed Ninette. In particular it was agreed that there should be a Joint Planning Committee, which was to meet monthly, to determine the allocation of time and to work out opera and ballet schedules. This committee met once in April, and then not again for many months, and agreed the dates for the coming November; and then by chance in August Ninette discovered that of the fourteen ballet evening dates agreed for the month of November no fewer than nine had been changed without her being consulted or informed, while the ballet dates for December had been fixed without any reference to her at all.

I was as angry as she was, and I sent a telegram to David, who was on holiday in Capri, asking for his comments. He replied in a characteristically soothing manner, telling me that there was no question of a *fait accompli*, and this, he said, George Harewood (who was in charge of opera planning) would 'make amply clear next week'. Things did improve, but it was only by dint of endless, tiresome pressure, which should have been unnecessary.

The best outcome of it all from my point of view was that I came much more closely into contact with Ninette de Valois than I might otherwise have done. This for me was pure gain. Of all the people connected with Covent Garden, she was outstanding. Her life was beautifully rounded, with everything that happened in it working towards her ultimate achievement. She was born in Ireland, coming of an Anglo-Irish family with a fine home in County Wicklow which became too costly to maintain, so that in 1906 the family moved to England, living first with Ninette's grandmother in the country, and then moving to a flat in London. At that time her name was Edris Stannus. It was only when she took up dancing professionally that she chose a name which was more evocative. From an early age she had shown an urge to dance as well as to invent romantic tales. She attended a dance academy and when only fourteen formed part of a group of dancers billed as the Wonder Children. Then, two years afterwards, she became the principal dancer in the Lyceum pantomime. Her father was killed in the war, and the need for her to earn was intensified. She became a pupil of Cecchetti, who had been one of the great Russian dancers and who had left his homeland with Diaghilev. In 1919, she was engaged as *première danseuse* for the season of international opera at Covent Garden, while at the same time also appearing in a musical comedy in a theatre in the Strand. After this she gained much experience in music halls and in West End revues, until in 1923 Diaghilev, who was in Paris, wanted a young classical dancer for his company. She was recommended to him by Cecchetti, although by then she was also known to other members of Diaghilev's company, among them Lydia Lopokova, the wife of Maynard Keynes, who was himself to become the first chairman of the Royal Opera House after the war, and who was largely instrumental in effecting the move to Covent Garden of the Sadler's Wells Ballet Company which Ninette was to create for Lilian Baylis after leaving Diaghilev.

There is little doubt that without her astonishing drive and determination British ballet as we know it today would not exist, nor would the ballet companies of many other cities throughout the world, for Ninette and her dancers have blazed a trail everywhere. Besides the Royal Ballet itself, she also created a school, attended by pupils from many foreign countries, and providing dancers for most of the companies in Great Britain.

Because of her tiring and modestly paid early years, she was never in the least grasping or greedy for money. Indeed her salary while she was director of the Royal Ballet was disgracefully low. She had nothing in the way of what are called fringe benefits, and since her husband, Arthur Connell, whom she married in 1935, was a successful doctor, any increase in her pay would have been virtually all taken from her in tax, owing to the absurdity of the rules as they then were. Arthur Connell practised at Sunningdale and occasionally visited us professionally at Englefield Green, having also the arduous task of attending Marilyn Monroe who once rented our house when she was making a film in England. The Sunningdale practice meant that Ninette commuted daily to work, returning on ballet nights by the last train from Waterloo; and then at weekends she had to handle the doctor's telephone calls for him. Yet if she grumbled it was never within my hearing. The truth was that she had an immense sense of pride and achievement, following with passionate interest the careers of all those who had passed through her companies or her school, and she sought no greater reward. I loved being with her, and admiring her fine head, which becomes ever more distinguished with passing years. I delighted in her warm-heartedness, her impulsive manner, her command over words and gift of oratory, her humour and her spirit. When she retired Jane Clark and I raised a small fund in her honour. This provided a modest capital sum to augment her meagre pension, and also financed the cost of her bust by a gifted sculptor, F. E. MacWilliam, whose name was proposed by Colin Anderson, a generous contributor to our fund. One cast of the bust adorns the grand staircase at Covent Garden, while another stands on a plinth at the Royal Ballet School, and a third she has at home.

As to opera, we were still suffering to some extent from the aftermath of the Kubelik row. During the 1958/9 season there were more good performances than the critics of Covent Garden wished to admit. Above all there was a landmark production of Verdi's *Don Carlos*, produced and designed by Lucchino Visconti, with whom David had established very good relations and through whom Covent Garden had first approached Franco Zeffirelli, Visconti's star apprentice. It was in these first performances of *Don Carlos* that Carlo Maria Giulini made his début before the opera-going public in London, making a sensational impact, for it seemed as though he really had inherited the mantle

of the great Verdi conductors of the past, with a faultless instinct for the composer's innermost intentions. The production was strikingly simple, deceptively
so, and an object lesson in one of Visconti's special skills, the art of conveying a
sense of perspective to the stage. As Don Carlos, Jon Vickers added greatly
to his budding stature. He was proving a real feather in David's cap, and
it was to be a serious blow when Vickers took against Georg Solti soon after he
had joined us as musical director, refusing to sing under his baton. These *Don
Carlos* performances were also memorable because they were the last occasions
when the brothers-in-law Boris Christoff and Tito Gobbi sang together on the
stage, certainly in London, perhaps anywhere, for soon afterwards they had a
disagreement of alarming proportions, and for a number of years would not
speak to one another. This too was a great disappointment for us. Fortunately
they both returned regularly, although never together, and both established a
particularly strong rapport with the Covent Garden public, deriving much
satisfaction from their visits and contributing a great deal to the general raising
of standards.

Not long after *Don Carlos* there came the triumph of Joan Sutherland in *Lucia
di Lammermoor* by Donizetti, where between them Tullio Serafin, the conductor,
and Franco Zeffirelli, who produced and designed, helped to transform her overnight into a major international star, with a voice of unique purity, agility and
range. This production, which uncannily conveyed the romanticism of Walter
Scott, was the first of a number contributed to the Covent Garden repertoire by
Zeffirelli, all of them visually beautiful and having, save for an over-heavy *Don
Giovanni*, considerable staying power, which cannot alas be said of many other
productions.

Visconti himself was to give us three other productions in coming years, a
handsome serviceable *Trovatore* in 1964/5, to the première of which I invited
Mrs Harold Wilson, who had been recently installed in 10 Downing Street and
of whom I had read in a newspaper profile that opera was among her enthusi-
asms. As company for her I thought that it would be a good idea to invite John
Betjeman, and I said to him, 'Please come and exercise your charm on the wife
of the Prime Minister. Covent Garden's grant may depend on you.' He duly
complied. During the music he was more hypnotized by the harpist in the
orchestra than by the action on the stage: but during the intervals Mrs Wilson
was captivated by him, with the result that regularly thereafter he was invited
for tea at No. 10. She most certainly enjoyed the evening. I remember her com-
paring it with some of her official functions where she said that she felt like a
tethered goat. She was obviously not in a position to determine our grant, but
at least her enjoyment at Covent Garden could not have hurt our cause.

After Visconti's *Trovatore* there followed two oddities. The first of these was a new *Rosenkavalier* in 1966/7 for Solti. Seeing the designs one could not help feeling that there was a degree of experimentation at Covent Garden's expense, for the whole thing was in *art nouveau* style, Visconti arguing unconvincingly that he was being true to the period of the music rather than to the period in which the story lay. Isaiah Berlin wrote to me on 7 May 1966, 'Obedient to your orders, as always, I dragged myself to CG in my feeble state. . . . If I had been an addict of Strauss, and adored *Rosenkavalier* as most people do, I should I think have been somewhat outraged. It is a very hostile treatment of it, deliberate, and uncalled for. But I was in fact fascinated.'

I too was fascinated, although far from happy for I felt it misconceived; and I had a rough time with my friend Raimund von Hofmannsthal, the generous and warm-hearted son of the librettist, who was extremely indignant. However, hope springing eternal, we all looked forward to Visconti's next production, promised for the following season, a badly needed new *Traviata*. When the designs for this were received even David Webster was shaken, and he did something which he would normally never have thought of doing. He asked the members of the board to come and inspect them in his office. Arriving there we found the room adorned with what appeared to be a newly discovered collection of Aubrey Beardsley drawings. 'Where's the colour?' we asked, getting the reply that there wasn't meant to be any. We all felt very let down. When Visconti was asked to produce *Traviata* for us, it had been because of a brilliant but traditional production which he had recently done in Italy. We had not expected black and white Beardsley. David agreed to fly to Algiers where Visconti was filming. His mission was in vain. 'Take it or leave it,' was effectively the reply, with a measure of comfort about the intended introduction of a little colour into some of the accessories and so on. Since we all had the deepest respect for Visconti for his *Don Carlos*, and since David convinced us that we should not see Visconti again if we rejected the *Traviata*, we agreed with some misgiving that we must go ahead. The reception was understandably mixed. Like everything that he did, the production had great style; but it was perverse, and I wish we had not done it, for we never saw Visconti again, and it cannot be long before the production has to be replaced, for nothing dates more easily than a quirky presentation of a basic masterpiece.

During the run of *Traviata* I witnessed a particularly impressive display of high professionalism on the part of Elizabeth Vaughan, a gifted British singer. The leading role was assigned to Mirella Freni, one of the most affecting and appealing of all artists. On the day of the third performance she fell ill, and at 5.30 in the afternoon Elizabeth Vaughan, who had sung the role at Cardiff but nowhere else, was asked whether she would come to the rescue. Within two hours she was on stage at Covent Garden, having to be more or less sewn into

Miss Freni's costumes, because although Freni was small Vaughan was tiny, having a ballerina's figure. She had a triumph, earning everyone's deepest respect.

The real triumph of *Traviata* was of course Giulini's, as it had been with *Trovatore*, and also with Zeffirelli's *Falstaff*. Joan and I used to see Zeffirelli regularly and when he was preparing his production he used often to visit the edge of Windsor Great Park in search of a suitable model for Herne's Oak (not that it helped him to find a perfection solution), while there is no doubt that the architecture of the Horseshoe cloister to the west of St George's Chapel greatly influenced his designs. From time to time I tried to revive the possibility of his returning to Covent Garden and he did in fact undertake to do a new production of *Norma* for us with Joan Sutherland in the title role, but he pulled back after he had accepted what was at least a moral commitment. A year or so before this episode, he rang me up from Italy at 3 a.m. one night in November 1966, saying, 'Garrett, I need your help.' The help was not for himself but for Florence, which was in the process of being inundated and devastated by the overflowing River Arno. Mercifully I had a brainwave. I thought of Ashley Clarke, who had been ambassador to Italy and who was living in London, retired but with numerous Italian links. As early in the morning as I decently could, I telephoned to tell him of Franco's call. He responded with alacrity, and within a short space of time the Italian Art and Archives Rescue Fund came into being, with an office, resembling a military headquarters, in the National Gallery, and Carla Thorneycroft the extremely effective deputy to Ashley. It would surely all have happened anyway but I was very glad that Franco enabled me to lend a hand.

In 1958/9 there were also high hopes that Maria Callas would sing regularly at the Royal Opera House. Her début with us had been in 1952/3 when she sang *Norma*, a concession to her, in the terms of those early days, being that the language used was Italian. Her appearance was striking. She was physically very large, but her mesmeric qualities overrode everything, and the public longed for her return. When she finally returned six years later to sing *Traviata* she had become slim and elegant: and if the loss of weight had perhaps taken some of the bloom from her voice it still retained its unmistakable timbre, while her credibility was immeasurably enhanced.

David Webster had established a very special relationship with her, and the board were led to expect that she would be appearing with great regularity at Covent Garden, so much so that Isaiah Berlin sounded a warning note about the possible difficulty of inviting other guest artists to sing roles that Callas regarded as particularly her own. It did not work out like that. She was in fact only to appear in two other operas. First was a dull production of *Medea* by

Bellini, in which she herself was magnificent, although it is debatable whether the production was worth the effort and the cost. The performances were memorable not only because of Callas but also because of a young Italian contralto, Fiorenza Cossotto, who was making her début in London and who was destined to rise to great heights. On the opening night Cossotto brought the house down in one scene and the applause was such that she felt obliged to acknowledge it, causing Callas to send a message to her dressing-room in the interval pointing out that it was not done to acknowledge applause in the middle of a scene. I remember her saying to me that whenever she herself was applauded at the end of an aria she regarded it as failure on her part, obviously because it meant that the audience were not spell-bound. Callas's greatest moment at Covent Garden came three years later with *Tosca*, a masterly production by Franco Zeffirelli, with Tito Gobbi quite unforgettable as Scarpia. This was the sort of performance that should have been recorded for all time. Act 2 was televised in black and white, and presumably that has been preserved. But why not the lot?

While she was in London she lunched with Joan and myself quietly at our house. We wanted her to talk about herself, which she readily did. What struck us most was her intensely practical and analytical approach to her work, and also the evident fact that despite her worldwide acclaim she was nervous and insecure, feeling that whenever she was on the stage the whole audience had eyes and ears only for her. It was perhaps understandable that when the opportunity to escape presented itself to her she seized it. It was, though, a fearful loss for the opera-loving public, and for David Webster a major disappointment.

To revert to 1958/9, the *Ring*, *Don Carlos*, *Lucia* and *Boris* were all performed in the original language, and the significance of this no one could deny. When it came to run of the mill repertoire, which largely continued to be given in English, there was plenty to criticize. The average level of attendances was still depressingly low. The opera committee, under its then chairman Jimmy Smith, met and thrashed out some principles which were approved by the board and which looking back on it were very cautious. The aim, it was said, should be to fill the house and above all to avoid half-empty houses. These were shown by figures prepared at the request of Jack Donaldson to cost almost as much as the most expensive successes (meaning expensive in terms of costly guest artists). The target figure for attendances, though, was set as low as $72\frac{1}{2}$ per cent of capacity, and from this were excluded what were called prestige operas, prestige meaning pretty well anything off the beaten track, where lower attendances were anticipated. On language there was a certain hesitancy. 'The policy of opera in English should not be discontinued, but if in the opinion of the administration better performances can economically be given in a foreign language there shall be no objection to this being done. In other words where there is a conflict between quality of performance and performance in English, the latter may be sacrificed.'

This careful phraseology was designed to assist the move towards what most of us knew to be the right policy for Covent Garden, without treading on too many toes. The analytical figures asked for by Jack Donaldson, which from then onwards were produced regularly, being simply labelled by us the Donaldson figures, did a great deal to help the change of attitudes, for they showed more clearly than any words the costliness, in terms of attendances and receipts, of rigid adherence to the policy of opera in English, and the need for what in commercial terms is known as trading up, which I was certain was the only direction in which we could or should move.

From the moment of his arrival on the scene Jack made a major contribution towards the well-being of Covent Garden, continuing to do so until he was obliged to resign on being made a Government Minister by Harold Wilson in 1974. He was also to become involved with Sadler's Wells Opera, the board of which he was asked to join in 1963, becoming chairman of a committee consisting of representatives of Covent Garden and Sadler's Wells which we brought into being in order to prevent or control careless duplications of repertoire. He devoted long hours to London's operatic affairs, and he would I think agree that my invitation to him to join me on the Covent Garden board probably helped in a real way to change the course of his life.

The first task to which he addressed himself at the time to which I am now referring, that is to say early 1958, concerned the opening of discussions with Walter Legge, a close friend of his who was known to be extremely vocal in his criticism of the running of the Royal Opera House. The outcome of these discussions was an invitation to Walter Legge to become a member of the board. Since Walter chose to place himself on record in *The Times* of 27 December 1975 that I invited him to join because I believed that he was advising his wife, Elisabeth Schwarzkopf, and Otto Klemperer not to appear at Covent Garden, advice which he says he was not giving, I must say categorically that my invitation had nothing to do with any such belief. The question of Klemperer conducting had not at that time arisen at all, and in fact he was far too ill in 1958 to conduct anywhere. I had known Walter slightly for a number of years, and I had always had a high regard for his brilliant achievements first of all in charge of the classical section of Columbia Gramophone records, and later as the creator and inspirational force of the Philharmonia Orchestra. He had himself before the war worked alongside Sir Thomas Beecham when short seasons of international opera were presented at Covent Garden. His knowledge of every aspect of serious music was extensive. He had a sharp wit and a lively imagination, and wide-ranging international contacts. I felt that by inviting him to join the board he would not only give us the benefit of his advice but also confine his criticism to a narrower audience, while at the same time coming closer to appreciating some of the problems with which we had to contend, notably the sharing of the theatre between the opera and ballet companies, and above all the inadequacy of the Government's grant.

Before I invited him to join the board the suggestion was mooted and supported by Jack Donaldson and one or two other colleagues that Walter should be offered the post of artistic director; and I fancy that he would have welcomed the opportunity of moving in, with Sir Thomas Beecham following close behind. But I was nervous of the possible repercussions on an organization which was improving all the time, and I was frightened of the shock effects of his appearance as a very senior member of the staff.

It was therefore decided, in the face of considerable opposition from David Webster, to invite Walter on to the board. He accepted the invitation, but he evidently regretted doing so, for, as he wrote in the same article in *The Times*, he found the experience of working with what he dubbed an establishment board, 'innocent amateurs on musical matters', one which filled him with horror. I fear that he had a constant desire to confuse his duties as a board member with those of general administrator and artistic director rolled into one. His advent caused some consternation among the artists' agents, and a deputation came to me to protest, quite needlessly, that his presence would mean no further employment for British singers at Covent Garden, their attitude being partly occasioned by the fact that so few of their artists were engaged for his various operatic recordings for Columbia. He heard of the deputation, and wrote to me to say that he was sure it had been inspired from within the Royal Opera House itself, which I frankly disbelieved. Anyway, I told them not to prejudge things, saying that in fact the result might be more gramophone recording engagements for their artists, as indeed proved to be the case. Had he himself had the overall responsibility, he might have been spectacularly successful, but I fancy that he would have had many fierce arguments with Ministers and with the Arts Council and others, and that he would not always have been in the right. I doubt whether he would have submitted for long to the numerous constraints imposed on us.

He stayed on the board for five and a half years. He produced some helpful suggestions, but he was very irregular in attendance at meetings: and always I felt that he looked down his nose at us. When his term of office was approaching its end I wrote suggesting that he should make way at the annual meeting for someone with more time to spare, in reply to which he resigned by return of

post. (The man who joined the board after Walter's departure was a very different type, Keith Falkner, the head of the Royal College of Music, and formerly
a distinguished singer. He was able and charming, but shy to a fault, finding it
hard to engage actively in our discussions, which tended to be somewhat
dominated by some of the stronger personalities among my colleagues.) A few
months after Walter left the board, he abandoned his own creation, the
Philharmonia Orchestra, in a very abrupt manner, to the dismay of its members,
who were taken by surprise by the announcement, of which they were only
acquainted a couple of days beforehand, while Otto Klemperer, the orchestra's
chief conductor, was told nothing in advance, despite the fact that he was in the
middle of recording the *Magic Flute* with the orchestra in London. I well
remember Gareth Morris, the principal flautist of the orchestra, ringing me up
on the day of the announcement and coming to see me to ask whether I could
do anything to help. I had to reply that I already had too many commitments,
and the most I could do was to suggest the name of Kenneth Cork, the well-
known City accountant, who was a friend and colleague of mine on the
board of the City Arts Trust. Although he had no intimate acquaintance
with the affairs of the Philharmonia Orchestra he immediately said that he
would join the trust formed to administer funds which the orchestra hoped to
accumulate for use in case of emergency, and he undertook to find other people
of substance to do the same thing. Also he for some time kindly lent his London
office for the trust's meetings, giving valuable advice on financial matters. The
name of the orchestra was changed to the New Philharmonia, but nineteen years
afterwards it became possible for the original name to be readopted.

There was one further and less controversial appointment to the board that
we made in October 1958, after which there were no additions for over two
years. The man was Gerald Coke, roughly my contemporary and a figure in
London musical life for many years. My reason for proposing his name was that
he was actively concerned with Glyndebourne, being a very close friend of its
founder, John Christie, whose attitude towards Covent Garden was far from
helpful, partly at least, one used to be told, because of his and Maynard Keynes's
mutual antipathy for one another. Christie resented the fact that Covent Garden
received a Government grant while Glyndebourne received none; and had he
been given the opportunity of taking charge of the Royal Opera House he
would I feel sure have welcomed it. But the time for any such solution to
Britain's operatic problems would have been soon after the war and not more
than ten years later. Nevertheless, it was self-evident that relations between
Covent Garden and Glyndebourne should at least be cordial, although it was
not until George Christie so ably succeeded his father, and recognized the basic
identity of interest, that matters really improved.

Gerald Coke himself was a very capable businessman. He had become an associate of Siegmund Warburg at an early stage in that creative man's rise to fame in banking circles in the City, and he had one or two other directorships, chosen with equal discrimination. For many years he had been a passionate music-lover, with a comprehensive collection of gramophone records, which he maintained in an orderly manner typical of his tidy, well co-ordinated way of life. He was extremely interested in the training of opera singers, and when the London Opera Centre was brought into existence two and a half years later, he agreed to become its first chairman, a decision that was to cause him some painful headaches.

Discussion about the appointment of a musical director continued in an inconclusive manner throughout most of 1958. The name of Rudolf Kempe was frequently mentioned, but he had made it clear that despite his attachment to Covent Garden and his willingness to conduct for us, he would not put on the harness. Nor would Carlo Maria Giulini, who had made such a tremendous impact by his performances of *Don Carlos* at the Royal Opera House. Rafael Kubelik's three-year tenure of the position ended in July, and after that the office became vacant.

At its October meeting the board formally agreed that 'consideration of the appointment of a musical director should be deferred for the time being'. Then, during the course of November, David Webster brought forward very strongly the suggestion that Benjamin Britten should be approached with an invitation to become a part-time adviser and consultant. His name had from time to time been discussed as a possible musical director but no one seriously believed that he would be willing to undertake an active executive role, or indeed that as a prolific composer of genius it would be right for him to do so. The nub of David's proposal was contained in the following sentences from his memorandum to the board:

The job I envisage for Britten is not an organisational job, it would not figure in one of these conventional ladders of responsibility and power. In fact he would have no executive power at all. His power would lie in the authority of his opinion.

His association with Covent Garden would have an obvious public relations value abroad and at home and it is with home that I am especially concerned.

After some weeks Britten accepted the invitation, and agreed to become musical consultant. It would be impossible for me to say how far his advice was sought or given. At opera committee or board level there was no visible sign. I am sure though that David welcomed the arrangement. For one thing it did effectively shelve for the time being the question of appointing a musical director, a post which he was not really anxious to fill, because his authority would be lessened. Also, the relations between Covent Garden on the one hand and Britten's English Opera Group and the rather rarefied Aldeburgh Festival on the other were already close; and in fact in the spring of 1959 Covent Garden was asked to take over the administrative responsibility for the English Opera Group, a proposal to which we readily agreed, chiefly because of Britten's pre-eminence, not to mention his great lovability, but also because, at least in my view, the new link might act as a kind of antidote to criticism of our move away from the opera in English policy.

During the second half of 1958 a great deal of time was devoted to the preparation of evidence to be given by Covent Garden to an independent Committee of Inquiry set up by the London County Council to advise on the question of financial assistance for Sadler's Wells from the London rates. The appointment of this committee followed from the decision of the Council in July 1958 to make an emergency grant of £25,000 to Sadler's Wells which despite the handing over of responsibility for its ballet company to Covent Garden a year previously was still in financial straits because of the inadequacy of the grant it was receiving from the Arts Council. Had Sadler's Wells not been in dire need, the probability is that no local authority money would have been forthcoming in the first instance; but as has so often happened a friendly gesture was to become an annual commitment, growing to a figure many times in excess of the original gift.

David Webster, Lionel Robbins and I appeared before the committee and urged that Covent Garden, even if it was a national institution in a way that Sadler's Wells then was not, played a major role in the cultural life of London, and was a very great attraction for people coming to London from abroad. We also pointed out the complementary nature of the two theatres, and stressed that so far as ballet was concerned Sadler's Wells had handed over its responsibilities to us.

Altogether, our case was very strong, but regrettably the committee stuck rigidly to their terms of reference and no proposal was therefore made for financial aid to Covent Garden. Paradoxically our case was weakened by the success which we had had in pleading for more generous treatment from the Treasury (for the finances of Covent Garden were every bit as parlous as those of Sadler's Wells). The Chancellor of the Exchequer at the time was Derek Heathcote-Amory, later Lord Amory, who in my experience was the first Chancellor to take a broad and imaginative view of our problems. He was one of the wisest and most balanced of statesmen, a man incapable of a mean or dirty trick, very enlightened and with a great sense of historical perspective. Encouraged by him, the Treasury had devised a formula whereby for a period of three years Covent Garden would receive annually a grant equal to 43 per cent of its 'approved' expenditure, an odd percentage fixed quite unscientifically, leaving us to find the remaining 57 per cent by box office and other takings. We argued for more, but accepted the 43 per cent, since it offered us a measure of security. I do not know why something similar was not proposed by the Treasury in the case of Sadler's Wells, but I fancy the explanation is that the percentage would have had to be very much higher in their case, and this would have strengthened Covent Garden's hand when arguing its own future needs. Periodically afterwards we at Covent Garden tried to raise with the London County Council, later inflated in title to become the Greater London Council, the possibility of a measure of support from the rates. The response was invariably negative, just as I am quite sure it would have been in the case of Sadler's Wells had they not obtained the initial rescue gift of £25,000.

It is a depressing fact that eagerness to give money for the Arts has always been confined to a small handful of politicians, local as well as national, for it is no vote-catcher; and I fear it may be a long time before attitudes change. Anyway, back in 1958 and 1959 we did the best that we could to argue what I am firmly convinced remains a very powerful case. But at the time we had to accept defeat, and twenty years later the attitude of the GLC remains equally negative towards the running costs of the Royal Opera House, although they give the English National Opera an annual grant of several hundred thousand pounds.

Before I became chairman, during my time first of all as secretary and then as a member of the board, I was often aware of a lack of contact between the artists working at Covent Garden and those responsible for the supervision of its work. I felt sure that to the singers, dancers and orchestral players we were just a bunch of faceless men. I urged upon David Webster that we should try regularly each year to hold a series of parties timed to take place in the artists' green room after selected board meetings at which members of the board would be enabled to meet the members of the resident opera company, including the chorus, and the principals of the ballet and of the orchestra. Finding convenient dates always seemed to be immensely difficult, but I persevered, and the first party, with members of the ballet company, was held in December 1959. The parties were too few in number, but I am sure they were appreciated and valuable.

Around the same period the board began to give preliminary thought to two other initiatives of mine which as time passed were to assume considerable importance in the development of Covent Garden's image. These were the creation of the Friends of Covent Garden and the inauguration of an annual opera gala. I had never understood why, although there was a benevolent fund for the ballet, nothing had been done to create a fund for the benefit of all the others working at Covent Garden. There was no general pension scheme, and despite repeated attempts over the years, and full agreement from the Arts Council and the Government about the need, the item always had to be sacrificed when we presented our yearly budget, because the grant was usually inadequate and something not of immediate operational moment had to go. It seemed to me sad that there was no annual opera gala in the same way that for a number of years there had regularly been a ballet gala. The view had been that the career of a ballet dancer was short, with only a limited prospect of employment in the profession after ceasing to dance; and this was a view with which one could not quarrel despite numerous examples, both at home and overseas, to controvert it. In any event the careers of singers were not always long, and the technical and other staff could all too easily fall victim to accident or illness. An earlier attempt had been made in 1952 when a gala performance of Beethoven's choral symphony raised a small sum, but the effort was never followed up. No one, it seemed, wanted to be bothered.

The Queen Mother had regularly attended the ballet gala, accompanied very consistently by Princess Margaret. It was self-evident that if we were to hold an annual opera gala there must be a guest of honour so as to assist the selling of tickets at high prices. Therefore in 1960 I approached Her Majesty and asked for her help. With the generosity of spirit which she had always shown towards Covent Garden she consented to attend. Princess Margaret I did not approach because she had never made any secret of the fact that, although she was devoted to the ballet, opera was not her favourite art-form.

It is axiomatic that any charitable gala performance needs a committee to help sell tickets and collect donations and advertising for the programme book. In order to give the thing a good send-off I asked Andrew Devonshire, bearer of a most distinguished name and generally liked and respected in all walks of life, to act as chairman. I also asked Miriam Marks, wife of the head of Marks and Spencer, the man who had already helped me so generously over my candelabra fund, to act as deputy chairman. Both agreed, he on the understanding that he would do it once but not annually, and she providing that she could be assisted by her dynamic sister-in-law Lois Sieff, a conscientious supporter of worthwhile causes, attractive, sympathetic and a great lover of the arts.

The Queen Mother said that she would like it to be a splendid occasion. The problem therefore was what the programme should be. I was against a bits and pieces evening, because these although unavoidable at times are usually pretty inartistic, something for everyone, leaving nobody satisfied. By a happy chance plans were in hand to revive a brilliant production by Franco Zeffirelli of the two one-act operas *Cavalleria Rusticana* and *Pagliacci*, good old *Cav.* and *Pag.*, which are traditionally given together, and which during the 1959/60 season had been performed no less than twenty times, always to packed houses.

For the revival in the summer of 1961 Victoria de los Angeles had been engaged to sing in *Cav.*, but she knew the leading role in both works, and the suggestion was made that for the gala evening she should sing in both, a proposal to which she most kindly agreed. With such a line-up I felt that we could not fail. We received great help from Leonard Wolfson, who contributed the cost of producing the programme. We managed to stuff it with advertisements: and we in fact cleared a sum of some £20,000 to get the Royal Opera House Benevolent Fund off to a flying start.

Regularly since 1961 there has been an annual opera gala, with an effort made to link the event to some important new opera production or happening in the life of Covent Garden; and now, twenty-six years later, the value of the fund exceeds £500,000. Since its inception it has done a good deal to help needy cases. With the introduction of an improved state pension scheme, and various schemes sponsored by the Arts Council, the importance of the fund has greatly lessened; and perhaps its range of beneficiaries should be in some way broadened (although to obtain a modification of the purposes of any charity is a daunting process), but in any event it would be sad if the annual opera gala were to be discontinued, for it has a value going far beyond its direct aim.

The work of launching the first gala was much helped by Lavinia Renton, the good-looking daughter of Sir Alan Lascelles, and herself a singer, whom I asked to act as secretary to the gala committee. She could not continue beyond the first year because she left to remarry. I therefore had to find someone to take her place, as well as a new chairman for the committee in succession to the Duke of Devonshire. In both cases I was more than fortunate. To act as chairman I approached Lady Diana Cooper, whose name alone quite apart from all her other qualities I knew would act as a magnet. For many years I had eyed her with awe. This was not only because of her legendary beauty, which bowled everyone over. More particularly it was because of her sophistication and quickness of wit, and her disconcerting habit of seeming to stare straight through one with her unnaturally pale blue eyes. She accepted my invitation to become chairman. We saw one another frequently, and I came to love her dearly. I loved her for her ability to rise above personal tragedy and disaster, and for her way of brushing aside those things she considered unimportant. She had a completely individual approach to every question. She was quite unwilling to be influenced by fashionable trends; and she judged people as she found them, regardless of their station in life. Towards those she loved, she was fiercely loyal. No one, I realized, could more completely exemplify Shakespeare's lines, 'Age cannot wither her, nor custom stale her infinite variety', words which I feel sure she must often have heard applied to herself, ignoring them in her characteristic manner. She did not enjoy performing the duties of chairman, and she forced me to guide her through the proceedings at each meeting: but she did a lot for the Benevolent Fund, for she was profoundly attached to Covent Garden, and she used regularly to tell me that it was one of the few things she would miss when she was dead.

As successor to Lavinia Renton there came the Hon. Kensington Davison, DSO, DFC. He had been christened Kensington because his father had been Mayor of the Borough, and then its Member of Parliament, but to all of us he was simply Ken. It was my *FT* colleague Pat Gibson, later and quite unforeseeably to become chairman of the Arts Council in 1972, who had asked me whether I might be able to suggest a job for him because he was not happy in the commercial air transport company he was working for and which he had presumably joined because of his distinguished career in the Royal Air Force as a night fighter pilot. It was clear that simply to come and run the annual opera gala was not good enough for him. He was high-powered though modest, and a passionate addict of both opera and ballet. The best I could say was that for some time we had been discussing launching the Friends of Covent Garden, although no date had been fixed; and if he would care to join on spec., with a view to running the Friends while also supervising the work of the gala committee, he would be most welcome. It was not quite as simple as that, of course, because he also had to be seen and approved by David Webster, as well as by Leon Bagrit, the head of Elliott-Automation, who had undertaken to get the Friends off the ground, and who was shortly going to join the board of directors. He was a man with extraordinary creative vision. His family had come to Britain because of Russian persecution of the Jews, greatly enriching the country of their adoption. He was an early pioneer in the field of electronics and automation, foreseeing the opportunities and possibilities. While his company was independent, and before it was taken over by the English Electric Company, it flourished, and he flourished with it. His tastes were eminently civilized. He bought Kenneth Clark's house in Hampstead, and he filled it with very well-chosen paintings and other subjects. Later he bought a house near Ascot racecourse named Ascot Place, which superficially appeared to be a nineteenth-century horror; but Leon removed the Victorian encrustations and revealed a splendid eighteenth-century residence. He and his wife Stella moved into it but not for long, for they found it a burdensome responsibility, and they sold the house to Jack and Dru Heinz, two close friends of mine who over the years have given much happiness to others through their kindness and hospitality; and it was most appropriate that in 1977 Jack should have been awarded a KBE, although he will never be able to use the title because he could never give up his American citizenship.

Music was Leon's first love. He was a good amateur violinist. With members of his family he used regularly to play chamber music. I forget now how I first met him, most probably through the *FT*, but in any event I was greatly intrigued and impressed by his quick imaginative mind, and his tense nervous personality; and when he volunteered to launch the Friends of Covent Garden I was overjoyed, feeling sure that he would prove an invaluable colleague. As his deputy chairman on the committee of the Friends, I proposed and he agreed to invite Roland Bird, who as I have earlier told was a key figure on the staff of *The Economist*, a great lover of opera, and above all calm, balanced and sensible. We also agreed that it would be generally welcome if we invited Marion Harewood to serve as president. She accepted, and proved most helpful and dutiful in her attendance at meetings, and so continued for over seventeen years, both as Lady Harewood and as Mrs Jeremy Thorpe, until she handed over the position to the Prince of Wales, whose interest in the work of Covent Garden was to prove a very gratifying aspect of Royal Opera House life. The most important thing about the launching of the Friends was that Leon and Ken Davison were able to work together, and Ken himself proved to be an inspired appointment. Nothing was too much trouble for him; and because he was single and had no family cares, he was able to devote an infinite number of hours to Covent Garden. He played the major part in building up the membership of the Friends to over 10,000, including a large number of young members, who were the audiences of the future. He produced a brilliant magazine. He organized lectures and every kind of activity designed to ensure the loyalty and enthusiasm of members. He regularly staged a hilarious annual Christmas party in the auditorium of the Royal Opera House, at which singers guyed dancers and dancers aped singers, and Sergeant Martin, Covent Garden's outsize mascot, was induced on to the stage to impersonate a Wagnerian heroine. There was no part of opera house life which did not concern Ken, and he went well beyond running the Friends and supervising the annual gala to covering the whole field of public relations. If he believed in what was being done there were no lengths to which he would not go to help something on its way; but he had to have his heart in it: and woe betide those who crossed his path.

One matter of constant concern to everyone connected with Covent Garden was the lack of rehearsal facilities. Matters were in a sense brought to a head by the appointment of Georg Solti as musical director, about which I write in the next chapter. He was insistent that something must be done. At more or less the same time, there was much discussion about the adequacy of the facilities for the training of opera singers. There was one specialized establishment attached to Morley College, the National School of Opera, which had been formed some years before by the distinguished singer Joan Cross, and Ann Wood, but the

49 The auditorium of the Royal Opera House as seen through a 'fish-eye' lens

50 The front entrance to the building

51 David Webster

52 Ava and John Waverley

53 Ninette de Valois

54 Rafael Kubelik

55 Margot Fonteyn

56 Frederick Ashton

57 Franco Zeffirelli

58 Georg Solti

59 Margot and Fred Ashton with Rudolf
Nureyev after his arrival in London, October 1961

60 The same trio, sixteen years later, after the
Queen's Silver Jubilee Gala

61 Antoinette Sibley and Anthony Dowell,
Titania and Oberon in Ashton's *The Dream*

62 Lynn Seymour in Macmillan's *Manon*

63 David Webster greeting the Queen Mother and Princess Margaret before a Royal Ballet Benevolent Fund Gala

64 Ninette de Valois with Sol Hurok

65 Otto Klemperer in the Crush Bar after a performance

66 On stage at the end of David Webster's farewell gala

67 Isaiah Berlin

68 Burnet Pavitt between myself and Bill Bundy, for many years the technical administrator

69 Jack Donaldson and John Sainsbury

70 John Tooley

Pictures taken at my farewell gala, July 1974

71 The Queen and Queen Mother with John Tooley

72 My shadow on stage

73 The Queen Mother talking to Jennie Lee and Ken Davison

74 The Queen with Colin Davis and his wife, Shamsi

75 John Sainsbury presenting my bust on behalf of The Friends of Covent Garden in the presence of The Queen. Beside him stands my successor, Claus Moser.

76 Sergeant Martin wearing his British Empire Medal

77 Joan seated at the piano, 1977

78 The Garter Procession, 1972. Beside me is Evelyn Howick with Hervey Rhodes behind.

79 Derry photographed by himself

Arts Council felt that with the growth in opportunities for opera singers there was a need for something on a larger scale, and they set up a committee under the chairmanship of Edward Bridges (wartime secretary of the Cabinet) who was generally respected for his objectivity and integrity if not for his knowledge of the subject.

The report was published in the summer of 1960. It proposed the formation of an advanced opera school, to be supported from public funds, giving intensive tuition in stage-craft and offering real scope for stage experience. The aims were basically those of Joan Cross's school, and it might have been thought that the simplest course would have been to strengthen her institution through the injection of public funds. The Arts Council, after serious consideration, rejected this course. Instead a proposal was pursued of acquiring the Winter Garden Theatre, which became available in the summer of 1961 and which had the great advantage of being within easy walking distance of Covent Garden, seeming to offer a very good way of providing the rehearsal facilities demanded by Solti as well as serving as the base for the new school advocated by the Bridges report. The theatre was on offer to us for a sum in the region of £180,000. However, the district surveyor had only valued the building at £120,000 and this was all that we were permitted to offer, nothing being allowed for the immense convenience of the nearness of the Winter Garden Theatre to the Royal Opera House, nor for its excellent auditorium. Despite very strong advocacy from the Arts Council, who were anxious to see the Bridges report implemented, public funds were not forthcoming and the deal fell through, a sad example of the all too frequent folly of red tape.

Georg Solti's determination regarding rehearsal facilities persisted; and in February 1962 David Webster told us that through friends of his in the Rank Organization he had found a large disused cinema in the East End which could be rented and adapted at moderate cost to serve both as the headquarters of the new opera training centre and to give Solti what he wanted for rehearsal purposes. I was not at all happy about the proposal. It was obvious that there would be many wasted hours travelling to and from the opera house, and the whole idea went against my instincts. But the Winter Garden proposal had collapsed, and I had no alternative suggestion to make.

The building had to be substantially modified, far more than was apparent at first. Indeed, I fancy that the money finally expended was more than would have been paid for the Winter Garden, and no long term asset was being created, because the premises were only rented.

The man appointed as director of the London Opera Centre was Humphrey Procter-Gregg, a professor of music and a pre-war colleague of Thomas Beecham. Gerald Coke was elected chairman of the board of governors, which included representatives from Covent Garden, Sadler's Wells, Glyndebourne, the English Opera Group, the main colleges of music, as well as one or two eminent singers. David Webster was given the title of administrator of the Centre, the idea being that he would provide a valuable link with the production and other departments of Covent Garden: but I fear that from the start he regarded the post too much as a sinecure, and this did not help what was to turn out to be a most unhappy situation.

Procter-Gregg knew a great deal about opera and about singing, but he was too kind and gentle in character to be asked to undertake the post of director. He took up his job optimistically in the belief that by making Joan Cross director of studies at the Centre and Ann Wood warden he would ensure continuity and harmony between the old school and the new Centre. At first they were unwilling to accept appointment, but later changed their minds. It would have been better had they not done so.

The task of converting the cinema took some time, and the Centre did not open for business until September 1963, a special subvention being made to the National School of Opera to keep it going during the period of waiting. There were many teething troubles, and the shortcomings of the building were all too apparent. However, these paled beside the clashes of temperament which developed; and by the end of the first term the board received Humphrey Procter-Gregg's resignation, partly because of failing health but also because as he stated at the time he 'found it difficult if not impossible to work with the warden'.

The board of governors met on 23 March 1964 to choose a new director. The name most favoured was that of James Robertson, who had been musical director of Sadler's Wells from 1946 to 1954; and despite a clear indication from Joan Cross and Ann Wood that if he was appointed they would resign he was offered and accepted the appointment. The two ladies were then true to their word and resigned, their resignations to take effect from the end of the summer term.

No public announcement regarding the resignations was made for nearly a month. David Webster then agreed a form of words with Ann Wood. He did not, however, anticipate that in addition the ladies intended to issue their own press statement and hold a press conference at which their grievances were ventilated. This created a very strained position. A special meeting of the governors was convened, with Gerald Coke in the chair although he had in fact by then handed over the chairmanship to Edward Pollitzer. Three members of the board of governors, George Harewood, Lois Sieff and Anthony Gishford, strongly supported Joan Cross and registered their displeasure by resigning. George Harewood was prevailed upon to suspend his resignation and agreed to serve on a committee set up to investigate the validity of the complaints; but within an hour of leaving the meeting his innermost feelings proved too strong, and he sent a telegram to Gerald Coke saying that he had decided that his resignation must stand *and* that he was conveying this news to the press. The result, not unpredictably, was that several unfriendly articles appeared, written with little effort to check the facts.

Lionel Robbins with his usual selflessness presided over the special committee, which included among others Ninette de Valois, Jack Donaldson and John Diamond, MP. The report endorsed some of the criticisms of the building, but did not uphold the complaints of Joan Cross and Ann Wood directed at Humphrey Procter-Gregg. Seen from his point of view the situation is best described in his confidential letter to the board quoted in the preface to the report: 'The Board, I knew, wished me to make and keep good relations with our members from the National School of Opera, and I did my best. By the end of the first term, I saw that practically nothing and no one I wished to introduce was acceptable to either Miss Cross or Miss Wood. Languages, my own classes, the acting classes, staff members not from their School, were opposed or disparaged. I lived in an atmosphere of frustration.' The governing body's comment, signed by Edward Pollitzer, the chairman, was to the effect that 'those who know Professor Procter-Gregg will infer that the frictions must have been indeed considerable to have evoked such a statement. There is evidence that they had become known to the student community.'

It was altogether an extremely sorry affair. James Robertson took up his appointment in the summer of 1964, calm was restored and plans were urgently put in hand for making the Troxy Cinema suitable for use as a rehearsal stage for Covent Garden and a production theatre for the Centre. It served a useful role for a number of years, despite the fundamentally inconvenient nature of the building. But I question how far the number of successful students produced justified the very considerable cost; and the decision has now it seems been taken to close it down after 1978, partly on account of ever-mounting costs, and also of the need instead for a smaller opera studio directly related to the main opera companies, which is just what the Winter Garden solution might have provided, a sad end to a sad story, made all the more so because it has not yet I gather even been decided where the new studio will be. Ultimately perhaps in the re-developed Royal Opera House, but who can say how many years away that is?

Chapter 21

For several years the board had more or less accepted the possibility that Covent Garden would be without a musical director for some while, and David Webster, I always felt, was far from wholehearted in his desire to find a successor to Kubelik. It was impossible to feel happy about the position. The two conductors who had most impressed themselves upon the board, the staff, the public and the critics, were Kempe and Giulini. Both more than once had made it clear that while they would be happy to conduct regularly they would not accept any greater responsibility. My first belief that a solution might be in prospect came towards the end of 1959 with the mention by George Harewood of the name of Georg Solti as a possible guest conductor. I had never heard him conduct, and I had never met him. I knew that he had been musical director at Frankfurt for a number of years, where he was well spoken of. It so happened however that the celebrated soloist and teacher Ilona Kabos, a woman of exceptional personality and talent, with whom Joan was studying the piano, knew Solti well from the old days in Budapest (although she was twenty years his senior). Through her I arranged to meet him, and I was instantly attracted. We had more than one talk together in her house in St John's Wood. David Webster likewise met him, and though hesitant was impressed. There was a mercurial quality (which of course still persists) that made an immediate impact. His mind worked with astonishing rapidity, and he always saw very clearly what he wanted. His knowledge of the operatic repertoire was extensive. He was also a splendid pianist. He studied conducting at the Liszt Academy in Budapest. When he was eighteen he was engaged as a *répétiteur* at the Budapest Opera and had minor engagements in Middle Europe including assisting Toscanini at the Salzburg Festival. He conducted once only at the Budapest Opera – a performance of *Figaro* on 11 March 1938, the day Hitler's troops marched into Vienna. By chance he was visiting Toscanini in Lucerne when war broke out. He was with great difficulty allowed to remain in Switzerland, but with no work permit was unable to continue his conducting career. For a while therefore he turned to the piano. When the war ended he made his way to Munich where for six years he was musical director of the Opera, before moving to Frankfurt for a stay of ten years. The ten years were due to finish in the summer of 1961 and thus the time was ripe for planning the next stage of his career. For him therefore as well as for us the moment was propitious. The Covent Garden job had obvious attractions, and Bruno Walter, I think, helped to tip the balance in our favour by pointing out to Solti how much he had to offer the opera-going public. David Webster and I saw him together in January 1960, after which he went off to America for a conducting tour. I pursued him with a letter almost fulsome in its content, but most sincerely meant. His wife Hedi replied on his behalf, as she often did, and letters passed to and fro between us. Then Solti was offered the post of principal conductor of one of the leading American orchestras. The question was whether he could do both Covent Garden and find time for the American orchestra as well. David quite rightly encouraged him, although in the event the particular job in America did not materialize, which was probably fortunate for Solti because it might have meant that the Chicago Orchestra (perhaps the finest in the world) would not have come his way as it did a few years later. After his return to Frankfurt he asked me to go and see him there. He was suffering agonies of doubt because he felt that David did not seriously wish him to come to London, and I persuaded him that however true that might once have been, it certainly was no longer the case. We went over the ground in great detail, staff, ratio of number of opera to ballet performances, rehearsal facilities, size of orchestra, employment of British and foreign singers and conductors (Giulini and Kempe he particularly wanted), policy regarding new productions, language policy, and so on: and it was agreed that he should come to London in May to go through every single point carefully with David in the hope that a contract could be signed before the end of June. On both sides we were anxious to finalize matters, and we duly succeeded despite a few hiccups, for instance arguments about his title, and explicit acceptance on his part that ultimate responsibility must rest with the board.

It was during the course of December 1959 that he made his début at Covent Garden, conducting *Der Rosenkavalier*, an engagement entered into before our talks with him started. He had a personal triumph. I remember Tom Armstrong saying that Solti made the orchestra's fingers tingle; and he was indeed one of that rare breed of conductors who could energize a whole performance and really hold the cough-free attention of the house. However, the *Rosenkavalier* performances had one real disappointment. Elisabeth Schwarzkopf sang the role of the Marschallin. The critics did not like her interpretation, and said so. As she was an artist of renown who had given important service to Covent Garden in the early postwar years, and as her husband Walter Legge had joined the board in 1958, we were anxious that she should be welcomed back with open arms. This was not to be. She sang beautifully, which she never failed to do.

But she was too arch and coquettish, and one of the critics compared her to 'a grand soubrette, too little the great lady'. To comfort her, her husband told her that the critics all liked to think of the Marschallin as a mother type; but the harm was done. She vowed that she would never expose herself again on the operatic stage in London, a vow that she kept. The loss of her talents was accompanied by a serious drop in her husband's interest in Covent Garden's doings, and this was only spasmodically revived.

Solti attended a board meeting for the first time in July 1960, and outlined his plans for his initial period as musical director, which was due to start in September 1961. It is fair to say that everyone was attracted by his friendly manner and impressed by his determined and astonishingly practical approach. He always had a very clear idea of what he wanted, yet he was not unamenable to reason; and if persuaded that what he wanted was wrong or impracticable, he readily agreed. The impression that he conveyed at his first meeting was not subsequently contradicted. One thing he made very clear, that the absence from the repertoire of Mozart, other than the *Magic Flute*, must be put right. We were at one with him over this. Indeed there had already been tentative discussions with Giulini in connection with the three most famous 'Italian' operas of Mozart. It was evident that if Solti himself wished to perform these works, he must as musical director have the prior claim, and it is perhaps true that without his insistence it would have been a long time before they were all introduced. There was a lingering feeling that Covent Garden was too large and that they should be left to Sadler's Wells, a feeling brought finally to an end when the Sadler's Wells opera company moved into the Coliseum.

However, Solti very intelligently decided that the first opera he would perform in the Royal Opera House after the announcement of his appointment (but before he formally took over) should be a modern British work, and in the early months of 1961 he conducted with notable success the first full-scale production of Benjamin Britten's *Midsummer Night's Dream*, which had had its première in a tiny theatre at Aldeburgh the previous summer, when Solti had attended, together with David Webster and myself. Producer and designer were John Gielgud and John Piper, and this got Solti off to a very good start.

At about the same time Otto Klemperer made his début at Covent Garden. He mounted a production of *Fidelio*, for me the most affecting of all operas, and since he was *the* authentic conductor of Beethoven and since he had only recently returned to work after a very serious indisposition the occasion was deeply moving. I had met Klemperer and his daughter Lotte in Lucerne, where I had gone on the advice of Walter Legge, Walter having given the great man his first engagement following a year's enforced absence, and he was in Lucerne to conduct the Philharmonia Orchestra in a programme which included Tchaikovsky's 6th Symphony. Lotte was about the most saintly person I had ever met, yet bubbling with humour, very honest and direct. She described to me how her father had dozed off one night in bed, smoking his pipe, had woken up, seen the sheet smouldering, taken a bottle from his bedside table, and without thinking had poured its contents on to the sheet, forgetting that it contained pure alcohol which he was using medicinally. This resulted in major chest burns, requiring skin grafts first from one thigh and then weeks later from the other, until eventually the maestro recovered. I remember saying to Lotte that this seemed to me one of the more grim examples of the inscrutable workings of providence, to which she half jokingly replied, 'Had you heard his recent conducting before it happened? It wasn't very good, you know!' as though he needed a shock to bring him to his senses. Anyway, there was no doubt that both the concert in Lucerne and above all the *Fidelio* performances were triumphantly successful. Klemperer developed a special sense of attachment to Covent Garden. David Webster handled him skilfully and persuaded him to return several times: and he certainly regarded London as his home from home. I always saw him when he was at the Hyde Park Hotel. I even induced him to come to hear Joan Sutherland singing in *Lucia di Lammermoor*, although I fear that he cut everything down to size in his rather devastating way by asking, 'Ist *das* ein Ewigkeitswerk?'*

Ever since I could remember Covent Garden had been very fortunate in the women occupying key positions on the staff, notably Muriel Kerr, David Webster's loyal Scottish secretary, Honor Thackrah, the orchestral manager, who never flustered and always looked serene whatever the stresses and strains, and Stella Chitty, the tireless stage manager, who happily worked round the clock if there was work to do. To these, Solti brought in his train two others, both of whom in their way contributed much to the well-being of the opera house. First was Enid Blech, his devoted personal assistant, whose death in 1977 after a gallant fight against cancer was a major deprivation both for him and for many more besides. The other was Joan Ingpen, a concert artist's agent, who sold her business in order to work for Solti as controller of opera planning, the post originally held by George Harewood. She stayed at Covent Garden for nine years, filling the most frustrating of all jobs with distinction, showing the tenacity of a terrier in her pursuit of singers. She left soon after Solti, moving to the Paris Opera where they benefited greatly from the experience she had gained with us. To succeed her John Tooley skilfully recruited another very gifted lady, Helga Schmidt from Vienna, whose knowledge of the international operatic scene was extensive. She was less matter of fact and far more elusive than Joan, but no one could deny that her methods achieved substantial results.

* Is *that* an eternal masterpiece?

Georg Solti's own first offering after he had actually taken over as musical director was *Iphigénie en Tauride* by Gluck, marvellous music but a disappointingly undramatic production. Next came *Don Giovanni*, with very splendid and beautiful sets by Zeffirelli which were too heavy and made the production move too slowly. Again the reception was mixed. Then in the following season Georg gave Verdi's *Forza del Destino*. He conducted with his characteristic verve, but the production looked absurd, translating the opera into a wrong period because the producer Sam Wanamaker had the notion of projecting Goya paintings on to a tiny picture frame suspended above the stage: while the soprano in the leading role sang consistently flat. I told Solti beforehand that I had serious doubts about the magic lantern slides, and also about the soprano. There was nothing to be done about the production, though, which had been entrusted to Sam Wanamaker following a very skilful production he had done for Covent Garden of Michael Tippett's *King Priam*. The plan had been for Renato Guttuso to do the designs, but Wanamaker rejected them, with sad results; and to rub salt into the wound they were put on display at a West End gallery where Walter Legge took great pleasure in buying one of the sketches. As for the soprano, Solti assured me she would be all right on the night, but alas he was mistaken, as became all too clear very soon after the ominous opening bars of the opera.

During this opening period of Georg's time at Covent Garden he had a great deal of unpleasantness to contend with. A small anonymous group engaged in booing from the amphitheatre, and he used to find things like 'Solti must go' written on the windscreen of his car. David and I both worked hard to reassure him. So did Isaiah Berlin, who at the time was chairman of the opera subcommittee and a tower of strength. The first term as musical director was only for a period of three years, and for me the important thing was to ensure that Georg would agree to stay on for a further term, for it is astonishing in the world of opera how quickly the time slips by, with everything having to be planned a good two years ahead.

Quite apart from the boos and the windscreen scrawls there were plenty of things with which Georg was displeased. I had every reason for fearing that he would not agree to renew his contract when the three years were up. I felt it essential to negotiate an extension, and in this my feeling was shared by Isaiah Berlin and the other members of the board most closely concerned. David Webster's position was unclear. Douglas Lund, the accountant and company secretary, had told me in September 1962 that David did not wish to discuss renewal for another year. I therefore pressed him strongly, and in the course of a letter which I wrote to him on 20 September I said:

I am personally very clear that we should be heavily condemned if we did not secure an extension of Solti's contract for at least a year or preferably two. You said, I believe, that he is already in the process of taking engagements at the Colon in the autumn of 1964 and at the Met. in the early months of 1965. This suggests that if we want him to stay we should not tarry in talking with him about the future. . . . What really matters is that he is quite outstandingly good and if he is allowed to be lost to us we shall stand to be heavily criticised. Indeed, a position of real crisis would arise, with widespread reper-cussions on the Board and throughout the organisation and this at a time when we are trying to get the Friends off the ground and the future looks bright. I really feel that we must do everything possible so to arrange matters that Solti stays on for another year or two. In my view we have an absolute duty to accomplish this for there is no conceivable alternative that would not mean a falling away from the high point we have attained – and from which we must still advance.

Watching him at rehearsal as I did last night, observing his fantastic grasp of detail without losing command of the broad sweep, his power to stimulate – his tremendous versatility, his practical and resourceful nature, one realises that to lose him would be a tragedy. Of course, there may be a few bloody noses from time to time but I would rather that than everyone being slightly or more than slightly below par.

Soon afterwards David told me that Solti had agreed in principle to an extension; but when I saw Solti together with David in December after his return from Vienna he began by saying that after careful discussion with his wife he had decided that he did not wish to continue. He then went on to outline some of his causes for dissatisfaction, in addition to his concern about the lack of rehearsal facilities of which I wrote in the last chapter. First of all, he complained of the conflicting claims of opera and ballet on the orchestra's time. He felt that the orchestra must be enlarged, but for this it was necessary to overcome the prejudice of the orchestra director, Morris Smith, against the engagement of women. The orchestra must also be given the opportunity of appearing regularly on the concert platform. He said that he was confused about the respec-tive duties of various people on the production staff. His chief complaint related to his personal position and his name, which he thought Covent Garden was doing far too little to build up in the eyes of the outside world, so that he felt that he was working almost anonymously. Much of what he said was justified. David turned on his avuncular reassuring manner, undertook that everything Georg had complained of would be attended to, and told him that before he next left London he would have signed on as musical director for a further three-year term. This, to the general contentment of the public, he duly did, being relentlessly urged and encouraged to do so by me: and the operatic way ahead seemed reasonably clear.

The failure of the *Forza* production exemplified some of the difficulties we experienced in the matter of design. They arose far more in the field of opera than ballet because in the main ballets called for few sets and minimal costumes. It was only with the handful of full-length 'classics', which largely means Tchaikovsky, that problems arose, and it was rare if not unknown to have a disaster in this department.

As to opera, it is first of all worth thinking how the choice of works to be produced is determined. In the early days after the war, and indeed at the start of my time as chairman, it was not unusual to give five or even six new productions a year: but with the steady rise in costs and the pressure of work the figure fell to three or four. This small number had to satisfy several competing needs: first, the filling of gaps in the repertoire, second, the replacement of an existing production because of dilapidation or obsolescence or sheer ugliness, third, the special predilections of the musical director or of any prominent guest condutor whom we wished to engage, and finally the presentation of newly composed contemporary operas. All the time of course we had to bear in mind box office implications because of our substantial dependence upon takings, but we never allowed this consideration to be the dominant one. The plans were the subject of regular monthly discussion at the meetings of the opera committee, attended by the general administrator, the musical director or his representative, and those members of the board particularly concerned with operatic matters. Through this there emerged a programme covering the next three or four years, which was continuously subject to variation as the availability of the desired artists fluctuated. At any given time there was naturally a programme which for say the next couple of years was firm. The first essential was to agree upon the conductor, and this for perhaps half the new productions would be the musical director himself. It was then necessary to agree upon the producer, after which would go forward the business of casting, and the choice of designer; and this was where the pitfalls chiefly lay, and too often we came to grief. The trouble was that we too readily accepted that in the choice of designer the decision of the producer should be paramount. In practice this was usually inevitable, because most producers, understandably enough, would only undertake a production with the designer of their choice; and even when accepting a designer whose name had been urged by us it was not unknown for the designs to be rejected by the producer, thus obliging us either to cancel the production or agree to whatever alternative he desired.

Hoping to find help with the problem, soon after becoming chairman in 1958, I invited Colin Anderson, whom I knew through Kenneth Clark, if he would join the board. He was a great lover of the fine arts, being chairman of the Tate Gallery, chairman of the Royal College of Art, a member of the Royal Fine Arts Commission, of which he later became chairman, and a host of other things. (For instance, we owe to him the choice of lettering used in motorway road signs.) He was a practical businessman, a director of P. & O. and other companies, urbane, cultivated and witty, with a delightful light touch. He joined the board of Covent Garden at the beginning of 1961, being quick to make his presence felt, and making a number of helpful proposals about the layout of our programmes and posters. In 1962 he agreed to become chairman of a new committee of the board, the need for which was strongly urged by Isaiah Berlin, to be called the design sub-committee. Its purpose was not only to keep the general question of design under regular review, but also to examine and advise on all proposals for the appointment of designers for particular works. The first members of the committee besides Colin were Burnet Pavitt, and William Coldstream. David Webster and I were *ex officio* members. After a short while Fred Ashton also joined the committee, but he was ill adapted to committee work and too busy to attend regularly. The committee started on its activities with high hopes. One interesting proposal was to build up a permanent reference library of photographs or drawings of sets and costumes by available living designers. David Webster welcomed the proposal, for he was all too aware of Covent Garden's shortcomings in this regard. Colin Anderson suggested that to get things going there would have to be someone specifically given the duty of getting the library started, and he asked Colette, the daughter of Kenneth Clark, whether she would be interested in taking on the job. She accepted, agreeing at the same time to become secretary of the committee so that she had some formal status. As things turned out, the compilation of the reference library never got very far. It was found to be too arduous a task, and the experience of the committee in proposing designers for particular productions was too dismaying to justify pressing harder for the library to be compiled. The best outcome in fact was that some years later Colette Clark was asked by me to join the board of directors; and she turned out to be a valuable addition, both intelligent and decorative, leaning rather towards the ballet but taking a passionate interest in everything to do with Covent Garden.

Early on in the work of the design sub-committee Burnet Pavitt produced a paper starkly listing some of the visually disappointing productions which had emerged from the policy of giving producers such a free hand in the choice of designers. It is worth quoting the following paragraph of his paper:

That the harmonisation of the three main elements for success in any new operatic production, namely the conductor, the producer and the designer, is immensely difficult for any administration to achieve goes without saying. I only plead against abdication to the producer on the question of design in all circumstances. Where harmony is found . . . the results have been first rate. And where the producer and designer have been men of double genius, such as Visconti and Zeffirelli, the summits have been reached. The problem, as I see it now, is how to bring in designers of quality, who are acceptable to good producers, when they are not one and the same man.

He went on to argue that the policy must be reversed, and recommended that before any actual engagement David Webster should discuss with the producer the names of two or three designers who through a knowledge of their work would be acceptable to Covent Garden; further, that if the producer insisted on anyone different the name must be considered by both the sub-committee and the board; and then if no agreement could be reached we must take the dramatic step of approaching another producer. Burnet's proposals were approved, and it was agreed that they must be adhered to. Alas, despite all the pious hopes, disappointments persisted; and these mainly arose because David Webster was not strong enough in enforcing what had been agreed. His visual sense was very erratic, and he allowed some terrible designs through; and we were apt to find ourselves committed in a way from which we could not escape. The position of the board was always difficult. If they had tried to exercise a power of veto, there would soon have been an outcry, somewhat analogous to the reaction to proprietorial interference with a newspaper editor's freedom. We were therefore bound to proceed with a degree of caution, not that this in any way excused the general administrator when he committed us without any kind of proper consultation.

1963 was a notably bad year from the point of view of the visual accept-ability of productions. In April there was the disappointment of Otto Klemp-erer's *Lohengrin*, musically marvellous but most depressing to look at, with really grotesque costumes, which should never have been accepted but which I suppose got through the net because of excessive reverence for the great man. In the following month came *Figaro*, where Solti insisted on having Oscar Fritz Schuh as producer; and this inescapably meant Teo Otto as designer. I felt strongly in my bones that he was quite wrong. We, that is the board, got to the point of insisting that at least the costumes should be designed in London, but of course they were not.

Two further productions were given in 1963, not beautiful to look at, but intelligently produced by a most delightful Yugoslav named Vlado Habunek. For Moussorgsky's *Khovanshchina* Isaiah Berlin, as a labour of love, wrote a splendidly erudite historical note for the programme. Edward Downes con-ducted. Very beautiful sounds came from the pit and the stage, and the final scene in which the so-called Old Believers sacrificed themselves in a blazing forest for the sake of their faith had a rare nobility; but the public stayed away. Likewise with the Shostakovich, which had been first performed in Leningrad in 1934 with the title *Lady Macbeth of Mtsensk*. It had then been banned from performance, and on its revival in London twenty years later a change of title to *Ekaterina Ismailova* was insisted upon, goodness knows why, but it was no help at the box office. It is fair to say, though, that Shostakovich himself, who was present in London for the rehearsals, thought that Covent Garden had done him proud. A couple of years later there was an example of a failure where the board itself had enthusiastically welcomed a proposal. Solti was eager to conduct *The Flying Dutchman*, a standard work which was wholly missing from the Covent Garden repertoire. At the time the stage designer Sean Kenny was all the rage. He was engaged, and produced models which filled David with excitement. However, the abstract end-product did not look in the least satisfactory, while the ugly hulk which represented the Dutchman's ship groaned and creaked as it moved.

I myself was always convinced that in the main with basic repertoire works it was quite wrong for Covent Garden to engage in experiment. Such productions were all right for a festival where they would be used for a handful of perform-ances and then probably scrapped, whereas with us when we introduced a basic piece we should expect to be able to revive it regularly for a number of years. The supreme example of this was *La Bohème*, the production of which dated back to 1897, and was only replaced in 1974, a task courageously and successfully undertaken by Julia Trevelyan Oman, whose collaboration with Fred Ashton also resulted in two superb ballets, *Enigma Variations* and *Month in the Country*.

The ideal, as Burnet Pavitt suggested in his note, was when we had as producer-designer, a doubly gifted man of genius: but the only examples within our experience were Lucchino Visconti and Franco Zeffirelli, and of these Franco alone was consistently reliable. It is lamentable that the last productions that he did for us were *Tosca* and *Rigoletto*, as long ago as the 1963/4 season. He was of course approached again after these and accepted to do three productions, *Norma*, *Fille du Régiment* and *Carmen*, but in each case he tiresomely withdrew, and then he was lured into film-making and was lost to us. Unfortunately Colin Anderson himself took against what he dismissed somewhat derisorily as Franco's *verismo** method, although the fact is that his productions have lived in a way that many others less '*verismatic*' have simply failed to do.

Colin was of course right that to have everything done in the same sort of style would have been dreadful. Occasionally my friend Harold Rosenthal, the editor of *Opera*, with whom I sometimes differed, mainly over language for he wanted opera sung in English, but also over the repertory versus *stagione* systems,† rebuked us for not developing a Covent Garden style, although he

---

* Strictly realistic representation.

† The argument concerned the method of planning the repertoire. The repertory system meant running a large number of different operas on consecutive nights, whereas *stagione* (literally 'season' in Italian) meant grouping a series of performances of one opera fairly closely together, performed with basically identical casts and conductor. Harold Rosenthal wanted the repertory system, which

never spelt out what he meant. To me diversity of approach seemed essential. It was all a matter of judgement and good sense. At heart I think that the ideal would have been to have had as general administrator a man of infallible judgement and taste, with the personality to impose his will. Rule by committee in aesthetic matters just does not work. I am clear that Colin Anderson's committee was useful in helping to improve the general standard of design. However, he found the frustration of making proposals which were so often ignored such that at the beginning of 1968 he recommended that the committee should cease to exist, leaving it to the opera and ballet committees to reassume the responsibility for the discussion of design problems in their respective fields.

In the early 1960s the Royal Ballet had been passing through a very good phase, although nothing diminished their poor relation complex, or removed their conviction that they kept Covent Garden going with their profitable foreign touring and because of their normally higher attendances and lower overheads. It was necessary to keep on stressing that the opera and ballet sides were complementary. I felt strongly that the existence of the two companies side by side helped to give Covent Garden its distinctive quality among the great opera houses of the Western world. Many of the leading opera houses on the Continent had their own ballet companies, but these were always in a very subordinate position, their first duty being to provide dancers for the opera. There were those who believed that the Royal Ballet should be installed in its own theatre in which it could perform nightly. An opportunity occurred to put this to the test when the Royal Opera House had to be closed for several months in 1964 in order to reconstruct the amphitheatre and to renew the electrical wiring both of which had been condemned as unsafe. The ballet appeared on its own at Drury Lane for five or six weeks, and the strain of nightly performances seemed to me to cause the enthusiasm for a separate home to die down noticeably thereafter. The idea is resurrected from time to time, but, regardless of artistic considerations, it will always be knocked on the head because of the financial implications, for it would require two orchestras, and involve the overheads of two theatres instead of one, while an effective doubling of the number of performances would surely mean more dancers *and* more singers. Indeed the idea could only become the subject of serious discussion if because of financial stringency there should be a request for a fresh study of the merits of merging Covent Garden and the Coliseum, not that I can see such a study having a positive outcome.

---

offered much greater variety during a given period of time. I was certain that for consistent quality of performance the *stagione* system was essential. It was the only way in which the public could be sure to see properly rehearsed performances with the same artists. The system is followed both at Covent Garden and very largely also by the English National Opera at the Coliseum.

In any event, in 1960 Fred Ashton was in supremely creative mood. At the beginning of the year he produced what to me is the greatest of all his ballets, *La Fille mal Gardée*, an evergreen masterpiece which from its first performance was clearly destined for immortality. The ballet's origins went back to the late eighteenth century, but the whole thing had been completely rethought. John Lanchbery had, as the Covent Garden report said, 'freely adapted and arranged Ferdinand Hérold's music from the 1828 version', and done it very well, while Osbert Lancaster designed sets and costumes which were beautifully apt and witty. The story, a simple rustic comedy, romantic and touching, conveying a sense of May Day happiness, enabled Fred with his uncanny knack to create roles perfectly suited to the two principals, Nadia Nerina and David Blair. The number of companies throughout the world who have added *Fille* to their repertoire has depended only on Fred's willingness to help them mount it. When the Royal Ballet went to Moscow in 1961 the success of *Fille* was overwhelming. I was lucky enough to be there because the major British trade fair organized by Industrial and Trade Fairs, of which I was chairman, took place at the same time. The Russians begged him to let them have it, but he was unwilling to return, finding the whole atmosphere antipathetic; and so they had to be disappointed.

A year later he produced for the second company another new ballet, *Les Deux Pigeons*, with music by Messager and extremely pretty sets and costumes by Jacques Dupont. At first the work did not have great success with the public, but it has stood the test of time, and is now very popular. He also produced a most ambitious ballet, Stravinsky's *Perséphone*, which was notable for two chief reasons. First, one of our most distinguished dancers, Svetlana Beriosova, both danced and recited (in impeccable French) André Gide's verse, her voice being amplified by means of an invisible microphone hidden in her corsage, which did not hamper her movements but was slightly erratic in its functioning. Secondly, the designs were by Nicolas Ghika, a well-known Greek artist who some twenty years ago married our old friend Barbara Rothschild. They brilliantly evoked the contrast between the springlike upper regions and the nether world, and they deserve to have been seen more often because of their visual beauty; but as the technical difficulty of presenting the ballet is considerable, I fear that limbo will be its fate.

During this same period Kenneth MacMillan, whose choreographic talent was steadily growing, produced, again for the second company, *The Invitation*, a highly original work possessing immense impact. It was the first ballet, at Covent Garden anyway, with rape as its basic theme, very explicitly presented yet in a way to which no one could take exception. For me *The Invitation* was most memorable for its revelation of the compelling qualities of Lynn Seymour.

a young Canadian who was then at the start of her career, but who already revealed extraordinary depths of emotion, as well as being a most poetic and versatile dancer, at home with both classical and modern dance. Later, it became clear that she also had skill as a choreographer. Of all the gifted dancers produced by the Royal Ballet, she seemed to me the one who save for Margot had the most to offer, not because of technique, where others outshone her, but because of her mysterious power to rivet attention and awaken the imagination.

MacMillan soon afterwards, in May 1962, produced a new version of Stravinsky's *Rite of Spring*, which had been performed originally by Diaghilev's company in 1913. This ballet showed an entirely new aspect of MacMillan's brilliance. As designer he engaged Sydney Nolan, and together they skilfully created an atmosphere of primitive ritual. The ballet was a particular triumph for Monica Mason as the sacrificial chosen maiden, and for the *corps de ballet* who for the best part of forty-five minutes had to concentrate unremittingly on a complex series of steps and movements in the execution of which the slightest flaw would be exposed. The main importance of *Rite of Spring* was that it gave such strong proof of MacMillan's ability to think and choreograph on a large scale, and provided fresh evidence of the originality of his mind.

Not long afterwards the whole world of ballet was to receive an electric shock. During the appearance in Paris of the Kirov company from Leningrad a young dancer on 17 June 1961 made his dash for freedom: and from that moment things could never be quite the same again. The dramatic escape of Rudolf Nureyev as his company were about to board the aircraft to leave Paris occurred a few months before Margot Fonteyn's annual matinée gala at Drury Lane in aid of the Royal Academy of Dancing. Hoping for an added attraction for the audience, she decided to ring up Nureyev and invite him to take part. Rather to her surprise, he agreed. Fred Ashton arranged a spectacular *pas seul* for him, in which he whirled dramatically round the stage, receiving an ovation. Ninette de Valois was quite bowled over by his looks, panache and effortless technique. Within a few weeks, Nureyev was appearing at Covent Garden as a sort of permanent guest artist, what in Fleet Street jargon would be called a regular casual, making his début in February 1962 with Margot Fonteyn in *Giselle*. This work was imaginatively selected by Ninette as one likely to show off Rudi to the greatest advantage. She quickly established a particular relationship with him, realizing what he had to offer as a stimulant, while recognizing that if he joined the company under contract he might throw it quite out of joint.

The force of his impact cannot be exaggerated. A certain initial resentment quickly succumbed before his dedication and devotion to the dance, his high professionalism, and his spirit of adventure. It is now over sixteen years since he first came to London, and he is a world star, yet his willingness to undertake new and challenging assignments has continued to grow. Indeed, the greater the challenge the greater his response. He has appeared and made friends with most of the leading ballet companies of the world, but it is fortunate for us that next to Russia his roots are more here than anywhere else, and we should all say thank you to him for what he has given us. In my Covent Garden days I always found him personally sympathetic, although with a caustic tongue. I first met him in Margot Fonteyn's dressing room after a performance in which he had not been dancing. (The ballet was Ashton's full-length work, *Ondine*, the story of a water sprite, with music by Hans Werner Henze, dating back to 1958, which seriously needs reviving.) While she was changing behind the screen, I said to Rudi, 'Wasn't she marvellous?' or some pedestrian words to that effect; to which he replied, '*She* knows what I think,' thus putting the poor old chairman firmly in his place.

Nureyev's most obvious effect was upon the general standard of male dancing in the company. He offered a kind of competition and a challenge which had not previously been met. His influence was also felt in the female *corps de ballet* for whom he introduced to the repertoire Act IV of *La Bayadère*, one of the favourite works performed by the Kirov Company, a great triumph for the girls, widely acclaimed, and capable of revival each season. Probably the ballet-going public would most thank him for prolonging the dancing career of Margot Fonteyn by ten or more years. When Michael Somes, her chief partner for many years, was obliged to give up dancing the leading classical roles, she was slightly stranded. The personality of David Blair, who inherited Somes's position, did not accord with Margot's, excellent dancer and delightful individual though he was. She could not accustom herself to the change, until Rudi appeared, almost young enough to be her son, and everything was transformed for her. His appearance in her life was of major significance because not long afterwards – in 1964 – her husband Tito Arias was shot in Panama, being as a result paralysed from the neck downwards, remaining entirely lucid mentally but incapable of movement or of speech above a whisper. Rudi's arrival therefore surely sustained her morale at a time of agony. If he gave, he also received; for in becoming the chief partner of the great Fonteyn, his career in the West was assured. For Margot is the most beautiful ballerina of her age, having remained so for almost forty years, with delicate features, expressive dark eyes, and a perfectly proportioned body incapable of a movement lacking grace. Perhaps I could quote Bernard Shaw from the *Saturday Review* of 9 January 1897:

The perfect dancer along whose limbs the rhythmic stream flows unbroken to the very tips of the fingers and roots of the hair, whose head moves beautifully, whose nape and wrists make the music visible, who can flex the spine at each vertebra more certainly than an ordinary person can flex his finger at each joint and who is the personification of skill, grace, strength and health.

I do not know whom he had in mind when he wrote those words eighty years ago, but they certainly fit Margot with her natural elegance and style, lovely low-pitched voice and radiant smile. With all her attributes she is loved by all and envied by none, never giving herself airs, and possessing true humility.

Not long after Nureyev's arrival in London Fred Ashton arranged a new ballet for him to dance with Margot, *Marguerite and Armand*, the story of *La Dame aux Camélias* compressed into a moving twenty minutes, the music an orchestral version of Liszt's piano sonata, with décor, which essentially meant an open shirt for Rudi and three dazzling costumes for Margot, designed by Cecil Beaton. The ballet received its first performance at the Royal Ballet Benevolent Fund Gala in March 1963. It was a great piece of melodrama carried off with total conviction by the two stars. So far no one else has danced their roles, and probably no one ever will.

In July of the same year came a moving occasion, the special performance marking the retirement of Ninette de Valois, when all the members of both companies and the students of the Royal Ballet School united to do honour to her on the stage of Covent Garden – although we all knew that retirement in her case was not really an admissible fact, and that so long as she lives her advice will be sought on every matter of significance bearing upon the Royal Ballet companies or the School, for they are all her creation, and her authority is supreme.

Several years before her retirement Fred Ashton had been clearly designated her successor by his appointment as associate director. There was therefore no problem or argument, and no call for the post to be advertised.

If it was obvious that without Ninette the Royal Ballet would not have existed at all it is every bit as obvious that without Fred the company would not have achieved the fame or distinction that it has done. Not only does he possess real creative genius, he also has to an extraordinary degree a natural sense of taste, both visually and musically, and an unerring feeling for what is appropriate to the occasion. He was born in Ecuador, where his father was working as British Consul. He first went to school in Peru, and therefore he speaks fluent Spanish. His education was completed in England. When he left school he went to work in an office, but already when he was only eighteen he knew that the career he wanted must be related to the dance. It is said that his imagination was first fired when he saw Pavlova dance while he was a boy in Latin America. His earliest opportunities came in various musical shows and he was made use of by C. B. Cochran. The scope for serious ballet work in England in the late 1920s scarcely existed. It was not until the foundation of the Camargo Society which was the inspiration of Maynard Keynes and his wife Lydia Lopokova, and then the entrancing Marie Rambert's little pioneer company at the Mercury Theatre that opportunities began to present themselves. Ninette was on the committee of the Camargo Society. Through her, Lilian Baylis became involved and the Vic-Wells company came into being. Fred, of course, was in evidence from the beginning, and already in his early twenties he produced a ballet, *Façade*, to the music of William Walton, which contained in embryo many of the qualities of sentiment and wit that he later developed to such splendid effect.

The key people in the early stages of the evolution of ballet in Britain were very few indeed. Together they formed a happy band, all of them poor and all of them dedicated. Fred was younger than the others, but he surely acted as a kind of catalyst. I used to go quite regularly to the Mercury Theatre in the early 1930s through Sacheverell Sitwell, whom I knew as a friend of both Emerald Cunard and Alice Wimborne. I enjoyed my visits, although more at that time I suspect because I thought it was the right thing to do than because of any genuine understanding. I often met Fred, but our worlds were too different in those days for me to have anything much to offer him. However, over the years I have been able to see him frequently, and he became an intimate friend of Joan's. I know no one who is more amusing or better company. His reactions are nearly always extremely subjective, but he has unerring judgement about people, seeing clearly through their pretences, and he can be very sharp-tongued. It goes without saying that he is astonishingly observant, and misses no nuance or foible, whether it be in talk, appearance or dress. When he wishes he is a devastating mimic. He loves social life and is very gregarious, yet he is essentially an extremely private person, with much kept locked up inside. He seldom shows his feelings strongly; and rebuffs and disappointments cause him to withdraw inside himself rather than to explode. The poverty of his early days created in him a kind of church-mouse mentality, which no degree of wealth or success will ever eradicate. But few people have contributed more to enhance the quality of life.

As artistic director of the Royal Ballet he was ably assisted by his three lieutenants, Michael Somes, John Field, and John Hart. Field had charge of the second or touring company, conducting a skilful, largely self-contained opera-tion. Hart had the intricate task of planning the basic layout of the rehearsal schedule in relation to the repertoire, often including the casting, always of course in consultation with Fred. Somes concerned himself particularly with the teaching of roles, and the development of artists. I tended to see him most often of the three. Field was mainly away from London with the touring group.

With Hart I never developed any real personal relationship. He was the least forthcoming, and an unknown quantity. Somes was most in evidence. At the end of any conversation with him I came away deeply conscious of my inadequacy as chairman of Covent Garden. 'How *can* you allow such and such to happen?' '*Why* does the ballet always have to put up with so and so?' Questions which usually hit some particular nail firmly into place, and then when he knew that the nail had been smartly driven home, he would draw back his distinguished head and a smile of disdainful triumph would cross his features. To Michael Somes more than to anyone else is due the credit for the maintenance of standards of performance. He was in fact almost impossible to satisfy. Because of this he sometimes had a depressant effect on weaker spirits. Yet everyone in Britain should realize our indebtedness to him for the enormous care and attention which he brought to his work, his refusal to be satisfied with the second best, and his unswerving loyalty to the Royal Ballet, extending over many years and regardless of the vicissitudes through which it might be passing.

Ashton's regime was to last from September 1963 until the summer of 1970. It was notable for a steady improvement in the quality of performances, and for the growing overseas recognition of the company's merits. The actual overseas work of the main Royal Ballet company was confined chiefly to the United States, which was visited at least once in every two years and where until recently profitable touring could be undertaken without any subvention. The touring company, which had evolved from the Sadler's Wells Theatre Ballet following assumption of responsibility for that company by Covent Garden in 1959, was tending to be called upon more and more by the British Council for overseas visits. They led a very exhausting life, seldom at rest in one place for any length of time. Their overseas touring was additional to their main responsibility which was to tour the provinces. Their London appearances were infrequent, their first appearance at Covent Garden being in 1957, when the main company was away in America. There was a certain amount of needless trepidation beforehand, but they covered themselves with glory, their dancing gaining greater freedom in a performing area a good deal larger than they were used to.

As things turned out, over the years Covent Garden's responsibility for two separate ballet companies was to add enormously to the work of the administration. Although when we first assumed the added responsibility we had stipulated that it must be on the basis that we should suffer no additional financial burden, the fact was that more than once we were obliged to put forward the inevitability of disbanding the second company as the only way open to us of making a saving of sufficient size to enable us to keep open the doors of Covent Garden. To have recourse to such a step would not have been realistically practicable, and it would have brought much justified criticism upon us. However, far too often time had to be wasted in arguing with the Arts Council that the grant they offered left us with no alternative. I fear that constant worry over finance resulted in many too many changes of policy in relation to the name, size and role of the second company, but to recount these changes would be otiose.

It was around 1961 that I made an unsuccessful effort to bring more sense into the planning arrangements of the British Council. Their involvement with cultural affairs caused a good deal of irritation. This was not because of the individuals concerned, who were always courteous and informed; the difficulty was that there was no co-ordinated policy between the Arts Council and the British Council. The Arts Council were only responsible for the UK while the British Council had to confine their attention to overseas; and although their total grant was very large, what they spent on culture, as narrowly defined, was relatively trifling. The theory was that the British Council should act as the Government's chosen instrument in helping to present the best of Britain's artistic endeavour to the outside world. They received broad guide lines from the Foreign Office which I never saw, but which from my limited experience struck me as being out of date by the time that any implementation became feasible, and also as having the idiotic effect that all too often those countries most friendly towards Britain tended to be taken for granted, save for visits undertaken on a purely commercial basis, hardly the way to retain friends.

I tried hard to persuade the British Council that one absolute necessity was to form some sort of co-ordinating committee to enable the handful of companies concerned with foreign touring to know what was being planned: and in fact a committee was set up, but it met very seldom, achieved very little, and faded away. It would have been far better, in my view, if responsibility had been transferred to the Arts Council, who were properly acquainted with the overall picture and who had the resources. However, it would have required a change in the Charter, and in any event the Foreign Office would never have agreed to a change in procedure hallowed by custom.

To return to Covent Garden, the first important production of Ashton's regime was a new *Swan Lake*, which he had misguidedly assigned to Robert Helpmann instead of doing it himself. Beni Montresor, a gifted Italian designer, had been asked to submit designs, a proposal I strongly supported because I had seen his beautiful *Pelléas et Mélisande* at Glyndebourne in 1962. Regrettably they were unacceptable to Helpmann, who preferred instead to use Carl Toms, the able assistant of Oliver Messel; but the result was unaccountably garish and vulgar and within a relatively short time there was a reversion to the old Leslie Hurry production, which had a simple richness and evoked memories of

Margot Fonteyn's early triumphs. I said that it was misguided of Fred to use Bobby Helpmann for *Swan Lake*. I still say so, although I recognize that there may have been layers of indebtedness beyond my understanding. Bobby was, I suppose, one of the most remarkable characters to rise to fame through the medium of the Royal Ballet. He was one of the early members of the company, and one with real star quality. He was not technically a great dancer, but he had a powerful stage presence which compelled attention. No one could be funnier. When he and Fred danced the roles of the ugly sisters in Ashton's *Cinderella*, they made the audience capsize with laughter. But his taste could be extremely capricious. He was very much a show biz personality; and in his hands drama could too easily become melodrama, not at all what *Swan Lake* called for.

Fred's first season consisted chiefly of revivals, including as a tribute to Ninette de Valois her *Rake's Progress*, with its brilliant Rex Whistler after Hogarth decor. The 1964/5 season, however, was to be rich in new works. There was the very splendid *Romeo and Juliet* by Kenneth MacMillan, with distinguished sets and costumes by Nicholas Georgiadis, a ballet which really revealed Kenneth's power of invention. Fonteyn and Nureyev danced at the première, although Lynn Seymour had above all been his inspiration, and she danced on the second night, with Christopher Gable as Romeo. Fred produced two new ballets. The first was *The Dream*, to Mendelssohn's *Midsummer Night's Dream* incidental music, a ballet destined to become another standard work of the Royal Ballet's repertoire, romantic, full of sentiment and humour, with a *pas de deux* for Titania and Oberon as moving as anything he had previously created, a perfect vehicle for Antoinette Sibley and Anthony Dowell, whose partnership together was then at its height, two kindred spirits complementing one another perfectly. His other ballet was a short, beautiful, abstract work, *Monotones*, set to Satie's music; specially choreographed for the Benevolent Fund Gala: just three dancers, two men and a girl each dressed in simple white tights, holding the audience spellbound.

He followed this work shortly afterwards by a companion piece, also to music by Satie. The two ballets are now always performed together, being entitled *Monotones I and II*. They show an entirely original aspect of the Ashton genius, bridging the gap between classical and modern dance, containing the best elements of both styles. Gratifyingly, they have been taken into the repertoire of several foreign companies.

Three ballets were brought into the repertoire from outside, George Balanchine's very beautiful abstract ballet to the music of the Tchaikovsky *Serenade for Strings*, and Bronislava Nijinska's two masterpieces, *Les Biches* and *Les Noces*, with music respectively by Poulenc and Stravinsky, both of them choreographed originally for Diaghilev. These three works are in their way classics, and they are regularly revived. They are excellent examples of the broad-minded approach of those planning the work of the Royal Ballet, an approach which has done much to develop the company's remarkable versatility, helping to set it apart from others.

The scope for new creative work was limited because of the amount of overseas touring undertaken during the early years of Ashton's regime. In 1965/6 the main company visited the United States and Canada, and also Italy. At that time North American touring was still profitable, and it made a significant contribution towards the balancing of the Covent Garden budget, as well as being welcome to the company for the boost given to both their morale and their earnings. In the following season they undertook a major tour of some of the Iron Curtain countries, Czechoslovakia, Poland, Rumania, Bulgaria and Yugoslavia, with significant help of course from the British Council. This tour was very worthwhile, and seemed to me the sort of thing that ideally we should more often have been called on to do.

In both seasons there were important visits from abroad at the Royal Opera House. In 1964/5 the New York City Ballet company came to us and had a huge success, acting as a powerful antidote to any complacency which might be creeping in. The company was the joint creation of Lincoln Kirstein and George Balanchine; while Balanchine was the creative force the driving power came from Kirstein, for whom I had the greatest admiration, although in my one dealing with him he was to cause me distress. I had met him through an American friend, Mrs Ogden Phipps, an ardent supporter of his company, and to whom I am indebted for many kindnesses, not least for introducing me to her stepdaughter-in-law, Diana, a subtle and perceptive beauty, whose decision after she was widowed to spend much of each year in England has greatly brightened many of our lives. My distress arose from an idealistic scheme conceived in Kirstein's brain for an interchange of visits by a wide range of companies, not confined to ballet. His main premise was that America had a plethora of new art centres and a shortage of talent, while in Britain talent abounded. What more natural, therefore, than to promote visits to the United States by British companies? There existed as a convenient instrument the American Friends of Covent Garden, a charitable entity established through the initiative of a kind and able New York lawyer named Henry Marx. There would of course be American visits to Britain, but the main movement would be in the other direction. Following a lengthy exchange of letters, Lincoln came to London, accompanied by Richard Clurman, who was chairman of the City Center for the Performing Arts. I arranged a luncheon to which I invited David Eccles, Minister for the Arts, Arnold Goodman, the chairman of the Arts Council, John Sainsbury, who had succeeded Leon Bagrit as chairman of the

Friends of Covent Garden, John Pope-Hennessy and John Tooley. Arnold was fired by Lincoln's enthusiasm, and agreed to convene a special meeting the next day. The meeting assembled, sat waiting, and just when timed to start received a message saying that Mr Kirstein and Mr Clurman were unable to be present. As the meeting had been called by Arnold simply to enable Lincoln to expound his plans his action was hard to swallow. Early the following morning he left London without explaining why he had behaved as he did, although some days afterwards he said that when sitting beside David Eccles at luncheon he had felt convinced that for 'political' reasons attention would be given to the British regions in preference to the United States, and that therefore attendance at the Arts Council meeting would have been a waste of time. But he gave no one a chance to prove otherwise; he simply upset everyone, which to me was sad and disappointing, for I had had high hopes of what might have flowed from Lincoln's concept.

In 1966/7, while the Royal Ballet were behind the Iron Curtain, the Kirov company from Leningrad, Nureyev's old company, came to Covent Garden for their second visit, the wound caused by his departure and his ready acceptance in London being by then healed. They had an enthusiastic welcome. Having less bravura than the Moscow Bolshoi company, they seemed to have greater artistry, while they were certainly more open-minded and less far removed from a cosmopolitan outlook.

Another significant event during the same season was the appointment of Kenneth MacMillan to be director of the ballet company of the Deutsche Oper Berlin. Four years later he was to succeed Fred as director of the Royal Ballet, although we did not know it at the time; and the experience of directing a company proved valuable to him. Very soon after he left London for Berlin he was followed by Lynn Seymour, the dancer with whom he felt a special sympathy, and by whom he was most inspired. Her departure was viewed by us in London with some concern, but happily she was not gone for long.

We also lost Nadia Nerina, who had been a pillar of the Royal Ballet from the early postwar years. Although she never explicitly said so she had hoped that when Margot Fonteyn ceased being a full-time member of the company – in view of Margot's frequent appearances abroad it suited her best to become a guest artist – she would inherit the position of *prima ballerina assoluta*, with her name standing alone at the top of the list of dancers. But, other than Margot, no dancer in the Royal Ballet had ever occupied this position, nor was it accepted general practice elsewhere to award such a title. Fred was opposed to it, fearing the possible repercussions on others, which in the case of Margot could not arise because no one questioned her supremacy. The upshot was that Nadia became very discontented. By agreement with David Webster I went to see her at the end of April 1966. She made various criticisms, mainly about casting, never of course raising the *prima ballerina assoluta* point. I suggested that it might suit her best to become a guest artist, thereby gaining greater freedom for herself. Her first reaction was adverse; and soon afterwards she went to the point of contributing an article which appeared in the July issue of the *Queen* magazine criticizing the lack of direction of the Royal Ballet Company, an intemperate piece which Jocelyn Stevens, the then proprietor, would have done better not to publish and which I have no doubt Nadia regretted writing. To my surprise she then telephoned and said that she would like to dicuss the guest artist proposal with David; and the upshot was that a satisfactory formula was agreed, made all the easier by the fact that at that time her husband, Charles Gordon, was prospering in his business career.

While we were having our excitements with Nadia, Kenneth MacMillan was mounting for us his ballet *Song of the Earth*, to the music of Mahler, with tenor and mezzo soloists, an inspired work epitomizing much of human experience. He had first mooted his proposal while Ninette de Valois was director of the company. Several members of the board had expressed doubts about the use for balletic purposes of a musical masterpiece not originally composed as a ballet, and seeming to them to stand on its own. As I recall it, the view of Sir Adrian Boult was sought, and he supported the doubters. Ninette agreed to be guided by him, and so the ballet had its première in Stuttgart, the loss being ours, for when it was finally given in London some months later, its reception was warm, for the ballet in no way diminishes the music, and it has become a valuable work in the repertoire.

As to the general issue of principle, I know of no way of deciding how far some of the great works of the concert hall should be used for ballet music. Before the war there were ballets to symphonies of Brahms and Tchaikovsky which proved quite unsatisfactory. Fred Ashton wanted to use *La Mer* of Debussy, but Constant Lambert dissuaded him with the argument that the movements were too long to sustain. Then in 1946 Fred used César Franck's *Symphonic Variations* to produce a masterpiece, a choice of music which the purists on the board might well have opposed. And after my retirement a further case arose when Kenneth MacMillan was director of the Royal Ballet. He wished to create a ballet to the music of the Fauré *Requiem*. Some doubts were expressed about the proposal, and he was asked to produce it in Stuttgart, where it seems to have been most successful, although I find it hard to imagine a less balletic work. Whether the critics would have been quite so rapturous had the ballet had its first performance in London is open to some doubt.

During the autumn and winter season following the company's return from North America in 1969 Fred Ashton produced a one-act version of his ballet

Sylvia. It had not been popular as a full-length ballet and the shortened version had the same fate. However, he had a surprise in store. He had come across a suite, *Jazz Calendar*, composed by Richard Rodney Bennett as a special commission for the BBC and certainly not intended for the Royal Ballet, but proving an absolute delight, setting the old nursery rhyme 'Monday's Child . . .' to syncopated classical steps, showing off the versatility of the company as well as of Fred himself, who seemed all the time to be subconsciously saying to the ballet world, 'Anything the others can do, I can do better'. I hope that *Jazz Calendar* will be revived.

Soon afterwards there was restored to the repertoire Tchaikovsky's third great balletic masterpiece *The Nutcracker* (companion to *Swan Lake* and *Sleeping Beauty*). For years Covent Garden had exercised a self-denying ordinance because the work had become the annual Christmas entertainment of the Festival Ballet, their Peter Pan, so to speak; but we finally decided after years of restraint that the work was of such basic importance that it was wrong for us never to include it. There was no generally accepted choreography as there was for instance with much of *Swan Lake* or *Giselle*. The version which had been performed in the old days at Sadler's Wells had been prepared by Serguëeff and was supposedly the traditional Mariinsky choreography; but it was thought desirable for the whole thing to be done afresh, and the task was entrusted to Rudolf Nureyev, who as well as producing also danced the principal role splendidly with Merle Park. Happily he elected to use as designer Nicholas Georgiadis, who was first introduced by Kenneth MacMillan as designer for two one-act ballets, *Noctambules* and *The Invitation*. Over the years he has, I feel sure, designed more productions for Covent Garden than any other single artist; and his record of success is exceptionally high. He has worked both for the opera and for the ballet, designing a sumptuous production of *Aida* as well as a very fine *Trojans*. Everything he has done has revealed a strongly individual personality, and one endowed with great versatility. His stage pictures are always pleasing, and he is brilliant at conveying a sense of richness with the simplest of materials.

If the production of *The Nutcracker* had a mixed reception, for me it was both splendid and beautiful; and ever since then it has gone on being regularly performed at Covent Garden, without in any way affecting the annual appeal of the Festival Ballet's far less sophisticated production.

There were two chief ballets in the 1968/9 season, a new production of *Sleeping Beauty*, and *Enigma Variations* to the music of Elgar. *Sleeping Beauty* was the work with which the ballet company had opened the Royal Opera House in 1946, and it had provided the basis for many of the company's triumphs. The 1946 production had been very beautifully designed by Oliver Messel in Louis xiv style, being used over and over again until it had to be freshly produced in 1960, when the designs of Messel, only slightly modified, were once more adopted. By 1968 the wear and tear on the production was such that renewal again became necessary. But on this third occasion it was decided to make a fresh start. Jointly with Fred Ashton, the task was entrusted to Peter Wright, who had started his career with the company and was then freelancing, after having been ballet master in Stuttgart under John Cranko. (Later Wright was to become associate director of the Royal Ballet in charge of the touring group.) They invited Lila da Nobili to do the designs; and she produced something of great distinction, departing from the epoch of Louis xiv and translating it all back into the Middle Ages, which to me was every bit as accessible. But the traditionalists grumbled and complained, and some of the leading members of the company objected to the inconvenience and unsuitability of the costumes; with the result that only a very few years later yet another production was to be embarked upon, with unhappy consequences.

Enigma Variations was Fred's last significant work while he was still director of the Royal Ballet, and in the view of many his greatest. He invited Julia Trevelyan Oman to be his designer, and between them they produced a gem which brought alive the most romantic aspects of the Edwardian era, and aroused a feeling of nostalgia in even the youngest members of the audience. Whatever the arguments about the validity of turning concert masterpieces to balletic use, Fred's *Enigma Variations* could only be regarded as doing honour to and even enhancing Elgar's music.

Chapter 22

In writing of some of Solti's causes of dissatisfaction when we were negotiating a renewal of his contract, I said that he felt the orchestra must have opportunities for concert performances. During the early months of 1963 a series of meetings took place at which the possibility of a merger of the Royal Opera House orchestra with one of the leading symphony orchestras was explored. Leon Bagrit urged the desirability of finding some kind of solution akin to that obtaining in Vienna where the Vienna Philharmonic served both the opera and the concert hall, its total size being large enough to cover the dual need. Solti was attracted by the idea and I felt that it must be fully examined, although I had great doubts about the practical aspects; and I did not think that there was a true parallel between London and Vienna because of the much larger number of orchestras in existence in London. First of all we talked with Bob Boothby, who was then chairman of Thomas Beecham's Royal Philharmonic Orchestra, Beecham himself having died in 1961. Bob himself was enthusiastic, and wrote a powerful memorandum covering every aspect; but a leak appeared in I think the *Daily Telegraph*, the members of the RPO were divided, and the discussions petered out.

Then a few months later the subject was reopened by my colleague Jack Donaldson who was concerned about the consistently hard working conditions of our orchestra, and talks opened with Ernest Fleischmann, the general manager of the London Symphony Orchestra. Once more, however, the outcome was negative. All that happened was a modest increase in the size of the Covent Garden orchestra, and things went on as they had done.

One thing constantly exercised me, the lack of recording possibilities. It annoyed me that, although Georg Solti was one of Decca's most important artists, a pitiably small amount of recording work was offered to our orchestra, for which admittedly he was doing much but which also was helping to display his talents to the public. I had for many years known Ted Lewis, the inspirational force behind the success of Decca, and I tackled him. He had been a friend of Brendan from 1928, and he had sentimental feelings about old friendships, and wanted to respond positively. There was no denying, though, that the Vienna

Philharmonic was better known internationally than the Covent Garden orchestra; and also there was the fact that with their hard-working schedule, playing for both opera and ballet, the time our orchestra could spare for recording work was very limited. Nevertheless, as time went by, with Covent Garden's growing renown, more recording work became available, from other companies as well as from Decca.

During the summer months of 1964, as I wrote in the last chapter, the theatre was closed to allow the amphitheatre to be reconstructed, the electrical wiring renewed, and new lighting equipment to be installed. We were given a special grant to cover the cost of the work, but as an example of Whitehall nonsense we were told that 10 per cent of the cost of the electrical work had to be regarded as representing an 'improvement' in our facilities and this we must cover from our own resources. Since they knew that we had no resources, and that if we ever earned a surplus this fact would be taken into account in fixing our next grant, the whole thing was absurd, for it would have been unnatural for us not to try to improve a hopelessly out of date stage lighting system. This was red tape at its worst. We did of course succeed in bridging the difference by a later adjustment to our grant, but it did show the idiocy with which we had to contend.

The ensuing season, after the closure, was a vintage one. Georg Solti opened it with his first full *Ring*, the production being by the illustrious Hans Hotter, with decor, which incorporated what to me was a particularly irritating symbolical 'ring', highly precarious for the singers, by Hans Schneider-Siemssen. Solti covered himself with glory, and had a triumph. Herbert von Karajan attended some of the performances surreptitiously, presumably to see the decor; and the sequel was that Schneider-Siemssen was engaged to design the Salzburg *Ring*. The performances were also notable for the appearance for the first time of David Ward and Josephine Veasey in the massive roles of Wotan and Fricka, providing certain proof of the importance of Solti's presence in London for the advancement of numerous British singers to international rank.

The season also included Visconti's *Trovatore*, which gave London some splendid performances by Giulini with a star-filled cast, drawing from Ted Heath the classic comment 'indifferent conducting of second-rate singing', a remark which he made to me when we met a day or two after he had attended a performance. For me the season's highlight was *Arabella*, one of the supreme examples of the collaboration of Richard Strauss and Hugo von Hofmannsthal. Solti conducted, giving us the first of a series of performances of Strauss operas which were truly revelatory, compelling even opponents of Strauss to admit his greatness. The production was by Rudolf Hartmann, a grand old master from Munich, who mercifully agreed to use a British designer, Peter Rice; and their joint endeavour resulted in a straightforward but authentic and imaginative production, splendid to look at, incapable of being bettered, meriting regular revival. The stars were Lisa della Casa, the most beautiful of all opera singers, and Dietrich Fischer-Dieskau, one of the greatest of living artists. The evening was altogether memorable.

While the 1964/5 season was pursuing its abridged but distinguished way a considerable argument was going on with Georg Solti over the question of Schoenberg's *Moses and Aaron*, a landmark work of great complexity which Georg had agreed to conduct during the following year. Having aroused all our expectations he began to have serious doubts about the competence of the Covent Garden forces to do the work justice, and about his ability to find enough rehearsal time. I felt deeply and strongly that he must not pull back, and I asked Isaiah Berlin to do what he could to persuade Solti. He nobly complied and wrote him a masterly letter, which deserves to be quoted:

... I see that with a new work, so controversial and discussed, which makes equally big demands – enormous ones, in fact – not only on the performers but on the audience too – why should they respond to it more readily than they have ever in the history of music to the genuinely revolutionary and original? – one had to be absolutely convinced of the value of the work to make so much effort and sacrifice so much of oneself, physically, emotionally, and in the case of the Opera House itself, financially. Our original motive for promising to do it still seems to me valid: it is, so far as I can judge (not that my views have the slightest aesthetic weight), a noble, austere, uncompromising work of major dimensions, artistically and historically important. ... Of course, it has to be prepared for, ... critics from abroad have to be invited; articles in the press, both musical and general, stimulated; lectures on Schoenberg and this opera in particular arranged, both for the Friends of Covent Garden and on the B.B.C. and perhaps at one or two universities as well. All these things I think the 'Schoenbergians' would be prepared to help with – they are as near to a fanatical musical sect as we have in these days – as the Wagnerians or Brahmsians were before them; and their help should on no account be scorned. In short I think that the 'right mood' for the work could probably be, by perfectly legitimate and honourable means, created. ... I am sure that records could be made of so authoritative a kind that these performances and these records would become the classical exposition of Schoenberg at his most ambitious and profound. In this sense, I do not see why the impact should not be cumulative and great. If this were done, you would surely and deservedly become a great opener of gates: no first-class performance of this work, as far as I know, has been performed in a great opera house; ... if Schoenberg even begins to be what his most passionate followers claim for him, there is surely a case for so permanent and conspicuous a service to music as the identification of Covent Garden and yourself with a magnificent exposition of this new chapter in the history of opera. I know of no musical development of similar *bahnbrechend*★ importance; ... to

★ epoch-making.

discard the whole thing and give the Schoenbergians and their friends the impression, which no amount of words from us however skilfully drafted will conceal, that we are not putting on this work, despite all their enthusiasm, because we do not like it quite enough to face all the technical and financial difficulties, will merely infuriate them. This, of course, is not to be considered if the work is genuinely not good enough, or even if you do not feel drawn towards it or simply do not like it. If that is so, there is nothing to be done: for certainly nobody else could do it – it would be foolish even to consider the possibility and we must then take our punishment like men. But I still have a feeling which will not leave me, that unless we go boldly forward and perform modern masterpieces – even if our main concern is still to establish a solid classical repertory – we shall stand still or retrogress; and that Britten, Shostakovich, even Henze, are not quite enough to ensure this, although of course Britten in particular is a very proper object of special devotion for us. . . . All I beg you to do, in all humility, is to look upon this as a truly critical decision. I won't say more. . . . But when will another opportunity to lead a great musical advance present itself?'

The letter had the desired result, namely that *Moses* went ahead. The original suggestion had been that Peter Brook should produce but in the event Peter Hall undertook the task, with his favourite co-adjutor John Bury as the designer. Hall at the time was in charge of the Royal Shakespeare Company. He was still only thirty-four years old, but he was widely experienced. Above all, he was intensely musical, and in fact nearly decided when he was at Cambridge to adopt music as a career. *Moses* was a spectacular success, although the realism of the Golden Calf scene caused the venerable Victor Gollancz to demonstrate in the stalls gangway where he stood up at the end of the first night performance, gesticulating wildly and shouting out, 'Filthy brutes!' as though sacrilege had been committed. More important, the success led directly to a close association between Peter Hall and Solti, their next collaboration together being a new production of *The Magic Flute* during the 1966/7 season.

Shortly before the production of *Moses and Aaron*, a turning point had come, not only for Covent Garden but for every artistic endeavour, with the change of Government in 1964, and the appointment by Harold Wilson in February 1965 of the first-ever Minister for the Arts, at the same time transferring responsibility away from the Treasury. His choice fell upon Jennie Lee, the widow of Aneurin Bevan. She had a very strong personality, and when young had been a real firebrand. I viewed her arrival with some trepidation. I felt that she would consider me as standing for everything of which she most probably disapproved; a hereditary peer with political leanings rather more to the right than the left of centre, connected with a newspaper which upheld the merits of free enterprise; something of a social gadabout; and chairman of the Royal Opera House, an institution that she was sure to regard as epitomizing élitism and privilege. Quite soon after her appointment I invited her to Covent Garden. I was delighted to notice that she beat time with delicate fingers while the music was being played, thus indicating enjoyment. I had never previously met her, but I instantly warmed to her. The general effect of her appearance was pleasing. It was easy to see that she had been very pretty. Her hair provided her face with an attractive white halo. I liked the Scottish burr in her voice, and her deep-throated laugh. Above all I liked her direct manner. What she at first thought of me I do not know, but as time went by we became friends. Early in 1967 I was moved to write a letter to *The Times* because some idiotic Tory MPs had tabled a motion censuring the Government for sanctioning an increase in Jennie's salary. This is what I wrote:

By their Motion they are in effect saying that it is wrong that Miss Lee, who is charged with the responsibility for the Arts, should be promoted from the rank of Parliamentary Secretary to that of Minister of State.

Miss Lee has been the Minister responsible for the Arts since the Labour Government was elected in 1964. She has done and is doing an outstandingly good job and everyone concerned with this most important branch of our national life respects her for her achievements. If a mistake was made it was in not giving her the rank of Minister of State when she was first attached to the Department of Education and Science.

Mr. Edward Heath is reported as having told the 1922 Committee that the Opposition are learning to pick the right issues to press and the ones to leave alone. There is no doubt into which category Mr. King's Motion falls.

She wrote thanking me. 'About salary I could not care less; but about leverage for the job, as you know, a very great deal.'

Later in the same year she said in another letter:

I know how much I owe to your influence in the City – a pillar of smoke by day and a pillar of fire by night you are when it comes to promoting the Arts.

Naturally I at once wrote thanking her:

What you said about me is far too kind, but thank you nevertheless very much for saying it. If I may return the compliment, I should like to tell you that no one can exaggerate the importance of the part you have played since you took Ministerial charge of cultural matters. You have been a triumphant success, and I can assure you that everyone would don sackcloth and ashes if you were to be translated elsewhere. I hope that you stay in the job as long as Mme. Furtseva has done, and goodness knows how many years that has been!

Not long after Jennie's appointment Mme Furtseva, the Soviet Minister of Culture, came to England on an official visit, and Jennie decided that she must take her to see the most exciting theatrical offering in London. She was advised that this was *Moses and Aaron* at Covent Garden. But I knew my Furtseva, and I knew that she would hate it. When I heard of the proposal I urged Jennie not to bring her, but she was adamant; so the two ladies came with an official party, and I received them. In Act 2, which contained the orgy scene and the sacrificing of four naked virgins (with their backs to the audience) I thought that the best thing I could do was to take Furtseva with me into the circle, so that she was as far from the stage as possible. It was clear, though, that she was miserable, and I fear that that evening Anglo-Soviet cultural relations suffered rather a setback.

Jennie used to come regularly with us to Covent Garden. Her visits seemed to give her pleasure; and at my farewell gala at Covent Garden she was kind enough to agree to appear with me on the stage, as I relate a few pages on.

Within a few months of her arrival as Minister for the Arts a White Paper entitled *A Policy for the Arts* (Cmnd. 2601, 7 Feb. 1965) was issued from the Prime Minister's office. This document made it clear that far more positive action could be looked forward to. It stated truthfully that hitherto Government aid had been on a relatively modest scale and had grown up in response to spasmodic pressures rather than as a result of a coherent plan. It then set forth four objectives, which are worth quoting:

(i) Today's artists need more financial help, particularly in the early years before they have become established. Their ability to develop and sustain a high level of artistic achievement lies at the centre of any national policy for the arts.

(ii) The Government hope to see a great increase in local and regional activity, while maintaining the development of the national institutions. They are convinced that the interests of the whole country will be best served in this way.

(iii) The Government appreciate the need to sustain and strengthen all that is best in the arts, and the best must be made more widely available.

(iv) There is need for more systematic planning and a better co-ordination of resources.

Since Covent Garden received special mention more than once in the White Paper I felt that we could take comfort, and rest assured that our financial needs would be adequately covered, as indeed proved to be largely the case, although it took an unconscionable time before we could make anything like proper pension provision for those working at the opera house, and even longer before anything could be done about the disgraceful backstage working conditions.

What pleased me about Jennie was that at no time during her tenure as Minister for the Arts did she attempt to bring politics into her job. She always held that there must be certain centres of excellence which needed generous support because it was for them to set standards, and she recognized that if they were financially starved they could not fulfil their task. So long as she was around, Covent Garden's position was therefore secure.

In the White Paper Arnold Goodman, who had already helped Covent Garden over the Charter for the Royal Ballet, was named as chairman of a committee set up to report on the needs of the London orchestras: not so long afterwards he was given a peerage, and appointed to be chairman of the Arts Council in succession to Lord Cottesloe, an able man with a careful precise manner, who had hoped to have his appointment extended but who was not cast in the right mould for Jennie. 1965 was therefore the year of Arnold's first entry upon the national scene. His partnership with Jennie was to persist for a number of years, and it certainly proved fruitful. Their relationship was very close. I remember her saying to me of him, 'It's a beautiful mind.' And if not exactly the same thing can be said of his build, his appearance, with his bulky frame, his thick arched eyebrows and his large brown eyes, is certainly very striking. Through my Covent Garden connection my contacts with him during the seven years that he was chairman of the Arts Council were frequent, and almost always rewarding. I developed other links with him when he succeeded me as chairman of the Newspaper Publishers Association, and when he gave up the Arts Council I invited him to join the board of Covent Garden to which he agreed.

Had Harold Wilson not won the 1964 election, Arnold might not have had the same opportunity to become the national figure that he has done. As chairman of the Arts Council he came increasingly into the public eye, and more and more people came to recognize his formidable gifts. No one else of my acquaintance has been able to express himself with such facility both in speech and in writing. I remember him addressing the Institute of Directors' Annual Conference in the Albert Hall when he spoke to an audience of five thousand for forty-five minutes without a single note. I have sat beside him while he has dictated a long and complex memorandum over the telephone to his secretary so that it could be ready for his signature on his return to his office, and not a word had to be changed. At meetings his one desire has always been to find a just and fair solution, and he believes that few problems are incapable of solution, given only patience, goodwill and a willingness to compromise. Intransigence, he believes, does not pay. Humour is among his most powerful weapons, and he is brilliant at taking the heat out of situations. Not only is he wise, but he has an essentially kind and generous nature, and no friend in need of help or advice has ever been denied it. Together he and Jennie made a very effective combination. Through her links with the Prime Minister she was able to cut many corners, while Arnold's balanced approach helped to modify her ardours.

At more or less the same time that Jennie Lee became Arts Minister, I made a most important addition to the board of directors. This was Claus Moser, who nine years later was to follow me as chairman. His name was first suggested to me by Lionel Robbins. They knew one another well because of their acquaintance at the London School of Economics, where Claus was Professor of Statistics; and their friendship had developed during Lionel's chairmanship of a Governmental committee set up in 1961 to consider the future demand for higher education facilities. Claus was the statistician on the committee, so that their contacts were frequent and intimate.

One of our needs at Covent Garden was for a really professional analysis of the level of attendances at particular performances at various seat prices in the different parts of the house. It was easy for anyone to tell that for certain artists in demand throughout the world price was never a limiting factor, while for certain operas it was impossible to ensure a full house, however low prices might be pitched. But between these two extremes a very careful study was required, more methodical than anything previously undertaken, because we were not in the happy position of most continental opera houses which seemed to be assured that however large their deficit it would always be met: and therefore we had to have constant regard to the box office.

Claus joined the board at the end of January 1965, and he set to work with a will. Within a short space of time he was providing us with invaluable analyses which were to have an important impact on our pricing policy, and also to some extent on our choice of repertoire. Beyond that, he was highly musical, and an excellent amateur pianist. His background was German Jewish, his parents having come to England at the time of Hitler, but he was mainly educated in this country and there was no trace of a foreign accent. In his political attitudes he was to the left of centre, but never extreme in his views. As soon as he joined the Covent Garden board he became very constant in his attendance at perform-ances, especially of opera. He joined Lionel Robbins's finance committee at once, and it was not long before I asked him to join the opera committee. He had inherited a Germanic *Pflichtgefühl*,* and he was a model of conscientiousness, although it would be invidious to say which of my colleagues deserved the prize in this regard. They were all busy people and yet they almost always attended the monthly board meetings, as well as the meetings of whichever committees they were on: and if the sole test of Covent Garden's excellence was the attendance record of the directors at meetings as well as at performances very high marks would be awarded. I myself tried to set a good example, for at board meetings I always felt keenly that I was presiding over a body of my intellectual superiors, and I thought that my best hope of maintaining any authority over such a formidably able group of men was by regular attendance at all committee meetings in addition to seeing at least one performance of every opera and ballet performed during the season, which meant that I spent fully some fifty evenings a year in the opera house.

* Highly developed sense of duty.

The ranks of my intellectual superiors on the board received an important addition within a year of Claus's appointment when I invited Noel Annan to join us. The suggestion of his name was likewise made to me by Lionel Robbins. He had been Provost of King's College, Cambridge, but was about to move to London to hold the same post at University College. I did not know him, but I met him and found him a most refreshing personality, easy, persuasive and articulate. Colleagues on the board who knew him were enthusiastic, while questioning the extent of his interest in musical matters. It was clear that he was well connected among the political intelligentsia, and he was said on all hands to be brilliant at committee work; and since Covent Garden had plenty of committees I felt that Noel could play a most useful role. So he duly joined us, becoming a valued colleague, placing the emphasis of his interest more particularly on the side of the ballet, which was rather under-represented on the board and in need of another champion. He had a disconcerting habit of burying his head in his hands, conveying the impression of either great boredom or dismay at the stupidity of the discussion. But I soon realized that he was always attending to what was being said, and his utterances were always relevant and usually constructive.

A couple of years later I made another most satisfying addition to the board. This was William Glock, who joined us in 1968. His claims were strong, and no one could call him an amateur. He had been a distinguished music critic with both the *Observer* and the *New Statesman*, and since 1959 he had been controller of music with the BBC, a post he was to hold until 1972; and during his time there he quite simply revolutionized the whole quality of music transmitted, giving an entirely new look to the Promenade Concerts, which became a major force in the musical life of Britain. He himself was a very good pianist, having studied with Artur Schnabel. The impression he conveyed to everyone was one of quiet, unassuming excellence. His judgement was always clear and sound. At meetings he was not particularly forthcoming, and he tended not to speak (I called him William the Silent) unless pressed by me to give his views. These when he spoke were always concisely expressed, and penetrating. He was in many respects most helpful, but particularly so in the early dealings with Colin Davis leading up to and after Colin's appointment as our musical director. Colin was the principal conductor of the BBC symphony orchestra, and therefore had frequent contact with William, who had been responsible for his appointment: and since in the early stages of his association with Covent Garden, Colin was peculiarly abrasive, tending to look down his nose at the board of directors, William was able to lubricate relationships to very good purpose. He would I suppose most wish to be remembered as director of the Dartington Hall Summer School of Music, which he really created, and where he bridged the great space separating classical and modern music; and for his time at the BBC where he was able to develop on a much larger scale the aims and policies of Dartington: but to single out any of his activities would be invidious, so generally significant has his impact been.

Not long after joining the board Claus Moser was seconded from the LSE to become head of the Central Statistical Office, the branch of the Treasury concerned with the collection and dissemination of a wide range of official statistics. His appointment was helpful for Covent Garden because it gave him easy access to all the senior civil servants in Whitehall. He did a great deal to overhaul their methods of collection and presentation, and he helped enormously to give new life to a dull department. The fact that the figures were fairly consistently depressing was not his fault: they merely reflected the follies of politicians and the steady decline in Britain's standing in the eyes of the world.

Fortunately Covent Garden was not in a state of decline. We were in fact in a reasonably healthy condition. Thanks to the assistance we had from Jennie Lee and Arnold Goodman our grant was kept at a realistic level, not, I could immodestly say, without a good deal of prodding from me; and a formula for paying off the large overdraft we had accumulated with Coutts & Co. was agreed. Artistically things were going well, not so much because of the new productions, which sometimes were visually disappointing, but because of the general quality of performance, for which above all we were indebted to Solti; and his popularity with the London public was very great. It seemed natural therefore that we should ask him and he should agree to stay on for a further three-year term covering the years from 1967 to 1970. It was for him a particularly happy time because in 1967 he re-married, his second wife being an intelligent and attractive girl named Valerie Pitts whom he had met when being interviewed by her for a BBC programme. Their marriage turned out most happily. She bore him two lovable little daughters and he became altogether more relaxed and at ease in himself than he had previously been: and this reflected itself in his music-making. Indeed during this period he gave us a series of splendid performances. Even to mention all the chief events of Solti's later years as musical director would be difficult, but there were some great highlights, if nothing perhaps to measure up to the *bahnbrechend Moses and Aaron*. For me I think that the most thrilling was *Die Frau ohne Schatten*, orchestrally the richest of all Richard Strauss's works, a strange mythical tale by von Hofmannsthal, with symbolic overtones of the complexities of marital love, set in a remote Eastern land. In *The Pendulum Years*, Bernard Levin's book about the 1960s, he more or less said that he was only saved from total disenchantment by three opera performances, Solti's *Frau ohne Schatten* and Klemperer's *Fidelio* at Covent Garden, and Reginald Goodall's *Meistersinger* at Sadler's Wells. Sceptics of the aesthetic and emotional power of opera when superbly performed should read the particular chapter in Levin's book, for he describes it better than I have elsewhere seen. For me to paraphrase him would be unbecoming, and to vie with him would be grotesque.

The producer of Solti's *Frau* was Rudolf Hartmann, to whom we were already indebted for the beautiful production of *Arabella*, and who in the following season, 1968/9, was to produce a new *Meistersinger* for Solti, when Geraint Evans, one of the handful of really distinguished British artists, made his début in the comic role of Beckmesser, in which he later excelled internationally. The designer for *Frau ohne Schatten* was Josef Svoboda, a Czech who worked mainly in Prague, but who visited England and elsewhere pretty regularly. He was a man of real versatility and huge output. I remember his telling me that since he started designing at the age of twenty-one or so he had been responsible for over two hundred and fifty productions, which I reckoned meant an average of nearly one a month, easily a record, I feel certain. He was highly skilled in the use of mirrors, of lighting and of projections, and was much sought after because he was both quick and imaginative. For Covent Garden he designed a number of productions, usually but not invariably with success. The most effective of his productions for us was *Pelléas et Mélisande*, conducted consummately by Pierre Boulez, with a superb cast, deserving a high place in the annals of the Royal Opera House. The designs were almost wholly abstract, but they evoked a distant, timeless past.

As to Boulez, would that he had conducted for us more frequently. No one else that I have heard could so seem to be coldly dissecting a piece of music and yet at the same time convey what one felt to be the composer's true intentions. Boulez is a true intellectual, with amazing clarity of thought, able to express himself with equal ease in French, English and German: and no opportunity of hearing him lecture should ever be missed.

Another of Georg Solti's productions during what was a fairly golden period was Mozart's *Cosi fan tutte*, one of the happiest and most delightful of evenings. The production was assigned to John Copley, the assistant resident producer at Covent Garden, who had been on the staff for several years but who previously had only been given the responsibility for mounting Puccini's one-act opera *Suor Angelica*. He is highly gifted and musical, with a remarkable memory, only able to produce an opera if he knows every part, bar by bar, being himself capable of singing every note. His trouble was that he was given to excess and would not allow the action to speak for itself, his imagination running riot, with a danger of slapstick creeping in. With the passage of time has come more restraint. His experience has broadened; and altogether he has done much to enliven the operatic scene, both in London and abroad.

During the 1968/9 season, and indeed during ensuing years, no one could say that Covent Garden did not more than do its duty by British opera. What we could not do was to force the public to fill the house, however low we fixed the seat prices. Solti conducted an impressive reworked production of Benjamin Britten's *Billy Budd*, atmospheric and theatrically telling, but no box office draw. This statement was equally true of Michael Tippett's *Midsummer Marriage*, revived in a new production conducted by Colin Davis with all the loving care that he devotes to everything composed by Tippett, who insists upon writing his own libretti, of doubtful literary quality but of quite undoubted obscurity.

Although latterly attitudes seem to have been changing, with Tippett's last opera *The Ice Break* playing to full houses, the unwillingness of the public to respond to modern British operas used to be one of the depressing facts that we had to accept. We were not however deterred by it from what we regarded as the fulfilment of an obligation, and regularly each year we presented one new production or significant revival. But one a year was all we could risk, which meant that contemporary operas by foreign composers were more or less excluded. The emphasis tended to be upon Benjamin Britten, or, as Colin Davis got into his stride, Michael Tippett: but in the three years between 1969 and 1972 new works by Humphrey Searle, Richard Rodney Bennett and Peter Maxwell Davies were also given their premières. Box-office-wise it was always the same story. I blessed my premium stalls scheme (whereby companies had seats on an all-the-year-round basis) for the help it gave in swelling the attendance figures. As far as I could, I tried to see to it that the seats were actually occupied, and if I saw an empty premium stall I used to pursue the offending company and point out to them that they were placing the whole scheme in jeopardy. But in the main the occasions for rebuke were rare.

Chapter 23

My last reference to ballet was about the triumph of *Enigma Variations*. This triumph made it all the more distressing that the atmosphere should have been clouded through the unhappy circumstances which led up to the announcement of the retirement of Fred Ashton and of the appointment of Kenneth MacMillan and John Field to succeed him as joint directors of the company.

In the summer of 1968 David Webster, whose health was already showing signs of failing, asked to see me urgently. He was in a very exercised state. He told me that John Field, the assistant director of the company with particular responsibility for touring, in connection with which he had been doing admirable work, had been offered the challenging post of director of the Festival Ballet. David's concern at the threatened loss of Field was understandable. Furthermore, he convinced me that Fred who was approximately the same age as himself, wished to retire when he did, finding the task of directing the company burdensome and distracting; and he emphasized that the loss of Field coupled with the retirement of Ashton could have serious consequences. Ninette de Valois was out of the country on her annual visit to the Turkish Ballet company, which she had founded. David attempted to contact her by telephone in Ankara but failed. When she returned to London she was presented with a *fait accompli*, although it is fair to say that she always accepted the necessity of retirement at a certain age, whether it be herself or anyone else; and I knew from a long talk with her that she believed that, when Fred retired from the post of director of the Royal Ballet, he should be succeeded by John Field and Kenneth MacMillan as joint directors. David impressed upon me his strongly held view that the problem should not be discussed formally by the board as a whole, and I therefore brought into consultation Mark Bonham-Carter, who was the chairman of the ballet committee, and Lionel Robbins, a member of the ballet committee and chairman of the finance committee. I also spoke privately to individual colleagues. For nearly a year nothing was actually discussed or minuted at a board meeting as such, although we all accepted the position. It was certainly the case that more than once Fred himself had told me of his wish to retire, and I had taken him at his word. It was therefore agreed that David should speak to him, so as to establish the position clearly. Unfortunately he baulked at doing this, and delayed for several months; and then when he finally did so it was in a brusque and insensitive manner, telling him in effect 'your time is up'. This took Fred completely by surprise, particularly because David said nothing about his own retirement, although Fred had convinced himself that David would be retiring at the same time, as in fact he did. Matters were made somewhat worse because David chose to make the actual public announcement while the Royal Ballet was appearing on tour in New York. Not surprisingly Fred was deeply offended, and told people that he had been fired.

I reproach myself that I did not personally speak to Fred at the time, but David was general administrator, and if I had usurped his function he would have had a legitimate grievance. Had I realized what had happened, or rather what had *not* happened, I should certainly have intervened. In any event in July 1970 a grand gala was held, indeed two galas, one for Fred and one for David: and in the course of my speech from the stage at the gala honouring Fred I announced that he had undertaken to produce one new ballet a year for us, which in fact for over four years after his retirement he simply could not bring himself to do. He needed the kind of stimulus his directorial responsibility had given him, and he laboured under a sense of injury and injustice, which made his good wishes to MacMillan at the farewell party given in his honour particularly moving and touching: 'May he have what every choreographer longs for – continued inspiration!' It was therefore a great moment for Covent Garden when he returned in 1976 to produce *Month in the Country*, a masterpiece based upon the Turgenev play, choosing most rewardingly Lynn Seymour for the principal role and using at the suggestion of Isaiah Berlin the music of Chopin, which was far more appropriate than anything Russian. With this ballet Fred proved all too clearly that inspiration was still welling up inside him. My sense of indebtedness to him is profound because, despite the way in which the matter of his retirement had been handled, he most generously undertook the overall artistic supervision of the farewell gala given for me when I retired from the chairmanship in the summer of 1974. Ironically, the partnership of Kenneth MacMillan and John Field lasted barely six months, temperamental incompatibility resulting in the departure of Field in the early months of 1971.

If the matter of the succession to Fred Ashton was clumsily handled by David Webster – for which I accept my share of the blame – the talks relating to the succession to David himself were also to cause me real anxiety and concern. The date of David's retirement had been agreed by me with him as the end of the 1969/70 season after he had reached his 67th birthday. His actual retirement date should have been two years earlier, but with so much change in the air it had seemed desirable that he should carry on for another couple of years. As things turned out, the final phase of his regime was a fairly agonizing time. Throughout it he was quite seriously ill, although coming regularly to the office. For nearly twenty-five years Covent Garden had been his life, and the prospect of retiring weighed heavily upon him. It would however have been out of the question for him to continue as general administrator beyond the date agreed. His power of decision-making and his grasp had been visibly slipping. Towards the end of 1968 I had discussed with David what he himself felt about his successor. It was evident that he regarded it as unthinkable that anyone other than his deputy, John Tooley, should succeed him. I shared this view very strongly, as did the whole board of directors. John had been effectively in charge for over a year. He had the confidence and trust of the staff, and no one had a wider ranging knowledge of the work of the house. Had anyone else been appointed instead of him the consequences could have been dire. There was however some strenuous argument with the Arts Council as to whether despite these considerations the post should be advertised, on the doctrinaire view that it was an important public appointment, although I knew that a similar demand had not been made of comparable institutions (for instance the National Theatre) and I felt that it would have been unreasonable to insist upon it in the case of the Royal Opera House. I held that Covent Garden was a going concern and what mattered was continuity of management. If I had been in doubt about John Tooley's adequacy it would have been an entirely different matter, but I was certain that he was more than equipped for the job, and I believed that to advertise the post would have created consternation among the staff as well as being humiliating for him and unfair to other applicants. In the event, a way of not advertising but nevertheless seriously reviewing a short list of conceivably possible other candidates was agreed; and it became clear that John Tooley was the right man and that his appointment should be confirmed as David Webster's successor. Looking back after eight years, I would certainly not wish any different decision to have been made.

In July 1969 Tom Armstrong, having completed his term of office as principal of the Royal Academy of Music, decided to retire to the country, and resigned from the Covent Garden board. From my personal point of view his departure was a cause for regret. Although I used to tease him for what I referred to as waving his little Union Jack (he always spoke up for British music and musicians) he was an extremely helpful colleague, whom I was very sorry to lose.

In his place I invited George Harewood, who had left the staff when he went to Edinburgh, to rejoin the board, and to my great satisfaction he agreed to do so. While he was in Edinburgh and after his return to London we met regularly, and there was one moment, I think in 1967, when my wife Joan and I were able to play a small part in assisting in relation to his private life. He was living in St John's Wood with Patricia Tuckwell, the sister of the famous horn player. For a while she and George were virtually besieged for two or three weeks by sections of the press, whose behaviour was shamefully unattractive, making it impossible for them to move without running the gauntlet of a posse of cameramen and reporters, the sort of behaviour that even the toothless Press Council would condemn (not that its condemnations achieve much in compensating the victims of monstrous intrusion or in improving standards of press conduct). Patricia telephoned us to say that George and she planned to leave England in order to be married. Could they stay with us at Parkside House the night before their departure? We gladly agreed. They left their house as though to dine out. A friend of theirs then brought out their luggage through an entrance at the bottom of the garden, while the representatives of the press were relaxing their vigil. The friend arrived at Parkside House, and then a little later George and Patricia appeared in another car. They slept at the house, and in the morning a Portuguese manservant then working for us drove them, heavily camouflaged, to Heathrow Airport, only twenty minutes away, and they managed to leave the country *incognito* and unobserved. They were safely married; and when they returned, they were left in peace.

George did not in fact stay on the Covent Garden board for long after rejoining it because in 1972 Stephen Arlen, the managing director of Sadler's Wells Opera, died suddenly. The appointment of George to succeed him seemed entirely natural. It gave him everything he wanted, a large company which by then was housed in the Coliseum, a theatre with three hundred more seats than Covent Garden, performing opera in English five nights a week, uniquely capable of fulfilling his ideals, perfectly suited for his strong and assured personality to exercise full sway.

Three months after George had rejoined us I invited John Sainsbury to become a member of the board. I cannot remember now how his name was suggested, but since he was married to Anya Linden, who had been one of the more gifted and beautiful ballerinas of the company, he was always considerably in evidence and enormously interested in our activities. I knew that Leon Bagrit was on the point of retiring from the board, and I thought that John would make an excellent successor as chairman of the Friends of Covent Garden, for he was young and forceful, used to getting his way, but with a good sense of humour. Fortunately he was willing to undertake the task, and together he and Ken Davison, the organizing secretary, made a most effective team, and the Friends went from strength to strength. It was evident that his family were equally aware of his capabilities, for not long after he came on to the Covent Garden board he was made executive chairman of his family business when he was barely forty, no mean compliment considering its size and importance.

John's association with Covent Garden began at a crucial time, only a few months before the retirements of David Webster and Fred Ashton, with the prospective retirement of Georg Solti a year later. The summer of 1970 was pretty agonizing for David. His health was steadily deteriorating, and the thought of retiring weighed heavily upon him. At meetings he made little sense, but this did not matter because in the main our discussions related to ensuing seasons. Two things happened which gave him a good deal of pleasure. First of all, in April the Royal Opera company, led by Georg Solti and Edward Downes, made a hugely successful visit to Berlin and Munich, our first overseas operatic appearance as a company. Secondly, the Queen made David a KCVO, an honour confined to those who have rendered personal service to the Monarchy, so that its conferment upon David gave him particular satisfaction. Then there was his farewell gala, which was held in June, attended by the Queen Mother and the Prince of Wales, in which a galaxy of operatic stars took part. I made a speech in his honour from the stage, with the company arrayed behind me, while David waited in the wings; and then when I led him out on to the stage he received an ovation, so much so that he was too moved to speak, beyond a solitary 'Thank you'.

David attended his last board meeting on 28 July, when I paid a further tribute to him. It had been agreed that to augment his pension he should continue to receive a modest fee as a consultant with special reference to fund raising. He clearly expected to go on attending board meetings, but I thought that there should be a brief interlude, until John Tooley was securely installed; and the question did not in practice arise again for the sad reason that David died within nine months of retiring. He had as I have said been ill for the past year or more before he retired, and the emotional stresses of his final months can only have worsened his state. I was in fact distressed that for six weeks after his retirement he did not send the board or myself any sign or word despite the numerous tributes we had paid him. When he did write he sent me the following letter which should be quoted in full:

18th September 1970

My dear Garrett,

I am sure you realise that the end of June and the whole of July were a difficult time for me. I had given very little thought to retirement and when I found myself the centre of a great deal of almost unstinted praise I became a bit emotional. I have reasonably good control of my feelings, but the resultant wave of such things as that wonderful Gala, the Friends' luncheon, an enormous amount of unexpectedly agreeable stuff from the Press, presentations and projected presentations from various sections of the staff, the award of the K.C.V.O. from the Queen, was to take me off a reasonably even keel. As time went on I realised I needed a short time at a health farm even before I went on holiday in August!

When I came to the last Board Meeting of the year in July I was scarcely aware that it was my last. I listened to your kind words but I was incapable of making a formal reply.

I have served under three Chairmen. The first was an inspiration, the second a huge tower of strength in the privacy of our affairs and in public representation but he left all the detail to me. You were a shock at first. Here was someone who wanted to know every detail and to have a hand in everything. You revelled in detail and expected all the Board and your officers to revel. You have a great love for Covent Garden. You have a tremendous flare for writing letters in which you make clear to each of us exactly what you think. In time these letters have become known as Droghedagrams. Your enthusiasm has been a fund of strength. If you took up an idea in which there is something that you should follow through with the authorities for Covent Garden then nothing would deflect you from your aim. In the last Droghedagram you pointed out to me that I had thanked everyone except the Board and yourself. A justified rebuke which I am doing a slight something to repair.

I would be glad if you would convey my thanks to the members of the Board for their constant support, kindness and understanding and thank you Garrett for all your warmth and generosity.

Yours,
David

This letter touched me greatly. Between David and myself there had always been a pretty close understanding. Our relationship could be called one of creative tension. At times he simply maddened me, as I think I have made clear in earlier pages. But I was genuinely fond of him. He was wise and wily, he had presence and he had humour, he was affectionate, and his outward calm concealed a very passionate nature. Above all he was deeply attached to his job at Covent Garden. Without it, his incentive for life departed. After his death a most moving memorial service was held on 2 July 1971 at the Church of the Holy Sepulchre, High Holborn, in which many of the singers who had grown to fame under his aegis took part, and Geraint Evans, whose contribution to opera in Britain cannot be exaggerated, gave an address that was a model of its kind, leaving the entire congregation in or on the verge of tears.

By then John Tooley had been in charge for the best part of a year, having effectively run Covent Garden for two years before that. Of him there is a good deal that should be said. First of all, he is a man of real ability. If he lacks David Webster's sheer presence, he more than compensates for this by a far greater willingness to follow things through; and he is far more musical. He is able to assimilate a mass of complex detail without allowing it to obscure the broad picture. His work at Covent Garden on both the opera and the ballet fronts has done much to put the theatre in the forefront of international opera houses. People have generally come to regard him as a man of his word and one who can be trusted. In his dealings with performing artists, whether of opera or ballet, he always takes a tremendous personal interest. Before the curtain rises he goes round the dressing rooms, and at the end of the performance he is the first on stage with words of appreciation. He has shown himself to be resourceful and ingenious; and once he is faced with a problem he will not let go until it is solved.

Apart from the abiding worry of finance, his greatest and most continuing problem has related to the improvement of the working conditions of the Royal Opera House. In 1961 the Government of the day decided that something must be done to reduce the traffic chaos caused by the presence in Central London of the Covent Garden fruit, flower and vegetable market. It was thought at first that the market could be replanned so as to improve the flow of traffic without moving it away, and the freehold of the land and buildings occupied by the market was compulsorily acquired. A new Authority was appointed headed by Ian Jacob, whom I had first met when I worked in the War Cabinet offices. Within a short space of time David Webster and I were calling on him to stake out a claim for the needs of the opera house to be borne in mind when the blueprint for the future was being prepared. Fairly soon, however, the impracticability of replanning the market on its old site became clear, and a decision was taken to build an entirely new market on a large area of land across the river not far from Battersea. This meant, of course, that the scope for the Royal Opera House would be far greater. Whenever I had an opportunity, either in debates in the House of Lords, or at meetings with the Arts Council or with Ministers, I emphasized the need for an improvement in our facilities; and our case was strengthened when a House of Commons committee under the chairmanship of the radical Mrs Renée Short, whom I personally conducted round the building, reported that working conditions at Covent Garden were a disgrace and should be improved. Throughout the period John Tooley was closely concerned with every detail of the discussions about what should be done. Indeed, David Webster left it all very much to him, partly because he found the endless points of detail arising over something like planning most irksome, but also because he knew that the likelihood was remote of anything visibly happening before his own retirement. John therefore spent countless hours in the preparation of plans and in making submissions to the numerous authorities requiring to be consulted in any matter relating to so important a building as the Royal Opera House. It is only very recently (as I write) that the way ahead has begun to seem in any way clear; the Government has made available the land adjoining the opera house; and the problem now appears more likely to be one of money than of anything else. I was therefore delighted when Claus Moser asked me to be chairman, with him, of a Royal Opera House development appeal committee; and I should certainly feel immensely pleased if while I am still around, and before too many more years have passed, Covent Garden has had some of the improvements carried out which are needed to take the theatre into the next century. Most delighted of all will be John Tooley, who has laboured so long and hard at the problem.

While I was still chairman, John brought off one major coup for which all the credit is due to him. It was in 1971 that he persuaded the Midland Bank to start sponsoring a series of 'promenade'-style performances of opera and ballet in the opera house itself, the essential idea being the removal of all the stalls in order to open the stalls area to promenaders who would be admitted up to the permitted capacity of some seven hundred, paying a small admission charge, the difference between that and the ordinary price for stalls being found by the Midland Bank. This was for the bank an original and valuable promotional exercise, while for Covent Garden it meant bringing into the theatre a largely new type of audience. The idea proved hugely successful. The number of 'promenade' performances given in a season has now risen to ten, which is probably as far as it can go without overstraining the Midland Bank's promotion budget or upsetting Covent Garden's regular clientele, including a vast number from abroad.

For John Tooley the venture was one with which he could feel thoroughly pleased and proud. In writing of him I have perhaps depicted him as too much of a paragon. To redress the balance let me say that like everyone he does have his faults. First of all, as was the case with his predecessor, I fear that his visual sense is unreliable, and he has approved some very indifferent designs. Then he can be quick-tempered and impatient, although that is perhaps hardly surprising in his job, with its wide-ranging responsibilities. But the worst is that his long period as number two to David Webster, when he had to attend to so many matters of detail, created in him an attitude towards his work in which he found it very difficult to delegate, and which forced him too much to handle everything personally. On top of this he had an incessant and laudable desire to be present in person at any important appearance of the opera company or of either of the two ballet companies, whether in London or the provinces or overseas. And he hated to miss major events at other opera houses both at home and abroad. He thus imposed far too much on himself. In 1976 he had a quite serious illness, which I refuse to believe was not in some way linked with the manner in which he drove himself; and I would hope that he has learnt a salutary lesson, for he is still far from old, with a great deal still to offer.

At the start of the Tooley regime in the autumn of 1970, urged I think by

Burnet Pavitt, I invited John Pope-Hennessy to join the board. I had known him, not well, for many years; while his brother James, who was to die so tragically, had once been an intimate friend of Joan's. We first knew them when they lived in Ladbroke Grove, round the corner from our house in Lansdowne Crescent, and their rather formidable mother Dame Una was still alive. The two brothers were alarmingly able. Both were scholarly, and both wrote brilliantly, but James defied authority whereas John conformed and accepted the conventional order of things. He had wide-ranging tastes and extensive knowledge of the operatic and balletic repertoire. His visual sense was highly developed, and he had a very clear view of what he liked and disliked. When he expressed his opinion it was always with great assurance. His strange hooded eyelids gave him a haughty and rather supercilious air, and he seemed to look down on lesser beings with disdain. People hung on his words, treating him with justified respect, and anyone who dissented was made to feel very small. To all he was known as the Pope. On the Covent Garden board, it was always reassuring when he thought something well done, for he did not bestow praise lightly. At the beginning of 1974 I was honoured by being invited to become a trustee of the British Museum, which I regard as the greatest institution in the land, and of which John had just been appointed director. I therefore had further opportunities of seeing him regularly. The rapidity with which he asserted his authority over the whole of that complex establishment was extraordinary. There was general regret when he asked to be released from his contract while it still had nearly three years to run, and it was a major blow to Humphrey Trevelyan, one of the most able, conscientious and witty chairmen under whom I have ever served. Soon afterwards John received an offer from the United States which he could not refuse. He was therefore obliged to give up membership of the Covent Garden board, although this was after I had handed over the chairmanship, and my successor had to bear the loss of John's talents and taste.

At the time of David Webster's memorial service, in which of course Georg Solti played a major part, he was himself on the point of retirement. Shortly after he had renewed his contract for a third three-year term he had expressed to me his strong wish to stay on for an additional year, thus making his total period of service with us a round ten years, equalling in length the time that he had been musical director at Frankfurt. I was delighted, so were my colleagues. Georg had by this time endeared himself all round. More important, he had given us a number of dazzling performances, and Covent Garden's international standing had risen markedly. Had he said that he would like to stay on for a further three years I should have been in favour. He was quite clear, however, that ten years was as long as he wished, or was desirable from either his own or our point of view.

The ten-year period was due to end in July 1971, but discussions relating to the problem of succession commenced in 1967 while David was still in the saddle. We all felt that we must appoint a British conductor. Since the war there had been three musical directors at Covent Garden and they had all been foreign. If we appointed a fourth, it would be tantamount to saying that despite all the years of operatic experience gained in London since the war there was still no native-born conductor worthy of the job. This would have been patently absurd. Had either Rudolph Kempe or Carlo Maria Giulini offered themselves we should have been in some difficulty because they were both very close to Covent Garden and greatly loved by the British public. They were, though, both edging away from opera, Giulini in particular, finding it too time-demanding and taxing, with too many ingredients, any of which could go wrong. Apart from these two men there was no other foreigner who ranked for consideration by us.

Looking nearer home, the number of British conductors of stature with the right experience was quite limited. On the staff of Covent Garden there were Reginald Goodall and Edward Downes. Goodall had conducted at the Royal Opera House a great deal during the early postwar years, but David Webster did nothing subsequently to promote his claims. His spiritual affinity was with Wagner, and Solti's own identification with Wagner did little to help Goodall. His moment of glory came when he was given the responsibility for the *Ring* at the Coliseum, and he had a wildly enthusiastic reception on the rare occasions that he reappeared at Covent Garden. Yet he would not have been right as musical director, being too shy and too introverted.

Edward Downes had given sterling service on the staff at Covent Garden. He had strong all-round capabilities. He was a very good musician, and also a linguist, for he had mastered Russian as well as other languages; furthermore he knew the opera house intimately, and altogether he had made himself indispensable. Charles Mackerras was an Australian whose qualities and attributes made him a powerful possibility. He was, however, shortly to become musical director of Sadler's Wells, and his attachment there was close. There were those who said that John Pritchard was the most gifted musician of all; and he had certainly given several impressive performances in the opera house. Others argued that he might find the intricacies of Covent Garden too daunting. In any event he was closely identified with Glyndebourne, where he was spiritually very much at home.

There remained Colin Davis. His name was the one strongly supported by David Webster and also by Solti and myself. By virtue of his experience and his talent he seemed the most obvious choice. As far back as 1959 he had made a great impact, taking over at very short notice a concert performance of *Don*

Giovanni with Walter Legge's Philharmonia Orchestra in place of Otto Klemperer who was ill. He was musical director of Sadler's Wells from 1961 till 1965, and then became chief conductor of the BBC Symphony Orchestra, in which position he gained popularity with an important musical public at the Promenade Concerts in the Royal Albert Hall. Thus he had both operatic and concert experience. From my point of view what mattered most was that he had a passionate intensity in all that he did, and one felt all the time that there was a fire raging inside him.

The board discussed the problem at length. Most of us agreed that Colin Davis was the better-known public figure, with wider experience. However, we also felt that it was important to retain the services of Edward Downes, and it was hoped that he might be persuaded to accept the title of associate musical director, working alongside of and complementing Colin Davis. This was not to be. He undertook to conduct regularly at Covent Garden, but only freelance, since he did not wish to accept a lesser title: and then before long he was offered and accepted the position of musical director of the new Sydney Opera House, which was to open its doors at the end of 1973, although he returned to London, disillusioned, after only three years. Now he is doing a great deal of work all over the world, including Covent Garden. Whatever he undertakes is sound, always musical, and absolutely reliable, while his direct no-nonsense manner is most refreshing.

Colin Davis, therefore, was appointed to take over the post of musical director in the autumn of 1971. Soon after his acceptance of our offer, I suggested to him that it would be a good thing for him to meet Peter Hall, who had been responsible, with Solti, for the masterly production of *Moses and Aaron* in 1965, as well as doing other valuable work for us at Covent Garden. I knew what charm he possessed, and I felt sure that they would be attracted to one another. They came for dinner with Joan and myself. After a short while we felt quite *de trop*, such was their mutual response. Within days Colin was more or less saying to me that unless he had Peter to work alongside of him he did not think he could undertake the position of musical director at all. This meant creating a new post of artistic director; and having persuaded David Webster, who was unenthusiastic but unresisting, since he was due to retire, and then getting my colleagues on the board to agree to what was effectively an increase in staff, I bent every effort to obtain Peter's agreement to join us. In this I thought I had been successful, for in March 1969 he duly signed a contract to take effect from the autumn of 1971. All the signs were therefore that on the opera side we should have a duumvirate, with Peter on the artistic side very much the dominant voice.

While these talks were going on, Solti's regime still had more than two years to run, with plenty of delights in store. The 1969/70 season opened with a fine new production of *The Trojans* designed by Nicholas Georgiadis and conducted by Colin Davis. It was given in honour of the centenary of the death of Berlioz, for whose music Colin had a special affinity and so was in constant demand. Covent Garden's contribution to the centenary was highly successful, and it was good to revive a work which had been a highlight of the Kubelik regime.

Among Solti's new productions was Gluck's *Orfeo*, produced by John Copley with skill, although the Elysian fields were a bit tinselly to look at; and simple white drapes would have been far preferable to gold and silver lurex. The title role was sung with dignity and style by Yvonne Minton, who was one of Covent Garden's chief assets, an Australian mezzo-soprano with a beautiful voice and a distinguished profile, with whom Georg had established a close working association. In his final years he also gave us a splendid *Ring*, and most satisfying revivals of two of Verdi's noblest masterpieces, the famous Visconti production of *Don Carlos*, and Zeffirelli's production of *Falstaff*, which seemed especially fitted to Georg's mercurial temperament. Quite rightly Richard Strauss figured prominently in his last offerings, with welcome revivals of *Frau ohne Schatten* and *Elektra*; and a new production of *Salome*, a powerful although strangely sick work, certain to be musically stunning with someone of Solti's calibre in the pit. His last two productions as musical director were Tchaikovsky's *Eugene Onegin* and Wagner's *Tristan and Isolde*. Somewhat ironically, these were both produced by Peter Hall. In fact, during the season before he should have taken up his duties with us as artistic director, Peter seemed to be constantly in the Opera House, because together with Colin Davis he was also responsible for the première of Michael Tippett's intriguing but obscure *Knot Garden*.

The *Eugene Onegin* production was distinguished by Julia Trevelyan Oman's authentic decor, the fruit of many days' study in and around Leningrad; and also by the début in London of a lovely Rumanian artist, Ileana Cotrubas, who at that time was little known but for whose claims, having heard her in Germany, Peter successfully fought, the sequel being that she and her husband Manfred Ramin were to make their home in England, while she was to become one of the most loved of all opera singers. The worst feature of the *Onegin* production was the maddening rhymed translation. Because the Pushkin libretto was in verse Peter thought that the English text must also be. There were some really ghastly couplets (one I recall is 'God sends us habit from above / To take the place of perfect love'), and at several points in order to produce a rhyme the sense of the original was varied. I pointed all this out to Peter in a long letter, but not I fear to much avail.

For *Tristan* Peter used his most frequent collaborator, John Bury, a very gifted designer who tends to eschew prettiness to the point of austerity. With Solti conducting and a fine cast there was little doubt of the success of the production, but it disappointed me. I felt that the attempt to introduce some quite unnecessary symbolism into the action was a mistake, while Peter's idea of resurrecting Tristan and making him peer over Isolde's right shoulder during her singing of the Liebestod was tiresomely distracting. For the last performance, in order to give a glorious farewell, Georg asked Birgit Nilsson to sing Isolde (Ludmila Dvorakova had sung the earlier performances), and to my relief Tristan was not required to resurrect. Afterwards I asked Nilsson what had happened, and she said: 'As it was the last performance, I told him that he could stay asleep.'

At the end of the evening a party in Georg's honour was given in the Crush Bar. He had been awarded a knighthood in the Birthday Honours List, and Ted Heath, the Prime Minister, presented the insignia to him at the party, thus creating what was unquestionably a precedent. The idea had emanated from Robert Armstrong, who had followed Denis Rickett at the latter's suggestion as secretary of the board of directors, and who had been appointed, later and quite coincidentally, the Prime Minister's principal private secretary. He happened by pure chance to be the son of Tom Armstrong, whom I had invited to join the board soon after I became chairman in 1958. We were outstandingly lucky to have as secretary someone of such ability, so obviously marked out for a distinguished career, in a position to play a helpful and important role in the affairs of Covent Garden. When he was first appointed principal secretary to the Prime Minister he rang me with typical modesty to ask me, of all things, whether *I* would allow him to carry on as secretary to the board. After Harold Wilson succeeded Heath as Prime Minister, Robert continued in the key position at No. 10, until he was eventually appointed to be the top civil servant at the Home Office, where he now is. Happily he still remains secretary of the board of Covent Garden, and will do so, I hope, until he becomes head of the Treasury.

When Georg Solti received his knighthood he was not a British subject, otherwise it would have been bestowed on him by the Queen; but receipt of the honour did help him to decide to assume British nationality, thus establishing a right to be addressed Sir Georg, a title justly his for the very considerable services he rendered to Covent Garden.

Chapter 24

While we were saying farewell to the new Knight, we were undergoing a pretty traumatic experience at the hands of Peter Hall. We confidently expected him to join us two months later as artistic director alongside Colin Davis, the incoming musical director, with whom Peter had worked out pretty full plans for the next two years. However, on 4 July 1971 I received a letter from him asking to be released from the contract he had signed over two years previously. This is what he said:

My dear Garrett,

I have to admit to a great mistake. The only course open to me is to recognise it and to apologise to you personally and publicly.

I have now been working for the Royal Opera for two years. During this last season, I have been particularly active and have had full opportunity to see how my future with you would develop.

I thought, as you know, that by giving the Royal Opera twenty-six weeks exclusive work each year, I could serve it fully under the terms of my contract, and collaborate with John and Colin in the exciting way we envisaged. I now know this was muddled thinking. To do the job properly, I would have to devote all my time to it.

As the number of my productions increases, revival will pile on revival, and unless I am with you full-time, other people will have to do them. I cannot face this, because I want to improve my work, not see it become something else. For audiences also, a production is in some sense mine, even if I haven't rehearsed it, and if I am your director with special responsibility for production, I *ought* to have rehearsed it.

Why, then, don't I ask you if I can be at the House for more weeks of the year? Because I cannot be. It has always been my intention to put the Royal Opera first (otherwise I would not have accepted the job), but everyone has recognised my need to work at other things as well. I could not exclude the theatre or the occasional film, even if it were asked of me.

I am therefore led to a sad conclusion. Twenty-six weeks is a compromise which does not work, and I should have known it. I should either be full-time or an occasional visitor, as in the past.

I must also recognise that temperamentally I am not suited to the needs of a Repertory Opera House. I have always worked very personally with the people I am directing and found my solutions through their individuality. There is nothing remarkable about this, but it needs time. This method is not possible where revivals have to be speedily mounted and moves and business given out quickly, no matter who is executing them. I hate doing this.

Yet unless the Royal Opera does speedy revivals, it cannot have the scope of repertory that it needs. So I am not criticising the House. With the exception of festivals, it has the best conditions for opera. I thought I could work happily in them: I was wrong. I believe that although musically revivals often improve on the originals, this rarely happens dramatically. And it can't; there isn't time, unless the cast is the same.

My heart has gone out of the future since I realised that I had put myself in this impossible position. The fault is mine and nobody else's, and I am dreadfully sorry. My optimism was unrealistic.

I realise that I am creating great difficulties for you, the Board and for John; and particularly for Colin. He gave me half his new kingdom gladly, and it is a poor way to answer his generosity. Working with him was one of the best experiences of my life.

But I have to ask you to release me from my contract. I feel that I would compound my mistakes by continuing.

If, in the light of all this, you ever want me to do a new production, or continue to work in any way on the new works started with librettists and composers, I want you to know I shall be delighted. But I shall quite understand if you find this impossible.

I am very sorry.

Yours ever,
Peter

There was of course no option but to accept his withdrawal. Some of my colleagues on the board took it less hardly than I did, having viewed with some alarm his imminent arrival on the scene. I was distressed because of the part I had played in introducing Colin and Peter to one another. I knew well what magnetic qualities Peter possessed; and I had seen Colin's sense of anticipation develop after what he called, in a letter he wrote to me in January 1969, 'our first excited meeting'. Then soon afterwards he was writing to me from New York:

The more I think about it the clearer it becomes to me that we must be seen to be responsible on completely equal terms. I know that in recent years the producers have had it too much their own way, but I think that this is because musicians on the whole are ill educated visually and are, besides, far too concerned with their own problems. The possibility we have here is of two men approaching the *whole* problem of opera from a shared attitude.

These words were written more than a year before their collaboration over Tippett's *Knot Garden*, which brought them even closer together.

Although Colin was not due to take up his post until September 1971 he used to attend meetings when matters bearing on the plans for his first season were under discussion. On occasion he was rather intemperate towards the board of directors, whose *raison d'être* somewhat escaped him; and if money was not available he would say in so many words, 'What are the board for if they can't raise the necessary funds?' He could be singularly unreasonable, but then he would disarm one with charm. For instance in February 1970 he gave an interview to the Oxford magazine *Isis* in which he was quoted as casting various aspersions on Solti's regime. He said that he and Peter Hall both felt that if one was going to give a theatrical performance one had to make some kind of statement about the condition of being a human being; therefore it wasn't very interesting when the whole thing was entirely decorative or appeared to be put on for the self-indulgence of the performers. Under Solti the new operas performed had been a peripheral activity. With Peter and himself they would be central: 'We are going to gradually try and turn the whole place upside down.' Then he was quoted as saying, 'Solti may have given the impression of having left a lot of young singers, but the company as such has never been smaller, only about a dozen people on the books.'

This last statement was untrue, and gave a most misleading impression. I wrote him a letter urging him not to ventilate criticisms of the person he was succeeding: I had spent a good deal of time asking people to support Covent Garden and I did not at all like it when their faith in what they were supporting was shaken. In his reply he said that the article had misrepresented him. His interview had been in response to a very gloomy previous article (which I had not seen). He was, he told me, 'indiscreet, somewhat ferocious, fairly honest, affectionate, insolent, but not wittingly treacherous'. As well as writing to me he also sent a note of explanation to Solti, which I appreciated.

During the period of drawing up plans for their first two or three years together (including the prospect of a production by that well-known iconoclast Ken Russell, from which in the event he withdrew), Colin and Peter had hopes of producing the main Mozart operas, and much else besides, not excluding of course the *Ring*. *Figaro* was to open the first season. They had broadly accepted Covent Garden's policy regarding the language in which opera was sung, but after the artistic success of the *Knot Garden*, with its very obscure libretto, they became convinced that to come close to the audience, to bring alive the social drama of *Figaro*, the opening performances must be in English. There had been a slight foretaste of a clash over language policy in September 1970 when plans for *Don Pasquale* were under discussion. Colin half wanted it done in English, because it was a comedy. I told him that I did not favour Covent Garden becoming a glorified Sadler's Wells; the jokes in *Don Pasquale* were basically situation jokes, calling for no great subtleties of language, and if we gave the opera in English, we should never be able to cast it with foreign singers. To this Colin replied that the language could be alternated from season to season, which I felt was an uneasy and impractical compromise, not in fact adopted, Italian being the language which was used. However, the matter of *Don Pasquale* paled into insignificance beside *Figaro*, where Colin and Peter adopted a very emphatic stance that English must be the language a year after the plans had been made and the artists engaged on the basis of singing in the original Italian. Letters were exchanged and rather tense meetings took place, the issue moving away from language to the question who had the ultimate power of decision.

On the question of language, George Harewood, who was still on the board, wrote me a long letter which deserves to be quoted at some length, because he is a great authority and feels deeply about this contentious subject. First of all he set out the arguments for and against translation into the language of the audience. The points in favour of using English, he argued, were immediacy of impact, understanding of individual phrase and situation, greater theatrical–musical possibilities, the fact that most composers have wanted their operas translated, and finally that the great nineteenth- and twentieth-century opera houses 'with a local, involved permanent type of audience' always sang in translation, and those that didn't, namely Covent Garden and the Met. in New York, 'tended to breed an audience with social, perhaps snobbish, certainly canary-fancying tendencies'. Against translation he recognized that 'the composer's full intentions cannot reach a listener since he (the composer) was inspired by the original language ...', 'certain texts had real merit ...', 'the great singers prefer singing in the original ... which takes them to international houses all over the world', and lastly that 'the audience is partly made up of visitors who are not interested in the English-speaking audience around them'.

George recognized that the problem could not be solved in isolation and would always divide people interested in opera. Covent Garden, he thought, 'could have the best of both worlds, with by and large international perform-ances of established works, and others maybe of a sharper impact in the English language, using British and English-speaking stars'. He said that he 'would not attempt to deny the successful aspects of Covent Garden's ten-year-old original-language policy. It has brought more international stars than before, and in so far as these are stars ... they enhance the stage and do little but good'. The snags, he said, were higher ticket prices and therefore richer and older audiences than desirable. By putting the emphasis on the performer rather than on the work performed a superficial approach was encouraged. He instanced *Arabella*, which he thought would have had a bigger impact in translation. On the particular question of *Figaro* he said that he sympathized with Colin and

Peter for wanting 'their performance to make the very strongest possible impact on the audience, thus in their view fulfilling Mozart's intentions' better than they otherwise could. He saw no reason why in revivals Italian might not be used, and he rejected as a pure red herring any suggestion that in using English Colin and Peter wished to put over Beaumarchais rather than Mozart. Finally he said, 'I hope that no policy would ever become so rigid as to get in the way of genuine artistic intention.'

William Glock, for whose opinion I also had profound respect, felt that before we departed from our agreed policy there must be a precise argument from Peter Hall why a production in English was going to be more creative. He simply did not believe that English was right if the audience were to have the most satisfying experience. If *Figaro* then why not *Don Giovanni*? There must surely be some sort of binding agreement for the future, and clear guidelines which must be adhered to, or only departed from after adequate warning.

I myself wrote to John Tooley, 'Our first duty is to give the great basic masterpieces as finely as possible, and this means drawing on the most outstanding artists available, regardless of their nationality.' Lionel Robbins, who was rather the elder statesman among us, wrote two long letters. On the question of language he said:

My judgement, for what it is worth, is quite definitely against the performance in English; this is for several reasons, some intrinsic, others concerning public relations.

The intrinsic reasons are simple. First, I am sure that an opera house which aspires to performances of the highest excellence ought to perform Italian opera in Italian. Any resort to translation, however good, must necessarily be a second best. Moreover, quite apart from the musical considerations involved, any other policy necessarily limits your casting. Suppose your Figaro goes sick, where do you immediately find someone equally capable of performing in English rather than the original language?

The public relations considerations are more various. I cannot believe that it is good policy for Covent Garden to seek to usurp the explicit function of Sadler's Wells in this respect. Sadler's Wells as the auxiliary company has always provided this service in English. We have definitely evolved in the other direction and if at this critical juncture in the relation between the two houses we reverse gear, this simply further complicates the excruciating question of our relative claims on the limited resources of the Arts Council.

On the wider question of the board's responsibility, Lionel stressed that while they must have the final say on any matter of controversy they would be very foolish to attempt to impose limitations on creative activity, and 'only big questions of principle . . . should be the subject of board rulings'. These questions, he said, obviously included broad questions of finance and the engagement of important officers. Beyond that, differences between the operatic and balletic sides of the house over access to the stage and so on would clearly involve the board, and anything calling for a dramatic change from established practice.

I am sure that there has to be a good deal of give and take ... but when there is involved our position in relation to Sadler's Wells, our position in relation to the engagement of foreign artists and the training of our own company in such a way that they are available for employment in foreign parts, when the position of the board in this respect has already been made very clear, I do not think that the artistic directors can claim full autonomy.

A week or two passed without any conclusion being reached. The board meeting approached, and I had letters from Claus Moser and John Sainsbury, both of whom were unable to be present. In the course of a lengthy letter Claus wrote:

We have argued about this at length, and I trust that Colin Davis and Peter Hall will have carefully considered our arguments against. But if, having done so, they remain keen on artistic grounds to try English, I think we should agree, and do everything to make it a success. After all, we have appointed them and can be proud of such an outstanding set of appointments. All the early signs are of an immensely exciting period ahead, and I think it is particularly important in these days, to give the new 'directorate' every chance and support to develop the work of the House in the ways which they feel to be right. ... I do not think that we should regard the single decision on *Figaro* in these early days of the new regime as calling in question the entire language policy, and therefore the point to stick at. ... Our policy should firmly remain original-language; it would be much better to stick to Italian for *Figaro*; but we should accept English as a definite exception to our policy, if after all our discussion this is what Colin and Peter still favour.

John Sainsbury said:

At the risk of simplification, I believe we should be guardians of the artistic policy and standing of the Opera House, as we are of its financial viability. To this end, we must seek to dissuade Artistic Directors from pursuing a policy which we feel to be inconsistent with the objectives, artistic or otherwise, of our Opera House. The one thing I believe we cannot do is to seek to veto what they do. If our persuasion fails, and the consequences are sufficiently serious, then the Board has in its power the ultimate sanction of replacing its Artistic Directors. However, this step is one which I believe and pray need never arise.

Peter Hall himself wrote to me, '*Figaro* is a particular. We fully appreciate that the important consideration is excellence of casting and maintaining Covent

Garden as an international house. Therefore the basic policy *must* be opera in the original language.' He went on, 'We need your support and your backing. We have a difficult task ahead of us and we can't do without you.'

I hated having to drag out all the old arguments, and I simply did not accept the practicability of performing *Figaro* in English in one season, and in Italian the next. Mercifully we were rescued from a most tiresome situation because, while the board accepted that in the last analysis those charged with the artistic responsibility must have the final say, they stipulated that our contracts with the artists engaged to sing in Italian must not be repudiated. If they were willing to learn their roles in English, well and good; but otherwise we must stick to what had been agreed a year before. Fortunately from my point of view, and I think from Covent Garden's, one of the artists flatly refused to accept the projected change, and that, in a rather lame conclusion after all the excitement generated, was the end of the argument.

The work of planning the coming seasons went ahead and everything seemed fine until the arrival several months later of Peter's letter asking to be released from his contract. This caused great distress, and the situation was not helped when the *Sunday Times* published an unworthy article in which it was darkly suggested that from the first 'the artistic tensions between the Covent Garden board and its directorate (Peter Hall and Colin Davis) were destructive'. They wanted, the article said, 'to move the opera house towards a twentieth century commitment, a group activity in which drama and music were equally deeply rooted'. And so on. 'Drogheda in bringing Davis and Hall together had created a monster he could not manage.' The distorted piece then turned to *Figaro*, saying that the idea of giving the opera in English had been scotched, quite omitting to state that when the opera was first planned it was on the basis of its being sung in Italian. The article was about as unfair as it could have been, and caused Peter to write to me: 'Yesterday's speculations in the *Sunday Times* were not inspired by me, or encouraged by me to masquerade as fact. They have not helped a very unpleasant situation which I alone am responsible for. . . .'

The simple fact was that Peter had asked to be released only a matter of weeks before he was due to start working for us; and I was deeply disappointed, while to Colin it was a harsh and bitter blow, for he had banked on their collaboration together, and all his plans seemed to him to lie in ruins. Nor was the blow softened when some months later it was announced that Peter had been appointed to succeed Laurence Olivier as director of the National Theatre.

Although Peter had said that he would always be available to do a production for us, it was obviously out of the question for him to produce *Figaro* with Colin as though nothing had happened. Instead he produced it two years later at Glyndebourne, where no argument about language arose, because their policy of adhering to the original Italian text was quite clear. For Colin as well as for the board it was a mercy that John Copley was available and willing at such extremely short notice to undertake Covent Garden's new *Figaro* production. He did it really splendidly, the sets of Stephanos Lazaridis were very handsome, indeed beautiful; and Kiri te Kanawa, the gorgeous Maori girl who had been training at the London Opera Centre, made a spectacular début as the Countess, Colin's boldness in giving her such a chance so early in her career being truly rewarded. She quickly went on to become a world star, captivating audiences with the loveliness of her voice, her natural unaffected manner, and her great dignity and sense of style.

Despite the success of *Figaro* Colin did not in his first year or two at Covent Garden have an easy time with the press. In a long and helpful article in the *Evening Standard* of 13 July 1973, written by Sydney Edwards, most benign of newspapermen, Colin was quoted as saying, 'Are they out to destroy me?' To me he used to say, 'In their eyes Sadler's Wells can do no wrong, and we no right,' and as with Solti in the beginning there was a certain amount of objectionable booing to put up with, obviously organized but by whom one never knew. It passed away, but for a while Colin preferred not to take a curtain call on his own, and when he did so he used rather stupidly to stick his tongue out at the booers. His second production failed to follow up the success of *Figaro*. It was Verdi's *Nabucco*, produced by Josef Svoboda, using projections rather than actual sets in a manner which in Svoboda's hands was by then in danger of becoming a cliché. And as with Solti's first Verdi production at Covent Garden the leading soprano was a disappointment. Such booing as there was should certainly not have been at Colin's expense. In the following season, the team of John Copley and Stephanos Lazaridis were asked to produce *Don Giovanni*, which like *Figaro* should have been produced by Peter Hall. Bearing in mind how visually pleasing their *Figaro* had been, we were full of hopeful expectations. Alas, though, we were to be sadly disappointed. Motivated by a desire perhaps to 'make some kind of statement' and to give us what I suppose was intended to be a misconceived timeless symbolism, the audience were treated to a singularly ugly abstract set consisting entirely of metal rods, with two squeaking meccano-like platforms on each side of the stage. By contrast the costumes were absurdly elaborate. I cannot think what possessed these two able young men to offer something so out of character with their normal work, but I am sorry that it was accepted by Colin Davis and John Tooley, and allowed to go forward at considerable cost.

During the same year Georg Solti returned to Covent Garden to give us a new production of *Carmen*. It had been hoped that Giorgio Strehler from Milan would be the producer, but in the event Franco Zeffirelli accepted the commitment, and then cancelled at short notice in a fairly maddening way. Michael

Geliot, then in charge of Welsh National Opera, stepped into the breach to produce, proposing as designer a talented young girl named Jennie Beavan, of whom
afterwards more should have been heard. It was good to have Solti back, and he
certainly made the orchestra's fingers tingle. The beautiful black singer, Shirley
Verrett, sang the title role, and with Placido Domingo and Kiri te Kanawa also
in the cast there was little cause for complaint.

If on the opera side we had to adjust ourselves to the failure of Peter Hall to
materialize, on the ballet side plenty of difficulties arose during the opening year
of Kenneth MacMillan's term as artistic director. Our hope that Kenneth could
work happily with John Field was short-lived. What went wrong I do not
know. A basic incompatibility developed, and the position was not helped by
the largely unfriendly press that Kenneth received. In any event, Field left and
Peter Wright rejoined the Royal Ballet as associate director, with particular
responsibility for the administrative side of things, which Kenneth found tiresomely distracting. Field went to a good job in Italy, returning to London two
or three years later and becoming the head of the Royal Academy of Dancing,
a body which exists to improve standards of ballet teaching, where he seems to
have found a satisfactory niche.

As to Kenneth, I found him a fascinating personality. In personal contacts he
was not easy; he often seemed downcast, and he did not always express himself
well in words. He certainly never met anyone as much as halfway. The rest of
us had to make the concessions. He is, though, a man of great artistic integrity,
sticking almost mulishly to his beliefs. The start of his regime was unfortunate
because in a BBC interview he criticized the standard of male dancing in the
company, not wholly without reason. His complex nature was considerably
helped through his marriage to Deborah Williams, a handsome Australian who
bore him a daughter, and whose warmth and receptiveness helped to bridge the
gap caused by his frequent difficulty in communicating with others. In any event,
I believe that, although the business was clumsily handled and done a year or
two too soon, it was right to appoint him artistic director of the Royal Ballet
after Fred Ashton retired. No one else had shown the same creative talent, capable of thinking on the large scale called for at Covent Garden, and despite his
complexity of character he was the man who merited the job.

Kenneth's first ballet after taking over the directorship was *Anastasia*, which
had its première in July 1971. It had started life as a one-act ballet when he was in
Berlin, the libretto being based on the legend that the youngest daughter of the
Imperial Russian family was still alive. It showed her perplexed state of mind,
assailed as she was by nightmarish memories. The music was by Martinu.
Kenneth had the idea of turning it into a full-length work, depicting in the first
act the idyllic life of the Imperial family until it was interrupted by the declara-

tion of war, and in the second Anastasia's coming-out ball disrupted by the outbreak of the revolution. For these new acts he used two of the early, beautifully
romantic symphonies of Tchaikovsky. The contrast with Martinu's music
worked very well for me. I found the ballet moving and full of imagination; and
Lynn Seymour, Kenneth's muse, upon whom the ballet was mounted, gave a
remarkable performance. However, the work was too long. His mistake was
that he felt obliged to use the whole of the two symphonies for fear of being
criticized for musical tampering, and when the ballet was revived, a few but not
enough cuts were made. With the public the ballet was popular from the start,
although the critics were in the main unfriendly, one notable exception being
Clement Crisp, the ballet critic of the *Financial Times*, a kindly and very humour-
ous man who was one of Kenneth's most constant protagonists.

In general Kenneth had to stand up to a good deal of ill-disposed criticism
during his early years as director of the company, much of it rather unfair and
really looking back nostalgically to the days of Ashton. I respected Kenneth for
the way in which he managed to overlook the criticism, but I have little doubt
that it affected his creative spirit, and indeed one of his ballets, *Poltroon*, produced
for the touring group, a kind of 'he who gets slapped' tragedy, was I felt
subconsciously influenced by his harsh treatment.

His productive output during the time that I was chairman and he was director
was in fact a little disappointing. There were two ballets with original and
colourful decor and costumes by Ian Spurling, the Brecht-Weill *7 Deadly Sins*,
and *Elite Syncopations* to Scott Joplin's ragtime music, a taste for which Kenneth
helped to revive. But these were lightish-weight works, and there was nothing
really substantial to place beside them. A full-length ballet, *Manon*, using the
music of Massenet but not from his opera of the same name, had superb décor
by Nicholas Georgiadis and much inventive choreography; but it was sugary
and sentimental and far removed from the profundity of which Kenneth
MacMillan was capable. *Triad*, to the music of Prokofiev's violin concerto,
scarcely compensated. Then he landed us with a very disappointing *Sleeping
Beauty*, having rejected the designs of Beni Montresor, as Helpmann had in the
case of *Swan Lake* some years before. The failure of the production was particularly regrettable because we felt that we could not take it on tour to the
United States although it had largely been financed by the American Friends of
Covent Garden, thanks to powerful help from Mrs Walter Annenberg, the wife
of the then American Ambassador, who while she was in London was very good
to the opera house and a very good friend to me; and had it been successful it
could have been most helpful for the future.

Against this it must be said that the general standard of dancing, both male and
female, was consistently pretty high during Kenneth's regime, and although I

was told that the morale of the company was low this was certainly not the impression that I formed when I flew to America with them in their charter aircraft in 1974, providing me with one of the most agreeable of all my memories of Covent Garden and telling me better than anything else could have done what is meant by *esprit de corps*.

To revert to the repertoire, four most rewarding ballets by Jerome Robbins were introduced to the repertoire, and an absorbing work, *Laborintus II*, by Glen Tetley, to highly original music by Luciano Berio. (Tetley also gave us *Field Figures*, to music of Stockhausen, for the touring group.) Kenneth's open-mindedness about the work of others was much to his credit. He deserved more support from his colleagues than he received, and largely because it was lacking he never really seemed at ease as director of the company. He found the general responsibility as well as the relative isolation of his position inhibiting to his creative work, the two things reacting adversely upon one another; and eventually, after my own retirement, he gave up the position of artistic director, becoming instead principal choreographer, Norman Morrice, formerly director of the Ballet Rambert, being brought in from outside to the top position, a hazardous step which, as I write, is evidently proving successful.

For much of the time after Kenneth had become director and while I was still chairman the affairs of the ballet loomed large in discussions with the Arts Council. Mark Bonham-Carter, the chairman of the ballet committee, devoted much time to a masterly paper outlining the problems, which revolved essentially around the size and role of the touring company. His chief recommendation concerned the need for giving the touring company a proper base of its own. When the chance of redeveloping beside the Royal Opera House became a serious possibility, we fought strongly for a second auditorium which could be built side by side, providing a base for the small company as well as giving scope for the performance of smaller scale operas and enabling young singers to have back the proving ground they had lost when Sadler's Wells opera was moved to the Coliseum. As the fulfilment of that hope was obviously at best far off, we suggested various theatres which might provide a temporary solution, among them Sadler's Wells. But the Arts Council, influenced by pressure from the Conservative Paymaster General and Minister for the Arts, David Eccles, who wanted the largest possible numbers to go out into the provinces, urged Covent Garden to put the two ballet companies into one, which we had already once unsuccessfully attempted in an effort to economize. We were clear that the two companies must be kept separate; and in any event, as we kept on telling the Arts Council, the theatres outside of London were in the main hopelessly inadequate and even in danger of disappearing from use. The pressure would have made more sense if David Eccles had found funds to enable the theatres to be acquired, adapted and modernized, or had provided money for putting up some new buildings. But the sum available for this purpose was grotesquely small. Fortunately, our view that the two companies must be kept as separate entities, with only a few principal dancers interchangeable, was allowed to prevail. And now, over two years after my retirement, the problem of the second auditorium has been solved, in so far as concerns the ballet, by basing the touring group once more upon Sadler's Wells, whence in a sense it sprang; although the theatre will of course continue with its valuable work of presenting other small dance and opera companies, including visitors from abroad. Needless to say, Covent Garden, tragically in my view, has been forced by the impact of inflation to abandon the idea of a second auditorium beside the opera house itself. Would that it could be revived.

I should not like it to be thought that I regard David Eccles as having done a bad job when he was Minister for the Arts between 1970 and 1973. He certainly put his foot in it badly over the subject of museum charges, and he failed to persuade the Chancellor of the Exchequer Tony Barber to exempt the live theatre from VAT, with the result that when VAT was introduced we had to add 10 per cent to our seat prices without any advantage to our receipts, and the fact that we were supposed to be compensated by an adjustment in our grant was little comfort; but so far as Covent Garden was concerned David Eccles was helpful over the level of our grant and he surely played the major part in securing the land adjoining the Royal Opera House, which was quite vital to us for redevelopment purposes. It was only in the matter of provincial touring, where no one could quarrel with his desire to see the provinces better provided, that he got his priorities wrong.

During his period as Minister he suggested one name as a possible addition to our board. This was John Thorn, the headmaster of David's old school, Winchester. I thought that John might be helpful in arousing interest among the public schools in the work of Covent Garden, and I never minded gratifying Ministers if an opportunity arose. He was elected to the board in 1971, and he was most co-operative in sending out a large number of letters, although the response was disappointing. He was as assiduous as his scholastic duties allowed in attending meetings and performances, and after my retirement he acted as host to the board for a working weekend at Winchester, which was to set a pattern for the future. However, as the work of the board developed, with so much work done by the various committees, those based away from London were at a disadvantage.

It is worth recording that in 1971 the Arts Council decided to commission Peat Marwick Mitchell to produce a detailed report on the workings of the four main subsidized theatres, Covent Garden, Sadler's Wells, the Old Vic and the Royal Shakespeare Company. So far as Covent Garden was concerned, I do not think that the report was very illuminating. It gave us a reasonably clear bill, although it said that there should be closer control over the cost of new productions, which we knew, and that John Tooley should delegate more, which we also knew. There was some discussion of the possibilities of effecting economies through joint working with Sadler's Wells Opera in the production and other departments, but the idea of a true merger and the establishment of complementary policies was not again examined as it had been in 1956.

Once the Sadler's Wells company had moved to the Coliseum the practicability of such policies was in any case remote. That move took place at the end of August 1968. Previously, in the early 1960s when the layout of the new National Theatre was at first under active discussion, there had been a proposal that Sadler's Wells Opera should be moved to the South Bank of the River Thames and incorporated within the complex of new buildings. This would have given them a new opera house with every modern facility, but with a seating capacity about the same as their old theatre, that is to say not more than 1,500 seats. I confess that I had viewed the proposal with a certain degree of alarm from the point of view of Covent Garden, although I kept absolutely silent. There was in fact no need for me to worry because Arnold Goodman, recently appointed chairman of the Arts Council, took strongly against the idea, regarding it as an absurdly extravagant proposition, and he effectively killed it. However, Stephen Arlen, who was then in charge of Sadler's Wells, was a very determined fellow and he was resolved that they should move to a new home. A year or two afterwards he came up with a proposal that Sadler's Wells should move into the Coliseum, belonging to Stoll Theatres Corporation, a subsidiary of ATV, containing 900 more seats than they would have had on the South Bank. Although the move meant a radical change in the nature of the Sadler's Wells operation, making it far more directly competitive with Covent Garden, and paradoxically turning Covent Garden into the more intimate of the two theatres, with four hundred fewer seats than the Coliseum, Arnold Goodman embraced the idea strongly. The result of the move was that there was no small auditorium in which young singers could try out their paces, while the Sadler's Wells (shortly afterwards renamed English National) Opera Company felt obliged to tackle most of the large-scale works in the repertoire. This gave rise to a certain confusion about the respective roles of the two theatres, and resulted in great duplication in the works performed, as well as inflating London's share of the Arts Council resources devoted to opera, and at the same time leaving the English regions relatively starved, except when the English National Opera Company goes on tour, as it does for ten weeks each spring and summer. An unpredictable postscript was that in 1977 Arnold Goodman himself became chairman of the Coliseum after its chairman Kenneth Robinson was appointed to the head of the Arts Council in succession to Pat Gibson.

Arnold gave up the chairmanship of the Arts Council at the end of April 1972, being succeeded by Pat Gibson, whose appointment was originated by David Eccles. I had been anxious to capture Arnold as quickly as I could for the Covent Garden board, and already before he handed over at the Arts Council he had agreed to join us as soon as he was free to do so. He joined us in May, and when I added him to our number it gave me a general sense of comfort, for I respected him greatly and loved him dearly even though on occasion he and I failed to see eye to eye, finding one another tiresomely obstinate if we disagreed on a matter of principle. But he had a great talent for reconciling differences, and I hope I can say that we have always remained good friends.

Arnold's first gesture as a member of the board was to present a new set of seats for the benefit of the orchestra, who for years had had to be content with a motley assortment of chairs. Although the Covent Garden grant was large, we were always short of funds. More and more it became clear that we had to try to raise money from private sources. I asked Arnold to suggest whom we might recruit to the board to help us in this regard. I put one or two names to him, but he dismissed them saying, 'I don't think they'd do any *work*.' He then proposed the name of Harry Kissin, a close friend of his whom I did not know. We met, I liked him, and in January 1973 he joined the board. His background was Russian Jewish, stemming I think from Danzig. He had acquired control of an old-established Far Eastern commodity business, Lewis and Peat. Not long after joining the Covent Garden board he merged it with a famous private merchant bank, Guinness Mahon, naming the holding company Guinness Peat, and then becoming its very active chairman.

Harry was a particular favourite of Arnold's; and while Arnold was still at the Arts Council he had made him chairman of the controversial ICA or Institute of Contemporary Arts. It was a post which accorded ill with Harry's suave and elegant appearance, and still less with his sleek beige Rolls-Royce, but he obviously enjoyed it and I believe rendered it good service. For some while after joining the Covent Garden board he seemed to me to be disappointingly slow in setting in train his fund-raising efforts. However, he had promised me that he would produce not less than £50,000 a year, and he was considerably better than his word. Taking as his starting point the Royal Opera House Society formed in 1962 by Leon Bagrit but allowed to become dormant, Harry modified the articles and changed the title to Royal Opera House Trust. He invited several helpfully effective people to become directors of the Trust, among them Francis Sandilands, head of the Commercial Union Assurance Company, who has done more than anyone to civilize the image of commerce, and whom later I was to propose for membership of the main Covent Garden board, although he did not join until after my retirement. It was thanks to Harry Kissin's initiative that we first started to make a serious effort to promote sponsorship of new opera and ballet productions by individual companies, a field where there is still far to go, but where we gave an important lead. Harry also actively promoted corporate membership of the Trust, with the dual purpose of providing the Trust with a steady income and building up a body of potential sponsors. In proposing his name, therefore, Arnold was most helpful.

Soon after Harry became a director my own retirement from the chairman-ship loomed up. In an earlier chapter I explained that when I became chair-man in January 1958 I was instrumental in altering the article relating to the term of appointment (which had previously been indefinite and theoretic-ally therefore perpetual) by specifying that election should be for a five-year term but capable of renewal. My appointment was therefore by agreement with the Arts Council renewed in January 1963; and when the question arose at the beginning of 1968, Arnold Goodman then being Chairman of the Arts Council, I went to him and told him that my colleagues had asked me to carry on for a further five years. His consent was necessary, and it was forthcoming. However, he said that 'we' (meaning I supposed Jennie Lee, the Arts Council and himself) normally believed ten years to be long enough for anyone to hold an important public appointment, but that since I was regarded as having given a reasonably good account of myself re-election for a further period of five years would be ap-proved, but not beyond that. Therefore towards the end of 1972 I told my col-leagues that my term of office would shortly be expiring and they must decide whom they wanted to appoint as my successor. The matter had not been the subject of any previous discussion, and there were no preconceived ideas. A committee of the board was formed (of which I was naturally not myself a member); and quite quickly the conclave agreed that Claus Moser should be in-vited to succeed me, providing of course that the necessary official consent could be obtained since he was head of an important Government department, and therefore his appointment would be creating a precedent. The consent was forthcoming, but it was thought desirable that I should carry on for a further full season, in other words until the summer of 1974, so that in all my term of office was to be sixteen and a half years.

Soon after Claus had been chosen as my successor, he was formally elected to the position of deputy chairman. I made it my business to ensure that I regularly consulted with him privately on any point of substance which arose, because of its possible impingement on the future. One important matter came to the fore in the autumn of 1973. This related to the artistic direction of the Royal Opera (we had obtained permission to give the title Royal to our opera company so that it could look the ballet company in the face, as by its achievements it was entitled to do). After Peter Hall had asked to be released, a major gap in the plans for new productions was Wagner's *Ring*, which Colin and Peter were to have done together. John Tooley approached Götz Friedrich, a highly gifted German producer who was supervisor of productions at Hamburg, after previously working with the famous Felsenstein for nearly twenty years in Berlin. When Colin met Friedrich and commenced discussions, he began once more to fall under a spell. Not only was Friedrich engaged for the *Ring*, Colin also decided that he would like him to take the part intended for Peter Hall. He believed, he said, that the artistic supervision was not what it should be, and he wanted someone with whom to share the responsibility. Discussions relating to the renewal of his contract were imminent: the board wanted Colin to carry on for a further period of three years; and it was on the cards that unless we agreed to engage Friedrich Colin himself might not stay. Claus and I saw Friedrich. So did one or two other members of the board. We liked him and were much impressed if slightly apprehensive. A start was not made on the *Ring* cycle until just after my retirement, but I saw the plans and designs and thought them really exciting. It was evident that there was a highly original and creative mind at work, and when the curtain rose on the first scene of *Das Rheingold*, to which Mary Moser, Claus's sympathetic and charming wife, had thoughtfully invited Joan and myself to accompany them as their guests, I believed that Covent Garden was on to a winner. Josef Svoboda was responsible for a most remarkable, adaptable set. The costumes were strange hybrids between the traditional and the space age, with Niebelheim making an almost too obvious political comment on the exploitation of the toiling masses as the gold was forged. The ingenuity was extraordinary, and when a couple of years later the whole cycle was completed Bernard Levin engaged in one of his rare raptures.

Rather surprisingly the collaboration between Colin and Götz did not develop into the kind of artistic supervision of the whole repertoire that had at first seemed likely. They worked together very well on their first productions, but because of heavy commitments with other opera houses it was not possible for Götz to exercise any kind of general oversight as was first envisaged, and it is unlikely now that he will be encouraged to do so.

My own last season as chairman, that is to say from the autumn of 1973 until July 1974, was mercifully a good one artistically, although the political and economic climate for much of the time could scarcely have been worse. There were three new opera productions, *La Clemenza di Tito* of Mozart, Wagner's *Tannhäuser*, and *La Bohème* of Puccini. The *Clemenza* and the *Bohème* were complete triumphs. Colin conducted *Clemenza* in a very handsome production by Anthony Besch, a producer too long neglected by Covent Garden. The singing was as fine as could be heard anywhere, dominated by three British ladies, Janet Baker and Yvonne Minton, with the glamorous Anne Howells skilfully disguised in a transvestite role. It was the sort of performance for which at Salzburg people would happily have paid four or five times the prices charged by us; and for Colin it was a big feather in his cap.

To undertake a new production of *Bohème* was a considerable gamble. The old production dated back to the first performance of the opera in London, that is to say 1897. It was simple and authentic, and it had a sort of mystique about it attaching to no other opera production that I can recall. However, it was battered and worn and had to be replaced. Silvio Varviso, a highly gifted Swiss conductor and a delightful man, who had already made his mark in London, undertook to conduct the opening performances. The production was entrusted to John Copley, with Julia Trevelyan Oman as designer. Save for Act 2, John curbed his occasional tendency to excess; the sets and costumes were both authentic and beautiful, and the scene changes were commendably swift. No one afterwards said that a mistake had been made, and goodness knows how rare *that* is.

As to *Tannhäuser*, Colin Davis was widely praised for the musical quality of the performances. The singing was fine, especially that of the black singer Jessye Norman, who were it not for her noble bulk would be one of the great prima donnas of the age. Visually, alas, the production failed, the sort of failure too often predictable when there is an attempt to depart from a traditional presentation of a traditional masterpiece. And during the course of rehearsals, producer and designer fell out, which scarcely helped. Their difference found its way into one of the popular newspapers, being as one might expect inaccurately reported and exaggerated. The main thing, though, was that Colin personally received wide acclaim.

In addition to the two new productions, Colin conducted revivals of *Don Giovanni*, *Falstaff* and *Fidelio*, Rudolf Kempe came back to do *Elektra*, and the versatile Charles Mackerras conducted Britten's *Midsummer Night's Dream*, Janacek's *Jenufa* and Verdi's *Otello*, in which the lovely Kiri te Kanawa sang the part of Desdemona for the first time at Covent Garden. Peter Hall's discovery Ileana Cotrubas sang Violetta in *La Traviata*, and also Norina in *Don Pasquale*, where she proved she was as good at comedy as at tragedy, and the interplay between Geraint Evans and herself gave a splendid foretaste of the delights in store for the coming season when they were to appear together in Donizetti's *Elisir d'Amore*, one of the happiest of all operas, beautifully produced by John Copley with very imaginative decor by Beni Montresor. The general standard of opera performance throughout was gratifyingly high, and the same can truthfully be claimed for the work of the Royal Ballet, although in terms of new productions 1973/4 was not rich.

So far as I myself was concerned the summer months were a period of pre-paration for my retirement. A proposal was made that my portrait should be painted by Lawrence Gowing, but he either found the setting of the Royal Opera House uncongenial or my features lacking in appeal; so instead I was sculpted by F. E. McWilliam who some years earlier had made a bust of Ninette de Valois. He was commissioned by the Friends of Covent Garden on the pro-posal of their chairman, John Sainsbury, who also organized a Friends' luncheon to say goodbye to me, at which their president Marion Thorpe spoke, as well as beloved Ninette de Valois, and to my agreeable surprise Tito Gobbi, the greatest of the great among opera singers.

The McWilliam bust was in fact unveiled in the Crush Bar at Covent Garden in the presence of Her Majesty The Queen on the occasion of the Royal Opera House Benevolent Fund Gala which, since each year it had to be tied to some special happening, it was decided in 1974 should be related to my retirement. From the moment that I had started these galas in 1961 they had always been honoured by the presence of the Queen Mother: and in giving her approval to the plan for the 1974 gala she told me that it was her intention to invite the Queen and Prince Philip to accompany her, as well as Princess Margaret. Knowing that I should be required to make a speech from the stage at the end of the evening I found the prospect of such an august array distinctly alarming. I had thought beforehand that to stand quite alone on the stage would be alto-gether too daunting and I therefore asked Jennie Lee, the first ever Minister for the Arts, who had given me such support, whether she would introduce me, to which she most kindly agreed.

John Tooley devised the programme in consultation with Fred Ashton. It was in three parts, opening and closing with opera, with a ballet section in the middle. The opera excerpts were conducted by Colin Davis and Georg Solti, who returned to London specially. The programme opened with the drinking scene from Act I of *La Traviata* conducted by Colin Davis, with the irresistible Ileana Cotrubas as Violetta, and the chorus raising their glasses towards the Royal Box, where we were seated, as they sang a toast. In the ballet section the girls of the *corps de ballet* stole the show with the Entry of the Shades from *La Bayadère*, a great test for them, and Nureyev's most important contribution to the repertoire. The final opera section opened with the Entry of the Matadors from *Carmen*, and again the chorus were asked to hail the Royal Box rather than the procession on the stage. To end the programme Solti conducted the trio and closing scene from *Der Rosenkavalier*, giving me a large lump in the throat. Supervision of the general presentation was in the hands of Fred Ashton and Bill Bundy, the technical administrator, who had charge of every-thing to do with the stage. When the curtains fell I was required to go on to the stage and stand at the top of the flight of steps with my back towards the auditorium, a long white gauze was lowered to hide me, and a brilliant spotlight was directed at me from the back of the stage. I questioned having to stand facing what I thought was the wrong way, but Bill Bundy said, 'You must remember that you are in the hands of the professionals now.' The purpose of the gauze was to present my silhouette to the audience, and it seems that to get a proper silhouette one must be turned away. I duly obeyed. When the curtains rose again, the audience saw a far larger than life-size outline of myself, feeling peculiarly sheepish. I was told to count six, and then turn round and descend the flight of steps as the white gauze against which I had been silhouetted was raised. The effect achieved by the professionals drew a suitable round of applause, and at that moment I beckoned from the wings on one side Jennie Lee, resplendent in gold, and on the other my successor, Claus Moser. Claus made a short and very kind opening statement, and then Jennie went into action, splendidly over-generous about myself, and launching fervently into one of her pet themes, the importance of promoting standards of excellence. Being a great orator, she was slightly carried away, and for the time of night her speech was a little long. When it was my turn I opened by saying, 'After Jennie's speech I really have to tear mine up,' whereupon there was a round of applause from the amphi-theatre, which gave me the opportunity of earning a laugh in saying, 'I'm not sure if I altogether like that applause – you should have been groaning.' I tried to say one or two serious things without being too pompous, and then I embarked on a series of thank yous to people who had helped me while I had been at Covent Garden, starting by saying what an honour and pleasure it was for me that the Queen and Prince Philip were present, and going on unpre-meditatedly, 'I'd love to think that they'd both make it a bit of a habit of coming here regularly,' which was very well received by the audience, so much so that I was prompted by some inner demon to say, 'I'm quite sure that my successor would see to it that the programmes were short and absolutely to their liking.' Mercifully Her Majesty did not send for me afterwards and have me thrown into the Tower of London; and I can only pray that I did not offend too deeply.

Then I came to the Queen Mother, 'our Patron in all but name', and in thank-ing her and saying that wherever she trod she spread light, having helped to spread light materially at Covent Garden through her contribution towards the cost of the third row of candelabra, I arranged for a small *coup de théâtre* by agreeing with Bill Bundy that when I said 'Hey presto' the third row of lights would be switched on.

Of Princess Margaret, the President of the Royal Ballet, I said that she too was a queen, the queen of the dance, so that we had three queens present; and indeed no one is more diligent than she in attending performances of ballet, classical or modern, wherever they may take place.

At the end of the speeches, there was a party on the stage attended by many members of the opera and ballet companies, and of the Royal Opera House staff. The next day I had a strange sense of emptiness and of wondering whether the kind things said were in any sense justified and what really would have been different had I had no connection with Covent Garden. And then I thought back to a long letter which I received from Isaiah Berlin in 1970, of which I quote a considerable part. Isaiah was a constant presence throughout my association with Covent Garden even when he was off the board (he came back in 1974 before I retired). His letter was written shortly before David Webster's retirement, and when we were awaiting the hoped-for partnership of Colin Davis and Peter Hall. These are extracts from what he said:

You ask me what I think all right about Covent Garden? You know perfectly well that the business of Committees such as ours is to goad the enterprise on to greater and greater heights. No doubt praise where praise is due is right, and it is ungenerous and wicked to refuse it: but the danger of complacency is far greater than that of excessive self-criticism – let the critics praise, let the public flock, let the artists express delight, let the Friends of Covent Garden display passionate loyalty, but the Board and the Committees must go on nagging and nibbling if they really do see something to nag and nibble at, and not be accused of carping and destructive criticism if they do. The older Covent Garden from which you as much as, and indeed, more than anyone else rescued us, was guilty of precisely that. What is right about Covent Garden is that (a) there are now very few really bad performances, (b) that we achieve heights, from time to time, that no other Opera House, on the whole, can out-climb: the original *Don Carlos* comes first, of course, and after that come such affairs as the original Sutherland *Lucia; Cav and Pag*; an excellent *Ring*, which I have sat through one and a half times with mounting admiration, if not pleasure; a matchless *splendid Tosca* with Callas, a good *Trovatore*, *Otello, Parsifal, Grimes*; a splendid *Wozzeck*; a very, very good *Billy Budd*, and a sensational *Moses & Aaron*, which, like *Carlos*, was a world event of the first significance, and so recognised by everybody. We have absolutely nothing to be ashamed of, indeed, the reputation of Covent Garden has shot up, as well you know, since those difficult and ill-attended, rightly attacked, early patriotic days. I think the brio has slightly gone out of our general condition, partly I think because of our very success: the Board is full of friends all of whom are fond of one another, like the staff and the Opera House, and the Administration, and we are all very happy and are doing perfectly well, save that an occasional injection of a strongly critical voice or two – Walter Legge did us no end of good I may say – helps.

What is chiefly wrong is that the Administration, in particular David (Webster), are insufficiently prepared to accept the no doubt sometimes idiotic but often valid opinions of the Board members, when they are not satisfied. They tend to sulk about this; but we ought to be the first to point to flaws – the feeling that it is caddish or unjust to harass a sorely tried and very worthy body of workers who are doing their best, is in the best British tradition, but not good for art. Never will I forget a moment in the Box when Ava criticized some dancer or other after a ballet, and the late Viscount Waverley said sternly to her: 'Don't crab them, Ava, they are doing their best.' There is a bit of that about us still: an effort to congratulate ourselves whenever this is at all possible. The two most just voices on the Board seem to me those of Burnet (Pavitt) and Claus (Moser). I sometimes disagree with them, but it seems to me that they are least affected by extraneous motives: Burnet is sometimes too nice to voice the objections that he deeply feels: but when he talks to one in private his opinions seem to me to be as penetrating and as un-biased as anybody's that I have ever met. Your tendency, if I may say this with the deepest respect, is at times a certain impatience of criticism in virtue of your acute sense of personal responsibility for the whole thing; one of mine is a narrowness of taste and an excessive passion for the beauty of the human voice at the expense of acting, decor, the personality of singers, human frailty, money, etc. We could go through most of the Board in this way; but on the whole, they need gadfly-like rather than punkah-like activity. If the critics are reasonably satisfied and the public does not abandon us, we tend to call it a day. The balance between purveyors and critical amateurs is hard to draw, nevertheless I think that a little more ferocity is occasionally called for. And although I admit I am an unabashed canary fancier, I have a feeling that our new management are a little too contemptuous of that; the contemporary search for contemporary 'relevance' in an art form which has not proved very amenable to this kind of treatment, makes me a trifle nervous. Still, we are all aged men, and it may be that Peter Hall and Colin are right. They must be given a free run without chivvying from us, I suppose. This contradicts my earlier remarks, but this is an exceptional situation, and if still alive, I shall write you another letter in 1972, about whether some Old Turk* action may not be required.

(c) On the credit side, and very heavily, we must place the fact that there is very little intrigue, that artists are not exposed to the horrors of La Scala or even New York, and that the general atmosphere is decent, friendly and absolutely OK so far as I know. Conductors love Covent Garden.

(d) On the credit side also is the fact that the British company and the singers we have trained have risen far beyond the hopes of realists, even fifteen years ago. If you think where we were musically at any time in the twentieth century, so far as singers were concerned, and compare that with the fact that there is today a highly respected resident company at whom foreign Opera Houses cast eyes – when the history of these years comes to be written not even the most biased critic will be able to attribute this mainly to the early post-war period, but to the subsequent dozen years.

(e) On the debit side we must place the fact that we don't search for singers with sufficient zeal: we don't find out about marvellous new young singers in Italy or Peru or Sweden as early as we might – Glyndebourne in that respect, sometimes does better, I do not know how, but they do. I think that even members of the Board could be

* In the early days of our association Isaiah used to refer to some of us as the Young Turks, meaning those who wanted to bring about a new order of things.

stimulated to roam Europe and report on what they hear – is this an absurd suggestion? Tooley is probably too busy to go about much, but he ought to have young men circulating and be in touch with our younger critics who do dash about, and with those people who write quite interesting special correspondents' reports in *The Times* and elsewhere about out of the way Festivals and the like.

(f) The real point is that Covent Garden has become an absolutely central part of London and indeed British culture as much as, and I think, rather more than, the National Theatre, and in that sense is quite unique; which it hasn't been since before the war. It is as intrinsic and traditional and national as the B.B.C. and that would not have happened without – as you very well know and do not need me to tell you although I do so with the greatest of pleasure – your administration. Long may you flourish.

Yours ever,
Isaiah

When I received this letter, it did my morale a power of good, and it continues to do so whenever I re-read it. There are I know plenty of people who think that a board of directors is a totally unnecessary excrescence. Not unnaturally I am not among them. I agree with Isaiah that what is needed is a group of people, unpaid it should be made clear, who go on 'nagging and nibbling' in an effort to correct faults, to prevent complacency from creeping in, to anticipate criticism, to sense trends, and to do it all in a helpful and friendly way, designed to ensure that public money is being properly spent, endeavouring to promote the efficiency of the administration and to assist the artistic direction. Without a board of directors, what is there to help and guide those in charge of the running of the theatre? There is nothing but the Arts Council, which has dozens of recipients of grants to supervise and is simply not in a position to give the sort of detailed attention needed. I do not say this in any disparaging sense. On the contrary, I regard the Arts Council as performing an essential function as a buffer between Whitehall and the various artistic enterprises and doing so with as much skill as they can within the limitations imposed on them by lack of adequate finance. And if they are unable to give detailed attention to all their clients, this was not so in the case of Covent Garden, which receives the largest single grant. Their music director John Cruft, and before him John Denison, was invariably present at meetings of the board, and they either attended or were represented at all committee meetings. They came basically as assessors, but they always gave advice if asked to do so, and they were most helpful in sounding a note of caution whenever they thought it called for. I used sometimes to get angry if their attitude seemed to me to be negative, but I had to recognize that shortage of funds weighed upon them constantly, and I have no doubt that to the limit of their ability they wholeheartedly supported Covent Garden.

What then of the Continent, where to the best of my knowledge there is nothing comparable to the Arts Council? Usually there is simply an Intendant in charge of the opera house, reporting direct to a Minister of Culture, who is a politician with all that that implies, liable at any moment to change, and having a multiplicity of other problems to contend with, so that either the Intendant has far more power than is desirable or he finds himself enmeshed in a lot of bureaucratic red tape. One almost certain consequence is, I believe, that much greater extravagance ensues, and this is borne out by the relative size of the grants received by most of the leading opera houses abroad, putting Covent Garden's grant well and truly into the shade.

If Covent Garden's grant does seem large it is only because it is greater in amount than that of any other subsidized theatre in Britain, yet in relation to what Covent Garden undertakes with *two* ballet companies in addition to its opera company the subsidy is modest. Those who grumble about the level of the grant do so essentially because of prejudice. 'The *Royal* Opera House? Must be élitist, and therefore *ipso facto* no good!' No one, well hardly anyone, grumbles about the level of the grant of the National Theatre, or indeed of the English National (formerly Sadler's Wells) Opera at the Coliseum, although in both cases the grant is very large in absolute terms and far larger as a proportion of their total expenditure than is the case with Covent Garden; and what is more they receive substantial sums of money from the Greater London Council, whereas hitherto, to the shame of the GLC, Covent Garden has received nothing.

There are people who ask why opera (and to a lesser extent ballet) is so costly to present. The first point to establish is that as a percentage of the total expenditure the money spent on new productions in the course of a year is relatively very low, not even 5 per cent; while in recent times much of their cost has been financed with the help of private sponsorship. The bulk of the money goes on wages and salaries, and fees to performing artists. If there were no new productions the grant would have to be virtually as large, perhaps even larger, for box office receipts would suffer badly, and the place would gradually atrophy. Were it possible to present one popular opera, say *La Bohème*, and one popular ballet, say *Swan Lake*, and run them on alternate evenings throughout the season then costs would drop dramatically; but few people would think that that was what Covent Garden existed for. During the course of twelve months Covent Garden in fact presents about twenty-four different operas, and a much greater number of ballets. Diversity is a vital ingredient for its success; and one role of the board of directors has always been to ensure that there is a proper balance in the fare provided.

In the case of Covent Garden, where opera and ballet of high international quality is presented, two significant factors have operated to push up costs. First of all there has been the calamitous fall in the value of the pound, a trend only reversed in the second half of 1977, which has meant that without any increase in the demands of foreign artists in terms of their own currency (and also British artists who are resident abroad) they have cost us much more. Secondly, there has been a world-wide discovery of the pleasures to be derived from great singing and conducting, and also great dancing, although the interchangeability of dancers is far less than that of singers because in the world of ballet there is relatively so little common repertoire. It would be unnatural if artists' agents were unaware of the trend. The result of this discovery has of course been that fees have risen, in some cases quite frighteningly. Occasional efforts have been made to get the leading opera houses to present a united front in the face of unjustified demands; but where particular singers are universally sought after these efforts can achieve little. Questions of repertoire and of casting are of course left to the administration and the artistic direction, but the plans are all submitted to the board of directors, and there have been plenty of instances where their views have been listened to to good purpose, as well as instances where they have been ignored with sad effects.

What matters in choosing board members above all is to select people who mind passionately about the work of the house, who can cover a broad range in their interests, who can find time to attend meetings and also performances, and who will not only uphold the administration but register their dissent in no uncertain terms if they think that a mistake is in prospect. I know that in the main those I invited to join me on the board lived up to these ideals. I certainly tried to do so, for I counted myself extremely fortunate to have been elected to such a responsible and privileged position as chairman of Covent Garden. Looking again at what I have written about the Opera House, I fear that I may be thought by some to have begged the question whether it matters that Covent Garden should have a high standing in the eyes of the world. But it must be self-evident that I do believe it to be one of the most important features of our cultural life, playing a significant part in drawing people to London. There are those who say that opera and ballet are not important art forms and that the annual grant is money wasted. These people are unfortunately impervious to argument, refusing to accept the evidence there for them to see if only they would look. To me it matters greatly that Covent Garden should be the home of what is perhaps the most famous ballet company in the world, with a diverse repertoire and very high standards of dancing, and of an opera company whose general level of excellence is so widely acclaimed and which in the opinion of many experts is perhaps more consistent in quality than anywhere else overseas.

After my retirement one really delightful thing happened which gave me infinite pleasure. Two very dear friends of mine whom I had known for many years, Joan Aly Khan and Ann Fleming, joined together in inviting other friends and close acquaintances who had come to Covent Garden as guests of Joan and myself to contribute towards a 'leaving present' for us; and as a result we received a splendid colour television set and what by now has become an indispensable video-cassette recording machine. Their spontaneous act of kindness touched me deeply. To have been able to give enjoyment as I had through the mere accident of my position as chairman was more than sufficient reward in itself. And there were certainly plenty of evenings where the element of duty predominated over pleasure!

Happily for me, although I had left the board of Covent Garden, I continued to be and to feel closely associated. From the moment of taking over from me Claus Moser used to consult with me regularly, which I greatly appreciated. In addition Claus and other colleagues on the board invited Joan and myself to attend performances quite regularly. I have already related that Claus asked me to become chairman with him of the Development Appeal Committee, a major challenge for both of us. I have become chairman of the Royal Ballet School in succession to Joe Lockwood, whom I have known in various guises for many years, notably as head of EMI, and who has always acted as a breath of fresh air wherever he is active. My involvement with the Friends and with the Royal Opera House Trust will persist. And all in all Covent Garden is destined to remain in my bloodstream until I die.

PART FOUR

Coda

Chapter 25

Nine months after giving up the chairmanship of Covent Garden I was destined to retire from the *FT*. At the end of 1970 Lionel Robbins had retired from the post of chairman on reaching his 72nd birthday, and I had been asked to succeed him, handing over the position of managing director to Alan Hare. I requested that I should be regarded as chief executive in order that in the unlikely event of a disagreement between us I should have the final say. But during the time that I was managing director and he was general manager we had each developed our own particular spheres of activity so that things fell naturally into place, and no difference arose, at any rate none of any significance that I can recall. On all important issues we usually saw matters in the same light. One change was that we no longer both went to meetings of the NPA as we had done when I was its chairman and Alan used to attend as spokesman for the *FT*. After I gave up being managing director I stopped going to the NPA unless there was some major crisis, in which case we would probably both attend. I did everything in my power to leave the day-to-day running of things to him, although, having had the responsibility for running the business as it grew from its relatively small beginnings in 1945, and being rather bossy by nature, it was inevitable that on occasion I had an irresistible urge to engage in matters of detail.

In practice of course the chief executive of a wholly owned subsidiary company has singularly little power, because no decisions can be taken without the approval of the parent company. Pat Gibson in fact ran things on a fairly loose rein, and interfered very little, for he was experienced in the newspaper business, and knew how quickly decisions often had to be taken. He also had shrewd and wise judgement. On top of that we at the *FT* were fortunate because it was decided to move the head office of Pearson Longman, our parent company, into Bracken House; and this gave us ready and free access to their small headquarters staff, notably Frank Taylor and later Robert Allan (created Lord Allan of Kilmahew in 1973).

Frank Taylor was the finance director, a Yorkshireman who had developed his career with the Westminster Press Provincial Newspaper group. His mind was a model of clarity and fairness. He was the sort of man who would have been invaluable in Whitehall, knocking sense into ministerial heads. He retired two years after me, and he will be missed.

Bobby Allan had first of all been recruited to our group in 1947 by Brendan Bracken, and like me he was one of Brendan's favourites. He was on the board of the *FT*, but his main duties had to do with the *Investors Chronicle*, which for a while he managed, and also with various aspects of the group's medical publishing interests, notably E. & S. Livingstone, a famous Edinburgh business, of which Bobby became chairman. Brendan had for years wanted to acquire Livingstones, but his ambition was only fulfilled in 1954. It was run by a redoubtable Scot named Charles Macmillan who had started life as an office boy and had made himself a great authority on the medical profession. Apart from the company's name and reputation, Brendan's imagination was particularly captured by their austere rule-book, which might have been drafted by John Knox himself. Bobby entered Parliament as member for South Paddington in 1951. He was given junior ministerial office by Harold Macmillan, but his chief role was as friend and comforter to successive Tory leaders. He was Parliamentary private secretary to Anthony Eden during the painful time of Suez, and held the same position with Harold Macmillan, although the relationship was not quite so close because of Macmillan's deep attachment to John Wyndham (later to become Lord Egremont), who had a special place straddling both Westminster and Whitehall, while being neither a member of Parliament nor a civil servant. Bobby Allan was later appointed treasurer of the Tory Party. He rejoined our group, being seconded for a while at the end of the 1970 election to act as Ted Heath's unofficial chief of staff. The secret of Bobby's appeal to three such very different leaders lay in his unobtrusive effectiveness, his absolute trustworthiness and lack of personal ambition, coupled with an appearance guaranteed to inspire confidence. During the war he had served in the Navy and his features had developed a nautical cut, with eyes clear and straight. Pat Gibson made him deputy chairman of Pearson Longman, and gave him various positions on the book publishing side of the group where his direct, sympathetic and comforting manner was most valuable.

When the matter of my own retirement was first put to me in 1974 I was rather shaken. It was not something I had ever thought of in relation to myself, because I had for so many years been going daily to the office and carrying the main responsibility. I suppose too that I had in mind the case of Lionel Robbins who had only retired when he was seventy-two. It was therefore rather like being forcibly uprooted. Pat asked me to stay on the board of the holding company, Pearson Longman, as a non-executive director, and also of *The Economist*, *Investors Chronicle* and ITF; but when I reached my sixty-fifth birthday in April 1975, he himself became chairman of the *FT* while Alan Hare

added chief executive to his title of managing director. At the end of 1977 John
Cowdray retired from the chairmanship of S. Pearson and Son, the top company of the group, and Pat, who was already deputy chairman, succeeded him;
while Alan was given the chairmanship of the *FT* as well as remaining chief
executive of the company, the changes all seeming to happen with surprising
rapidity.

As to myself, several activities mercifully emerged to help fill the vacuum
created by my departure from the *FT* and Covent Garden. In his capacity of
chairman of the Arts Council Pat asked me to take on two appointments, the
presidency of the Contemporary Dance Trust, and the chairmanship of Youth
and Music. Both assignments opened up new vistas for me.

The Contemporary Dance Trust was the brainchild of Robin Howard, an
Old Etonian of imposing appearance and great independence of thought, a
bachelor with a certain amount of money which he devoted to the creation in
Britain of a school of dance and a dance company based on the ideas and techniques of Martha Graham, the queen of modern dance in the United States.
His personal drive and impetus have been matched by the creative talent of his
most engaging artistic director, Robert Cohan, an American dancer and
choreographer who before he came to Britain was a member of Martha
Graham's company. Together these two men have made The Place, as the
headquarters of the Contemporary Dance Trust is known, a significant force
in the artistic life of London.

When I became president there was a chairman named Gabriel Harrison who
was engaged in the property business; but he had to undergo an operation,
suffered an embolism, and died abruptly, barely fifty years old. No successor
was appointed, Robin acting as chairman, and I myself doing what I could to
help him. After Harrison's death a large building at the back of The Place
became vacant, and the possibility arose of acquiring the freehold both of it and
of The Place itself. The opportunity could not be missed. Robin sold his valuable
collection of books, his attitude being that the Contemporary Dance company
was his true family for which he happily parted with his possessions. His self-
less gesture largely covered the cost of the freehold. However, there remains the
problem of adapting the new building and modernizing the old premises, and
for this an appeal for funds is taking place. I pray that it will succeed.

Youth and Music is the creation of another remarkable man, Sir Robert
Mayer, who came to Britain from Mannheim early in the century, prospered
in the metal business, retired when he was forty-five years old, and decided to
dedicate the rest of his life to promoting the enjoyment of music among the
young. The work of Youth and Music consists in the main in subsidizing
concert, opera and ballet seat prices for young people, but other forms of

stimulating interest are also pursued. When I was asked to become chairman Robert was ninety-five. I said that so long as he was alive the most I could do would be to act as co-chairman with him, and this proposal was accepted. Lois Sieff was a member of the board. She and I thought that it would be a good idea to arrange a concert to celebrate Robert's ninety-sixth birthday, asking ninety-six companies or individuals each to contribute £100 for one year of his life; and thus we raised a tidy sum to augment Youth and Music's meagre resources. Not much arm twisting was required, because the name of Robert Mayer has real charisma; and no wonder, for he is endowed with infinite charm, and despite his great age he is in full possession of pretty well all his faculties and brimming over with fun. We did not hold a concert in 1976, but I thought that it would be fitting to hold one in 1977, not with a view to fund-raising but because his birthday fell right in the middle of the Queen's Silver Jubilee celebrations, so that it gave Youth and Music the opportunity to do double honour. By the time this book is published Robert will be in his hundredth year, and the fifth of June 1979 is his red letter day.

I had a particular interest in the Silver Jubilee because I was chosen as chairman of the London Celebrations Committee. This arose by pure chance in the autumn of 1975 after the *Evening Standard* had carried on its front page a letter from Illtyd Harrington, a Welshman of great originality who was at the time deputy leader of the Greater London Council, although he wrote in his personal capacity. His object was to remind people that 1977 was looming up, and The Queen's Silver Jubilee would offer London a chance to shake off its gloom and rejoice. Charles Wintour, one of the most enlightened figures in Fleet Street, who was at the time editor of the *Evening Standard*, arranged a luncheon to which he invited a handful of people representing some of the interests most likely to be concerned, throwing in for good measure two others who had no special reason for being present, the versatile publisher George Weidenfeld and myself. I undertook to act as chairman for the duration of the lunch, but without any further commitment, beyond agreeing that we should meet again in a few weeks' time.

I did in fact have one particular personal reason for welcoming an opportunity of becoming involved. This was that in the spring of 1972 I had received a letter from the Queen's principal private secretary saying that he had it 'in command' to inform me that it was Her Majesty's wish to appoint me a Knight of the Garter. His letter reached me on 1 April, when I happened to be feeling low in spirits, and my immediate reaction was that it must be some kind of leg-pull, for I could not think what I had done to justify the conferment of this high honour. However, I recalled that Lord Melbourne was supposed to have said of the Order of the Garter that there was 'no damn merit about it', which made me reflect that the letter might conceivably be seriously intended, although I took the precaution of ringing up Michael Adeane to make quite sure. Two other Knights had been appointed at the same time as myself, Evelyn Baring, Lord Howick, who had been Governor-General of Rhodesia, and Hervey Rhodes, a Labour peer, who had started work in a textile mill at the age of fourteen, had been wounded in the Flying Corps during the first war, and after the war had built up his own business, becoming a Member of Parliament and then Lord Lieutenant of Lancaster. I remember him saying to me in his Yorkshire accent, while we were donning the splendid raiment before the service, 'D'you think we'll be the last?', which since the summer of 1972 was one of serious discontent seemed all too possible. After the awesome service, Gerald Templer, one of my sponsoring Knights, came up to me and said, 'I suppose you feel very virtuous now!' I replied, 'I certainly should,' to which he comfortingly observed, 'You'll find it wears off,' as of course it must do.

I nevertheless felt a strong obligation to do something to express my sense of gratitude, and I was therefore anxious that Charles Wintour's initiative should be followed properly through. After the first luncheon, soundings were taken in Westminster and Whitehall, and I saw Martin Charteris, who had followed Michael Adeane as principal private secretary to the Queen; (in both cases no monarch was ever better served). A second luncheon was held, by which time we had established that the amount of public money to be spent in connection with the Silver Jubilee would be very small, and Roy Jenkins, then Home Secretary, had announced in Parliament: 'The Government are considering how the occasion might most appropriately be marked in compliance with the Queen's express wish that undue public expenditure should be avoided.' This made it obvious that if there were to be a real display of rejoicing it would have to be done with private funds. I thought that this should be possible, and that something worthwhile could be achieved, providing that we were able to obtain the active encouragement of the GLC and of the London Boroughs. I knew that many of the county councillors lacked enthusiasm for the Monarchy, and there was one in a key position, I was told, who whenever he saw a picture of the Queen would turn its face to the wall. The director-general of the GLC, Sir James Swaffield, a very adroit man, was at the Wintour luncheons and it was clear that he was an enthusiast for our cause. Through him I saw the leader of the GLC, Sir Reg Goodwin, who made sympathetic noises, while leaving me in no doubt that County Hall funds would not be made available. I therefore had to seek for an honorary treasurer who could engage actively in fund-raising. Initially I approached John Sainsbury, whom I knew well from my Covent Garden days, and whom I had little conscience in approaching since at the end of 1974 he and David Harlech had persuaded me to be chairman of a committee to raise funds for the Britain in Europe referendum campaign. John was too heavily committed with his family business, however, and accordingly I turned to Jeffrey Sterling. He had served on the Britain in Europe committee, and I knew from my experience then that he was a true entrepreneur, energetic, resourceful and persistent. He accepted my invitation, and went further because he also agreed to become my deputy chairman and helpfully offered office accommodation for the small planning staff which we needed to recruit.

The referendum campaign, let me say in passing, was a heart-warming experience. As chairman of the finance committee I attended meetings of the policy forming group which was presided over by Roy Jenkins. It pleased me to see some of the most temperate and balanced leaders of the three main parties sitting round the table and agreeing together on common courses of action. I could not help regretting that something like it could not persist; for they were the people occupying what David Watt always referred to as the middle ground, those with whom I always felt myself most in sympathy.

In any event, at the time of the referendum campaign Jeffrey Sterling gave me much help, and I was therefore delighted to have him as my deputy on the London Celebrations Committee for the Queen's Silver Jubilee. We assembled a large committee, with members drawn from many branches of activity, including religious leaders headed by the Bishop of London and the Chief Rabbi, the House of Commons (with a representative from the two main parties), the army, the police, the arts, sport, the media, the river, the GLC, the City of London, and the London Boroughs Association. The Silver Jubilee Appeal Trust were regularly represented because one of the difficulties with which we had to contend in raising funds for our modest efforts was the fact that a massive charitable appeal was being launched – the Prince of Wales's Appeal on behalf of the Queen's Silver Jubilee Trust – and confusion arose in the minds of some of the companies we approached who thought that they were being asked to contribute twice to the same thing. Fortunately we had started to make our approaches before Prince Charles's appeal got under way, otherwise there would have been precious little in the way of celebrations to enjoy; and as it was, the sum we raised was only a tiny fraction of the figure achieved by those in charge of his appeal.

The Prime Minister made a statement in the House of Commons in the course of which he gave us an encouraging pat on the back. I kept him informed of our plans; and because I thought it essential to see the maximum number of buildings floodlit, especially along the river, I appealed to him for support. So many of the buildings were in Government hands that by ourselves our committee could achieve very little. Jim Callaghan responded enthusiastically, and the Thames by night became a fairyland. And since, now that the equipment is installed, the cost of the actual current used is very low, it would be folly not to repeat the display regularly each summer.

The work of our main celebrations committee was broken down into a series of groups, and I appointed chairmen to the different working committees. The principal people who agreed to help were Bernard Delfont, impresario extraordinary, who made himself responsible for the so-called popular events; and John Denison, who was on the point of retiring from running the Royal Festival Hall complex, and who undertook to supervise the cultural side, that is to say music, theatre, opera, ballet and exhibitions, an enormous programme. For sport we recruited Jimmy Hill, although in the main the work of planning the various sporting events was undertaken by Boris Garside and Roger Bottomley of the Sports Council. William Bowey of the Port of London Authority gave tremendous impetus to a whole series of river events. Max Nicholson, a well known environmentalist and naturalist, who had been closely involved with the 1951 Festival of Britain, took charge of the environmental committee, recruiting to it Hugh Casson, the most engaging of all Presidents of the Royal Academy, Misha Black, a brilliant industrial designer, and others; and collectively they instigated a large number of 'improvements', leaving one hopes some lasting impression. Finally, Charles Wintour, who had really instigated the whole thing, formed a committee to co-ordinate all matters concerning what are most horribly referred to as the media, stimulating competitions, assisting with publicity and so on; and few would disagree that they worked to very good effect. To tie it all together we appointed as honorary secretary-general a semi-retired diplomat, Sir Paul Wright, who, whatever we needed, always seemed to know the right person in the right place. Aided by a tiny staff he did a remarkable job.

There were not many events that we ourselves sponsored, but we made financial contributions towards the cost of a very large number of happenings, incorporating them into a programme of events which we published and put on sale. We also made a kind of pump-priming grant to each of the thirty-two London Boroughs, as well as to the City, which was not too proud to accept our £1,000; and we recruited an invaluable young man, Tom Petzal, whose job it was to go round the boroughs and urge them to help and encourage local manifestations of loyalty, even the most republican of councillors finding him hard to withstand.

An early decision that we made was to have our London emblem and flag. It was designed by a design consultant named Professor Richard Guyatt of the Royal College of Art, and flags were manufactured for us on a considerable scale. We had fearful difficulty getting them delivered on time because flags in general were greatly in demand; but by mid-summer our banner was flying over a large number of buildings, and I think that it assisted London's adorn-ment. In my subjective view it had a good deal more distinction than the official decorations, which were pretty meagre and shoddy.

The actual date of the Queen's accession to the throne was 8 February 1952. As it was planned that she should visit Australasia in February and March I suggested that before her departure she should undertake a symbolical planting of a tree to mark the 25th aniversary of her accession. I engaged in considerable discussion about a suitable location. The site finally chosen was in the gardens to the south of the Houses of Parliament. For the most suitable tree I thought it right to consult Harold Hillier, the greatest nurseryman in Britain. The result was that on 9 February the Queen planted a handsome Lucombe Oak, supplied by Hilliers of Winchester, in a situation where the tree has ample space to spread its branches, and very fine it will grow to look behind its green slate plaque.

As to the celebrations, there were two major events where we took the initi-ative, and the Queen herself agreed to attend, accompanied by nearly all the other members of the Royal Family. These were a grand gala at Covent Garden, and a mammoth fireworks display.

It would have been unnatural if I had not pressed for a gala at Covent Garden, and wrong if there had not been one. While it was not an official function, the hosts being Claus Moser and myself, we were clearly obliged to invite a number of official guests, although the bulk of the seats were sold to the public at prices ranging from £1 to £25. The whole of the centre of the grand tier was removed, with the space converted to one large Royal Box in which the Queen, Prince Philip and the rest of the Royal Family were seated. It was agreed that there should be an hour of opera and an hour of ballet, with one long interval. The production was supervised by Frederick Ashton and John Copley. The evening as a whole was generally judged a success, but I regretted Covent Garden's decision to end the opera section with the closing scene from *Fidelio* which was too long and disappointingly sung; while their idea of having the dances from *Gloriana* re-choreographed as part of the ballet section thoroughly misfired. At the end, rather than formal presentations, the Queen and her family went on to the stage to meet the artists and technical staff, and in a way that was the most pleasing part of the evening. One of those singing in the opera section was Boris Christoff, who sang a famous aria from *Don Carlos*. Sitting beside the Queen I reminded her that some years previously she had agreed to come to hear Christoff in *Boris Godunov*, my inducement having been that his death scene was memor-able, overlooking the fact that it took over three hours to get there: and with that irresistible smile of hers Her Majesty replied, 'I shall never forget it!' The BBC televised the entire evening live, including the arrival of the Royal Party, and the visit backstage afterwards; and the programme was transmitted to the

United States as well as to many other countries, giving much pleasure to most of those who saw it.

In the case of the fireworks it seemed to me that three things mattered. First, the River Thames must form part of the setting; second, it must be possible for large numbers of people to enjoy the display; and third, I thought it would appeal to the Queen if she could watch from a high place rather than from ground level so as to have a panoramic view all round London. I therefore arranged to take Martin Charteris to the 30th floor of the Vickers building in Millbank where Lord Robens held sway. Unfortunately the weather was atrocious and there was a visibility of about one yard, so that no decision could be reached. This was perhaps as well because further consideration of the surroundings made me feel that the Shell Building on the other side of the river, with a panoramic view embracing the Houses of Parliament, Whitehall and Somerset House, and a great curve of the Thames, would be more suitable. I knew too what extraordinary amenities the building possessed. Therefore I asked David Barran to discover from his colleagues whether they would be agreeable to a proposal that the Queen should view the fireworks display from the top floor of their building. To this they readily agreed, and so I went one lovely spring day with Martin Charteris to survey the scene, the upshot being that we were able to start to prepare plans.

The chief problem was who should mount the display; and here I was very lucky because the ever resourceful Jacob Rothschild had told me of a clergyman who had recently undertaken a display for a cousin of his with conspicuous success. Thus I came into contact with the Reverend Ronald Lancaster, a chaplain at a boys school in Norfolk, whose hobby was fireworks and whose assured manner gave me an immediate sense of confidence. He brought with him the head of the well-known firm of Pains-Wessex, and we began the work of planning. I urged upon them above all that it must be the finest display of fireworks ever seen in London. Secondly, I suggested that the artist John Piper should be asked to be a kind of artistic consultant, since I knew he had experience in this field, and I thought too of his Coventry Cathedral stained-glass window achievement. Third, I asked that there should be some kind of musical accompaniment for the benefit of people watching the display. (In the event John Piper personally compiled a tape of musical excerpts which was transmitted through loudspeakers.) Fourth, I conceived the idea of there being a sort of diadem of light, with fireworks sent up not simply in front of the Shell building, but also in smaller displays from the four points of the compass around London, so that there might be a very large audience and the Queen could see the sky ablaze. Everything worked out as I wished, except that on 9 June, the chosen day, the weather was quite awful; and, although the rain stopped in time, visibility was too poor for her to be able to see more than the one main display. That display, however, really was magnificent, both lavish and beautiful, *and* cheap (only some £20,000) in relation to the millions of people who viewed it, for the fireworks were televised live both at home and also world-wide. At the end the Queen and her family returned to Buckingham Palace in a horse-drawn carriage procession, the skies had cleared, and although it was late at night the route was lined with cheering crowds who converged on the Palace to roar their approval when she appeared on the balcony at midnight.

I had experienced something of these crowds when I escorted her to the Shell building before the start of the fireworks. At the beginning of the evening, in driving rain, the Queen had unveiled a plaque inaugurating our Silver Jubilee walkway, and then from County Hall had watched an ill-lit procession of boats, which formed part of the official celebrations and was not the responsibility of my committee. The walk was a few hundred yards long, passing through a new Jubilee garden financed with money raised by Jeffrey Sterling from the Hayward Foundation, with contributions also from Shell and the GLC. I walked slightly behind the Queen, and I felt the full force of the cheering. The noise was deafening, and in a way quite alarming; but all the time the Queen smiled dazzlingly, and I could observe at first hand what was aptly described to me by a member of her entourage as her love affair with the British people. The depth of their affection for her had not previously been displayed so vividly, perhaps because there had never before been such an opportunity; certainly the men of the extreme left, to whom the mere idea of Royalty is anathema, kept very quiet in the summer months.

During the months of planning and preparation, and throughout the period of the celebrations, which extended for a good six months, with the main effort concentrated in June and July, our steering committee met fortnightly, and the large main committee at intervals of two or three months: and in between meetings there was much to be done. If we had not done it, others would surely have stepped forward. Whether they would have been more successful than us can never be known. All I know is that everyone on my committee felt glad to have been able to play a part, and I am sure that they would like to have the opportunity of doing so more often than every twenty-five years. For myself it was not merely my personal sense of obligation. More especially, it was an awareness of the unifying force embodied in the person of the Queen, who happens to be in appearance and example everything that a queen should be.

As the Silver Jubilee celebrations recede, my life resumes its fragmented pattern, with many ties and responsibilities, some new and very interesting, but none ever likely to compare with my two main absorptions, the *FT* and

Covent Garden, with both of which I was for so many years identified, and which complemented one another so marvellously. To have had the opportunity of being simultaneously managing director of the one and chairman of the other is a perfect example of supreme good fortune, and I can only hope that I succeeded in repaying something of what they both gave to me. It is not for me to judge whether I contributed anything of value to either organization, and impossible for me to say to what extent if at all the course of their history would have been in any significant way different had my association with them not occurred. What I *can* say – and I hope that it does not sound insufferably smug – is that I tried hard to guide them both in directions which I believed to be right. There were terrible mistakes and setbacks and disappointments, some of which I have related; but there were also successes of which I feel proud, while recognizing that little credit for them is due to me personally, but rather to the many able and devoted colleagues with whom I worked.

For the rest, I have been supremely lucky in my marriage and in my family, in my health, in the friendships I have made, and in the possibilities I have had for meeting people and visiting places. I have plenty of regrets, and I am all too well aware of opportunities missed, often because of a lack of adequate faith in my own judgement. Had I had the self-assurance, I should have liked to play more part in the political life of the country. But I have always felt inhibited by the possession of a hereditary title; and my failure to attend the House of Lords more regularly was only in part the result of my commitment to the *FT* and to Covent Garden.

As to the uncertain future, I can only pray that Providence will grant that I shall retain my faculties, and stay alive on this earth, with my wife Joan still beside me, until in twenty-two years' time the new millennium arrives. I shall then be on the verge of ninety, still several years younger than my dear colleague Robert Mayer, who more than anyone else possesses the secret of eternal youth and from whom therefore I constantly beg a wave of his magic wand; for I really should rather like to welcome in the New Year on the First of January 2000 AD.

Index

Abdy, Sir Robert, 118, 125
Abdy, Lady Diana, 118
Abdy, Valentine, 118
Aberconway, Lady, 74
Adeane, Lord, 360, 361
Admiralty, 91
Advanced Air Striking Force, 74, 76
Advertiser's Weekly, 164
Aga Khan, H.H. The, 156
Agar, Mrs Herbert, 105
Agar, Herbert, 105
Aherne, Brian, 57
Aida (Verdi), 233
Aitken, Sir Max, 198, 203
Albanian Legation, in London, 52
Albert Hall, 185
Albery, Sir Bronson, 147
Aldeburgh Festival, 271, 282
Aldershot, 79, 80
Aldwick (Bognor), 21
Aldwych Theatre, 173
Alecto, Editions, 169
Aley (Bracken's driver), 160, 161
Alington, Dr Cyril, 18
Allan, Robert (Lord Allan of Kilmahew),
    357, 358
Alloa (Scotland), 28, 29, 30
Alsop, Joseph, 124
Alton (Hampshire), 84
Aly Khan, HH Princess Joan, 353
American Friends of Covent Garden, 299,
    339
American Smelting and Refining Company,
    32
American War Production Board, 91
Amery, The Rt Hon. Julian, 124
Amory, The Rt Hon. Viscount, *see*
    Heathcote-Amory
Anderson, Lady (Ava), (Viscountess
    Waverley), 230, 243, 254, 349
Anderson, Sir John, (Viscount Waverley),
    87, 88, 89, 158, 230; as chairman of
    Covent Garden, 226–31, 236, 237, 240,
    241, 242, 246, 247, 249, 349; death, 254

Anderson, Sir Colin, 219, 258, 262, 286–7,
    289
Andreu, Mariano, 248
Angeles, Victoria de los, 274
Anglesey, The Marchioness of, 35, 59
Anglesey, The Marquess of, 23, 35
Anglo-American co-operation, 91, 98, 99,
    100, 104
Anglo-American relations, 105, 121
Anglo-Persian Oil Company, 128
Annan, Lord, 312
Annenberg, Mrs Walter, 339–40
Apollo (magazine), 168, 169
Apollo Society, 27
Arabella (Richard Strauss), 234, 305, 314, 332
Arborfield (Reading), 74, 75
Arco, Count and Countess, 59
Argus Press, 44
Arias, Tito, 293
Arlen, Stephen, 319, 337
Armenian Circus, 177
Armstrong, Robert, 328
Armstrong, Sir Thomas, 259, 281, 318, 328
Arran, Lord, 231
Arts Council, 250, 254, 255, 258, 260, 268,
    271, 274, 277, 322, 340, 350–1; and Lord
    Gibson as chairman, 147, 203; Charter,
    173, 297; Music Panel, 235; co-ordinated
    policy with British Council, 297; and
    Lord Goodman as chairman, 337; and
    Rt Hon. Kenneth Robinson as chairman,
    338
Ascot Place, 275
Ashby St Ledgers (Near Rugby), 58
Ashcombe House, 67
Ashcroft, Dame Peggy, 27, 106
Ashton, Sir Frederick: *Fille mal gardée*, 244,
    291; *Enigma Variations*, 288, 303, 316;
    Month in the Country, 288, 317; *Les Deux
    Pigeons*, 291; *Ondine*, 293; *Marguerite and
    Armand*, 294; as Dame Ninette de
    Valois's successor, 294–5; *Façade*, 295;
    Swan Lake, 297, 298; *Cinderella*, 298;
    Rake's Progress, 298; *The Dream*, 298;

Monotones I and II, 298; *Symphonic Variations*, 301; *Sylvia*, 301–2; *Jazz Calendar*, 302; retirement, 316–17, 320, 338; contribution to Jubilee gala, 364
Astor of Hever, Lord, 190, 192, 193
Attlee, The Rt Hon. Clement, 88
ATV, 182, 337

Bagrit, Sir Leon, 275–6, 299, 304, 319, 342
Bagrit, Lady, 275
Baillieu, Sir Clive, 90, 92
Baker, Dame Janet, 345
Balanchine, George, *Serenade for Strings*, 298; and the New York City Ballet company, 299
Ballet Rambert, 340
Bangkok, 181
Bank of China, 178
Bank Rate Tribunal, 148
Banker, The (magazine), 44, 65, 151
Banker's Magazine, 44
Barbados, 122
Barber, Lord, formerly Rt Hon. Anthony, MP, 341
Barbirolli, Sir John, 236
Bareau, Paul, 64–5
Baring, Francis, 16, 28–9, 210
Baring, Maurice, 17
Barnetson, Lord, 187, 188
Barry, Edward, 258
Baruch, Bernard M., 57–8
Bax, Sir Arnold, 37
Baylis, Dame Lilian, 262, 295
BBC, 236; Symphony Orchestra, 312, 326
Beardsley, Aubrey, 264
Beaton, Sir Cecil, 67, 294
Beatty, Countess (Dorothy), 76
Beaumarchais, Jacques and Marie Alice de, 125
Beavan, Jennie, 337
Beaverbrook, Lord, 43, 49, 50, 87–9, 90, 105, 133
Beddington-Behrens, Sir Edward, 54, 55, 56, 62
Beck and Pollitzer, 172, 173
Beecham, Sir Thomas, 37, 38, 70, 108, 245, 246, 247, 267, 268, 278, 304; and Royal Philharmonic Orchestra, 304
Beethoven, Ludwig van, 282, 283, 345
Behan, Tim and Bridget, 9
Behrman, Sam, 57
Beilby, Alec, 171
Beit, Sir Alfred and Lady, 115
Belgium, 6, 7, 76
Bell, Clive, 42
Bellini, Vicente, 266
Belvoir Castle, 35, 123

Benenden (Kent), 3
Bennett, Arthur, 167
Bennett, Richard Rodney, 302, 315
Benson, Mrs Rex, 76
Benthall, Michael, 148
Berio, Luciano, 340
Beriosova, Svetlana, 291
Berlin, 72–3, 130, 135, 256
Berlin, Lady, 258
Berlin, Sir Isaiah, OM, 240, 241, 264, 265, 284, 287, 288, 317, 348–50; letter to Georg Solti, 306–7
Berlioz, Hector, 327
Bernales, Claude de, 132
Berners, Lord, 38
Berry family, 54
Berry, Hon. Michael, (Lord Hartwell), 173, 198
Besch, Anthony, 344
Betjeman, Sir John, 263
Betty, Aunt (father's sister), 8, 9
Bevan, The Rt Hon. Aneurin, 307
Bevin, The Rt Hon. Ernest, 87, 88
Biallaid House (Kingussie), 22, 23
Biarritz, 20–1, 78
Biches, Les (Poulenc), 298
Billy Budd (Britten), 230, 315, 348
Bingham, Stanley, 172
Birch, Rt Hon. Nigel (later Lord Rhyl), 34
Bird, Roland, 155, 156, 276
Birkbeck, Winifred, 21
Birkenhead, The Earl of, *see* Smith, F. E.
Birmingham, 175; Chamber of Commerce, 175; Repertory Theatre, 229
Black, Sir Misha, 363
Black, Sheila, 170
Blair, David, 291, 293
Blakenham, The Rt Hon. Viscount, *see* Hare, The Hon. John
Blech, Enid, 283
Blech, Harry, 36
Bliss, Sir Arthur, 240, 259; *The Olympians*, 240
Blore, W. P., 11–12
Board of Inland Revenue, 129
Board of Trade, 104, 114, 116
Boardman, Robert, 175
Bodnant house (North Wales), 74
Bognor Regis, 21, 22
Bohème, La (Puccini), 289, 344, 345, 351
Bolshoi Ballet company, 176, 300; first visit to London, 243–4
Bolshoi Theatre, 176
Bonfield, John, 202
Bonham-Carter, The Hon. Mark, 259, 316, 340
Bon Marché store (Liverpool), 232
Boosey, Leslie, 225, 228, 230

Boothby, The Rt Hon. Lord, 304
Boris Godunov (Moussorgsky), 233, 266, 364
Bottomley, Roger, 363
Boughton House (Northamptonshire), 120
Boulez, Pierre, 314
Boult, Sir Adrian, 301
Bowes-Lyon, The Hon, Sir David and
  Lady, 93, 94
Bowey, William, 363
Brabazon, Sir William, 3
Bracken, Brendan (Viscount), 41, 43–4,
  45–9, 105, 219, 255; as director of *FN*, 43,
  45, 46; extends the 'empire', 44–5;
  peerage, 47; and Churchill, 48; as
  godfather of Lord Drogheda's son, 63;
  and Lombard column in *FN*, 65; note to
  Lord Drogheda in Arborfield, 74; as
  Churchill's PPS, 81; appointed
  Minister of Information, 81, 85, 152;
  moves from Information to Admiralty,
  113; as Chairman of *FT*, 115, 195; as
  Chairman of Union Corporation, 115;
  influence on Hargreaves Parkinson, 128,
  129; 'Men and Matters' column, 128–9,
  131; posthumous bust of, 133; and new
  FT building, 141–4; conflict with Sir
  Oliver Crosthwaite-Eyre, 145–6, 160;
  reply to Drogheda about new job, 150–1;
  illness and death, 160, 161
Bracken House, 144, 153, 165, 169, 191, 220,
  221, 357
Brand, Lord, 94–5
Brand, Leila (Viscountess Hampden), 93, 94,
  103
Brand, Tommy (Viscount Hampden), 93,
  94, 95, 98, 100–1
Brecht, Berthold, *7 Deadly Sins*, 339
Bridges, Alvilde, 25, 26, 28, 30, 33
Bridges, F. W. & Co., 175
Bridges, Lady, 25, 30, 33
Bridges, Lord (formerly Sir Edward), 85, 86,
  87, 96; report, 277
Bridges, Sir Thomas, 30, 33
Brighton, 137
Briginshaw, R. W. (later Lord), 201
Britain in Europe, referendum campaign,
  361, 362
British Aluminium Company, 149
British Council: Charters, 173, 297
British Exhibitions, in Moscow and Peking,
  176–80
British Food Mission, 94
British Institute of Management, 185
British Printing Corporation, 155
British Supply Council, in North America,
  98
Brittan, Sam, 209, 210, 214
Britten, Benjamin, 226, 230, 239, 240, 270,

281, 307, 315, 345, 348; English Opera
  Group, 271
Broackes, Nigel, 155
Brockman, Harold, 219
Brod gallery, 169
Broken Hill (South Australia), 48
Brook, Sir Norman (Lord Normanbrook),
  87
Brook, Peter, 235, 307
Brooks, John, 219
Brooks's Club, 43, 71
Brown, Winthrop, 104
Bruce-Lockhart, Robin, 134
Bruce-Lockhart, Sir Robert, 134
Brussels, 154
Buccleuch, Duke and Duchess of, 120
Bull, George, 136
Bundy, William, 346, 347
BUPA centre, 184
Burgess, Sir John, 187
Burn, Charles Maitland Pelham, 4
Burn, General Harry Pelham (uncle), 22–3
Burn, Jim Pelham (uncle), 23
Burn, Katherine Pelham (aunt), 22
Burn, Kathleen Pelham (mother), 4, 6, 12,
  22; marries father, 5; parts from father, 6,
  9, 12; visits Eton, 14; marries de Landa,
  19; divorces from de Landa, 25;
  daughter's marriage, 51, 52; new
  companion, 52–3, 68; camp follower
  existence, 79–82; death, 189
Burn, Ronald Pelham (cousin), 23
Burnet, Alastair, 154
Burnham, Lord, 196, 198
Bury, John, 307
Bury Farm cottage, 93, 103
Busch, Fritz, 70
buzz-bombs (or V1's), 111

Callaghan, The Rt Hon. James, 362
Callas, Maria, 265–6, 348
Camargo Society, 295
Cambridge, 10, 25, 26, 27–8, 228; Marlowe
  Dramatic Society, 27; King's College, 70,
  312; Appointments Board, 135; Master's
  Lodge at Churchill College, 161
Cameron, Rory, 21, 125
Campbell, Donald, 12
Camrose, Viscount, 49–50, 111, 112, 113,
  196
Canada, 299
Cannes, 21
Cannon Hall, Hampstead, 116–17
Canton, 178
Caraman Chimay, Prince and Princess
  Jean de, 75, 76

Carl Flesch violin competition, 173
Carl Rosa Opera company, 250, 251
Carl Rosa Sadler's Wells, 250–1
Carmen (Bizet), 244, 289, 336–7, 346
Carr, Joan (wife), 54–5; meets Garrett
    Moore, 56; marries Garrett Moore, 56–7;
    ill on honeymoon, 59; son born, 63;
    broadcasting work, 72; visits Berlin with
    husband, 72–3; joins BBC staff, 73, 74;
    Red Cross job in Paris, 76, 78, 252;
    escapes from France to England, 78;
    leaves for America with son, 79; piano
    concerts in New York, 81, 89, 91; goes to
    Washington to meet husband, 92; returns
    with son to England, 93; gives concerts
    in Germany, 135; heart attack, 162; son's
    marriage and divorce, 197–8
Carr, Sir William Emsley, 197
Carrick, Dr David, 165
Casa, Lisa della, 306
Casa Maury, Marques de, 69
Casa Maury, Marquesa de, *see* Dudley
    Ward, Freda
Casson, Sir Hugh, 363
Castlerosse, Viscount, 68, 125
Cattley, Thomas, 13, 14, 15, 16, 17
Cavalleria Rusticana (Mascagni) and
    Pagliacci (Leoncavallo), 273, 274, 348
Cazenove & Co., formerly Cazenove,
    Akroyds & Greenwood, 112, 146
CBI, *see* Confederation of British
    Industry
Cecchetti, Enrico, 261
Cecil, Lord David, 120
CEMA, *see* Council for the Encouragement
    of Music and the Arts
Chamberlain, The Rt Hon. Neville, 72, 74
Chamber Music Society, 36
Chandos, Viscount, *see* Lyttelton, Oliver
Channel Tunnel Company, 125
Channon ('Chips'), Sir Henry, 59–60
Charles, HRH The Prince of Wales, 185,
    276, 320; Jubilee Appeal, 362
Charteris, Lord, formerly Sir Martin, 361,
    365
Chelsea Flower Show, 219–20
Cherrington, John, 167
Chicago, 155; orchestra, 281
Chisholm, Archie, 128, *128*, 138
Chitty, Stella, 283
Chobham, 79
Chopin, Frédéric, 317
Christie, George, 269
Christie, John, 70, 71, 247, 269
Christie's, 153
Christoff, Boris, 248, 263, 364
Churchill, The Hon. Mrs Randolph, 98, 105
Churchill, Randolph, 98

Churchill, The Rt Hon. Sir Winston, OM,
    7, 43, 47, 48, 81, 143, 182, 230; offer of
    joint citizenship with France, 77, 78; Map
    Room and Cabinet War Room, 86; and
    Beaverbrook's appointment as Minister
    of Supply, 87–8, 90; in Washington for
    the Arcadia Conference, 90; and Article
    VII of Lend Lease Agreement, 104;
    Ditchley Park house made available to,
    121
Churchill Club, 105, 106
City Arts Trust, 168, 269
City Center for the Performing Arts (New
    York), 299
City Corporation, 142, 173
City of London, biennial arts festival, 168,
    173
Clark, The Hon. Colette, 287
Clark, Lady, 106–7, 116, 118–19, 227, 262
Clark, Lord, formerly Sir Kenneth, 105,
    106–7, 116, 118–19, 168, 275, 286, 287;
    as member of Covent Garden, 225, 227,
    228; as chairman of the Arts Council, 240
Clarke, Sir Ashley, 265
Clarke, Sir Richard (Otto), 86, 166
Clarke, William, 151
Cleethorpes (Lincolnshire), 79–82, 85–6, 89
Clements, E. H. (Mrs T. S. G. Hunter), 139
Clemenza di Tito, La (Mozart), 344
Cleveland-Belle, Jimmy, 232
Clurman, Richard, 299, 300
Cobham (Surrey), 25, 80, 117
Cochran, C. B., 294
Cohan, Robert, 359
Cohen, Harriet, 37
Coke, Gerald, 269, 270
Coldstream, Sir William, 252, 287
Cole, A. G., 128
Cole, G. D. H., 31
Colefax, Lady, 122
Coliseum, 235, 240, 272, 282, 290, *290*, 319,
    325, 337, 338, 340, 351
Collins, William, & Co., 259
Columbia Gramophone records, 267
Combined Exports Board, 104
Combined Production and Resources
    Board (CPRB), 90, 91, 93, 98
Combined Raw Materials Board, 90
Commercial Union Assurance Company,
    155, 342–3
Common Market, 212, 213, 220
Confederation of British Industry (CBI),
    175, 202, 218
Connoisseur (magazine), 168, 169
Contemporary Dance Company, 359
Contemporary Dance Trust, 359
Cooper, Lady Diana, 124, 274
Cooper, The Rt Hon. A. Duff, 124

Cooper, Martin, 244

Copley, John, 364; *Suor Angelica*, 314; *Cosi fan tutte*, 314; *Orfeo*, 327; *Figaro*, 336; *Don Giovanni*, 336; *La Bohème*, 345

Cork, Kenneth, 269

Coronation Gala Performance Book (1953), 235

Cossotto, Fiorenzo, 226

Costa Smeralda (Sardinia), 155–6

Cotrubas, Ileana, 327, 345, 346

Cotter, E. P. C. (Pat), 171

Cottesloe, Lord, 310

Council for the Encouragement of Music and the Arts (CEMA), 225

Country Life (magazine), 119

Courcel, Geoffroi (Baron) and Martine (Baronne) de, 125

Courtauld-Thomson, Lord, *see* Thomson, Sir Courtauld

Courtaulds, 51

Coutts and Co., 162, 237, 313

Covent Garden (Royal Opera House): Lady Cunard and, 38; Drogheda as secretary to board of directors of, 137, 161, 168, 202, 203, 221, 227; Drogheda acts as chairman of, 158, 254; Opera Trust, 225, 226, 227, 228, 229; converted into Royal Opera House, 225, 239; first financial crisis, 226; Drogheda's first board meeting of, 228–31; opera in English policy, 233, 234, 271; grants (1952 and 1977/8), 237; and Sadler's Wells revenue, 238; integration with Sadler's Wells, 250–1, 262; articles of association, 255, 256; Royal Box occupancy, 256; chairman's term of office, 256, 343; Premium Stalls Scheme launched, 257, 315; auditorium, 258; Arts Council grant, 260, 271, 350–1; Joint Planning Committee, 261; financial aid to, 271–2, 313; annual opera gala, 273, 274; annual ballet gala, 273; Benevolent Fund, 274, 275, 346; lack of rehearsal facilities, 276–7, 279, 285; Sir Colin Anderson's design sub-committee, 287–8, 290; working conditions of orchestra, 304–5; lack of recording possibilities, 304; reconstruction at, 305; Government grant to, 313, 342; improvement of working conditions at, 322–3; development appeal committee, 323; promenade-style performances, 323; language policy, 331–4; Peat Marwick and Mitchell's report on, 337; second auditorium, 340–1; Jubilee grand gala at, 364–5

Covent Garden Properties Ltd., 258

Coventry Cathedral, 143, 365

Cowdray, Viscount, 147, 149, 192, 208, 359

Cox, Alan, 191

Craigweil House (Aldwick), 21

Cranborne house (Dorset), 120

Cranko, John, 302

Craxton, Harold, 55

Crisp, Clement, 339

Critics' Circle, 243

Cross, Joan, 226, 277, 278, 279

Crosthwaite-Eyre, Colonel Jack, 43

Crosthwaite-Eyre, Sir Oliver, 145, 146, 147

Crowther, Lord, 45, 97, 106, 152, 153, 155–6, 208; *An Outline of Money*, 152

Cruft, John, 350

Cudlipp, Lord, 156, 197, 198

Cunard, Lady (Emerald), 37, 38, 70, 106, 108, 118, 295

Cunard, Sir Bache, 37

Cundell, Edric, 237, 259

Curzon Cinema (London), 69

Daily Express, 154

Daily Mail, 202

Daily Mirror, 195, 196, 201

Daily Mirror Group, 195, 197, 198, 200, 203

Daily Telegraph, 50, 64, 111, 112, 168, 170, 190, 195, 215, 244, 304; and Thomson's acquisition of *The Times*, 193, 194

Dalton, The Rt Hon. Hugh, 122, 226, 227, 230, 237

Dartington Hall Summer School of Music, 312–13

Daubeny, Sir Peter, World Theatre Season, 168, 173

Davenport, Nicholas, 44, 66

Davenport, Olga, 66

Davies, Peter Maxwell, 315

Davis, Colin: appointment as Covent Garden musical director, 312, 325–6, 327, 329–31, 344; *Midsummer Marriage*, 315; *Don Giovanni*, 325–6; *Knot Garden*, 327, 330; association with Peter Hall, 326, 327, 329, 330, 331, 332, 333, 335, 344; new *Figaro*, 336; *Nabucco*, 336; collaboration with Götz Friedrich, 344; *Tannhauser*, 345; *La Traviata*, 346

Davison, Hon. Ken, 275, 276, 319

Dawnay Day and Co., 116

Dawnay, Major-General Guy, 116

Dearlove, Leslie, 138, 150

Deauville, 21

Debenham, Gilbert, 34

Debenham, Martin, 35

Debussy, Claude, 301

Decca Ltd, 130, 304, 305

Delfont, Lord, 363

de Liagne, Alfred, 57

de Valois, Ninette, see Valois
Denison, John, 350, 363
Dent, Professor E. J., 228
Deutsch-Englische Gesellschaft, 135
Deux Pigeons, Les (Messager), 291
Development Appeal Committee, 353
Devonshire, Duke of, 273, 274
Diaghilev, Serge, 261, 262, 298; company, 292
Dialogues des Carmélites (Poulenc), 244
Diamond, Lord, 279
Director, The, 136, 184, 186
Ditchley Park (Oxfordshire), 121
Domingo, Placido, 327
Don Carlos (Verdi), 262–4, 266, 270, 327, 348, 364
Don Giovanni (Mozart), 263, 284, 325–6, 333, 336, 345
Don Pasquale (Donizetti), 331–2, 345
Donaldson, Lady (Frances), 178, 260
Donaldson, Lord (Jack), 28, 34, 36, 56, 61, 62, 259–60, 279, 304; becomes Government Minister, 267
Donizetti, Gaetano, 263, 345
Donne, Michael, 167
Dorchester Hotel (London), 52
Dorn, Marion, 53, 62, 106
Dorneywood House, 43
Douglas, The Hon. Lewis, 48–9, 155, 258
Douglas, Mrs Lewis, 49
Dowell, Anthony, 298
Downes, Edward, 288, 320, 325, 326
Drake, Fabia, 56
Draper, Ruth, 22
Drayton, Harley, 183
Dreebin, David, 184
Drogheda, Charles, sixth Earl of, and first Marquess of, 4
Drogheda, Edward, fifth Earl of, 4
Drogheda, Henry, first Earl of, 3
Drogheda, Kathleen, Countess of, see Burn, Kathleen Pelham
Drogheda, Ninth Earl of (grandfather), 4
Drogheda, Garrett Moore, eleventh Earl of: birth, 3, 5; early life, 6–10; schooling at Ludgrove, 11, 13; goes to Eton, 13–25; cruise to Spain, 15; holidays from school, 19–25; love affair with Alvilde, 25, 26, 28, 30, 33; goes up to Cambridge, 26–31; car accident, 28; starts career in London, 32–3; social life, 34–42; meets Bracken, 43–4; job with Financial News, 43, 45, 46–7, 54; on board of FN, 54, 63; friendship with Bracken develops, 54; meets future wife, 54–5; marriage in New York, 56–7; as Bracken's emissary in NY, 56–8; son born (1937), 63; colleagues in the FN, 64–5; responsibility for

business oversight of Investors Chronicle, 65; portrait by Princess Marina, 69; takes up still photography, 69–70; decides to join Army, 72; visits Berlin with wife, 72–3; mobilization, 73–4; regiment embarks for Cherbourg, 74; appointment in Reims, 74–5; wife's visit in Reims, 76; return from France to England, 78; granted 3 months leave from Army, 81, 85; visits to Bracken at Ministry of Information, 85; work for Oliver Lyttelton in War Cabinet, 85–7; work at Ministry of Production, 89, 90; journey to Washington, 91; promotion at Joint American Secretariat, 99, 101, 102, 103, 104, 111; and acquisition of the FT, 111–13; released from Government to concentrate upon FN/FT, 116; addiction to gardening, 120; golf outings with father, 123–4; holidays with wife in France and Italy, 124–5; and Gordon Newton at FT, 131; on Covent Garden board, 137, 161, 168, 202, 203, 227–8, 240, 242; offer of new job, 149–51, 158; father's death, 158–9; and Bracken's death, 160–1; as chairman of ITF, 174; visits to Moscow and Peking, 176–82; association with Institute of Directors, 182–3; nomination to board of Reuters, 186; as chairman of the NPA, 196–7; 198, 202, 218, 357; son's marriage and divorce, 197–8; as temporary secretary to Covent Garden board, 227, 235; elected chairman of Covent Garden, 254–5; and extension of Georg Solti's contract, 284–5; and Frederick Ashton's succession, 316–17; becomes a trustee of British Museum, 324; retirement from Covent Garden chairmanship, 343, 346; succession, 343, 353; bust, 346; 1974 gala related to retirement, 346–8; Sir Isaiah Berlin's letter to, 348–50; retirement from FT, 357; Knight of Garter, 360–1
Drogheda, Tenth Earl of (father), 4, 13, 21; first marriage, 5; divorce, 6, 9, 12; marries Olive, Lady Victor Paget, 13, 23; and Olive's death, 25, 123; and son's car accident, 29; change of job, 30; letter to son at start of career, 32–3; letters of introduction for son, 46; work at Ministry of Economic Warfare, 83–4, 159; as Chairman of Committees in House of Lords, 123, 158; golf outings with son, 123–4; death, 124, 158; letter to son, 158–9; Lord Home's tribute to, 159
Drumlanrig House (Dumfriesshire), 120
Drury Lane, 290, 292
Dubois, Madame, 80

Du Cros, Sir Arthur, 21
Dudley Ward, Angela, 39
Dudley Ward, Freda, 38, 39–40, 48, 49, 53, 56, 68–9, 93
Dudley Ward, Penelope, 38, 39, 40, 41, 49, 62
Duff, Lady Caroline, see Paget, Lady Caroline (Lord Anglesey's daughter)
Duncan, Sir Andrew, 87
Dundas Castle (Linlithgowshire), 5
Dunkirk, 77
Dunlop Rubber Company, 21
Dupont, Jacques, 291
Dusseldorf, 135
Dvorakova, Ludmilla, 328
Dykes, F. J., 27
Dyson, Sir George, 228, 229

Eccles, The Rt Hon. Viscount, 299, 300, 340–1, 342
Economist, The, 84, 97, 115, 136, 156, 175, 186, 208; building, 34, 152–3; Bracken's acquisition of 50 per cent share in, 44, 45, 163; printing of, 139; growing circulation, 152, 153, 154, 157; Financial Report, 154; Foreign Report, 154; Bookshop, 154; Weights and Measures Guide, 154; World in Figures, 154; rule of anonymity in, 211
Economist Intelligence Unit (EIU), 153, 155
Eden, The Rt Hon. Anthony (The Earl of Avon), 358
Edinburgh, 29, 30, 318; Festival, 124, 229
Edward VIII, Prince of Wales, 40, 62; King of England, 178
Edwards, Sydney, 336
Egremont, Lady (Pamela), 181
Einzig, Paul, 65, 105, 212
Elektra (Richard Strauss), 251, 327, 345
Elgar, Edward, Enigma Variations, 302, 303, 316
Elisir d'Amore (Donizetti), 345
Elizabeth, HM The Queen Mother, 258, 273, 320, 346, 347, 364
Elizabeth II, HM The Queen, 239, 346, 360, 361, 364, 365–6
Elizalde, Fred, 28
Elliott, Maxine, 6–7
Elliott-Automation, 275
Ellis, Havelock, Studies in Psychology of Sex, 31
EMI, 333
Encyclopedia Britannica, 155
English Electric Company, 275
English Life (magazine), 44
English National Opera Company

(formerly Sadler's Wells), 235, 271, 272, 290, 338, 351
English Opera Group, 271, 278
Enigma Variations (Elgar), 302, 303, 316
Epstein, Jacob, 133
Erlanger, Leo and Edwina d', 125
Eton, 13–18, 70, 83, 117, 229
Eugene Onegin (Tchaikovsky), 327
Evans, Sir Geraint, 314, 321, 345
Evening Standard, 336, 360
Exbury Gardens, 219
Eyre, James Bristow, 43
Eyre and Spottiswoode, 43, 44

Falbe, Vera de (Vubby), 22, 23
Falbe, William de, 22
Falkner, Sir Keith, 269
Falstaff (Verdi), 265, 327, 345
family motto, 3, 11
Fauré, Gabriel, Requiem, 301
Feather, Vic, 218
Feathers Clubs, 40
Festival Ballet, 302, 316
Festival of Britain (1951), 127, 363
Fidelio (Beethoven), 282, 283, 313, 345, 364
Field, John, 295, 316, 317, 338
Figaro (Mozart), 280, 288, 331, 332–3, 334, 335
Fille du Régiment, La (Donizetti), 289
Financial and Provincial Publishing Company Ltd, 208
Financial News (FN), 43, 44; Drogheda's offer to work with, 43; holding, 45; Drogheda collects financial advertising for, 45–6; Lombard column, 65, 212; in war-time austerity, 84; merger with FT, 112, 114, 115–16, 127–8, 146; Lex investment column, 128, 130, 169, 211
Financial Times (FT): Bracken buys control of, 50; competition with FN, 54; post-war success, 64; Alan Hodge to the editorial staff of, 85; Camrose wants to sell, 111–12, 113; and FN merger, 112, 114, 115–16, 127–8, 146; regarded as leading City paper, 114; editorship, 128; 'City Men and Matters' column, 128, 210; industrial coverage, 131; advertisement revenue, 131–3, 165, 167, 214–15; 'Whitehall Industrial issues', 133–4; complete theatre coverage, 137–8; recruitment methods, 138; offices in Coleman Street, 139; and the St Clements Press, 139–40; new building, 141–3; transfer of control of, 145–7, 149, 160; after Bracken's death, 161–71; launch of Medical News, 164;

Policy Committee, 165; overseas coverage, 166; overseas circulation, 167; Queen's Award for Export, 167, 215; Technical Page, 167; coverage of the Arts, 167–70; coverage of sporting events, 170–1; Saturday issue, 170; share in *Management Today*, 186; possible merger with *The Times*, 189–93, 194; impact of Thomson's acquisition of *The Times* on, 194; increase in circulation, 211; Stock Exchange share index, 211; Lex investment column, 211, 212; Lombard column, 212; Business Enterprises division, 216; celebration of 25,000th issue, 217; Industrial Architecture Award, 219; gold medal for garden at Chelsea Flower Show, 219, 220

Finch-Hatton, Lady Daphne, *see* Straight, Lady Daphne

Firth of Forth, 124

Fischer-Dieskau, Dietrich, 306

Fisher, E. C. 46

Fisher, M. H. (Fredy), 171, 212, 213

Fischer, Harry, 64

Fishlock, David, 167

Flagstad, Kirsten, 234

Fleetwood-Hesketh, Cuthbert, 27

Fleischmann, Ernest, 304

Fleming, Mrs Ian, 353

Fleming, Peter, 34

Fletcher, Michael, 151

Florence, 124; floods, 265

Flying Dutchman, The (Wagner), 289

Fonteyn, de Arias, Dame Margot, 239, 243, 292, 293, 297, 300; in *Giselle*, 292; in *Marguerite and Armand*, 294; in *Romeo and Juliet*, 298

Foot, The Rt Hon. Dingle, 159

Foot, The Rt Hon. Michael, 205

Foreign Office, 297

Fort Belvedere, 40

Forte, Sir Charles, 156

Forza del Destino (Verdi), 284, 285

Foster, Eric, 184

Fournier, Alain, *Le grand Meaulnes*, 67

Fowler, John, 122

Francis, Alfred, 148

Franck, César, *Symphonic Variations*, 301

Franckenstein, Clemens von, 39

Frankfurt, 280, 281, 324

Franks, Lord, 240, 241

Frau ohne Schatten (Richard Strauss), 313, 327

Freni, Mirella, 264–5

Freud, Sigmund, 31

Friedrich, Götz, 344

Friends of Covent Garden, 272, 275, 276, 285, 299, 306, 319, 346, 353

Furman, Louis, 80, 81–2

Furness, Viscount, 125; Yacht *Sapphire*, 22

Furtseva, Mme Ekatecinar, 308–9

Gable, Christopher, 298

Gabriel, Wilfred, 214

Gagarin, Yuri, 177

Galliner, Peter, 134–5

Games, Abram, 127

Gardiner, John, 169

Garside, Boris, 363

Gaulle, General Charles de, 220

Geddes, The Hon. John, 218, 219

Geliot, Michael, 336–7

General Election (1945), 113, 122

General Election (1964), 310

General Election (1966), 189

General Election (1974), 209

Georgiadis, Nicholas, 298, 302, 327, 339

Germany, 25, 26, 48, 59, 199

Getty, Paul, 52

Ghika, Nicolas, 291

Gibbings, Peter, 203

Gibson, Lady, 147

Gibson, Lord, 147, 149, 161, 162, 168, 169, 188, 205, 208, 219, 358; as member of *FT* board, 190, 357; as chairman of Pearson Longman, 208, 358; as chairman of Arts Council, 275, 338, 342, 359

Gide, André, 291

Gielgud, Sir John, 56, 248, 282

Gilliat, Jack, 123

Gilliat, Virginia (later Lady Sykes), 35

Gishford, Anthony, 225, 278

Giulini, Carlo Maria, 229, 252, 262, 265, 270, 280, 281, 282, 305, 325

Gladwyn, Lord, 176

Glasgow Academy, 92

Glock, Sir William, 312, 333

Gloriana (Britten), 239, 240, 364

Gluck, Christoph, 284, 327

Glyndebourne Opera Society, 70, 147, 247, 269, 297, 325, 335

Gobbi, Tito, 263

Goldsmid, Sir Henry and Lady d'Avigdor, 123

Goltz, Christl, 251

Goodall, Reginald, 325; *Meistersinger*, 313

Goodman, Lord, 147, 188, 192, 203–7, 217, 239; as chairman of Arts Council, 299, 300, 310, 342; partnership with Jenny Lee, 310; as member of Covent Garden board, 310, 337, 338; becomes chairman of Coliseum, 338

Goodwin, Sir Reg, 361

Goossens, Eugene, 235

Gordon, Charles, 301

Gowing, Lawrence, 346
Goya, Francisco de, 284
Graham, Martha, 359
Granger, Derek, 137, 138
Graves, Robert, *The Reader over Your Shoulder*, 85
Greater London Council (GLC), 272, 351, 360, 361, 366; *see also* London County Council
Green, Maurice, 63–4, 84, 128
Greywalls house, 66, 124
Grimsby, 79, 80, 81
Grosvenor House, Ford Motor Company's flat in, 160
Guardian, The, 203; *see also Manchester, Guardian*
Guest, The Hon. Cynthia (Lady Wimborne's daughter), p. 36
Guggenheim, Solomon, 32
Guildhall School of Music, 237
Guinness, Honor, 59
Guinness, Patrick, 156
Guinness Peat Company, 342
Guttuso, Renato, 284
Guyatt, Professor Richard, 363

Hadley, Patrick, 37
Hailsham, Lord, 206
Hall, Sir Peter, 307, 327, 331, 332, 333, 334–5; contract with Covent Garden, 326, 329–30, 335, 338, 344
Haley, Sir William, 186, 191, 192, 193
Hallé orchestra, 236
Hallgarten and Co., of New York, 30
Hampden, Viscount and Viscountess, *see* Brand, Leila and Tommy
Hampstead, 107, 116
Hanover, 25–6
Hare, The Hon. Alan, 174, 215, 219, 357, 358–9
Hare, The Hon. John, 174
Harewood, Countess of, Marion, *see* Thorpe, Mrs Jeremy
Harewood, Countess of, *see* Tuckwell, Patricia
Harewood, The Earl of, 228, 229, 248; as Controller of Opera Planning, 229, 237, 239, 244, 251, 261, 280, 283; as director of Edinburgh Festival, 229, 237, 318; as member of London Opera Centre board of governors, 278–9; on Covent Garden board, 318–19, 332–3; as managing director of Sadler's Well's Opera, 319
Harlech, Lord, 361
Harling, Robert, 151–2
Harriman, Kathleen, 98

Harriman. W. Averell, 98; *Special Envoy*, 99–100; Mission, 100
Harrington, Illtyd, 360
Harris, Ralph, 130
Harris, Sir Ronald, 86
Harris, Tony, 214
Harrison, Gabriel, 359
Harrod, Sir Roy, 136
Hart, John, 295–6
Hartmann, Rudolf: *Arabella*, 305, 314; *Frau ohme Schatten*, 314
Hartwell, Lord, *see* Berry, Michael
Haskell, Arnold, 250
Hasler, W. J., 98, 99, 101, 104
Hatfield House, 120
Haugwitz-Reventlow, Count Kurt, 79
Hawkes, Ralph, 225
Hayward Foundation, 366
Hayward, John, 10
Hazell Watson and Viney, 155
Head, Viscount, 180–1
Head, Viscountess, 180–1
Heath, The Rt Hon. Edward, 209, 212, 220, 305, 328, 358
Heathcote-Amory, The Rt Hon. Derek, 271
Heinz, Mr and Mrs Jack, 275
Heller, Robert, 186
Hellyer, Arthur, 219
Helpmann, Sir Robert, 297, 298
Henman, Philip, 173
Henschel, Sidney, 131–2, 137, 138, 190, 191, 193, 214, 216
Henze, Hans Werner, 293
Herbert, The Hon. David, 15, 56, 67, 119
Hérold, Ferdinand, 291
Heron Bay (Barbados), 122
Higgins, John, 167, 168
Hill, Derek, 69
Hill, Heywood, 34
Hill, Jimmy, 363
Hill Samuel, 190
Hillier, Harold, 364
Hillingdon Estate (Glasgow), 133
Hills, Colonel Jack, 63
Hills, J. D. (Eton master), 16–18
Hilton Hotel (London), 217, 218
Hinchingbroke, Victor (became Victor Montagu), 34
Historical Association, 151
History Today, 151
Hitler, Adolf, 59, 63, 64, 67, 73, 76, 85, 134, 183, 184, 280
Hobson, Sir Oscar, 46–7, 63
Hodge, Alan, 85, 129, 151; *The Reader over Your Shoulder*, 85
Hodgson, John, 7
Hofmannsthal, Hugo von, 305
Hofmannsthal, Raimund von, 234, 264, 313

Holmes, G. J., 44, 65
Holt, Harold, 225
Hong Kong, 178, 181
Honiton quarry, 143
Hooper, Geoffrey, 140, 141
Hopwood, Neville, 199, 201
Horlick, Colonel James, 124
Horrocks, General Sir Brian, 251
Hotter, Hans, 234, 305
Houghton, Lord, 205–6
House and Garden (magazine), 151
House of Commons, 204
House of Lords, 47, 92, 188, 204, 205, 206,
    322, 367
Howard, Robin, 359
Howells, Anne, 345
Howick, Lord, 361
Huddleston, Father Trevor, 115
Hudson, Stephen, *see* Schiff, Sydney
Hulton, Lady, 108
Hunter, Ian, 173
Hunter, T. S. G. (Jim), 138–9, 150, 174, 217
Hurok, Sol, 237–8, 258
Hurry, Leslie, 297
Hurstmonceaux Castle (Sussex), 51, 56, 58
Hussey, M. H. (Dukie), 202–3
Hutber, Patrick, 136
Hutchinson, Barbara (later Barbara
    Rothschild), 41, 42, 46, 68, 124, 291
Hutchinson, St John, 41, 68, 73
Hutchinson, Mrs St John, 41–2
Hutton, Barbara, 20–1, 78–9, 81

Ice Break, The (Tippett), 315
Imperial Tobacco Company, 92
Independent Television (Broadcasting)
    Authority, 85
Industrial and Trade Fairs (ITF), 155, 172,
    174, 175, 177, 291
Industrial Relations Act (1971), 204
Ingpen, Joan, 283
Innes, Hammond, 64
Institute of Contemporary Arts, 342
Institute of Directors, 182, 183, 184, 185,
    186; first annual conference, 184–5;
    conference in Albert Hall, 310
Institute of Economic Affairs, 130
Institute of Journalists, 205
International Press Institute, 135
International Publishing Corporation
    (IPC), 151, 164
Investors Chronicle, 44, 64, 65–6, 84, 130,
    132, 151, 170, 358
IPC, *see* International Publishing
    Corporation
IPEX (printing machinery exhibition), 176
Iphigénie en Tauride (Gluck), 284

Ireland, 3, 8, 9, 10
Ironside, Robin, 248
Isis, Oxford University Magazine, 136, 331
Italian Art and Archives Rescue Fund, 265
ITF, *see* Industrial and Trade Fairs
Iveagh, Lord, 59

Jackson, Sir Barry, 228, 229
Jacob, Sir Ian, 87, 91, 322
Janacek, Leos, 234
Jardine, Matheson & Co., 178, 179, 180
Jarvis, Ralph, 34
Jay, Peter, 209
Jenkins, The Rt Hon. Roy, 361, 362
Jenufa (Janacek), 345
John, Augustus, 62
Johnson, Christopher, 216–17
Johnstone, 'Crinks' Harcourt, 121
Joint American Secretariat, 99, 101, 102, 103,
    104
Joll, James, 169
Jones, Jack, 218
Jones, Sir Roderick, 186
Joplin, Scott, *Elite Syncopations*, 339

Kabos, Ilona, 280
Kanawa, Kiri te, 336, 337, 345
Karajan, Herbert von, 305
Kauffer, E. McKnight, 53
Kempe, Rudolf, 229, 251, 252, 270, 280,
    281, 325; *Tannhäuser*, 251; *Elektra*, 251,
    345; *Ring*, 251
Kemsley, Viscount (Gomer), 50, 190
Kenmare, Countess of (Enid), 21, 125
Kennedy, Jackie, 197
Kenny, Sean, 289
Kensington Housing Association, 40
Kent, HRH Prince George, Duke of, 69
Kent, HRH Princess Marina, Duchess of,
    69, 123
Kerr, Muriel, 283
Keswick, Sir John, 178, 180
Keyes, Admiral Sir Roger, 80, 95
Keynes, J. Maynard, 105, 136, 152, 269, 295;
    General Theory, 31, 47; as chairman of
    Covent Garden Opera Trust, 225, 226;
    as first chairman of Royal Opera House,
    261
Kildangan Castle, 8
Kinross House (Loch Leven), 25
King, Cecil, 151, 196, 197, 198, 243
King Priam (Tippett), 284
King, Wilfred, 64
Kipping, Norman, 97
Kirov, the, 244, 292, 293, 300
Kirstein, Lincoln, 299–300

Kissin, Lord, 342, 343
Kleiber, Erich, 235–6
Klemperer, Otto, 213, 229, 267, 269, 282, 283, 326; *Lohengrin*, 288; *Fidelio*, 313
Klemperer, Lotte, 282
Knight, Andrew, 154
Knock, Albert, 84
Knopf, Alfred, 57
Knot Garden (Tippett), 327, 330, 331
Knoydart (Scotland), 145
Koestler, Arthur, 119
Kokoschka, Oscar, 83
Koo, Fritz, 178, 179, 180
Korda, Sir Alexander, 41, 49, 66
Khrushchev, Nikita, 176
Kubelik, Rafael, 236, 244–8, 251, 252, 262, 270, 280; *The Trojans* and *Boris Godunov*, 248
Kuala Lumpur, 180, 181
Kvergic, Mrs Gerti, 154

Labrot, Eleanor (Mrs Brian Aherne), 57
Lacroix (near Hyères), 69
Lady Macbeth of Mtzenk (Shostakovitch), 288–9
Lammers, Gerda, 251
Lancaster, Mrs C. G., *see* Tree, Nancy
Lanacster, Sir Osbert, 105, 291
Lancaster, Reverend Ronald, 365
Lancastria, 78
Lanchbery, John, 291
Landa, Billy de, 19–21, 30
Landa y Escandon, Don Guillermo de, 20
Landmark Trust, 162
Lane, Sir Allen, Penguin Books, 208
Lane Fox, Robin, 219
Lang, Fritz, 69
Lascelles, Sir Alan, 274
Latham, Sir Paul, 51–2, 58, 79, 93
Latham, Richard, 79
Latham, Thomas, 51
Lavender, Miss (nurse), 6
Law, Victor, 168
Lawson, Fred, 196
Lawson, Hon. Harry, 195
Laycock, Lady (Angie), 107
Laycock, Sir Robert (Bob), 15, 39, 107
Layton, Lord, 44, 84, 89, 91, 97, 98, 115, 152
Lazards merchant banking house, 147, 149
Lazaridis, Stephanos, 336
Lee, Jennie (Baroness Lee of Asheridge), 203, 217, 255, 257, 307–9, 310, 313, 346, 347
Leeds, 173
Leeds, Duke of, 121
Legge, Walter, 267, 268, 281–2, 348; Philharmonia Orchestra, 326
Leigh, Vivien, 137

Leigh Hill House (Cobham), 25
Leighton, Frank, 65
Lend Lease Agreement, Article VII, 104–5, 106
Leningrad, 292, 300
Leverson, Ada (the Sphinx), 55
Levin, Bernard, 194, 344; *The Pendulum Years*, 313, 314
Lewis, Cecil Day, 27, 106
Lewis, Sir Edward, 130, 304
Lewis, Wyndham, 5
Lewis's department store group (Liverpool), 232
Lhevinne, Josef, 81
Lilley, Mrs Thomas (Vera), 108
Linden, Anya (Mrs John Sainsbury), 319
Livingstone, E. and S., 358
Llewelyn-Davies, Lord, 122
Lloyd, Eliza, 197
Lloyd, Stacey, 198
Lloyds Bank, 61, 217
Lockwood, Sir Joseph, 353
Loftus, Jane, 3
Lohengrin (Wagner), 288
London Celebrations Committee, 360, 362
London County Council (LCC), 272; Committee of Inquiry, 271; *see also* Greater London Council
London Opera Centre, 37, 251, 270, 277–8, 279, 336
London scale of printing charges, 199
London School of Economics, 139, 154, 162, 163, 311, 313; Library, 163
London Symphony Orchestra, 304
London University, 162, 163
Long, Gerald, 187
Longman, Mark, 208
Longmans, Green Co., 165, 208
Lonsdale, Frances (Frankie), 61, 62; *see also* Donaldson, Lady
Lonsdale, Frederick, 61
Lopokova, Lydia, 261, 295
Lowenstein, Bobby, 21
Lucerne, 280, 282, 283
Lucia di Lammermoor (Donizetti), 258, 263, 266, 283, 348
Ludgrove school (New Barnet), 11
Lund, Douglas, 284
Lutyens, Sir Edwin, 66, 105
Lyons, Derek, 175
Lyttelton, The Rt Hon. Alfred, 66
Lyttelton, Lady Moira (Viscountess Chandos), 66, 67, 121
Lyttelton, The Rt Hon, Oliver (Viscount Chandos), 48, 63, 66–7, 107, 121, 148, 182; as Minister of State in Cairo, 85, 86, 87; as Minister of Production in London, 87, 89, 90, 98; mission to the United States,

90–1, 95; parliamentary position, 95–6; second visit to Washington, 99–100

Mackerras, Charles, 325, 345
Maclean, Sir Fitzroy, 8
Macmillan, Charles, 358
Macmillan, The Rt Hon. Harold, 54
MacMillan, Kenneth: *The Invitation*, 291; *Rite of Spring*, 292; *Romeo and Juliet*, 298; appointment at Deutsche Oper Berlin, 300; *Song of the Earth*, 300; as director of Royal Ballet, 301, 316, 317, 338, 340; *Anastasia*, 338–9; *Poltroon*, 339; *7 Deadly Sins*, 339; *Elite Syncopations*, 339; *Manon*, 339; *Triad*, 339; *Sleeping Beauty*, 339
MacWilliam, F. E., 262, 346
Maeterlinck, Maurice, 234
Magic Flute (Mozart), 35, 233, 269, 282, 307
Maginot Line, 76, 77
Malaysia, 180, 181
Mahler, Gustav, *Song of the Earth*, 301
Management Today, 136, 186
Manchester Guardian, 132, 186
Manon (Massenet), 339
Mansion House, 176
Mar and Kelly, Lady, 28
Marconi scandal, 62
Margaret, HRH Princess, 259, 273, 346, 347
Marks, Lady (Miriam), 273
Marks Lord (Simon), 258
Marks and Spencer, 258, 273
Marshall, Alfred, *Principles of Economics*, 31
Marshall Field estate, 122
Marten, C. H. K., 15
Martin, Sergeant, 276
Martin-Turner, Grahame, 132
Martinu, Bohuslav, 339
Marx, Henry, 299
Marx, Carroll, 116
Mary, Queen of Scots, 25
Mariinsky Theatre, 302
Maschwitz, Eric, *No chip on My Shoulder*, 72
Massenet, Jules, 339
Massigli, Odette, 125–6
Massigli, René, 125
Matthew, Francis, 139–40
Maugham, W. Somerset, 125
Maurier, Sir Gerald du, 116
Maxton, The Rt Hon. James, 95
May, Olive, *see* Olive (stepmother)
Mayer, Lady (Dorothy), 258
Mayer, Sir Robert, 258, 359–60, 367
McAsee (house carpenter), 9, 52
McClean, Richard, 214
McClean, Stuart, 214
McCloy, The Hon. John J., 48
McCormack, Count John, 9, 52, 58

Mellifont Abbey, 3, 8
Medea (Bellini), 266
Medical News, 164
Meinertzhagen, Daniel, 146–7
Meinertzhagen, Luke, 146–7, 208
Meistersinger (Wagner), 233, 313, 314
Mellon, Mr and Mrs Paul, 197–8
Mendelssohn, Felix, *Midsummer Night's Dream*, 298
Mer, La (Debussy), 301
Mercury House Group, 164
Mercury Theatre, 295
Messager, André, 291
Messel, Oliver, 66, 297; *Sleeping Beauty*, 226, 302
Metal Box Company, 97, 226
Metcalfe, 'Fruity', 178
Metcalfe, Lady Alexandra, 178
Methven, Sir John, 202
Metropolitan Opera, in New York, 248
Meynell, Hugo, 154
Midland Bank, 323
Midsummer Marriage (Tippett), 315
Midsummer Night's Dream (Britten), 281, 345
Mildenhall golf course, 28
Mildmay, Audrey (Mrs John Christie), 71
Mills, The Rt Hon. Viscount, 97
Ministry of Aircraft Production, 88, 91, 133
Minister for the Arts, 255, 257, 260, 307, 340; White Paper, 309–10
Ministry of Production, 91, 96, 111, 114, 116; Industrial Division, 97; Industrial Information Division, 97
Ministry of Supply, 64, 87, 88, 91, 96, 232, 241
Ministry of Works, 96
Minton, Yvonne, 327, 345
Mission for Economic Affairs, 100
Mitford, Nancy, 34, 70
Mitford, Tom, 34
Moffat Cottage Hospital, 29
Moir, Ann (grandmother), 4, 5
Monasterevin (County Kildare), 3
Monckton, Viscount (Walter), 105
Monnet, Jean, 99
Monopolies Commission, 192
Monte Carlo, 21; Opera, 21
Montgomery, Sir Basil and Lady, 25
Montresor, Beni, 297, 339, 345
Moore Abbey, 7, 8, 9, 10, 16, 52, 58
Moore, Charles, 3
Moore, Dermot (Derry), Lord Drogheda's son, 63, 70, 73, 74, 79, 92, 93; education, 93–4, 103; marriage, 197–8; divorce, 198
Moore, Edward, 3
Moore, Garrett, Viscount, 3
Moore, Henry, *see* Drogheda, Henry, first Earl of

Moore, Henry (artist), 106
More O'Ferrall family, 8
Morgan-Grampian company, 165
Morison, Stanley, 140; *History of the Times*, 140
Morley College, 277
Morrice, Norman, 340
Morris, Charles, 91
Morris, Gareth, 269
Morrison, John (later Lord Margadale), 14
Moscow, 176–7
Moser, Sir Claus, 213, 310–13, 323, 334, 343, 344, 347, 349, 353, 364
Moses and Aaron (Schoenberg), 306, 307, 309, 326, 348
Mottisfont Abbey (Hampshire), 121
Mount Isa Mine (Queensland), 32
Mountain, Sir Brian, 258
Moussorgsky, Modest: *Boris Godunov*, 233, 244, 266; *Khovanshchina*, 288
Mozart, W. A., 233, 282, 314, 331, 333, 344
Muirfield golf course, 66, 123–4
Munich, 26, 39, 135; State Opera House, 39, 280
Murdoch, Rupert, 203
Murray, The Rt Hon. Len, 218
Myers and Co., 54
Myers, Mossie, 54

Nabucco (Verdi), 336
Nantes, 77, 78
Nantes Base Sub-Area Staff, 77, 78
Nast, Condé, 57
Nation, The, 66
National Enterprise Board, 195
National Exhibition Centre, 175
National Gallery, 17, 106, 265; paintings, 119
National Graphical Association, 202
National Management Game, 218–19
National Theatre, 148, 335, 337, 350, 351
National Trade Press, 172
National Trust, 163
National School of Opera, 277, 278, 279
National Union of Journalists (NUJ), 138, 205, 207
Nelson, Mr Donald, 90–1
Nerina, Nadia, 291, 300–1
New Brutalists, 153
New Philharmonia Orchestra, 269
New Statesman, 66, 247, 312
Newnes (George) printing works, 140–1, 164, 172
Newton, Sir Gordon, 129–30, 134, 137, 138, 163, 166, 167, 168, 170, 171, 190, 210–12,

214; takes over *FT* editorship, 131, 135–6; and Thomson's acquisition of *The Times*, 193, 194; retirement, 213
Newton, Ivor, 37
News Chronicle, 84, 214
News of the World, 197, 203
Newspaper Proprietors Association, 186; *and see* Newspaper Publishers Association
Newspaper Publishers Association (NPA), 186, 195, 196, 197, 198, 199, 200, 202–3, 239, 357
Newsweek, 98
Newton Ferrers (Cornwall), 118
New York, 56, 57, 81, 169, 197
New York City ballet company, 299
New York Herald Tribune, 103, 104
New York Theatre Guild, 55
New York Times, 169
New Yorker, The, 136
Nichols, Sir Philip, 240, 259
Nicholson, Max, 363
Nijinska, Bronislava, *Les Biches* and *Les Noces*, 298
Nilsson, Birgit, 328
Nimptsch, Uli, 133
Nobili, Lila da, 303
Noces, Les (Stavinsky), 298
Nolan, Sydney, 292
Norma (Bellini), 265, 289
Norman, Jessye, 345
Norman, Lord (Montagu), 44
Normanbrook, Lord, *see* Brook, Sir Norman
Normandy landings (1944), 99, 111
North American Supply Committee, 98
Northampton, 133
Noyes, Charlie, 104
NPA, *see* Newspaper Publishers' Association
Nureyev, Rudolf, 292, 294, 298, 302; in *Giselle*, 292; in *La Bayadère*, 295; in *Marguerite and Armand*, 294; in 1974 gala, 346
Nutcracker, The (Tchaikovsky), 302

Oakley, W. J., 11, 22
Observer, 142, 171, 187, 191, 203, 210, 312
Ocean Trust, 54
Old Vic theatre, 147, 148, 337
Olive (stepmother), 13, 23, 25, 123, 158, 159
Olivier, Edith, 67
Olivier, Lord (Laurence), 56, 67, 137, 335
Oman, Julia Trevelyan, 289, 303, 327, 345
Opera (magazine), 229, 251, 289
Order of the Garter, 360–1
Orfeo (Gluck), 327

Otello (Verdi), 244, 345, 348
Otto, Teo, 288

Paget, Celia, 119
Paget, Lady Caroline, 35, 36
Paget, Lady Elizabeth, 35, 36
Paget, Lord Victor, 23, 24, 35
Paget, Mamaine, 119
Paget, Peggy, 23, 159
Paget, Sandy, 23, 159
Pains-Wessex Fireworks Co., 365
Palmer, David, *see* Prior-Palmer, David
Pan American Airways, 122
Paris: Red Cross, 76, 78, 252; American
    Embassy, 124; British Embassy, 124;
    Times office, 217; Opera, 283
Paris cinema (London), 69
Park, Merle, 302
Parker, Grahame, 212
Parker, Lord Justice, 148
Parkinson, Hargreaves, 65, 84, 105, 128, 129,
    155, 212
Parkside House, Englefield Green, 117, 118,
    262, 319
Parsifal (Wagner), 21, 348
Pasmore, Victor, 106
Patsy, *see* Patricia (sister)
Patten, Bill, 124
Patten, Susan Mary, 124
Patricia (sister), 6, 7, 10, 19; marries Sir Paul
    Latham, 51, 58; leaves for America with
    son, 79; divorce, 93; remarries, 93
Pavitt, Burnet, 252-3, 287-8, 289, 324, 349
Pavlova, Anna, 294
Pears, Peter, 226
Pearson Longman Group, 226
Pearson, S. & Son, 147, 149, 160, 190,
    192-3, 194, 208, 218, 359
Peat, Marwick, Mitchell & Co., 337
Peggy Guggenheim Gallery, *see* Venice,
    Palazzo Morosini
Peking, 177, 178, 180
Pelléas et Mélisande (Debussy), 234, 297, 314
Pembroke family, 24, 67
Pembroke, The Countess of, 23, 24
Penguin Books, 208
People, The, 237
Persephone (Stravinsky), 291
Perth, The Earl of, *see* Strathallan, David
Peter Grimes (Britten), 226, 270, 348
Petzal, Tom, 363
Philharmonia Orchestra, 269, 282, 326
Philip, HRH Prince, 185, 346, 364
Phipps, Mrs Diana, 299
Phipps, Mrs Ogden, 299
Pickering, Edward, 195

Pioneer Health Centre (Peckham), 61
Piper, John, 106, 239, 282, 365
Piper, Robert, 214
Pitlour house (in Fife), 23
Pitts, Valerie (Lady Solti), 313
Plas Newydd House, 35, 36, 58
Plesch, Janos, 83
Poland, 299
Pollitzer, Edward, 278
Pollitzer family 172, 173
Pollitzer, George, 172, 173
Poniatowski, Jean, 75-6
Ponsonby, Lady Sarah, 4
Poole, Lady (Daphne), 162
Poole, Lord (Oliver), 147, 148, 149, 161,
    162, 190, 192, 195
Pooley, Sir Ernest, 225
Pope, Sir George, 191
Pope-Hennessy, Dame Una, 324
Pope-Hennessy, James, 324
Pope-Hennessy, Sir John, 138, 299-300,
    324
Port of London Authority, 231
Portal of Laverstoke, Lord (Wyndham),
    96-7
Portarlington family, at Emo Park, 8
Porter, Andrew, 138
Portmeirion hotel (Wales), 119
Poulenc, Francis, 244, 298
Powell, Sir Richard, Bt., 183, 184, 185
Poynton, Sir A. Hilton, 89, 91
Practitioner, The, 45, 84, 151, 164
Press Association, 186
Press Charter, 205, 206, 207
Prices and Incomes Board, 209
Prices Commission, 209
Priestley, J. B., 240
Primrose Hill, 74
Primrose, Ruth, 35
Princess Royal, HRH, 229
Printing House Square, 191, 193
printing trades unions, 217
Prior-Palmer, David, 171
Pritchard, John, 325
Pro Arte Quartet, 70
Procter-Gregg, Professor Humphrey, 37,
    251, 277-8, 279
Prokofiev, Serge, 339
Promenade concerts, 312
Puccini, Giacomo, 314, 344

Quarter Society (London), 36, 37, 61, 260
Queen (magazine), 301
Queen's Award for Export, 167, 215
Queens Hall, 38, 70
Quennell, Peter, 151

Rambert, Dame Marie, 295; *and see* Ballet Rambert
Rampling, A. J., 140–1
Ramsay, Dr A. B., 15
Rank Organization, 277
Rankl, Karl, 235, 236, 245
Rattigan, Sir Terence, 107
Raw Materials Allocation Committee, 96
Rayne, Lord (Max), *188*
Reckitt's (Liverpool), 231
Reddish, Sir Halford, 130
Redpath, Anne, 169
Reed, Philip D., 100, 103, 104, 106
Rees-Mogg, William, 136, 137, 194
Reims, 74–5, 76
Reiss, Sir John, 183
Renoir, Jean, 69
Renton, The Hon. Lavinia, 274, 275
Renwick, Lord (Bob), 182, 183, 185
Reuter, Julius, 186
Reuters agency, 177, 186–7
Rhodes, Cecil, 115
Rhodes, Lord, 361
RIBA, 219
Richardson, Professor Sir Albert, 142, 143, 220
Rickett, Sir Denis, 89, 227, 328
Rigoletto (Verdi), 289
Ring, The (Wagner), 266, 305, 325, 327, 331, 344, 348
Robbins, Jerome, 340
Robbins, Lord (Lionel), 161, 162, 190, 195, 218, 260–1, 310–12, 316; as chairman of *FT*, 163–4, 165; elected to Covent Garden board, 241, 242, 271, 333–4; chairman of committee over London Opera Centre affair, 279; on language policy, 333; retirement as chairman of *FT*, 357, 358
Robens, Lord, 365
Roberts, William, 62–3
Robertson, Diana Forbes, 7, 7
Robertson, Professor D. H., 31, 152
Robertson, Doris Howard, 53, 62
Robertson, James, 278, 279
Robinson, Austin, 97
Robinson, The Rt Hon. Kenneth, 338
Robinson, W. S., 48, 49
Roche Products, 252
Rockefeller, Nelson, 57
Rodgers, Sir John, 97
Rogaly, Joe, 209, 210
Rogers, Frank, 198, 199
Rootes, Lord, 40, 72, 73
Rosenkavalier (Richard Strauss), 234, 264, 281, 346
Rosenthal, Harold, 229, 289, *290*
Rosslyn, The Earl of, 125
Rothermere, Viscount, 195–6, 198

Rothschild, Barbara, *see* Hutchinson, Barbara
Rothschild, Edmund de, 219–20
Rothschild, Evelyn de, 156
Rothschild family, 186
Rothschild, The Hon. Jacob, 365
Rothschild, Leo de, 258
Rothschild, Lord, 10, 27–8, 41, 56, 67–8
Royal Academy of Dancing, 292, 338
Royal Academy of Dramatic Art (RADA), 55
Royal Academy of Music, 259, 318
Royal Ballet, 238; and Sir Frederick Ashton, 239; appearance in Drury Lane, 290, 292; visit to Moscow, 291; Benevolent Fund Galas, 294, 298; touring the USA, 296, 299; touring Canada, Italy and Iron Curtain countries, 299, 300
Royal Ballet School, 173, 250, 294, 353
Royal Bank of Canada, 155
Royal College of Arts, 286, 363
Royal College of Music, 229, 269
Royal Commissions, 156
Royal Festival Hall, 363
Royal Fine Arts Commission, 286
Royal Institute of International Affairs, 210
Royal Opera company, 320
Royal Opera House, *see* Covent Garden
Royal Opera House Trust, 342–3, 353
Royal Shakespeare Company, 337
Rubinstein, Nash, 239
Runciman, Sir Steven, 27
Russell, Isabella Romanes, 4
Russell, Sir John, 169
Russell, Ken, 331
Russell, Mrs Gilbert, 121
Russell, Victor (KC), 30
Russia, 32
Rutland, Duke of, 35, 123
Ryan, Mrs John Barry, 258
Ryder, Lord, 195, 199
Rylands, George (Dadie), 27

Sackville-West, Hon. E. J., 228, 248; *Classical Record Guide*, 229
Sadler's Wells Ballet Company: moved into Covent Garden, 226; Foundation, 228, 229; regular tours to the USA, 237–8; integration with Covent Garden, 250–1
Sadler's Wells ballet school, 238
Sadler's Wells Opera Company, 235, 282, 319, 337, 340
Sadler's Wells theatre, 240
Sadler's Wells Theatre Ballet Company, 238, 296, 337; Royal Charter, 238, 239, 310; *and see* Royal Ballet

Sainsbury, The Hon. John, 319–20, 334, 346, 361–2
Salisbury, The Marchioness of, Betty, 120
Salisbury, The Marquess of, Bobbety, 120
Salome (Richard Strauss), 327
Salzburg, 35, 305, 345; Festival, 280
Sandilands, Sir Francis, 342
Sarachi, Chatin, 52–3, 68, 79, 80, 83
Sargent, Sir Malcolm, 37, 106
Satie, Erik, 298
Saturday Review, 293–4
Savill Gardens, 117
Savill, Sir Eric, 117
Savory, Archie, 75
Scanlon, Hugh, 218
Scharrer, Irene, 229
Schiff, Sydney, 55, 56
Schiff, Violet, 55, 56
Schmidt, Helga, 283
Schnabel, Artur, 70, 312
Schneider-Siemssen, Hans, 305
Schoenberg, Arnold, 306
Schoeters, Ted, 167
Schuh, Oscar Fritz, 288
Schwarzkopf, Elisabeth, 234, 267, 281–2
Scott-Moncrieff, C. K., 55
Scotland, 22–3, 25, 123
Searle, Humphrey, 315
Secker, Adrian, 215
Sedbergh public school (Cumberland), 43, 161, 255
Self, Sir Henry, 96, 97, 100
Sendall, Bernard, 85
Serafin, Tullio, 263
Seraglio (Mozart), 233
Serenade for Strings (Tchaikovsky), 298
Serguëeff (choreographer), 302
Seymour, Lynn, 291, 298, 300, 317, 339
Shakespeare, William, 27
Shapland, Leonard, 84–5
Shaw, Bernard, 293–4
Shawe-Taylor, Desmond, 229, 247
Shell building, 365, 366
Shell-Mex, 232
Sherren, Graham, 164, 165
Sherren, Vere, 164–5, 172, 174
Shonfield, Andrew, 210–11
Short, Mrs Renée, 322
Shostakovitch, Dmitri, 288–9
Shuard, Amy, 248
Sibley, Antoinette, 298
Sieff, Mrs J. Edward (Lois), 273, 278, 360
Silver Jubilee Appeal Trust, 362
Simon, Norton, 168–9
Simon, Sir Ronald, 167
Sinclair of Cleeve, Lord, 91–2, 93, 97, 98, 100–1, 102, 114
Singapore, 177

Sinn, Robert, 187
Sitwell family, 37
Sitwell, Lady (Georgia), 58, 106, 120–1
Sitwell, Sir Osbert, *Who's Who*, 19, 106
Sitwell, Sir Sacheverell, 58, 106, 120–1, 295
Skene, Colonel Moncrieff, 23
Skene, Dorothy Moncrieff, 23
Skene, Helen Moncrieff, 23
Skinners' Company Hall, 218
SLADE (Society of Lithographic Artists, Designers, Engravers and Process Workers), 202
Slade School of Art, 42, 252
Sledmere House (Yorkshire), 122, 123
Sleeping Beauty (Tchaikovsky), 226, 302
Smetana, Friedrich, 234
Smith, F. E., 43; biography, 107
Smith, G. O., 11
Smith, Hon. James, 228, 229, 266
Smith, John, 162–3
Smith, Morris, 285
Smith, Lady Pamela, 43, 124; *and see* Berry
Smith, Peter Dallas, 153
Smith, Sir Henry Wilson, 114
Smith's Lawn, 117
Smithson, Alison and Peter, 153
SOGAT (Society of Graphical and Allied Trades), 201
Solihull (Birmingham), 175
Solti, Sir Georg, 263, 264, 276, 277; early career, 280–1; as musical director of Covent Garden, 282, 288, 289, 305, 306–7, 313, 314, 315, 324, 327, 328; renewal of contract, 284–5, 304; association with Peter Hall, 307, 326; remarries, 313; retirement, 320, 324; identification with Wagner, 325; succession, 325–6; knighthood, 328, 329; new production of *Carmen*, 336–7; and 1974 gala, 346
Solti, Hedi, 281, 285
Somerhill house (Kent), 122–3
Somerset House, 129
Somes, Michael, 293, 295–6
Sophiatown, 115
South Africa, 115, 150
Speaights (Eyre and Spottiswoode company), 139
Spears, Sir Edward L., 182, 183–4, 185
Spencer House (London), 153
Spender, Mrs Stephen (Natasha), 106
Spiegel, Sam, 53
Spira, Dr Jack, 83
Spira, Peter, 83
Springer, Axel, 135
Spurling, Ian, 339
Stanley, Charles, 183
Stannus, Edris, *see* Valois, Ninette de

St Clements Press, 139, 140, 141, 145
Sterling, Jeffrey, 362, 366
Stevens, Jocelyn, 301
St Evin Monastery, 8
St Jean Cap Ferrat, 21
Stock Exchange, 215
Stock Exchange Gazette, 151
Stockhausen, K.-H., 340
Stoll theatre, 233
Stoll Theatres Corporation, 337
St Malo, 78
St Nazaire, 78
St Paul's Cathedral, 141, 220
St Paul's Walden, 93, 94, 101, 116
Strachey, Jack, 72
Straight, Camilla, 63
Straight, Lady Daphne, 61, 62, 63
Straight, Whitney, 62
Strakosch, Sir Henry, 115
Strand House, 163
Strassner, Joe, 73
Strathallan, The Viscount (later Earl of
    Perth), 98, 99, 102
Strathallan, The Viscountess, 99
Strauss, Richard, 264, 305, 313, 327
Stravinsky, Igor, 291
Strehler, Giorgio, 336
Stuart, Sir Campbell, 75
Studholme, Joe, 169
Stuttgart, 301, 302
Sun, 203
Sunday Telegraph, 173
Sunday Times, 137, 139
Sunley, Bernard, 132-3
Svor Angelica (Puccini), 314
Sussex Daily News, 137
Sutherland, Graham, 106
Sutherland, Joan, 244, 263, 265, 283,
    345
Sutton, Denys, 168, 169
Svoboda, Josef, 314, 336, 344
Swaffield, Sir James, 361
Swan Lake, 297, 298, 351
Sykes, Camilla, 94
Sykes, Christopher, 48, 94
Sykes, Mark, 94
Sykes, Sir Richard and Lady, 123
Symphonic Variations (Franck), 301

Tangier, 119
Tannhäuser (Wagner), 251, 344, 345
Tate Gallery, 286
Taverne, Dick, 136
Tawney, R. H., 31
Taylor, A. J. P., 88
Taylor, Frank, 357

Tchaikovsky, Peter, 286, 298, 302, 327
Technical Information on Microfiche
    (TIM), 163
Templer, Sir Gerald, 361
Tether, C. Gordon, 212
Tetley, Glen, *Laborintus II* and *Field Figures*,
    340
Thackrah, Honor, 283
Thatcher, The Rt Hon. Margaret, 206
Thayer, Walter, 103
Thebom, Blanche, 248
Thomson, Dr William A. R., 151
Thomson, Sir Courtauld (later Lord
    Courtauld-Thomson), 43
Thomson, Pinkie, 104
Thomson of Fleet, Lord, 193, 194
Thorn, John, 341
Thorneycroft, Lady (Carla), 265
Thorneycroft, Lord (Peter), 148-9
Thorpe, Mrs Jeremy, 276, 346
Tidworth Camp, 15
Tiger Balm, 178
Times, The, 64, 84, 94, *128*, 136, 138, 140,
    202, 203, 211, 244; Roman type, 140;
    possible merger with *FT*, 189-93;
    Thomson acquisition of, 193, 194;
    Business News section, 194; price
    increase, 211; Paris office, 217; Rafael
    Kubelik's letter to, 246, 247
Tingay, Herbert, 172, 173
Tippett, Sir Michael, 284, 315, 327, 330
Toms, Carl, 297
Tooley, John, 216, 237, 283, 300, 318, 320,
    321-3, 333, 336, 337, 344, 350; in 1974
    gala, 346
Tosca, La (Puccini), 266, 289, 348
Toscanini, Arturo, 70, 280
Trade Unions, 199, 201, 202, 204, 209, 213;
    and Labour Relations Act (1974), 204,
    205, 207
Trafalgar house (Hampshire), 121
Trafalgar House Investments, 155, 165
Trafford, Ian, 155, 174-5
Transport Development Group, 173
Traviata, La (Verdi), 264, 265, 345, 346
Treasury, 254, 260, 271; Central Statistical
    Office, 313
Tree, Mrs Ronald (Marietta), 122
Tree, Mrs Ronald (Nancy), 121, 122
Tree, Ronald, 121-2
Trevelyan, G. M., 151
Trevelyan, Lord, 324
Triggs, Harold, 81, 92
Tristan and Isolde (Wagner), 327
Trojans, The (Berlioz), 248, 327
Trovatore, Il (Verdi), 263-5, 305, 348
Troxy Cinema, 279
Trust Houses, 156

TUC (Trade Unions Congress), 148, 202, 217, 218
Tuckwell, Patricia (Countess of Harewood), 319
Tugendhat, Christopher, 163, *163*
Turandot (Puccini), 233
Turgenev, Ivan, *Month in the Country*, 317
Tyerman, Donald, 97, 152, 154–5

Ueberlacher, Dave, 104
Ulanova, Galina, 243
Ullstein publishing company (Berlin), 133
Union Corporation, South African, 115, 150
United Services Club, 185
United States of America, 28, 52, 56, 78, 85, 296, 299; sale of *The Economist* in, 152
Urquhart, Leslie, 32, 33

Vaizey, Marina, 169
Valois, Dame Ninette de, 238, 239, 250, 260-2, 279, 292, 294, 295, 301, 316; *Rake's Progress*, 298; bust, 346
Varviso, Silvio, 345
Veasey, Josephine, 305
Vechten, Carl van, 57
Venice, Palazzo Morosini, 68
Verdi, Giuseppe, 262, 327, 336
Verrett, Shirley, 337
Vezelay, Abbey of, 124
Vichy, 32
Vickers Company, 183; building, 365
Vickers, Jon, 248, 263
Vienna Philharmonic Orchestra, 304–5
Villa Florentina (St Jean Cap Ferrat), 21, 125
Villamediana, Conchita, 15–16
Villa Mauresque, 125
Viollet-le-duc, 124
Visconti, Lucchino, 289; *Don Carlos*, 262–3, 327; *Trovatore*, 263, 264, 305
Vogue (magazine), 57

Wagner, Richard, 325, 327, 344
Wakehurst, Lord, 228–9
Wakhevitch, Georges, 244
Wall Street Journal, 128, 214
Walpole, Hugh, *The Portrait of a Man with Red Hair*, 232
Walter, Bruno, 235, 281
Walton, Sir William, 106, 107, 228; *Façade*, 37, 295; *Troilus and Cressida*, 228
Wanamaker, Sam, 284
War Office, 85–6; Army Requirements at, 92
Warburg, Sir Siegmund, 83, 149, 150, 270

Ward, Barbara, 97
Ward, Dame Irene, 251
Ward, David, 305
Ward, The Hon. Edward (Eddie), 119
Ward, of Witley, The Rt Hon. Viscount (Geordie), 119
Wardlaw-Milne, Sir John, 95
Warrens house (New Forest), 145
Washington, 154, 197; Arcadia Conference in, 90; CPRB headquarters in, 91; Treasury delegation in, 94; War Production Board in, 98; British Embassy in, 227
Waterlows, 44
Watt, David, 209, 210–11, 362
Waugh, Evelyn, 48, 75
Waverley, The Viscountess, *see* Anderson, Lady
Waverley, The Rt Hon. Viscount, *see* Anderson, Sir John
Weaver, John and Ursula, 124
Webster, Sir David, 106, 236, 282; as general administrator of Covent Garden, 225, 229–33, 235, 237, 243, 244, 248, 249, 251, 254, 258, 259, 261, 268, 270, 271; and Maria Callas, 265, 266; as administrator of London Opera Centre, 278; and Kubelik's successor, 280, 281; and extension of Solti's contract, 284–5; and board design sub-committee, 287; and Nadia Nerina's status, 300–1; and Ashton's succession, 316–17; retirement, 317–18, 320; own succession, 318; made a KCVO, 320–21; death, 320; memorial service, 321, 324
Weeks, Lord, 183
Weidenfeld, Lord, 360
Weill, Kurt, *7 Deadly Sins*, 339
Welsh National Opera, 337
Westminster Hospital, 160
Westminster Press Provincial Newspaper group, 147, 193, 208, 357
Westminster School, 105
Weston Hall, 58, 120
Wexford Festival, 115
Whistler, Rex, 67, 298
White, Harry, 105
Whitehead, Arthur, 133–4
Whitehead Industrial Trust, 133
Whitney, Jock, 103
Wigan, Dare, 171
Wigan, Dominic, 171
Wilde, Oscar, 55
Wilding, Tony, 7
Williams, Deborah, 338
Williams-Ellis, Clough, 119
Wilson, The Rt Hon. Sir Harold, 47, 62, 96, 148, 195–7, 209, 213, 217, 218, 255, 307, 310

Wilson, James, 44
Wilson, Lady (Mrs Harold), 263
Wilson, Sir Steuart, 236–7, 247
Wilton House (Wiltshire), 24, 67, 119
Wimborne House, 36, 228
Wimborne, Viscountess (Alice), 36–7, 58, 295
Wincott awards, 130–1
Wincott Foundation, 130
Wincott, Harold, 64, 130, 131
Windlesham, Lord, 206
Windsor, 117; Park, 117; St George's Chapel, 265
Winfield House, 79
Winter Garden Theatre, 277, 279
Wintour, Charles, 360, 361, 363
Wittersham (Kent), 66
Woburn Abbey, 142
Wolfson, Sir Leonard, 274
Wolfson College (Oxford), 240
Wood, Ann, 277, 278, 279
Wood, Michael, 249–50

Woods, Sir John Henry, 101, 114, 116
World Bank, 155, 156
World Medicine, 165
World Theatre Season, 173
Worsley, Cuthbert, 137
Worst Play Club (London), 34
Wozzeck (Alban Berg), 236, 348
Wright, Dr H. Beric, 184
Wright, Peter, 338; *Sleeping Beauty*, 302–3
Wright, Sir Paul, 363

Yeo, Peter, 214
Yorkshire Post, 132
Youth and Music, 359, 360

Zeffirelli, Franco, 262, 289, 336; *Lucia di Lammermoor*, 258, 263; *Falstaff*, 265, 327; *Tosca*, 266; *Cavalleria Rusticana and Pagliacci*, 273; *Don Giovanni*, 284
Zimmerman, Philip, 163–4

THE
FINANCIAL
NEWS
Map of
THE STOCK EXCHANGE

1 Gilt Edged.	5. Banks.	10 Breweries.	13 Foreign Rails.	17 West African	19 Miscellaneous
2 Shipping, Canals,	6. Insurance	9 Distilleries	14 Investment Trusts	Mines.	Mines.
5 Gas.	7 Oils	11 Rubbers.	15 Electric Light	18 Australian	20 Rhodesian
3 Home Rails	8 Industrials	12 Iron, Coal,	8 Power	Indian,	21 S. African
4 Yankees	9 Foreign Bonds	9 Steel.	16 Teas	Malayan Mines	Mines